Writing Sentences and Paragraphs
Integrating Reading, Writing, and Grammar Skills

Joy Wingersky
Glendale Community College, Arizona

Jan Boerner
Emerita from Glendale Community College, Arizona

THOMSON
™
WADSWORTH

Australia   Canada   Mexico   Singapore   Spain   United Kingdom   United States

Writing Sentences and Paragraphs:
Integrating Reading, Writing, and Grammar Skills
Joy Wingersky / Jan Boerner

Publisher: *Michael Rosenberg*
Acquisitions Editor: *Stephen Dalphin*
Development Editor: *Cathlynn Richard Dodson*
Editorial Assistant: *Stephen Marsi*
Production Editor: *Samantha Ross*
Director of Marketing: *Lisa Kimball*

Executive Marketing Manager: *Carrie Brandon*
Senior Print Buyer: *Mary Beth Hennebury*
Compositor/Project Manager: *Lachina Publishing Services*
Cover Designer: *Ha Nguyen*
Cover Printer: *Lehigh Press*
Text Printer: *QuebecorWorld*

Cover Image: © Michael Pawlyk/ Index Stock

For more information contact Wadsworth, 25 Thomson Place, Boston, Massachusetts 02210 USA, or you can visit our Internet site at http://www.wadsworth.com

For permission to use material from this text, contact us:
Tel 1-800-730-2214
Fax 1-800-730-2215
Web www.thomsonrights.com

ISBN: 0-15-508530-1
(Student Edition)

Printed in the United States of America.

1 2 3 4 5 6 7 8 9 10   07 06 05 04 03

Page xv constitutes an extension of the copyright page.

Library of Congress Control Number: 2003108316

Contents

Chapter 2 Developing Paragraphs with Examples and Details 77

Chapter 7   Editing for a Final Version   321

Preface

An Integrated Approach

In *Writing Sentences and Paragraphs,* we have integrated writing, reading, and grammar concepts in each chapter. Therefore, as students learn writing skills, they also learn the grammar skills that they can apply as they write their own paragraphs.

- *Writing Instruction:*
  (1) In this textbook, we help students learn to write effective sentences that are grammatically correct as well as varied. Students are asked to write simple, compound, complex, and compound-complex sentences that are interesting as well as effective.
  (2) We also teach students to write well-developed paragraphs that include a topic sentence, support sentences, and a concluding sentence, but, most importantly, are informative and appealing.
- *Writing Assignments:* We include a variety of writing assignments that are integrated within each chapter.
- *Writings by Professionals:* In each chapter, we include an essay. These essays are written by knowledgeable men and women who work at professional jobs in society and who write well but do not make their living exclusively as authors. We believe that these professionals serve as role models for students and inspire them to work hard so that they, too, can become successful writers.
- *Readings:* We include examples of effective writing that reinforce what is taught in each chapter.
  (1) Paragraphs from students who have learned to write well.
  (2) Paragraphs from writers who are published professional authors.
- *Grammar:* In this textbook, we include grammar and mechanics that students need to understand to write fluidly and effectively.

Organization and Key Concepts

This textbook is organized into seven chapters, each divided into four separate yet related parts.

Part 1   Deals with writing skills, whether isolated or combined with grammatical concepts. Part 1 of each chapter (except Chapter 1) is followed by a practice test in context of a paragraph. Also, Part 1 of each chapter is followed by a summary and a writing assignment.

Part 2   Includes a professional essay that starts students thinking about possible writing topics that they can use in their own writing. All of these professional essays are followed by a brief vocabulary exercise and a writing assignment related to that essay.

Part 3   Includes paragraphs written by students and professional authors. These paragraphs, that can be used to generate discussion in class, model the concepts taught in that chapter. Each paragraph is followed by questions that ask the students to analyze and discuss content and form. Because the authors of these selections have a wide range of writing experience and come from diverse backgrounds, their writing appeals to students of different ages, gender, and ethnic backgrounds.

Part 4   Is dedicated to grammar and mechanics instruction. Here students learn and practice the grammatical concepts aimed at improving writing skills. Because students have already started writing before they get to this section, they have the chance to reinforce what they learned in Part 1 of each chapter. Part 4 in each chapter ends with a summary, a practice test in context of a paragraph, and a writing assignment.

Step-by-Step Process

Students learn in a step-by-step process so that they do not feel overwhelmed by having to learn everything at once. *Writing Sentences and Paragraphs* emphasizes the importance of understanding basic grammar so that students will have a clear understanding of how words can fit together in a logical order, resulting in effective sentence patterns. While beginning writers are learning sentences, they are also fitting them into effective paragraphs.

Our emphasis goes beyond simply having students memorize definitions for parts of speech. We help them analyze words so they understand how they function in the context of a sentence. Our goal is to help students build confidence in their ability to understand the way grammar works rather than have them memorize definitions and examples of that definition. We try to teach students that grammar is sensible and that if they understand and work effectively with their own sentences, they can understand basic grammar.

Students learn to prewrite, organize, write, edit, and rewrite, one step at a time, until they have an effective paragraph that includes examples and details that support a topic sentence. While students are composing paragraphs, we continually emphasize the importance of sentence variety. Our goal is to help students build the confidence they need to write effective paragraphs and, thus, believe in their own ability.

Focus on Better Paragraphs

Instruction in *Writing Sentences and Paragraphs* is dedicated to helping students write with confidence as they combine words into sentences and sentences into paragraphs.

- We include intense writing instruction of sentences and paragraphs, leaving essay instruction for a higher-level text.
- We concentrate on topic and support of strong expository paragraphs.
- We constantly emphasize having students write and revise sentences in the context of their own paragraphs.

Major Features of Writing Sentences and Paragraphs

Integrated Approach to Writing

In *Writing Sentences and Paragraphs,* the writing, readings, and grammar instruction are blended together. For example, readings are not separated from the material that they model. Grammar is integrated so that students can see how grammar fits into what they are trying to do rather than being an isolated skill. When developing strong sentences, students learn editing skills that will help them build effective and varied sentences that result in interesting sentences.

Step-by-Step Process to Learning Writing

In *Writing Sentences and Paragraphs,* we emphasize having students learn one skill at a time so that they build confidence in their ability to write. We model these skills early in the text by showing multiple drafts of a single paragraph. We stress the patience and commitment needed to becoming a better writer.

Readings That Model What Students Learn

We have chosen reading selections that will interest students and at the same time serve as models for the skills they are learning.

Exercises That Require Thinking Skills

Although the exercises we have developed for *Writing Sentences and Paragraphs* include simple identification exercises, they also include exercises that require more complex thinking skills, such as combining sentences, sorting out scrambled sentences, and generating topic sentences. Students progress from identifying concepts, such as parts of speech, to applying this learning to their own sentences and paragraphs.

ESL Material

Throughout *Writing Sentences and Paragraphs,* we have been mindful of material that is appropriate and useful for ESL students. Appendix B includes additional information for ESL students.

Appendices

Appendix A	Confusing Words, Including Exercises
Appendix B	ESL: Gaining Confidence in Using English
Appendix C	Spelling, Including Exercises
Appendix D	Answers to Odd-Numbered Exercises, in Version A of Each Exercise

Supplements

Annotated Instructor's Edition
Instructor's Manual
Test Bank
Writer's Resources CD-ROM, Version 2.0

Acknowledgments

We thank our colleagues at Glendale Community College who provided support and encouragement, especially Marti Moraga whose commitment to her own students was transferred to us. She was always ready to read our drafts and make valuable suggestions as our book evolved. We also thank Char Howey, who offered suggestions regarding the ESL material, and Casey Furlong, who helped us with in-class testing. We also appreciate the encouragement and positive comments from our other colleagues.

We will always be particularly indebted to our students whose commitment and dedication to learning as well as their trust in us made this book possible. We thank the students who allowed us to include their paragraphs as models: Benny Alvarez, Hanan Al-Shakhrit, Patrina Begay, Mark Bethke, Veronica Carmelo, Joseph Ronald Fahoome, Ellen J. Gary, Christian Kelly, Valerie Lewis, Nereyda Martinez, Travis Mays, John McMurray, Amanda Moreno, Kalli Mussetter, Mark Sanchez, Joshua Sewell, Josh Seyfert, Tarya Tjernagel, and Ashleigh Wolfe.

We also thank the professionals who were willing to share their writing with others: Larry Bohlender, René Díaz-Lefebvre, Shyrl E. Emhoff, Elizabeth R. Minnich, Russell F. Proctor II, Jim Reed, and Kathy Sins. Their articles enrich our textbook and encourage students to respond thoughtfully and creatively to ideas for writing.

We especially thank our families for their patience and on-going support, especially George Wingersky for his understanding of and help with historical references. We also thank Anne, LaJuana, and Bob for their contributions and suggestions.

The staff at Wadsworth has also been outstanding. We will always be grateful to Steve Dalphin for his insight and desire for a quality publication, Cathy Richard Dodson for making helpful suggestions and creating a positive environment in which to work, and Samantha Ross for her attention to detail and willingness to take the time to get things right. We thank Lachina Publishing Services for their dedication and flexibility.

We also thank the reviewers of our text:

Kristine Anderson, *Riverside Community College*
Jessica Carroll, *Miami-Dade Community College*
Robin Daniel, *Broward Community College*
Stella Fox, *Nashville Community College*
Wanda Lockwood, *Monterrey Pacific College*
Marti Moraga, *Glendale Community College*
Victor Turks, *City College of San Francisco*
Teresa Ward, *Butte College*
Susan Warrington, *Phillips Community College*
Audelia H. Williams, *DeVry Institute of Technology*
Michelle Zollars, *Patrick Henry Community College*

Text Credits

Thanks are due to the following authors, publishers, and agents for permission to use the material indicated.

Page 39: Excerpt from *Wouldn't Take Nothing for My Journey Now* by Maya Angelou. Copyright © 1992. Reprinted by permission from Random House, Inc.

Page 39: Excerpt from "Graduation" in *The Pact* by Sampson Davis, George Jenkins and Rameck Hunt, with Liza Frazier Page. Copyright © 2002 by Three Doctors LLC. Reprinted by permission of Riverhead Books, an imprint of Penguin Group (USA), Inc.

Page 110: Excerpt from *THEFWORD, How to Survive Your Family* by Louie Anderson. Copyright © 2002 by Louie Anderson. Reprinted by permission of Warner Books, Inc.

Page 111: Excerpt from *Angela's Ashes* by Frank McCourt. Copyright © 1996 by Frank McCourt. Reprinted by permission of Scribner, an imprint of Simon & Schuster Adult Publishing Group.

Page 171: Excerpt from *A Long Way from Home* by Tom Brokaw. Copyright © 2002. Reprinted by permission of Random House, Inc.

Page 172: Excerpt from *If I Die in a Combat Zone, Box Me Up and Ship Me Home* by Tim O'Brien. Copyright © 1975 by Tim O'Brien. Reprinted by permission of Random House, Inc.

Page 206: Excerpt from *A Walk Through the Year* by Edwin Way Teale. Copyright © 1978. Reprinted by permission of Dodd Mead, Publishers.

Page 207: Excerpt from *Or Perish in the Attempt: Wilderness Medicine in the Lewis & Clark Expedition* by David J. Peck. Copyright © 2002 by David J. Peck. Reprinted by permission of Farcountry Press.

Page 252: Excerpt from *Mother Tongue* by Amy Tan. Copyright © 1990 by Amy Tan. First appeared in *The Threepenny Review*. Reprinted by permission of the author and the Sandra Dijkstra Literary Agency.

Page 253: Excerpt from *The Seasons of a Man's Life* by Daniel J. Levinson. Copyright © 1978. Reprinted by permission of Random House, Inc. and Ballantine Books.

Page 294: Excerpt from *Walden*, "The Ponds" by Henry David Thoreau. Copyright © Walter Scott, London, 1886.

Page 353: Excerpt from "Housekeeping in the Klondike" by Jack London. First published in *Harper's Bazaar*, 1900.

Page 353: Excerpt from *Healing Harmonies* by Tim Wendel. Copyright © 2001. Reprinted by permission of the author.

Professional essays by Dr. Russell F. Proctor II, Dr. René-Díaz Lefebvre, Kathy Sins, Shyrl E. Emhoff, Lt. Col., USAR, Ret., Dr. Jim Reed, Elizabeth Minnich, and Larry Bohlender. All Copyright © 2003. Used with permission.

Student essays by Hanan Al-Shakhrit, Amanda Moreno, Ellen J. Gary, Mark Bethke, Joshua Sewell, Kalli Mussetter, Tarya Tjernagel, Ashleigh H. Wolfe, Travis Mays, Christian Kelly, Joseph Ronald Fahoome, Valerie J. Lewis, Patrina Begay, Benjamin T. Alvarez, Josh Seyfert, Veronica Carmelo, John McMurray II, Nereyda Martinez, and Mark Sanchez. All Copyright © 2003. Used with permission.

Chapter 1

Understanding the Essentials of Writing and Grammar

Introduction to Writing
Attitude Toward Writing and the Writing Process

Objectives

Attitude Toward Writing

- Understand the importance of writing well
- Understand the importance of commitment to writing
- Understand the importance of a positive attitude in writing

The Writing Process

- Understand the importance of prewriting

    Freewriting

    Brainstorming

    Talking

- Understand the importance of organizing a paper

    Grouping in chronological or time order

    Grouping like ideas together

    Grouping in order of importance

- Understand the importance of drafting
- Understand the importance of revising and rewriting

    Changing content and rearranging order

    Adding coherence

      Key words

      Time words

      Transition words

- Understand the importance of editing

Attitude Toward Writing

One of the most important skills you can have in life is the ability to communicate with others. You need this skill when you talk to others and when you write to or for other people. Many people prefer to talk rather than write because they can also use facial expressions and gestures to get their point across. Sometimes, however, it is impossible to communicate everything in person, so being able to communicate through writing is extremely important.

One of the biggest hurdles you might face as a writer is being able to put down on paper what is in your head. Ideas may be flowing, but writing down your ideas can seem like an impossible task. You might be surprised to know that this happens to many people. Sometimes even professional writers say, "I am experiencing a dry spell." What they mean is that they are having a difficult time writing. When this happens to you, you have two choices. You can give up and say, "I just cannot do it right." Your other option is better. You can start writing down anything you can think of because one idea often leads to another. Everyone has to start somewhere, and sometimes writing just involves getting started. You have to start before you can be successful. What, then, is involved in being a successful writer?

Realizing the Importance of Writing Well

Before you decide that you want to be a better writer, you need to realize how important writing is in your life. Many times before you can reach a major goal in your educational years, professional career, and personal life, you will need to depend on writing.

Getting an education means being able to write papers successfully, not only for your English classes but for your other classes as well. In college, you will be asked to write essay tests, reports, and research papers.

Once you are out of college and looking for a job, you will most likely put together a resume that will often require a one-page personal history. Once you get a job, you may continue writing in whatever profession you choose.

- If you have your own business, you will need to communicate with your employees in writing.
- If you are a child-care provider or a teacher, you will need to write well to do your job.
- If you go into the medical profession, whether you are a doctor, a nurse, a paramedic, or a technician, you will need to write reports.
- If you go into research, you will need to present your results.
- If you are an attorney, you will need to present your cases.
- If you work on or with computers, you will need to write many types of papers, including directions that others can understand.

Throughout your personal life, you will have occasions when you need to explain situations through writing. For example, if your child is ill and you need to receive the proper medical treatment, you will feel comfortable knowing you can write the type of letter that will get the desired results from your insurance company. Sometimes you may want to write to someone who has helped because you want to show your appreciation. No matter where you are going in life, you will find it is helpful to be able to express your ideas in writing. Knowing how to write effectively can serve you well.

Committing to Your Goal

The people who are the most successful in any area are the ones who are willing to make a commitment. Talk to the people who are already successful, and they will tell you that they were willing to take on the responsibility to work hard toward their goal. Professional athletes, for example, have already made a pledge to a particular sport to be the best possible player. How many times have you seen a baseball player slip a cell phone into his pocket before going onto the field to pitch so that he will not miss a telephone call? How many times have you seen a football player put on headphones, turn up the volume on his CD, and dance onto the field so he can play better football? Never. Next time you watch a baseball game, look at the transformation and the total concentration on the face of the pitcher just before he throws the ball.

Perhaps you can think of individuals who have moved to the United States because they already have a goal in life: they want to provide an opportunity for themselves and for their children to have a better chance to be successful than they had somewhere else. They have already made sacrifices and are dedicated to their goal.

Perhaps you can think of returning students who always wanted an education but never had the opportunity to go to college because personal circumstances kept them from making a commitment to education. Today, however, they are focused on working hard day-by-day to reach their educational goals.

Think about how successful you can be when you decide that you want to get an education badly enough to make a promise to yourself to work hard and focus on your goal. Learning to concentrate and focus on the job at hand is necessary if you want to become a better writer. You are the only one who can make your education your first priority. Becoming a better writer is part of your dedication to your own education.

Having a Positive Attitude

How many times have you started something only to wonder if you could actually do it? But then you worked hard and, after accomplishing your goal, you said to yourself, "I don't understand why I ever thought I couldn't do it." Right now, writing may seem hard and intimidating for you, but believing in yourself will make your efforts pay off. You should not be intimidated by anything in writing, including the required length of a completed paper. You should just move forward one step at a time until you reach your goal. You will relax about getting started and not worry about problems you may have had in the past.

 ## *Summary*

Look at the following chart, which shows the steps necessary to become an effective writer. Once you realize the need to write well, make a commitment to do so, and assume a positive attitude about writing, you will find many benefits throughout your educational years, your career, and your personal life.

Steps to Becoming an Effective Writer

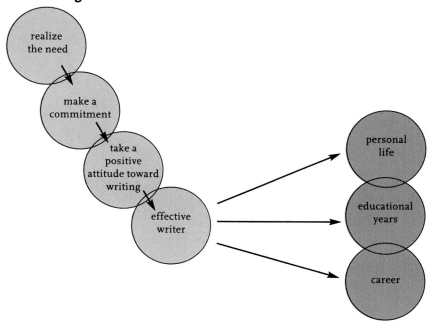

 Collaborative Activities

In groups of three or four, work through the following activities.

Activity 1
Discuss occupations in which people have to write something almost every day. Then list three occupations, and give examples of what they have to write.

Example:

home-health nurse	**write a report on each patient, including conditions, changes, recommendations for the patient and the family.**
Occupations:	Examples of what these employees have to write
_____	_____
_____	_____
_____	_____

Activity 2
A. Discuss a time in your life when you wanted or needed to write a letter, but you didn't do it. Explain the situation and describe the results of not writing the letter.

Example:

Situation:

Your homeowner's association sent you a warning saying your car was parked in front of your house overnight. Writing a letter was important because you had not left your car there overnight.

Results of not writing the letter:

Instead of writing a letter to explain the situation, you ignored the warning, and two months later you were fined.

Situation:

_____

_____

Results of not writing a response:

_____

B.   Give an example of when you wrote a letter that was successful for you.

Example:

Situation:

You wanted to get a job at Wal-Mart, but, in addition to your application, you had to write a paragraph that included your personal history.

Results:

You were able to write an effective paragraph, and you got the job.

Situation:

_____

_____

Results:

_____

The Writing Process

Writing well is easier for some people than for others. Most people, however, are able to write effectively if they put enough time and effort into the process. Most successful musicians, sculptors, and ceramists do not sit down and complete a project in an hour. Rather, they sometimes spend weeks creating a piece of art that is something they wish to share with others. They go through a process that is very painstaking but that gives them a great deal of pride when they have a finished product. The same is true of writing. Taking the time to complete a piece of writing is demanding, but the end result is rewarding. If you are willing to learn the writing process, you will be able to write paragraphs that communicate what you want to say. The more you practice writing, the easier it becomes and the faster you can write effectively.

Because this class will focus on helping you write better sentences and paragraphs, you will learn how to work step-by-step to reach these goals. As you remember and practice these steps in the writing process, you will create effective sentences and paragraphs, building a strong foundation for longer papers. Though these steps should become automatic later, you need to concentrate on completing one step at a time for now. The following overview of the writing process shows how you will move smoothly from one step to the next. You will learn this process clearly as you master these steps one by one.

- **Prewriting**—Getting started
- **Organizing**—Putting ideas into clear order
- **Drafting**—Writing a first draft
- **Revising/Rewriting**—Making changes in the draft
- **Editing**—Correcting spelling/other mechanical errors

Prewriting

Prewriting is extremely important to help you generate ideas that lead to a main idea for your paragraph. **Prewriting can be defined as any activity that you use to help you get started writing.** Prewriting can help you find out how much or how little you know about a topic. It can help you find a direction for your paragraph as you select the main idea you want to explain. It can help you find effective supporting examples and details for your writing.

This text will give you some prewriting activities. By doing these activities carefully, you will find the method that works best for you. Try them all, and then use one or two of these activities whenever you need to write a paper.

The three prewriting activities you will learn in this chapter are *freewriting*, *brainstorming*, and *talking*. All of these activities require thinking skills, so be patient as you work through each one. Your patience will pay off, and over time what at first seems difficult will become natural to you.

Freewriting

Freewriting to find a main idea means just what it says, writing freely with no restraints. Once you have a topic, you write whatever comes to mind without worrying about spelling, grammar, or even complete sentences. You just start writing without stopping. You probably do not know where you are going with the topic, but that is fine. If you are really stuck, you can write about being stuck. Often the first few sentences are simply for warming up and might be eliminated later anyhow. After you finish freewriting, you will want to read over what you have written. Once you see some ideas that interest you, you can concentrate, this time, on **one of the ideas** you discovered in your freewriting. This idea may end up being your direction for further writing.

Look at the following example of freewriting.

Firefighters—I do not know what to say about them. They always wear dark blue shirts and pants. Everytime I see a firefighter, Sometimes when I am at the grocery store I run into firefighters shopping for food. My neighbor is a firefighter and he says they always cook good meals **at the station.** Yesterday I read about station ten who **saved a little boy** who had been mauled by two pit bull dogs and later took gifts to the little boy and then they showered him with gifts. They fight fires. I remember the September 11, 2001 attack on America and the firefighters who **died trying to save others** who were trapped in the Twin Towers in New York. I wonder if it is hard to be a firefighter? I thought about—sometimes I think about being a firefighter. They spend 24 hours shifts **at the station**. I wonder who does the cooking and how they stay busy when they are not out on a call? Everyone likes firefighters. I wonder if they enjoy being at the station so much. I like to cook but who decides who will clean things up.

Notice that this example of freewriting seems to ramble and go in several directions, but that is part of the process. If you reread what has been written, you might find several ideas that have enough similarities to fit together into a possible idea that can become the direction for more freewriting. One idea might be the ***many heroic acts of a firefighter.*** Another idea might be ***life at a fire station.***

The ideas that support the topic, the ***many heroic acts of a firefighter,*** include

the firefighters who died in the September 11 attack on America and the firefighters who saved the little boy from the pit bulls.

The ideas that support the topic, ***life at a fire station,*** include

cook good meals,
spend 24-hour shifts at the fire station,
clean up the station, and
stay busy when they are not on a call.

These supporting ideas can be included in your paragraph, but now you will want to keep working to find additional support for further writing. This can be done by freewriting on one of these narrowed topics. If you have never been to a fire station, you can only guess what life is like there, so you will not want to use that idea unless you talk to a firefighter or spend some time at a fire station. However, you might want to write about the other idea, the ***many heroic acts of a firefighter.*** If you choose to go in this direction, you will use only the information that describes the heroic acts of firefighters. You will need to freewrite again for additional information, which is called ***freewriting with a direction.***

The example below shows how to freewrite with a direction. This freewriting is more narrow than the first one because it focuses on firefighters who perform heroic acts.

Firefighters perform many heroic acts. I remember my neighbor talking about the first time he had delivered a baby because the mother could not get to the hospital in time. He was so proud that he had delivered a beautiful six pound two ounce baby boy. It seems that I always hear about a firefighter on the news. Whenever a car gets into an accident, the paramedics perform life-saving procedures. I still remember the day my brother was involved in a roll-over accident and the paramedics kept him alive until they could get him to the hospital. Later we took my brother to the station to see those paramedics and to thank them for what they had done. Once when my grandfather was sick, the firefighters came to his house. They gave his oxygen and took him to the hospital. I think they saved his life. I know they do other things too because they often go to schools and talk to the kids about the dangers of drugs and alcohol.

This example of freewriting with a direction shows how more ideas emerged to give examples of heroic acts by firefighters. Freewriting is only one type of prewriting activity, but doing this not only helps you focus on one topic but also helps you recall additional ideas that support that one idea.

Brainstorming

Brainstorming for a main idea, which is very similar to freewriting, **is simply writing down words or simple phrases as they come to mind.** Be sure to write down everything that comes to mind even though you will not use every idea you put down. Using this prewriting activity can be fun because you can work alone or you can brainstorm in a group. Once you are finished, your next step is to search through your ideas to see if any of them fit together. If several words or phrases seem related, then you simply decide what makes them similar. Think of a general word or phrase that describes the related ideas. This thinking process prepares you for writing paragraphs. Look at the following ideas that were generated using the same topic, firefighters.

dangerous job   wear uniforms   die in a fire

fight fires   spend time at a station   cook good meals

take care of each other   grocery shop together   fitness equipment

work one day on, two days off   save people and their property

If you write a paragraph on everything listed above, you will have a hard time putting all the information into one paragraph, so you need to limit the information to a group of words that are in some way similar or *related to one another*. Look at the above thoughts to see which of the words go together. This common thread or the way these ideas fit together becomes your *direction or controlling idea*. You will probably find several controlling ideas, each with a topic and a direction. The brainstormed list above can be sorted into the clusters *shown below*. The general idea that describes the cluster becomes a possible direction (important idea) for a further writing.

Cluster #1:   Spend time at a station,   **relationships**
               cook good meals, and   **at the fire station.**
               take care of each other

Direction #1:   Firefighters at a station often develop good relationships.

Cluster #2:   Die in a fire,   **dangerous parts**
               dangerous job and fight fires   **of being a firefighter.**

Direction #2:   Firefighters have dangerous jobs.

Cluster #3: Work one day on,
two days off,
fitness equipment,
cook good meals, and
take care of each other } **positive parts of
being a firefighter.**

Direction #3: Firefighters have great jobs.

Note The brainstorming ideas "cook good meals" and "take care of each other" are included under both **direction #1** and **direction #3** above. This is possible because cooking great meals and taking care of each other both lead to good relationships. These ideas also support the idea that firefighters have great jobs.

After finding the way some of these words and phrases fit together, you will want to brainstorm again, this time with a specific direction in mind. Look at the following brainstorming, which focuses only on the dangerous jobs of firefighters.

Firefighters have dangerous jobs.

roofs collapse   trapped in burning buildings   oxygen tank can run out

going through intersections in a fire truck   rescuing hikers off cliffs

exposed to blood   go on calls late at night   violent situations

All of these points are examples of dangers on the job, but they need to be developed with strong, specific examples and details. Brainstorming, like freewriting, is a useful way to find more ideas or examples, but you might also decide to talk to someone about your topic.

Talking

Another way to start a writing project is to talk to others to find ideas for your paper. **Talking simply means discussing your topic with others to get a main idea and supporting ideas for your paragraph.** You have just seen the possible results that come from freewriting and brainstorming about firefighters. Now observe how talking to other people can provide even more information about firefighters. You might talk to other people who know firefighters, or you might decide to call someone at a fire station or even go down to a fire station and talk to the people there. As you talk to others, you will want to take notes that you can write more about later. Read the following notes that resulted from spending some time at the firehouse.

I went down to station 10 to talk to the firefighters. They were eating leftovers. They offered me a doughnut. They told me they might have to leave suddenly if a call came in. Everyone talked to me but one guy seemed to be doing all the work. He was washing dishes when I got there but then he swept the floor. When the telephone rang, none of the guys tried to get it except the one guy doing all the work. I asked why he was staying so busy, and everybody laughed. He is the booter they said. I asked what a booter was and they told me he was a rookie, a first year firefighter and then they told me he had the first year to prove himself and build his character. He could not sit down or watch television. He had to stay busy. That booter started moping the floor, but they said he had been there nine months. In three more months he would be off probation and be a regular at the station. Then a new booter would come aboard and do all the jobs. I asked about the other jobs he had and was surprised—put up and take down the flag, clean everything, including the floors—*yes, this would be my subject for my paper–first year firefighters*. I could get all the information I needed right here. Then I can go home and talk to my neighbor to see what his first year as a firefighter was like.

As you can see, the notes above have some excellent information that could be developed further. No matter how much you freewrite or brainstorm, you will almost always get more information through talking to others who know something about your subject. Look what happens when this same person talks to someone else about the **narrowed topic of booters or first-year firefighters**.

After getting home from the fire station, I talked to my neighbor who is a captain at Station 6. I wanted to see if he remembered his first year as a firefighter and how he felt being a booter. He told me this probationary year instills character and a sense of responsibility. Firefighters have to have high standards in their lives off the job as well as on the job. They need to earn the trust of the public because many times they have to go into people's homes. During their first year, their work ethic is important both during shifts and even when they are not on duty. Firefighters live and work together on a 24-hour shift so they need to be pleasant to each other. **Their off-duty life is also carefully monitored.** If they drink and drive even when they are not on duty, they will lose their job. If they get a eight points on their license, they will probably get terminated. If they get in a brawl somewhere and the police are called, this could be terms for getting fired. They will most likely be called in by their battalion chief. No one can steal, but probationary firefighters jeopardize their jobs when they are caught stealing even when off duty. When they first get hired, the rules are presented so they know what is expected. He told me about one young recruit who was doing an excellent job at the station, but he spent his off day at the beach and had a few beers. Instead of letting someone else drive, he unwisely decided to drive home. This turned out to be the unpardonable crime because he got stopped and ticketed. That was also the end of his dream job.

This talking with a narrowed topic revealed even more information about probationary firefighters. The additional examples suggest that the life of first-year firefighters is monitored even when they are not working. This is also a possible topic for a paragraph.

Information to support the statement that firefighters are bound by a code of ethics that extends to their personal lives includes the following information.

drinking and driving

getting eight points on their driving record

getting into a fight

stealing

Both occasions of talking through a topic result in useful information, and you as a writer have additional possibilities for writing a paragraph about the duties of first-year firefighters while at the station or the code of ethics firefighters must follow in their personal lives.

All of the prewriting activities explained can help you get information that you will need in your writing.

Prewriting

Freewriting—Writing freely with no restraints

Brainstorming—Listing words or phrases as they come to mind

Talking—Talking with others

Once you feel you have enough information to start a paragraph, you are ready to move on to the next step, but first work through the following exercise for practice in prewriting to generate ideas for writing.

Exercise 1

Choose one of the following topics:

Winter or summer where I live

My college

My home

A. Freewrite on one of the above topics.

_____

_____

_____

_____

_____

Direction or controlling idea from the above freewriting:

_____

Freewrite again using the above **direction**:

_____

_____

_____

_____

_____

_____

B. Brainstorm on the same topic you chose for freewriting.

_____

_____

_____

_____

_____

Direction or controlling idea from the above brainstorming:

_____

Brainstorm again using the above **direction**:

_____

_____

_____

_____

_____

C. Talk to someone about the same topic you chose for freewriting and brainstorming. Then make notes on the conversation.

_____

_____

_____

_____

_____

Direction from the above conversation:

_____

Talk again using the above **direction**:

_____

_____

_____

_____

_____

As you complete these prewriting activities, notice that each activity helps you think of the topic in a different way. You will probably prefer one or two activities. This is a natural part of developing your own writing process, so use whatever is most productive for you in your own prewriting, and continue until you decide on a **direction or controlling idea** that can be expanded in a paragraph or paper.

Organizing

Organizing, the second step in the writing process, refers to the way you arrange the information in a paragraph. Once you are satisfied with your prewriting, look at the ideas you generated, and decide on the best way to write your ideas.

Learning how to organize your ideas is one of the most important skills you can have as a writer. **Organizing** simply means **putting ideas into a clear, logical order** that your reader can easily follow. You already know a lot about order because you instinctively tell stories in chronological or time order, telling what comes first, second, third, and so on. However, there are other ways to put ideas into order. Study the following review of logical patterns of organization or order.

- Grouping in chronological or time order
- Grouping like ideas together
- Grouping in order of importance

Chronological or Time Order

As mentioned above, **chronological order is putting first events first and then moving along in the order that they actually occurred.** Stories usually rely on this kind of organization. Most of your writing, however, will be the kind of writing that explains an idea rather than tells a story. Nevertheless, when you use examples to help explain the main point in your paragraph, you probably will use examples of events that really happened, and in that case, you will want to present the information in the order that it occurred. In other words, your example is like a small story that uses details to show the order in which the events occurred. To do that effectively, you will need to be able to use time order clearly and effectively so that your reader can understand the examples and see the connection to your main idea.

To start, look at the following sentences, and notice how one event logically follows the other. The reader understands what happened first because there are time clues in the sentences.

This morning **Roger got up at** 6:00 A.M.

He was eating breakfast by **6:30**.   (correct order)

Then he went to work at **7:00**.

If the sentences were mixed up, you could still tell what the logical time order should be, and then make the appropriate revision.

> He was eating breakfast by 6:30.
>
> Then he went to work at 7:00. (incorrect order)
>
> This morning, Roger got up at 6:00 A.M.

You could understand right away that getting up comes first, eating breakfast comes second, and going to work comes last. You may not always want to use exact clock hours. Sometimes you will not know or need the exact time. However, clear chronological order means that you will need to use other **time** words and phrases. These appropriate time signals are **transition** words that will help your reader follow your ideas easily.

Once you have arranged your ideas in chronological order, you can help your reader follow this order by using time words. These words also add coherence to your paragraph.

Become familiar with the following time words that can help you organize the supporting ideas in your paragraph.

- Referring to time without using clock hours:

afternoon	morning	today
dawn	night	tonight
dusk	noon	twilight
evening	sunset	yesterday
midnight	tomorrow	

- Other useful words that also signal time:

day	later	then
early	month	week
first	next	year
last	now	
late	soon	

  names of days of the week

  names of months

  names of other words that signal a certain time, such as holidays and seasons

---

Using these time words helps you move from one idea to another smoothly and avoids confusing your reader about the order in which the events occurred.

The following exercise will help you practice identifying time words.

Exercise 2

Circle the time words and phrases in the following sentences.

Example:

(After) the movie (last night), we stopped for ice cream.

Version A

1. How many times did you call me yesterday?
2. Harrison wants to leave tomorrow, but his car will not be ready until next week.
3. We wanted to have a picnic at sunset tonight, but a storm is coming.
4. Next month, Maria and Tony will be married.
5. During spring break, Nikki wants to go to the mountains.
6. Watching the race yesterday morning was exciting, but after lunch we just sat around and talked.
7. After breakfast, Sandy went shopping but came home soon after she bought a pair of shoes.
8. Jill had a wonderful vacation in Bermuda last year.
9. Wilbur's big dog Jake always has his dinner in the middle of the afternoon.
10. The tulip bulbs came in the mail this morning, but I will not plant them until next week.

Version B

1. I planned to visit my cousins last week, but I will not be able to go until later in the month.
2. The last thing he did every night was call his girlfriend.
3. After we clean out the garage, we can fit both cars inside.
4. If Sara trims the grass before she mows the lawn, the yard will look neater.
5. On weekends, gunshots and police sirens are often heard late into the night.
6. The skies are the most beautiful at sunset.
7. The little boy was tired yesterday, but today he has endless energy.
8. Soon summer will arrive, and the days will seem longer.
9. Her baby was due yesterday, so it should be born soon.
10. Everyone loves springtime because the flowers bloom and the baby birds hatch.

Keeping time sequence in mind, practice putting information in the correct chronological order.

Exercise 3

Version A

Number the support sentences in chronological order. The sentence that identifies the event and the sentence that gives a sense of closure are already marked.

_1_ I will always remember helping my grandfather feed his chickens.

____ While I did this, Granddad always cleaned up and got everything organized for their next meal.

____ Then he would take my hand in his, and we would go back into the house.

____ As soon as I scooped out the first spoonful and put it down for them, they began to peck at the mash.

____ Though I was only four years old, I remember his calling my name and leading me to the backyard to see his chickens roaming around.

____ I still remember the sweet smell of the corn and wheat as he mixed the dry chicken feed with water.

____ Then my job was to put the feed on a long log, spoonful by spoonful.

_8_ Today, I remember these events as though they were yesterday.

Version B

_1_ I still remember parking in the college parking lot in the heat of summer.

____ As I headed out the classroom door, the noon heat surrounded me.

____ I drove around for thirty minutes before I could find a parking spot.

____ The real test, however, came when class was over.

____ Even though I was far from my classroom building, I quickly zipped into the empty spot, grabbed my backpack, and locked up my car.

____ Then I half-walked half-jogged to my class.

____ Once again, I picked up my backpack, preparing to head home.

____ I had to walk all the way back to my car in the suffocating heat, but once I got there, it was even worse.

_9_ As I opened my car door to go home, I realized that parking was the worst part of summer school.

As you just learned, time order can be explained by using such words as *then, first, morning, next,* and *soon,* but sometimes doing this can be monotonous and mechanical. To avoid being obvious, you can make your writing smoother and clearer by blending in time indicators at the same time that you relate the actual incidents or events.

Now look at the following paragraph about firefighters. It is organized using time order that is not mechanical because the sequence of events after firefighters arrive at a burning building is clear as you read through the paragraph. Notice that the words in bold make the sequence of events clear.

Paragraph That Is Organized Using Time Order

When arriving at the site of a burning building, firefighters must work rapidly and efficiently to save lives. **Once the truck reaches the fire**, the captain **immediately** designates one firefighter to get off the truck and hook the fire line to the hydrant. **While he is doing this**, the engineer **instantly moves** the truck to the fire, and as quickly as possible, firefighters, already clad in protective gear, put on their breathing apparatus and grab an ax or pike pole. The **first firefighter finished with these preliminary tasks** grabs the fire hose. The firefighters **then** quickly assess the situation and the fire condition. If conditions permit, they will enter the building in pairs for search and rescue. **At the same time** this is happening, a **ladder truck arrives**, and these firefighters cut power to the building and go up to the roof to horizontally vent the ceiling by cutting a hole in the roof. This allows the hot gases and smoke to come out, improving visibility for the firefighters inside the building. **As soon as possible**, firefighters inside the building bring the hurt and injured victims out to safety where firefighter emergency crews **are waiting** to perform lifesaving procedures. **As soon as they are sure no victims are left**, some firefighters will use their pike poles and axes to pull sheet rock from the ceiling and walls to check for hot spots **while** other firefighters open the hose onto the fire. They **continue to work** until every spark is extinguished.

Time order is a very effective way to organize a paragraph that depends on a clear sequence of events to prove the important or main idea in a paragraph. Now look at another way of organizing the support in a paragraph.

Grouping Like Ideas Together

Grouping like ideas together means organizing your paragraph by putting together examples that are similar. Suppose once again you decide to write about firefighters, and after you have completed freewriting, brainstorming, and talking, you come up with the idea that firefighters practice teamwork. Following is a paragraph that illustrates how to organize the supporting examples and details for the main idea that firefighters practice teamwork.

Paragraph That Is Organized by Grouping Like Ideas Together

station
(examples clustered)

public work area
(examples clustered)

fire
(details)

Being a firefighter demands teamwork. *Working together begins* at the station. Since firefighters work 24-hour shifts, they need to be good roommates. This involves understanding the other coworkers' beliefs and ethnic backgrounds and respecting them for who they are, building camaraderie. While at the station, everyone must get along and work together to keep the station clean. In the morning, everyone pitches in to help with housecleaning. Also, to prevent delays, everyone needs to work together to keep the truck ready just as each firefighter must keep his or her own gear in order. *This same teamwork overflows into the public work area.* When they are with the public responding to a call, teamwork is essential, especially when lives are at stake. *When responding to a fire,* firefighters go in as pairs, trusting that if something happens, his or her partner will be there as backup. If they are inside a burning structure together, both team members must stay beside each other and work together. *Also, when responding to an accident*, the firefighters must work

accident (details)

as a close-knit group. For example, when working on an injured person, one person's job is to set up the IV; another team member starts the IV; another might take blood pressure and vital signs; and another does the paperwork. When firefighters work together as one unit and can trust one another to do the job, everyone benefits, including community members as well as the firefighters themselves.

All the information about teamwork at the station was discussed first, and then everything about going out on public calls was explained next. The switch from teamwork at the station to teamwork in the public work area is clearly shown by the words, **This same teamwork overflows into the public work area.** Also, the information about responding to calls was grouped into details about responding to a fire and details about responding to an accident.

Grouping in Order of Importance

The ideas in support sentences are often presented in the order of importance. Many times, after looking at your examples, you might want to start with the most important example and then continue adding examples from most important to least important.

Other times, you might prefer to start with the least important example and end with the most important idea. Trying different approaches is helpful and gives you a feel for writing effective paragraphs.

The following paragraph moves from the most important to the least important duties of a firefighter. All the duties are important, but most people agree that **saving lives is more important than saving buildings.** Look at this paragraph to see how the examples and details are presented.

Paragraph That Is Organized According to Order of Importance

people

pets

buildings belongings

Firefighters perform many heroic acts. When fighting a fire, no act is more important than protecting lives. Before trying to save a building, firefighters look for trapped or lost victims. If they attempt to rescue victims at the same time they try to put out the fire, they will only make the fire hotter and increase the danger from smoke inhalation because when this happens, the victims' lungs will fill with smoke and they may die. Firefighters risk their lives a lot as they go into these burning, smoke-filled buildings and carry people outside to safety. Many times, when firefighters go into flaming structures for search and rescue, they also find terrified family pets and will do their best to pull them out of the fire, too. Once rescue is complete, firefighters perform other valiant acts by preventing any further damage to the burning building. If possible, firefighters go back into buildings so they can put people's personal belongings in the center of the room and cover everything with salvage covers. This prevents water and falling debris from destroying everything inside the building. When they are one hundred percent sure that it is too late to save anyone or anything, firefighters will not go into a building because they will not put their partner at risk when there is no hope; however, if there is even a slim chance that they can pull someone from the fire, they will go in.

In the previous paragraph, the heroic acts were arranged in the following order of importance: saving human lives first, saving pets second, and saving property last. This order seems the most effective for showing examples of the courageous acts performed by firefighters everywhere. The paragraph also included time words when needed.

Drafting

After all the careful thinking and prewriting you have done, you are ready to write your paragraph. This step in the writing process should really be easy for you now. Before you actually begin to draft your paragraph, you need to do a simple outline.

Main Idea: _____
Support Idea 1: _____
_____
_____
_____
Support Idea 2: _____
_____
_____
_____
Support Idea 3: _____
_____
_____
_____
Ending Sentence: _____

The outline helps you to identify the kind of pattern you need for your particular paragraph. For example, it is much easier at this point to sort out the most important from least important example or to group like ideas together. You can see now if time order is the best pattern to use.

Remember that once you have a draft, you can go on to the next steps in the writing process—revising and editing.

Revising

Once you have drafted your paragraph, you will want to be sure that it is clear and flows smoothly. Sometimes you have a very promising paragraph, but the ideas in your paragraph need to be rearranged before going any further.

Changing Content

The first draft of your paragraph is usually not your best work. You may need to add to your content or take out ideas that do not seem to fit. Even if you did a thorough outline, you may need to revise by rearranging ideas. Read through the following draft of a paragraph about first-year firefighters. This paragraph could be organized by time or chronological order. Study the following paragraph, paying close attention to the order in which the support is presented.

First Draft—Rough Copy

Booters

(1) In the fire department, probationary firefighters are often referred to by a nickname. (2) In the city of Phoenix, probationary firefighters are known as booters. (3) The responsibilities of booters are tremendous. (4) *As the sun goes down, probationary firefighters are responsible for taking down the flag*. (5) Their responsibilities include being the first person at the station and putting the flag up. (6) Booters are responsible for cleaning the station and doing the station duties such as cleaning the kitchen and bathrooms and mopping all the floors. (7) ~~When Keith was a~~ ~~booter, he made delicious chicken enchiladas and chocolate chip~~ ~~cookies.~~ Booters are responsible for mopping the apparatus bay floor where the fire trucks are kept. (8) The booters are responsible for keeping the fire truck clean and restocking it with supplies. (9) Booters are responsible for any other things that may need to be done around the station. (10) *Another responsibility of booters is to make the morning coffee and bring in the paper*. (11) Booters are responsible for answering the telephone and taking messages. (12) As booters, the new recruits must stay busy throughout this first year on the job. (13) This means that booters cannot sleep very much or sit on the recliners and watch television. (14) This first year is part of tradition and gives the booters a good work ethic as well as lets others know they are serious about the job.

The two sentences in the above paragraph that are italicized (4 and 10) are obviously out of order and break the flow of the paragraph. These sentences need to be rearranged.

Also, sentence #7 does not seem to belong, so it needs to be taken out and replaced with information that might have come from the prewriting activities.

Second Draft—Order Rearranged

Booters

(1) In the fire department, probationary firefighters are often referred to by a nickname. (2) In the city of Phoenix, probationary firefighters are known as booters. (3) The responsibilities of booters are tremendous. (4) Their responsibilities include being the first person at the station and putting the flag up. (5) *Another responsibility of booters is to make the*

morning coffee and bring in the paper. (6) The booters are responsible for cleaning the station and doing the station duties such as cleaning the kitchen and bathrooms and mopping all the floors. (7) Booters are responsible for mopping the apparatus bay floor where the fire trucks are kept. (8) The booters are responsible for keeping the fire truck clean and restocking it with supplies. (9) Booters are responsible for any other things that may need to be done around the station. (10) Booters are responsible for answering the telephone and taking messages. (11) *As the sun goes down, the probationary firefighters are responsible for taking down the flag*. (12) As booters, the new recruits must stay busy throughout this first year on the job. (13) This means that booters cannot sleep very much or sit on the recliners and watch television. (14) This first year is part of tradition and gives the booters a good work ethic as well as lets others know they are serious about the job.

Moving the two sentences eliminates the break in the chronological order. Now the time order is logical because making the coffee and bringing in the paper are morning activities just as taking the flag down occurs at the end of the day. Taking out sentence #7 and replacing it with a related idea strengthens the paragraph.

Also, note that similar ideas are grouped together. For instance, all the cleaning duties are grouped together (6, 7, 8), and sentence 9 actually serves as a connection to sentence 10, which is about different types of duties, answering the telephone and taking messages. Sentence 13 tends to complete the day, and, as such, completes the responsibilities of a booter. The concluding sentence provides closure for the paragraph by summarizing the firefighter's first year and serves as a commentary on what has been said in the paragraph.

Adding Coherence

One of the most important steps in revising is adding words and phrases to make your paragraph flow more smoothly. Every sentence should be clearly and logically connected to the one that comes before it as well as to the one that comes after it. This smooth flow is called **coherence**. It is possible to add coherence to a draft by using one or more of the following:

Key words
Time words
Other transitional words

Key Words   One of the simplest yet most effective ways to add coherence to your paragraph is to use key words. **Key words refer to the important words in the main idea** often stated in the first sentence of a paragraph.

If you wish to emphasize a word, you might use that word more than once in your paragraph, but most of the time, you will want to find other words that mean the same thing. Using other words that mean the same thing lets you thread the topic idea throughout the paragraph without repeating the same word over and over. It is actually exciting to see a paragraph go from boring and mechanical to interesting and creative while it supports the main idea of the paragraph.

The last draft of "Booters" has the potential to be a strong paragraph with many examples, but it can be made stronger through the use of **key words**. Look at the main idea, "The **responsibilities** of **booters** are **tremendous**" (sentence #3). The key words are "responsibilities," "booters," and "tremendous." Look at the following example that shows how other words can take the place of key words in the sentence. If you want to emphasize that these firefighters are called booters, you might use this word more than once, but you probably should not use the other words more than once. A form of the word "responsible" is used nine times, and this becomes monotonous.

responsibilities	first-year firefighter	tremendous
tasks	rookie	huge
duties	first year at the station	large number
jobs	new recruits	enormous
obligations	amateur	immense
requirements	new firefighter	
expectations		
liable for		
work they are counted upon to do		

Now look at the same paragraph after other words with a similar meaning have replaced the key words "booters" and "responsibilities" throughout the paragraph.

Third Draft—Key Words Added

Booters

(1) In the fire department, probationary firefighters are often referred to by a nickname. (2) In the city of Phoenix, probationary firefighters are known as ⟨booters.⟩ (3) The responsibilities of ~~booters~~ these new members of the station are tremendous. (4) Their obligations ~~responsibilities~~ include being the first person at the station and putting the flag up. (5) Another ~~responsibility~~ task of ~~booters~~ new recruits is to make the morning coffee and bring in the paper. (6) The ~~booters~~ newcomers are ~~responsible~~ accountable for

cleaning the station and doing the station duties such as cleaning the

kitchen and bathrooms and mopping all the floors. (7) Booters are
required to
~~responsible for~~ mopping the apparatus bay floor where the fire trucks are
rookies   expected to
kept. (8) The ~~booters~~ are ~~responsible for~~ keeping the fire truck clean and
They   counted upon to complete
restock~~ing~~ it with supplies. (9) ~~Booters~~ are ~~responsible for~~ any other
They
things that may need to be done around the station. (10) ~~Booters~~ are

responsible for answering the telephone and taking messages. (11) As
in charge of
the sun goes down, the probationary firefighters are ~~responsible for~~
first-year firefighters
taking down the flag. (12) As ~~booters,~~ the new recruits must stay busy

throughout this first year on the job. (13) This means that booters cannot

sleep very much or sit on the recliners and watch television. (14) This
new firefighter recruit
first year is part of tradition and gives the ~~booters~~ a good work ethic as

well as lets others know they are serious about the job.

Time Words   You learned previously that time words can actually make the connections clear between events. However, you do not need to use exact clock hours. As you have already learned, there are other ways to indicate time order. Now look at this draft of "Booters," and see how appropriate time words have been added.

Fourth Draft—Time Words Added

Booters

(1) In the fire department, probationary firefighters are often referred

to by a nickname. (2) In the city of Phoenix, probationary firefighters are

known as booters. (3) The responsibilities of these new members of the

station are tremendous. (4) Their obligations include being the *first*
in the morning
person at the station ^ and putting the flag up. (5) Another task of a new

recruit is to make the *morning* coffee and bring in the paper. (6) The

newcomers are accountable for cleaning the station and doing the

station duties such as cleaning the kitchen and bathrooms and mopping

all the floors. (7) Booters are required to mop the apparatus bay floor

where the fire trucks are kept. (8) The rookies are expected to keep the

fire truck clean and restock it with supplies. (9) They are counted upon

to complete any other things that may need to be done around the
station. (10) _{Throughout the day, t}They are responsible for answering the telephone and
taking messages. (11) _{At the end of the day a}*As the sun goes down*, the probationary firefighters
are in charge of taking down the flag. (12) As first-year firefighters, the
new recruits must stay busy throughout *this first year* on the job. (13) This
means that booters cannot sleep _{during the day} ~~very much~~ or sit on the recliners and
watch television. (14) This first year is part of tradition and gives the new
firefighter recruits a good work ethic as well as lets others know they are
serious about the job.

Note The above words and phrases in italics are time words that were already in
the first draft.

Transitional Words Another very important way to add coherence to your paragraph is to add transitional words and phrases. **Transitions** are words and phrases that show a clear connection between ideas in a paragraph. These words or phrases may add clarity and meaning to your writing and help your reader follow your ideas. Look at the following words that are often used to add coherence.

in addition	however	on one hand	first	for example
in the same way	therefore	on the other hand	second	for instance
in another way	consequently	also	finally	
in other words	furthermore	too	later	
	as a result		next	

Look at the fifth draft of this same paragraph to see how transitional words
and phrases have helped to add coherence.

Fifth Draft—Transitional Words Added

Booters

(1) In the fire department, probationary firefighters are often referred
to by a nickname. (2) _{For example, i}In the city of Phoenix, probationary firefighters are
known as booters. (3) The responsibilities of these new members of the
station are tremendous. (4) _{In addition to going on emergency calls, they have other obligations, including} ~~Their obligations include~~ being the first
person at the station in the morning and putting the flag up. (5) Another
task of new recruits is to make the morning coffee and bring in the paper.

(6) The newcomers are $\overset{also}{\wedge}$ accountable for cleaning the station and doing the station duties such as cleaning the kitchen and bathrooms and mopping all the floors. (7) Booters are required to mop the apparatus bay floor where the fire trucks are kept. (8) $\overset{Furthermore,\ t}{\wedge}$he rookies are expected to keep the fire truck clean and restock it with supplies. (9) They are counted upon to complete any other things that may need to be done around the station. (10) Throughout the day, they are responsible for answering the telephone and taking messages. (11) At the end of the day as the sun goes down, the probationary firefighters are in charge of taking down the flag. (12) As first-year firefighters, the new recruits must stay busy throughout this first year on the job. (13) $\overset{In\ other\ words,\ t}{\wedge}$his means that booters cannot sleep during the day or sit on the recliners and watch television. (14) This first year is part of tradition and gives the new firefighter recruits a good work ethic as well as lets others know they are serious about the job.

Now look at the completed draft that has been revised for coherence. Remember, however, that you can go back and revise a paragraph as many times as you wish.

Sixth Draft—Revisions Added

Booters

(1) In the fire department, probationary firefighters are often referred to by a nickname. (2) For example, in the city of Phoenix, probationary firefighters are known as booters. (3) The responsibilities of these new members of the station are tremendous. (4) In addition to going on emergency calls, they have other obligations, including being the first person at the station in the morning and putting the flag up. (5) Another task of new recruits is to make the morning coffee and bring in the paper. (6) The newcomers are also accountable for cleaning the station and doing the station duties such as cleaning the kitchen and bathrooms and mopping all the floors. (7) Booters are required to mop the apparatus bay floor where the fire trucks are kept. (8) Furthermore, the rookies are expected to keep the fire truck clean and restock it with supplies. (9) They are counted upon to complete any other things that may need to be done around the station. (10) Throughout the day, they are responsible for answering the telephone and taking messages. (11) At the end of the day as the sun goes down, the probationary firefighters are in charge of

taking down the flag. (12) As first-year firefighters, the new recruits must stay busy throughout this first year on the job. (13) In other words, this means that a booters cannot sleep during the day or sit on the recliners and watch television. (14) This first year is part of tradition and gives the new firefighter recruits a good work ethic as well as lets others know they are serious about the job.

Editing

The last stage in the writing process is editing. Before you can consider a paragraph finished, you will need to find and correct any errors in mechanics and grammar such as errors in spelling, punctuation, use of verbs and pronouns, and sentence structure. As you practice writing sentences, you will learn how to find and correct these problems. You should not expect to have everything perfect at the beginning, but you will get better as you continue to study different sentence patterns. However, writing sentences in the context of a paragraph can only help you become a more competent writer.

For now, you can use a dictionary to check your spelling. If you have a computer with a good word processing program, you can use the spell check. Your instructor may also have you use a grammar check program.

All in all, be patient with yourself as you practice the writing process. Be willing to take the time necessary to make your writing clear and meaningful.

Formatting

Having a good paragraph is your goal; however, making it look polished is also important and leaves the message that you have worked hard and been careful about the details. Standard requirements for handing in papers often include the following formatting:

- Use 8 1/2 × 11-inch high-quality typing paper.
- Use 1-inch margins on all sides of the paper.
- Heading

  Single-space heading, using a flush left margin:

  > Name
  >
  > Instructor's name
  >
  > Course number
  >
  > Date

- Title

  Center the title one space below the heading.

  Capitalize the first and last word of the title.

  Capitalize all main words in the title except articles (*a, an, the*), short prepositions (*at, by,* etc.), and short connecting words (*and, or,* etc.).

  Do not use quotation marks (" ") around the title or underline (___) it.

- Paragraph

  Skip a line between the title and the first line of the paragraph.

Indent the first sentence in the paragraph approximately half an inch or five spaces.

Double-space the paragraph.

- Put a period at the end of each sentence, and leave one or two spaces before the next sentence.

Sample Paragraph Format

1" ↓

Patricia Dowell
Professor Bill Cherrington
ENG061
17 March 2003

My Son's First Birthday Party

1" →

← 1"

1" ↑

Summary

Working through the writing process helps you write effectively throughout your life, whether you are going to college, working in a career, or solving problems in your personal life. If you take the time to write carefully, you will find success. Think through this review of the writing process.

Prewrite for information—Prewriting includes any activity that helps you generate ideas for writing, including freewriting, brainstorming, and talking.

Organize ideas—Organizing involves grouping ideas together in one or a combination of the following ways: chronological order, similarity, or importance.

Draft paper—Drafting means writing the first copy of your paragraph.

Revise and rewrite—Revising refers to rewriting your paragraph by rearranging ideas and adding coherence by using key words, time words, and other transitional words.

Edit carefully—Editing refers to correcting grammatical and mechanical errors, including punctuation and spelling.

Format carefully—Use a standard style such as MLA to format your papers.

Practice Test

Read the following three paragraphs that all describe two young brothers who spent many enjoyable summer days at the beach. Notice the organization of each paragraph, and then answer the questions at the end of Beach Paragraph #3.

Beach Paragraph #1

Summers at the Beach

The beach was a wonderful place for my brother and me to spend our summers. Whether the tide was coming in or going out, we always found something exciting to keep us busy while we were there. When the tide was coming in, we watched the water move closer and closer until waves began to hit a huge rock on the beach. My brother and I discovered that we could climb up on the rock, and as the water rose higher and higher, we could dive into the ocean. For maybe an hour or two, we continued, scrambling to see who could climb the rock the fastest until the water eventually covered our rock, making it disappear from our sight. Gradually, the water came so close that even the sandy beach itself began to fade away, and all we could see was blue water, waves flanked by sea gulls, and ships. When the tide was going out, we also found plenty of enjoyment. As the water receded, we would quickly dig holes in the sand looking for clams. On some days, we would find lobsters that were begging to be cooked, and we quickly filled our bucket ready to dash home and have our mother boil them in salt water. Sometimes, when the tide was completely out, it seemed as though we could walk miles out on the sand bars, admiring barnacle-covered rocks jutting out of the sand. On the best days, however, the tide would leave little pools, and we would leisurely swim with the baby mackerels or whatever fish were trapped in these little tide pools. Today, that beach is thousands of miles away, but I would give anything for one more carefree day on the beach with my brother.

Beach Paragraph #2

Summers at the Beach

The beach was a wonderful place for my brother and me to spend our summer days. At midmorning, when we first got to the beach, we knew the cold salt water would bring relief from the heat of summer, but instead of diving right in, we carefully tested the water with our toes. Within a few minutes, our excitement grew as we ventured out knee deep. Before long, a wave came gently tearing at us, and we found ourselves laughing and splashing as we rolled around in the surf. Later in the day, we swam out to the breakers so we could sit on the rocks, soak up the sun's warmth, and watch the big cargo ships come in from different countries as they headed for Boston Harbor. Though we could not read the foreign names on the ships, we would look for glimpses of their flags to see if we could identify the different countries they sailed out of. Once we had soaked in enough heat, we would then slide back into the water and swim back to the beach, once again reveling in the refreshing ocean water. When we had had enough water for the day and our lips were turning purple, we got out of the water and rolled in the sand to warm our bodies. At sunset, when our stomachs could no longer stand being empty, we headed home, knowing we would return the next day.

Beach Paragraph #3

Summers at the Beach

There were many things that lured my brother and me to the beach that summer, but perhaps the most enticing was swimming in the ocean. Nothing compared to the satisfaction we got from feeling the cold salt water cool our bodies. We loved to float up and down on the waves, following the rhythm of the ocean water. Totally relaxed, we did not have a care in the world. Some days we would dive under the waves or dive straight into the top part of the waves to avoid being pulled under. While we were enjoying the water, we were also drawn by the many opportunities to explore the marine life that surrounded us. Some days we could swim with the small fish left in tide pools. On many days, we found crabs, sand dollars, and clams, and once in a while I was fortunate enough to hold a starfish. I was both awed and honored to watch the beauty of the porpoises gracefully jumping in the water. Once I found a little baby octopus and held it in my hands as its little suction cups tickled my hand, and its tiny tentacles wrapped around my fingers. Another attraction that tempted us both back to the beach was the many treasures we found that had washed to the shore. I still remember my brother running toward me with a glass bottle that had a note inside. Another time, I found a rod and reel with the line stuck around a rock. Sometimes we found unusual seashells that we would take home and stash under our beds. Today I feel privileged for these times I spent with my brother.

Answer the following questions by circling the letter of the correct answer. Take your time and think carefully.

1. Beach Paragraph #1 is organized by grouping like ideas together. What are the two ideas?
   a. tide coming in and tide going out
   b. found enjoyment but had to go home
   c. became cold but were warmed by the sun

2. Beach Paragraph #2 is organized using chronological or time order. What words show progression from morning to night?
   a. we found ourselves laughing and splashing as we rolled around in the surf, when our stomachs could no longer stand being empty
   b. soaking up the sun's warmth, foreign names on the ships
   c. at midmorning, within a few minutes, later in the day, then we, once we had soaked in enough heat, we would then, at sunset

3. Beach Paragraph #3 is developed through order of importance, although it also groups like ideas together. Which support idea is the most important?
   a. the cold salt water that cooled our bodies
   b. the marine life
   c. treasures on the beach

4. In Beach Paragraph #1, what examples center around the tide **coming in**?
   a. clams, lobsters, barnacle-covered rocks, little tide pools
   b. big rock on the beach, sandy beach disappears, blue water, sea gulls, ships

5. In Beach Paragraph #1, what idea centers around the tide **going out**?
   a. clams, lobsters, barnacle-covered rocks, little tide pools
   b. big rock on the beach, sandy beach disappears, blue water, sea gulls, ships

6. In Beach Paragraph #1, what words or phrases go back to the key words "tide was coming in"?
   a. water rose higher and higher, water came so close that, eventually covered
   b. for an hour or two, water rose higher and higher, blue water
   c. water rose higher and higher, blue water, waves flanked by sea gulls

7. In Beach Paragraph #1, what words or phrases go back to the key words "tide was going out"?
   a. leisurely swim with the baby mackerels, sand bars
   b. quickly filled our buckets, walk miles out on the sand bars
   c. water receded, completely out, would leave little pools

8. In Beach Paragraph #2, what is the first phrase that refers to time order?
   a. within a few minutes
   b. when we first got to the beach
   c. once we had soaked in enough heat

9. In Beach paragraph #2, what final time word indicates the end of the day?
   a. first
   b. within a few minutes
   c. at sunset

10. In Beach Paragraph #2, what words provide transition from watching the ships and their flags to deciding to swim back to the beach?
    a. once we had soaked in enough heat, we would then slide back into the water
    b. we got out of the water and rolled in the sand
    c. we headed home

11. In Beach Paragraph #3, what words go back to the key word "lured"?
    a. baby octopus, cold salt water, swimming
    b. enticing, drawn by, tempted us both back
    c. awed and honored, baby octopus, rod and reel

12. In Beach Paragraph #3, the baby octopus is an example of which support idea?
    a. the cold salt water that cooled our bodies
    b. the marine life that surrounded us
    c. treasures on the beach

13. In Beach Paragraph #3, the rod and reel are examples of which support idea?
    a. the cold salt water that cooled our bodies
    b. the marine life
    c. treasures on the beach

14. In Beach Paragraph #3, which transition sentence provides a transition from the cold salt water to the marine life?
    a. I was both awed and honored to watch the beauty of the porpoises gracefully jumping in the water.
    b. Some days we would swim with the small fish left in tide pools.
    c. While we were enjoying the water, we were also drawn by the many opportunities to explore the marine life that surrounded us.

 ## *Writing Assignment*

Write a paragraph on one of the following topics.
1. A child's birthday party
2. New Year's Eve
3. First day on a new job
4. Most important quality of a neighbor
5. Favorite high school memory

Begin by prewriting to find a direction, and then follow all the steps necessary to have a finished paragraph. Be sure to spend as much time as necessary on revision.

Part 2

Something to Think About, Something to Write About

Professional Essay to Generate Ideas for Writing

This section of your textbook includes writing by well-educated, knowledge-able professionals who share their knowledge about various topics. As you read through each selection, think about what the author has to say, and then complete the writing assignment at the end of the selection.

It is not important for you to agree with what is said, but it is important for you to think about what is said and then try to relate that information to what you have experienced or learned.

How to Impress Your Professor
Some Tips for Guaranteed Success in This Class

Dr. Russell F. Proctor II, *Professor of Communication,*
Northern Kentucky University

1 It has been said that we usually learn rules by breaking them. Unfortunately, the breaking of unspoken classroom rules can be a source of frustration and embarrassment. Most college instructors expect, or as least desire, certain behaviors from their students, but rarely are those expectations communicated openly. Thus, students may only learn of an instructor's "pet peeves" by violating them.

2 It occurred to me a few years ago that these encounters could be avoided by informing students of my "unspoken rules" **before** they broke them. I knew, however, that it would be important to communicate my expectations without sounding picky about rules. I decided to try using humor; the result was a handout entitled, "How to Score Points with Dr. Proctor."

3 I was a bit concerned the first time I passed it out—would it be perceived the way I intended it? My fears were calmed as I heard chuckling (and even a few chortles) from the students. I was careful then and now to elaborate on each item, telling stories of classroom encounters that led to the handout's creation as each point has a history of its own. When read with the right tone of voice, the handout becomes a series of humorous hints rather than a strident list of do's and don'ts.

4 The reaction to the handout over the years has been quite positive. In addition, I am happy to report that students no longer ask, "Did I miss anything important?" (#12), nor do they request early exams to accommodate their vacations to Florida (#15). I discovered that by communicating rules with a grin, my students and I know what we can expect from each other.

1. Be sporadic in your attendance. It's not a good idea to "wear out your welcome," and your professor won't mind if you drop by class only occasionally.

2. Arrive at class a few minutes late each day. That way, your professor will be sure to notice you.

3. This class is a good place to catch up on your work in other courses. Class time can also be well spent by reading the newspaper, talking with a friend, or taking a nap. Your professor loves to see students use their time efficiently.

4. Avoid coming to class prepared. Reading the text in advance, for instance, means you'll lose a sense of spontaneity. Besides, your professor will cover the material anyway, so why bother?

5. Your professor is really flexible about assignment due dates. If you turn in something late, don't worry—it actually helps him spread out his workload. Penalties? Never!

6. Only the things your professor puts on the board or the overhead are important. Keep this in mind, and you'll take fewer notes.

7. Don't participate in class unless your professor calls on you. It's rude to ask questions and inappropriate to express your opinions. Remember—this is education, not a talk show.

8. When someone else asks a question in class, pay no attention. Your professor will be happy to answer the identical question when you ask it a minute later.

9. When you make spelling errors, inform your professor it's because your computer's spell-checking program didn't catch them. Learning how to spell on your own is a waste of precious brain cells.

10. Remember, personality is more important than performance. If your professor likes you, you're guaranteed a good grade.

11. No one, including your professor, still believes a C means "average." Anyone who comes to class regularly deserves at least a B.

12. If you're going to be absent, don't notify your professor in advance. Just show up a week later and ask, "Did I miss anything important?" (one of your professor's favorite questions). Being the nice guy he is, he won't hold you responsible for anything you missed while you were absent.

13. Here are some other comments your professor loves to hear:

    If you miss a question on an exam: "It's a trick question."

    If you do poorly on an assignment: "My mom thought it was great."

    If you won't be in class: "I need to study for another course."

14. Be sure to use class time to ask your professor questions that are answered on the syllabus, such as, "When is our paper due?," "What are we supposed to read for the next session?," or "How much is this exam worth?" Asking questions is a lot easier than reading the syllabus.

15. Your professor will be delighted to hear that you are planning to take a vacation while school is still in session. Feel free to take a break while the rest of the class abides by the schedule.

16. Don't bother your professor with questions during his office hours; he has work to do. Instead, approach him one minute before class and ask him to look over the paper you've written.

17. Your professor needs help remembering what time it is, so begin packing your books five minutes before the period is over. He will appreciate the reminder and be impressed with your concern.

18. Wait until you are at the crisis point before asking your professor for help; otherwise, he will not consider your problem important.

19. If you have a complaint or concern, don't discuss it with your professor—he won't listen or try to understand (after all, he doesn't really believe in this communication stuff). Instead, talk about it with as many classmates as possible. Better yet, give your professor no clue that you're upset, then unload on him in your course evaluation. Now *that's* effective communication!

20. Don't drop by your professor's office to chat—he's far too busy to be concerned about you. Remember, he's not a professor because he loves working with students; he's in it for the money.

21. Don't keep this handout or a copy of the syllabus: Your professor doesn't expect you to take them seriously. He made them just to keep busy and waste paper. Deposit them in the trash on your way out of the room.

Understanding Words

Briefly define the following words as they are used in the selection.

1. chortles
2. strident
3. sporadic
4. spontaneity

 ## *Writing Assignment*

Make a list of ten tips for success for one of the following people. Number each tip, and use complete sentences. Single-space your sentences, but double-space between each entry.

1. Boyfriend or girlfriend
2. Husband or wife
3. Son or daughter
4. Parent
5. Boss
6. Teacher
7. Brother or sister
8. Neighbor
9. Sales associate
10. Public bus driver

Part 3

Student and Professional Paragraphs for Discussion and Analysis

Reem Al Bawadi

Hanan Al-Shakhrit, *Student*

Reem Al Bawadi is the best restaurant that I have ever experienced. I especially remember that night five years ago when my friend invited me to have dinner at this restaurant. As soon as we arrived, the valet staff took care of our parking, and the host welcomed us inside. Within ten minutes, we sat down; soon our order was taken with lots of welcoming words and very nice smiles from the service people. After that, we started to notice our surroundings. Wherever I looked, something attracted my eyes and touched my feelings, especially those huge palm trees that had been planted everywhere as well as wonderful waterfalls and nice soft music playing in the background. The best part about this place was a very good taste of Arabian decoration, which made me feel as though I was invited to the king's palace. The floors were covered with very expensive rugs full of colors and designs, and the room was filled with rich-looking antique furniture. The interesting thing was that whoever decorated this place had added the Arabian cultural touch to every corner of it. An old lady was sitting on the floor baking and serving the fresh Arabian bread, using an old-fashioned oven that was made out of clay. While I was enjoying every corner of the restaurant, the waitress served the tastiest meal I have ever had. Later at the end of the wonderful night, I thought that my friend was going to pay a large amount of money, but I was surprised that it was just a very regular bill and it was very reasonable. I left the restaurant and went home, but I kept thinking of it for a long time, and I am still waiting for the day when I can go back and invite my friends to my favorite restaurant.

Understanding Words
Briefly define the following word as it is used in this selection.

valet

Questions on Form
1. What did the author do to add coherence?

2. What did the author do to help the reader visualize the restaurant?

3. What makes the concluding sentence effective?

Questions on Content

1. What were five examples of things she enjoyed at the restaurant?

2. What was the oven made of?

3. Why was she surprised at the bill?

Poverty in My Country

Amanda Moreno, *Student*

In my country, Nicaragua, there are many children working in the street, wiping windows, sweeping the streets, and selling food. These things break my heart. Poverty makes me sad because it is hard to see unfortunate kids who cry because they do not have food or water. Instead of going to school and enjoying their childhood, they are working hard to help support their families. I went back to my country last year, and I talked to a child who lived on the street. He told me he had not eaten for two days. He asked for money, and when I gave him the money, I saw happiness in his face. Two weeks later, a little girl about eight years old had been selling avocados, and she told me that somebody stole them. She was crying because her mother was going to punish her. I gave her some money to help her for the avocados she lost. I felt very happy to help her, and after this, we became good friends. I wish I could be rich so I could help all poor children.

Questions on Form

1. Identify the main idea.

2. What are the details surrounding the example of the little girl selling avocados?

3. Identify the concluding sentence.

Questions on Content

1. What is the effect on the writer of seeing poor children in the street?

2. Why was the little girl crying?

3. What does the author wish she could be?

Korea

Ellen J. Gary, *Student*

Korea is a very interesting country because some traditions are so different from the ones in America. When my husband and I visited Korea, we soon learned firsthand about some of these traditions. The Koreans believe that when people give a gift, that it is a reflection of their soul. One day, as we entered the elevator at the hotel, I spoke to a man and his young son. The young lad grinned, so I gave him the orange that I had in my hand. That evening when we were dining, this gentleman came over to our table and grabbed my hand and gave me two Korean dolls. I did not recognize him until his son came from behind him; it was the little boy that I had given the orange to. His father explained that because I was friendly to his son, he and his wife wanted to give me a gift also. Upon accepting the gift, I grasped his hand with both of my hands and bowed. That is the traditional way of saying thank you in Korea. We also found that the marriage customs, especially for girls, were different from ours. We learned that a thirty-year-old girl was considered an old maid because it is their custom that by the time a girl is thirty she should be married and have at least three children. This was a surprise to us because we have three daughters, and we have encouraged them to wait until they are older before marrying. Though Korean customs are different from ours, we learned to respect them because we were visitors in their land.

Questions on Form

1. What is the main idea of the paragraph?

2. What two examples does the author use to support the main idea?

3. How did the author add closure to the paragraph?

Questions on Content

1. What is the Korean custom regarding marriage?

2. What gift did the author give to the little boy?

3. By the time a woman in Korea is thirty, what is expected of her?

Excerpt from Wouldn't Take Nothing for My Journey Now

Maya Angelou

Because of the routines we follow, we often forget that life is an ongoing adventure. We leave our homes for work, acting and even believing that we will reach our destinations with no unusual event startling us out of our set expectations. The truth is we know nothing, not where our cars will fail or when our buses will stall, whether our places of employment will be there when we arrive, or whether, in fact, we ourselves will arrive whole and alive at the end of our journeys. Life is pure adventure, and the sooner we realize that, the quicker we will be able to treat life as art: to bring all our energies to each encounter, to remain flexible enough to notice and admit when what we expected to happen did not happen. We need to remember that we are created creative and can invent new scenarios as frequently as they are needed.

Questions on Form
1. Identify the author's main idea.

2. Give three specific examples of the main idea.

3. How does the author conclude the paragraph?

Questions on Content
1. What does she call life?

2. When things get rough, how do people survive?

3. What do people need to remember about how they were created?

Excerpt from "Graduation" in The Pact

George Jenkins

As I watched Sam walk across the stage, I sat still and quiet. Pride swirled through my body. I was thinking, "Man, we really did this." I thought of all we had been through together, from boys comparing sneakers on the schoolyard in junior high to men walking across the stage to become doctors. We had leapt into the unknown together and locked hands and pulled one another up, over, and through the rough spots. I remembered how much I had hurt for him when he had failed the state board exam, how I'd driven to Camden one and a half hours each way nearly every weekend after that to be there for him. I tried to get him to play basketball and just have some fun to get his mind off the results of that test. It was all I could do to show him that I cared and that he wasn't alone.

Questions on Form

1. What is the main idea of the paragraph?

2. What examples strengthen the topic idea?

Questions on Content

1. What is the distance to Camden?

2. What had they done as children?

3. Why was Sam walking across the stage?

Part 4

Understanding Grammar
Nouns, Pronouns, Prepositions, and Verbs

Objectives

- Review brief definitions of the eight parts of speech
- Understand, identify, and use nouns correctly
- Understand, identify, and use pronouns correctly
- Understand, identify, and use prepositions correctly
- Understand, identify, and use verbs correctly

Being able to write well means you understand how words fit together to form sentences, how sentences fit together to form paragraphs, and how paragraphs fit together to form longer papers.

Reviewing the parts of speech and understanding how words fit together to form sentences gives you the opportunity to understand and create effective sentences. As you build your own sentences, you have control over the English language and what you want to say. Reviewing grammar should be more than memorizing parts of speech. It should be thinking through words to find the most effective combinations you can use to communicate your ideas to others. Part of your commitment to being a better writer depends on your willingness to spend time and thought on revising the individual words and phrases in your sentences.

Overview of the Parts of Speech

All sentences are made up of words, and each word in a sentence functions as a specific part of speech. The eight parts of speech are defined simply.

Noun—A noun is the name of a person, place, or thing. It names anything that may be the topic of discussion.

Pronoun—A pronoun is a word that takes the place of a noun. It replaces a noun without naming it.

Preposition—A preposition is a word that is used with a noun or pronoun to form a phrase that shows location, ownership/identification, time, or exclusion within the sentence. A prepositional phrase begins with a preposition and ends with a noun or pronoun, or both, which is called its object.

Verb—A verb is a word that shows action, existence, or a state of being. It may be one word or a verb phrase with two or more words.

Adjective—An adjective is a word that describes or modifies a noun or pronoun. It answers which one, what kind, or how many. (The articles **a**, **an**, and **the** are adjectives.) An adjective is usually found before the noun that it modifies; however, it may be after the verb if a form of the verb **be** is used.

Adverb—An adverb is a word that describes or modifies a verb, an adjective, or another adverb. It answers when, where, how, why, or how much. It may be found in different places in the sentence if it modifies a verb but not if it modifies an adjective or other adverb. **Very** and **not** are always adverbs.

Conjunction—A conjunction is a word that joins one part in a sentence to another part. It may join words, phrases, clauses, or sentences.

Interjection—An interjection is an exclamatory word that shows strong feeling.

It may be written as a sentence by itself and followed by an exclamation point:

"Look! That house is on fire."

The interjection may be part of a sentence and set off by a comma:

"Oh, I forgot to mail this letter."

Usually you will not want to use interjections in formal writing.

Note Adjectives, adverbs, and conjunctions are covered in more depth later.

Though you may read or even memorize the above definitions for the eight parts of speech, you need to see these words in the context of a sentence because one word may serve as more than one part of speech. For example, think about the word "work." Immediately, you want to identify it as a verb, but it is not limited to being a verb.

Work can be satisfying.	(*Work* used as a noun)
Eddie **works** every day.	(*Work* used as a verb)
Eddie has an excellent **work** ethic.	(*Work* used as an adjective)

Not only can a word function as more than one part of speech, but that same word may have different forms that also function in different ways. Consider these additional sentences.

Working hard every day builds discipline.	(*Working* is used as a noun.)
Eddie likes **to work** on his car.	(*To work* functions as a noun.)
That certainly is a **workable** solution.	(*Workable* is an adjective.)

Most words have many different forms, but thinking about words and how they operate in sentences gives you the foundation you need to understand each part of speech.

Not all sentences contain all eight parts of speech though all sentences must have a noun or a pronoun as well as a verb. Also, being able to identify prepositional phrases often helps you identify subjects. Because of this, nouns, pronouns, prepositions, and verbs are covered in detail now.

You will study adjectives, adverbs, and conjunctions after you understand basic simple sentences. Just remember that being able to recognize these parts of speech can help you write effective sentences and paragraphs because you will be able to understand how words fit together to create sentences.

Nouns

A **noun** is any word that names a person, place, or thing.

person	place	thing
Laura Scott pilot	library store garden	elephant stereo car
mom son	Walgreens stadium	computer book
police officer friend	building World Trade Center	Mustang patriotism love

      person   person   thing   place
Jason Stevens became an attorney and practiced law in the city.

            thing   place
Cellular telephones cannot be used in some hospitals.

A noun can be common or proper.

Common nouns are general words and are capitalized only when they come at the beginning of a sentence.

     common   common
The team plays an exciting game.

     common   common
The dealer sells new cars.

   common   common
Dealers advertise on television.

Proper nouns name particular people, places, or things. Proper nouns are always capitalized.

       proper   common
The Phoenix Suns play exciting basketball.

     proper   proper
Crescent Motors sells Buicks.

    proper   common
Marie Williams is a wonderful administrator.

A noun can be concrete or abstract.

Concrete nouns are words that can actually be visualized or touched. They can be either common or proper.

      concrete   concrete
The snowflakes fell gently on the trees.

concrete   concrete

Peggy studied the assignment carefully.

Abstract nouns are words that name a quality or an idea. They are usually common nouns.

abstract   abstract

Love keeps a relationship alive.

abstract   abstract

Happiness and success often fall together.

A noun can be a verb form.
  -ing verb forms used as a noun

noun   noun

Swimming keeps the body toned.

noun   noun

Sleeping refreshes the mind.

  to before a verb used as a noun (infinitive)

noun noun

To sleep at night is great.

noun   noun   noun

To run on the forest path calms raw nerves.

noun   noun   noun

Carol likes to hike around the lake.

- A noun can be common or proper.
- A noun can be concrete or abstract.
- A noun can be a verb form.

Exercise 1

Circle the nouns in the following sentences.

Example:

The ⟨circus⟩ is enjoyed by both ⟨children⟩ and ⟨adults⟩.

Version A

1. Tiger Woods is an incredibly talented athlete.
2. Testing takes place during registration.
3. Uncle Mike made a delicious pie.
4. Excitement always follows Danny Griego and his band.
5. Many people prefer natural foods.
6. Unidentified flying objects fascinate many Americans.

7. Kevin likes apple pie.

8. Exercising keeps the body healthy and fit.

9. The computers in the lab were all busy.

10. The commuter train from New York to Boston set a record for efficiency.

Version B

1. Learning English can be a real challenge for international students.

2. Rose spent three hours in the museum.

3. Dancing is great exercise.

4. The beginning of each semester brings excitement for students and teachers.

5. Jodi works for the Internal Revenue Service.

6. The children enjoyed the light rain.

7. My cousins live in California, Oregon, and Kansas.

8. The ducks swam in the lake and searched for food.

9. Jalon and Kevin accepted the challenges of school.

10. Golfing is becoming popular among young people.

Exercise 2

Write two sentences that contain common nouns. (Circle the common nouns.)

1. _____
   _____

2. _____
   _____

Write two sentences that contain proper nouns. (Circle the proper nouns.)

1. _____
   _____

2. _____
   _____

Write two sentences that contain concrete nouns. (Circle the concrete nouns.)

1. _____
   _____

2. _____
   _____

Write two sentences that contain abstract nouns. (Circle the abstract nouns.)

1. _____
   _____

2. _____
   _____

Write two sentences that contain **–ing** verb forms used as nouns. (Circle the **–ing** noun forms.)

1. _____

_____

2. _____

_____

Write two sentences that contain **to** before a verb used as a noun. (Circle the **to + verb.**)

1. _____

_____

2. _____

_____

Pronouns

A pronoun is a word that takes the place of a noun. You use pronouns because you do not want to keep repeating the same noun over and over again. Some frequently used pronouns are in bold type in the following sentences.

Justin wanted to see a movie, so **he** invited his friend Stephanie to go with **him.**

She agreed, and **they** went to an early show.

They both enjoyed **it.**

You can easily see the connections here between the nouns and the pronouns. If pronouns had not been used, these sentences would have sounded monotonous:

Justin wanted to see a movie, so Justin invited Stephanie to go with Justin. Stephanie agreed, and Justin and Stephanie went to an early show.

Being aware of how pronouns take the place of nouns will help you later so you know which personal pronoun to use in your sentence. You can find more information about this in a later section on pronouns.

Exercise 3

Circle the pronouns in the following sentences.

Example:

Mia found a turtle in (her) back yard. (She) gave (it) water and fed (it).

Version A

1. Jeremy bought a new CD player. He played it nonstop for a week.
2. Heather found old coins in the attic. She sold them to a collector.
3. Katrina made three runs on the giant roller coaster. It roared down the steep dips and hurled her around the curves.

4. Brian, Steven, and I spent the weekend camping near the lake. We sat around the campfire and roasted marshmallows.

5. With so many homes being built, the wildlife are being forced from their habitat.

6. Toni and I went to the wedding. We congratulated the bride and groom afterward.

7. Tom has a test tomorrow. He expects it to be difficult.

8. Marsha and I left for our trip to Mexico early in the day.

9. The owls were nesting in the tree. They kept me awake at night.

10. My children and I are planning a camping trip. We are looking forward to it.

Version B

1. Kesha bought a new car. She washed it every day.

2. Donald took his dog to the veterinarian. They were there all afternoon.

3. The artist came from Guadalajara. She demonstrated her pottery-making techniques.

4. The students made red, white, and blue flowers. They put them on their float.

5. The little girl was sick. She watched television and read her favorite book.

6. Kelly and Brandon left the party early. They had to drive to his grandmother's house.

7. Pedro and Esther were chosen to be in the play. They worked well together.

8. Natalie took her children to the circus. They enjoyed it.

9. Justin applied for the job in January. He was not hired until May.

10. Maria found a parrot in her backyard. She fed it pieces of apple.

Knowing more about how pronouns work will help you feel more confident about your writing.

Kinds of Pronouns

Pronouns can be put into several groups or categories. In this text, you will become familiar with personal, possessive, indefinite, reflexive, intensive, and demonstrative pronouns.

Personal and Possessive Pronouns

Personal pronouns are probably the most frequently used pronouns in English. Persuasive, confident writers and speakers know them well and know how to use them correctly. Some forms of the personal pronouns are referred to as *possessive* because they show ownership. When personal possessive pronouns come before a noun or modify a noun, they are called adjectives. However, it is more important to make the clear connection between the pronoun and the noun being replaced than to worry about whether or not the word functions as a pronoun or an adjective. Look at the following list so that you are familiar with these types of pronouns.

	Singular			Plural		
	personal		*possessive*	*personal*		*possessive*
1st Person	I	me	my, mine	we	us	our, ours
2nd Person	you	you	your, yours	you	you	your, yours
3rd Person	she	her	her, hers	they	them	their, theirs
3rd Person	he	him	his			
3rd Person	it	it	its			

Pronouns must always clearly refer to the nouns they replace. Work through the next exercise to practice substituting pronouns for nouns.

Exercise 4

Using the knowledge you already have, complete the following sentences by writing in the appropriate personal pronouns (from the list above).

Example:

Marlisha called _her_ friends before _she_ left home.

Version A

1. Henry dropped the pizza before _____ could put _____ into the oven.

2. The new cars were delivered to the dealer at midnight. _____ were dirty from the storm.

3. Angela is taking a class in college. _____ asked _____ son to help _____ with more tasks around the house.

4. Last night the play opened on Broadway. _____ received good reviews in the newspapers.

5. Two women and one man refereed the first game of the new basketball season. The crowd booed _____ only twice.

6. Alice is my neighbor. _____ asked me to pick up _____ mail while _____ was on vacation.

7. My grandmother is learning to use a computer. _____ wants to use _____ to keep track of stocks and bonds.

8. Sara's aunt and uncle use the subway from Oakland when _____ visit _____ .

9. Tarya went to her senior prom with Dan. _____ had pictures taken that night.

10. The little girl loves to bake cookies. _____ often makes _____ for _____ family.

Version B

1. My brother had a special cancer treatment. _____ had to go to the hospital for _____ .

2. Steven studied the weather reports. _____ hoped _____ would show good weather for the party.

3. The drivers waited patiently at the red light. _____ knew _____ would soon change to green.

4. Penny enjoyed playing the organ every evening. _____ helped _____ to relax.

5. My ferret, Molly, loved to burrow under the carpet. _____ thought _____ made a nice den.

6. I bailed my brother out of jail. _____ promised to pay _____ back soon.

7. All the clocks stopped when the power went off. _____ started again when _____ came back on.

8. The planes from the airport flew low over my house. _____ drowned out _____ music.

9. The brother and sister started a new business. _____ opened _____ in the spring.

10. Denise and I went to the fitness center. _____ had a good workout.

Exercise 5

Write five sentences that contain one or more personal pronouns.

1. _____

_____

2. _____

_____

3. _____

_____

4. _____

_____

5. _____

_____

Indefinite Pronouns
Another kind of pronoun that you use very frequently is called an **indefinite pronoun.** This type of pronoun does not refer to a specific noun.

personal pronoun
He understands the instructions. ("He" refers to a specific person.)

indefinite pronoun
Everyone understands the instructions. ("Everyone" does not refer to a specific person.)

Following is a list of the most common indefinite pronouns. Some indefinite pronouns are singular; some are plural; some can be either singular or plural. Just like personal pronouns, these indefinite pronouns may sometimes function as adjectives. Do not be concerned with making that distinction at this point. Just read through the lists to become familiar with these pronouns.

Singular Indefinite Pronouns

each	anyone	anybody	anything
either	everyone	everybody	everything
neither	someone	somebody	something
one	no one	nobody	nothing

Plural Indefinite Pronouns

few	many	several	others

Singular or Plural Indefinite Pronouns

all	any	more
most	some	

For now, just learn to identify these pronouns by working through the following exercises.

Exercise 6

Circle the indefinite pronouns in the following sentences.

Examples:

One of the cars has something wrong with the brakes.

Everyone wants to go with somebody.

No one wants to go alone.

Version A

1. Yesterday, I worked with each of my brothers.
2. In class, no one wanted to write questions on the board.
3. A few of the restaurants closed early.
4. Everybody at the picnic enjoyed the barbecue.
5. Richard lost everything in the fire.
6. Justin read many of his favorite books over the summer.
7. He was not able to save anything from the flood.
8. Neither of the vacation trips appealed to anybody.
9. The detectives asked everyone at the scene to describe the crime.
10. Nothing at the scene escaped their attention.

Version B

1. Several of the doctors volunteered their services for the Peace Corps.
2. Did anyone hear anything about the new requirements for financial aid?
3. Jarad visited some of his favorite relatives last summer.
4. I did not see either of the lost dogs in my neighborhood.
5. Do you think everybody will show up at the party?
6. Someone knocked the cups off the shelf.
7. We saw nothing in the pool.
8. The stray cat would not eat anything.
9. Some of the front yard was under water.
10. Something raced across the roof last night.

As you learned earlier, some words can be used as more than one part of speech. When these indefinite pronouns are used before nouns, they function as adjectives. Look at the following sentences to see how indefinite pronouns sometimes are pronouns and sometimes are adjectives.

adjective
Many children enjoy watching cartoons.

indefinite pronoun
Many enjoy watching cartoons.

adjective
All books must be turned in by tomorrow.

indefinite pronoun
All must be turned in by tomorrow.

adjective
Phil would like **some** roast beef for lunch.

indefinite pronoun
Phil would like **some** for lunch.

Now work through the following exercise to determine which words are used as indefinite pronouns and which are used as adjectives. If you need more explanation, read the section under adjectives.

Exercise 7

Read the following sentences, and decide if the word in bold is used as a pronoun or as an adjective.

Examples:

adj. **Some** people like to take vacations in the winter.

pron. Please save **some** for me.

Version A

____ 1. We went to **several** computer stores and compared prices.

____ 2. **Several** were having sales.

____ 3. We watched **all** of the movie before going to bed.

_____ 4. **All** students in this class use computers well.

_____ 5. **Most** of the children are playing in the backyard.

_____ 6. **Most** children look forward to Saturday cartoons.

Version B

_____ 1. **Many** autumn leaves floated gently to the ground.

_____ 2. **Many** landed on the sidewalk.

_____ 3. **Most** of the apple was rotten.

_____ 4. We have **more** than we need.

_____ 5. Only **one** store carries the brand of shoes I prefer.

_____ 6. **Another** carries many brands of shoes.

Exercise 8

Write five sentences that contain one or more indefinite pronouns.

1. _____

_____

2. _____

_____

3. _____

_____

4. _____

_____

5. _____

_____

Reflexive and Intensive Pronouns

Reflexive and intensive pronouns end in **-self** or **-selves.** They usually refer to the subject of a sentence and add emphasis to the sentence. Here are the most common of these pronouns:

Reflexive and Intensive Pronouns		
Singular: myself	yourself	himself, herself, itself
Plural: ourselves	yourselves	themselves

Read through the following sentences to see how these are used as reflexive pronouns.

George bought **himself** a wallet.

I saw **myself** as the leader of the band.

David and Rachel comforted **themselves** with music.

Mark scolded **himself** for crying.

Marsha taught **herself** to be independent.

Sara cut **herself** out of her father's will.

Read through the following sentences to see how these are used as intensive pronouns to add emphasis to a noun or a pronoun.

I **myself** will handle the real estate sale.

I will handle the real estate sale **myself**.

Jason has to do his homework **himself**.

You **yourself** can take care of the details.

You **yourselves** can learn these skills (more than one person).

The children **themselves** cooked breakfast for their parents.

Note Remember that the plural of **-self** is **-selves**. There are **no** such words as **ourself** or **themself**.

Now, practice identifying the reflexive and intensive pronouns in the following exercise.

Exercise 9

Circle the reflexive and intensive pronouns.

Examples:

He hit ⟨himself⟩ in the foot with the falling brick.

She could not blame anyone but ⟨herself⟩ for losing the money.

The children ⟨themselves⟩ can clean their rooms.

Version A

1. The ribbon curled back on itself and became tangled.

2. We can paint the house ourselves.

3. He himself wanted to change the oil in his car.

4. The rocket cannot launch itself into space.

5. The dirty clothes are not going to wash themselves today.

6. The teacher took the test himself before giving it to his students.

7. The young child called 911 herself for her mother.

8. The zoo itself receives no tax funds for its operations.

9. I gave myself a reward for graduating from college.

10. Jerry taught himself to use the Internet.

Version B

1. Sam earned the money himself for the down payment on the car.
2. I wrote a note to myself to pay the bill on time.
3. The golfers themselves had to be sure to sign their score cards.
4. Life itself can be frustrating or encouraging.
5. The association president told herself that she needed to greet the new owners.
6. Larry wanted to train his puppy himself.
7. We cannot solve the problem ourselves.
8. The parents found themselves in a lot of trouble.
9. The director herself was interviewed on television.
10. The flag itself boosted the country's spirits.

Exercise 10

Write five sentences that contain one or more reflexive or intensive pronouns.

1. _____
   _____

2. _____
   _____

3. _____
   _____

4. _____
   _____

5. _____
   _____

Demonstrative Pronouns

Demonstrative pronouns are very common pronouns that point out nearness to or distance from particular objects or ideas. The object is in sight either physically (something concrete like roses) or figuratively (something abstract like dreams). There are only four demonstrative pronouns, two that are singular and two that are plural.

Demonstrative Pronouns		
Singular:	this	that
Plural:	these	those

Speakers and writers use **this** and **these** to refer to nearby objects or concepts. These words refer to something actually close in location to the speaker.

singular demonstrative pronoun
This is the best idea I have had today.

plural demonstrative pronoun
Please plant **these** in the front rose bed.

People use **that** and **those** to refer to objects or concepts farther away from the speaker. Read through the following sentences for differences in meaning.

singular demonstrative pronoun
That is the book I had trouble reading.

plural demonstrative pronoun
Save **those** for the backyard.

If **this**, **that**, **these**, or **those** is used directly before a noun, it is considered an adjective rather than a demonstrative pronoun.

This makes a lot of sense. (demonstrative pronoun)

This idea makes a lot of sense. (adjective)

Work through the following exercises to help you become familiar with demonstrative pronouns.

Exercise 11

Circle the demonstrative pronouns in the following sentences.

Example:

I need to think (this) over for a couple of days.

Version A

1. This is the last vacation we have planned.
2. Could you distribute these to the students in your classes?
3. That is the puppy who could be a champion.
4. We plan to distribute the food to those who are in need.
5. This is the street where we can catch the subway.
6. When New Year's Eve arrives, this is what I hope we can do.
7. Do you really want to give this to your instructor?

Version B

1. These are the records found in the old file cabinet.
2. Those fell before I could react.
3. How did these end up on the floor?
4. That is the highest temperature ever recorded in Phoenix.
5. This is the night we will never forget.
6. I told you about this the other day.
7. When I agree to babysit, I always take these with me.

Write five sentences that contain one or more demonstrative pronouns.

1. _____

   _____

2. _____

   _____

3. _____

   _____

4. _____

   _____

5. _____

   _____

Prepositions

A preposition is a word that is used with a noun or pronoun to form a phrase that shows location, ownership/identification, time, or exclusion within the sentence. A prepositional phrase begins with a preposition and ends with a noun or pronoun, or both, which is called its object. These phrases are very important parts of basic sentences because of the precise meaning they add to the sentence. These phrases are also important because they are usually closely connected to subjects and verbs.

Location:

                                  prep.   noun

The dolphin swam **in the ocean.**

                            prep.   noun

I will meet you **inside the library.**

Ownership or identification:

                        prep.   noun

The blouse **with an ink stain** could not be worn.

                           prep.   noun

He bought a car **without a front fender.**

Time:

                          prep.   noun

Shawn will meet me **after chemistry class.**

                        prep.   noun

The class ends **at four o'clock.**

Exclusion:

                        prep.   noun

All the children **except Beatrice** slept late.

                        prep. noun

Everyone was there **but me.**

Note Most of the time, careful writers try to avoid putting a preposition at the end of a sentence. At times, a preposition is used alone at the end of a sentence, but it should add meaning to the sentence.

Acceptable:	What do you want me to put the salad in?
Unnecessary:	Where do you live at?
Less wordy:	Where do you live?

Prepositions

about	between	onto
above	beyond	out
across	but	out of
after	by	outside
against	down	over
along	during	since
among	except	through
around	for	throughout
as	from	to
at	in	toward
because of	inside	under
before	into	underneath
behind	like	until
below	near	unto
beneath	of	up
beside	off	with
besides	on	within
		without

Even though a prepositional phrase may have more than one object, it is still one phrase.

Jeremy gave roses **to his girlfriend and his mother.**

Every day, the little girl played **with the dog and the cat.**

Everyone **except Brian and me** knew about the party.

I will meet you **in the parking lot or the parking garage.**

If you can, park your car **near the library or the gym.**

Consider again how important prepositional phrases can be in building sentences. Without them, the meaning in each of the above sentences would be vague or even entirely different. Learning to recognize prepositional phrases clearly will help you to write more interesting sentences.

Note When **to** is followed by a noun, it is the first word in a prepositional phrase.

The students went **to** the concert.

However, when **to** is followed by a verb, it is the first word in an infinitive and functions as a noun or adjective form.

infinitive   prep. phrase
Justin wanted to win the free trip to Hawaii.

infinitive
The little boy chose a book to read.

Exercise 13

Identify the prepositional phrases in the following sentences by putting a line through each phrase.

Example:

~~During intermission~~, the audience walked ~~to the lobby~~.

Version A
1. Before the game, the players stretched for half an hour.
2. After class, the students continued to work in groups.
3. Without a doubt, Jeff became an excellent president of the school.
4. Jill always saw the positive view in life, so she was recognized as optimist of the month.
5. Everyone in my family will be home within an hour or two.
6. After the dinner, the dean gave the table decorations to the students and their guests.
7. At the beginning of the meeting, the leader of the organization spoke to the members.
8. The large truck went slowly around the curves of the mountain road.
9. Because of its action, the movie thrilled the audience.
10. The ball of fur running through the house was a ferret.
11. Investing money in the stock market should provide income during retirement.
12. Going to the lake relaxes everyone in my family.
13. I do some of these tasks on a daily basis.
14. The saguaro cactus grew on the side of the mountain.
15. The tallest player on our basketball team stood a full foot above the coach.
16. We often enjoyed walking on the path around the lake.
17. On Saturdays, my family and I often go to the zoo.
18. Remaining hopeful in times of tragedy is very important to people.

Version B

1. The jury reached its verdict after many hours of deliberation.
2. The energetic young colt raced through the pasture.
3. The picnickers ran for shelter from the storm.
4. The sandwich was served with potato chips and Dr. Pepper.
5. In the middle of the night, the phone woke me from sound sleep.
6. Bank customers can access their accounts through the Internet.
7. The landscaper trimmed the hedges around the yard.
8. I finally found the misplaced bill under the newspaper.
9. In the morning sun, the hikers walked along the trail.
10. By the end of the movie, the audience was in tears.
11. Unfortunately, I locked the keys in my car.
12. The little girl in the front row watched the production of *Peter Pan* with total awe.
13. My father, an immigrant from Germany, worked hard for his family's future.
14. Children with confidence believe in themselves and their own abilities.
15. Getting a degree in psychology is my first priority.
16. At this time of my life, I am able to concentrate on college.
17. On our walk through the fields, we saw a mother cow and her calf standing in the middle of the stream.
18. Many of the students in my class were born in other countries.

Exercise 14

Write 10 sentences that include nouns, prepositional phrases, and pronouns. Label the nouns with an N; put a line through the prepositional phrases, and circle the pronouns.

1. _____
   _____

2. _____
   _____

3. _____
   _____

4. _____
   _____

5. _____
   _____

6. _____
   _____

7. _____
_____

8. _____
_____

9. _____
_____

10. _____
_____

Verbs

Being able to identify verbs is important because all sentences must have at least one main verb. Verbs carry significant meaning in sentences, and part of your ability to write well will depend on your use of verbs. Sometimes, in fact, others will even judge your writing by the verbs you use. Learning to identify verbs will help you be a more effective writer.

Action Verbs

A verb is a word that can show **action**.

The wolf cubs **tumble** in the grass.

A double rainbow **filled** the sky with vibrant colors.

Non-Action Verbs

A verb can show **being** or **existing** (*am, are, is, was, were, been, being*).

The pale lavender orchid **is** superb.
I **am** the oldest player on the softball team.

A verb can show a **state of being** (*seem, feel, appear*).

The national park **seems** quiet and peaceful.
Jake **felt** relaxed after a week on the beach.
The students in the class **appear** exhausted.

All the verbs in bold in the above sentences are main verbs. The main verb in a sentence may be simple or compound.

A **simple verb** is one action or non-action word or a verb phrase.

       action   action

Rob **ate** all the peanut butter.   Lisa **sang** her favorite songs.

non-action	non-action verb phrase
Tony **was** happy.	Tony **has been** happy for weeks.

Compound verbs are two or more action or non-action words or verb phrases.

Rob **ate** all the peanut butter and **drank** all the milk.

Lisa **sang** her favorite songs and **danced** all night.

Tony **was** happy and **was** tired at the same time.

Tony **has celebrated** his son's birth and **has started** saving for his education.

Helping Verbs

The **verb** may be one word or may be combined with a **helping verb** to form a verb phrase.

Forms of the verb **be** used as helping verbs:

Forms of Be	
am, is	are
was	were
been	being

Alberto **is walking** his dog.

Alberto's dog **was groomed** yesterday.

Other words can also be used as helping verbs:

Other Helping Verbs		
can	have	must
could	has	shall
do	had	should
does	may	will
did	might	would

Alberto **does walk** his dog every day.

Alberto **has been walking** his dog in the park.

Alberto's dog **has been walked** regularly.

Alberto's dog **should have been walked** before bedtime.

Read the following sentences. Underline the verbs.

Example:

The earthquake _shook_ the city for several minutes.

Version A

1. On her eighty-eighth birthday, Polly sang a solo.
2. The tiny sea turtles have hatched on the shore.
3. They immediately could walk into the ocean.
4. Harrison is throwing his fast ball ninety-five miles an hour.
5. Two peanuts rattled in the bottom of the can.
6. Jeremy must drive his car home and then work on it there.
7. Roxanne should be happy with the concert.
8. Carol may spend the afternoon at the mall.
9. Eric has been chosen captain of the team.
10. The young mother had pushed her baby in the stroller.
11. The famous poet will arrive on Friday and will read her poetry the same night.
12. Sara saved money during the summer and then enrolled in college in the fall.
13. The eager visitors hiked into the Grand Canyon and camped overnight.
14. The washing machine sounded strange and then stopped abruptly.
15. I would like to finish my project today.

Version B

1. Music came softly from the radio on the table.
2. Ben manages an ostrich farm in Arizona.
3. Gene should read the newspaper every day.
4. The new highway will go across the mountain.
5. The candy store specialized in lollipops and jelly beans.
6. Driving in the city requires a lot of concentration.
7. I heard the church bells and stopped to listen.
8. The center fielder jumped higher than the fence and caught the ball.
9. Because of the flowers, the twins have been sneezing all morning.
10. The peregrine falcons have nested on the second-story ledge.
11. She should have been given first prize for her presentation.
12. The speedy shortstop bunted the ball and then made it to first base safely.
13. Lea and Eric explored the cavern and took many unusual pictures.
14. My son lost three Palm organizers in less than two years.
15. The pomegranates on the tree grew into beautiful large fruit.

Verb Tense to Show Time

Verb forms change to show time. The word **tense** is used to talk about the concept of time for verbs. For instance, verb tense can show that something happens in the present, happened in the past, or will happen some time in the future. One of the writing skills you will need is to be able to use different verb forms correctly and accurately.

You already know how to use many verbs correctly, but you may not be aware that verb tense problems occur. Because errors in verb forms are very distracting, you will want to edit your writing carefully and eliminate any incorrect verbs. Learning to use verbs correctly should be part of the commitment you make to yourself as you work to become a better writer. Following is a review of the verb forms you need to use correctly.

Present Tense in Verbs

The **present tense** shows an event happening right **now** or happening **continually.**

> I **walk** to school in the fall.
>
> Maresha also **walks** to school.
>
> We usually **walk** together.
>
> I **eat** lunch at school.
>
> Maresha **eats** lunch with me almost every day.

Present tense does not cause any problems except when you are writing about one person [Amanda (she), Tom (he), Bank of America (it)] doing something in the present. In that case, you add the *-s* ending on the verb form. For instance, when you say, "She **sits** at the front of the room," you are talking about one person doing something in the present, so you need to add an *-s* to the basic verb form "sit." Look at the present tense verb forms below:

I eat	we eat
you eat	you eat
she, he, it eats	they eat

Exercise 16

Fill in the blank with the correct verb form.

Example:

Jodi __*eats*__ in the school cafeteria. (eats, eat)

Version A

1. Tourists _____ Holiday Inns in most states in America. (finds, find)
2. The dolphins _____ the vibrations of the boat motor. (follows, follow)
3. Working out at the gym _____ people energy. (gives, give)

4. My daughter _____ spending time at the beach. (likes, like)

5. The newspaper _____ people a lot of important information. (provides, provide)

6. The orange and black butterfly _____ by the hedge. (flutters, flutter)

7. The little lizard often _____ across my morning path. (scurries, scurry)

8. The little boy _____ happily in his mother's arms. (sings, sing)

9. Searching for seashells _____ the kids busy. (keeps, keep)

10. Rachel _____ ice hockey for the University of Wisconsin. (plays, play)

Version B

1. Mosquitoes often _____ people in the evenings. (attacks, attack)

2. The beautiful orchids and roses _____ the table. (decorates, decorate)

3. Many evenings, Karen and David _____ the dog at the beach. (walks, walk)

4. Maggie often _____ time with her grandparents. (spends, spend)

5. Many species of fish _____ in the ocean. (lives, live)

6. The boat-shaped restaurant at the pier _____ many tourists. (attracts, attract)

7. The fresh, blackened grouper _____ delicious. (tastes, taste)

8. The deep-sea fishing boat _____ every morning at 6:00 A.M. (leaves, leave)

9. The giant sea turtles _____ free in the ocean. (swims, swim)

10. Going out in a boat _____ some people seasick. (makes, make)

Just remember that when you use **he, she,** or **it** with a **present tense** verb, you need to add the *–s* to the basic form.

Past Tense in Regular Verbs

To show the past tense of the verb "walk," just add an *-ed* or *-d* ending. This ending makes the verb **regular**. All regular verbs add *-ed* or *-d* to show an event that happened in the past.

Yesterday, I walk**ed** to school as usual.

Last year, Marisha and I walk**ed** to school almost every day.

We refus**ed** to wait for the bus.

Past Tense in Irregular Verbs

To show the past tense for "eat," you do more than just add an ending. You use a different form of the verb.

I **ate** lunch at school.

Marisha also **ate** lunch at school.

We **ate** lunch together frequently.

This kind of change makes "eat" an **irregular** verb. Most irregular verbs change form in the past tense.

I **go** now.	(present tense)
I **went** yesterday.	(past tense)
I **am** here.	(present tense)
I **was** here.	(past tense)

Future Tense in Verbs

To show an action that will happen in the future, you use a helping verb. You use "shall" or "will" before the verb. Traditionally, "shall" has been used with the pronouns "I" and "we," and "will" has been used with all other words. However, "shall" has taken on a more pretentious meaning and is often no longer used, even in scholarly writing. "Will" is now usually considered acceptable.

I **shall** (or **will**) **eat** lunch with Marisha.

The president of the college **will speak** tomorrow evening.

Present Perfect Tense in Verbs

To show action that has happened earlier but is now completed, you use "has" or "have" before the verb form. The action may still be going on in the present.

Albert **has finished** his history paper.

Sara **has worked** at Motorola for two years. (She is still working there.)

Past Perfect Tense in Verbs

To show action that was completed before another event occurred, you use "had" before the verb form.

When I saw Tony, he **had** *already* **eaten** lunch.

I **had received** my engineering degree from college *before* Motorola **hired** me.

Future Perfect Tense in Verbs

To show action that will be completed before another event has occurred in the future, you use "shall have" or "will have" before the verb form. As stated earlier, "shall" has been used with "I" and "we," and "will" has been used with all other words. Most of the time, "will" is acceptable

He **will have eaten** lunch *before* we **arrive** in Tucson.

By the end of the project, I **shall** (or **will**) **have spent** many hours working hard on it.

Following is a summary example of these six frequently used verb tenses. The first box shows a regular verb; the second box shows an irregular verb.

Regular Verb (mow):

Present:	Luis often *mows* his yard on Saturdays.
Past:	Luis *mowed* his yard yesterday.
Future:	Luis *will mow* his yard tomorrow.
Present Perfect:	Luis *has mowed* it several times lately.
Past Perfect:	Luis *had mowed* it before I arrived home.
Future Perfect:	Luis *will have mowed* it before we arrive.

Irregular Verb (eat):

Present:	Luis often *eats* pizza for lunch.
Past:	Luis *ate* pizza for lunch every day.
Future:	Luis *will* always *eat* pizza.
Present Perfect:	Luis *has eaten* lots of pizza.
Past Perfect:	Luis *had eaten* all of the pizza before we got there.
Future Perfect:	Luis *will have eaten* the pizza before we arrive.

Keep in mind that regular verbs form the past tenses by adding *-ed* or *-d* to the verb. Irregular verbs have no set pattern, so they are harder to remember. For reference, use the following list of irregular verb forms to help you edit your papers. The last two columns show the past participles and the present participles.

Participles are the forms of the verb used in all the perfect tenses shown in the above boxes. Remember that when participles are used as main verbs, they must have helping verbs. (When they are not used as main verbs in a sentence, they function as adjectives. You will learn more about adjectives later.) Here is a summary of the helping verbs used with participles:

Past participles may use such helping verbs as **had, has,** or **have.**

He **had become** a father for the third time.
Many of the graduate students **have continued** their education.

Present participles may use such helping verbs as **am, is, are, was,** or **were.**

The toddler **is being** very cooperative at the moment.
The police officers **were writing** many speeding tickets.

Irregular Verbs

Present	Past	Past Participle	Present Participle (-*ing* form of verb)
am	was	been	being
become	became	become	becoming
begin	began	begun	beginning
bite	bit	bitten	biting
blow	blew	blown	blowing
break	broke	broken	breaking
bring	brought	brought	bringing
buy	bought	bought	buying
catch	caught	caught	catching
choose	chose	chosen	choosing
come	came	come	coming
dig	dug	dug	digging
do	did	done	doing
draw	drew	drawn	drawing
drink	drank	drunk	drinking
drive	drove	driven	driving
eat	ate	eaten	eating
fall	fell	fallen	falling
fight	fought	fought	fighting
fly	flew	flown	flying
freeze	froze	frozen	freezing
get	got	gotten	getting
give	gave	given	giving
go	went	gone	going
grow	grew	grown	growing
hang	hung	hung	hanging
have	had	had	having
hear	heard	heard	hearing
hide	hid	hidden	hiding
know	knew	known	knowing
lay	laid	laid	laying
lead	led	led	leading
lie	lay	lain	lying
lie	lied	lied	lying
pay	paid	paid	paying

Present	Past	Past Participle	Present Participle (*-ing* form of verb)
read	read	read	reading
ride	rode	ridden	riding
ring	rang	rung	ringing
rise	rose	risen	rising
run	ran	run	running
see	saw	seen	seeing
set	set	set	setting
shine	shone	shone	shining
sing	sang	sung	singing
sit	sat	sat	sitting
speak	spoke	spoken	speaking
sting	stung	stung	stinging
steal	stole	stolen	stealing
swear	swore	sworn	swearing
swim	swam	swam	swimming
take	took	taken	taking
think	thought	thought	thinking
throw	threw	thrown	throwing
wake	woke	woken	waking
wear	wore	worn	wearing
win	won	won	winning
write	wrote	written	writing

In the following exercises, you will have more practice in using verb forms.

Exercise 17

In each blank, write the correct simple, past tense form of the verb in parentheses. The verbs in this exercise are all **regular** verbs.

Example:

We _painted_ the living room in pale blue. (paint)

Version A

1. We _____ for a table by the window. (ask)
2. After lunch, I _____ my research paper for school. (finish)
3. The boiling water almost _____ the chef. (burn)
4. The captain in the Navy never _____ his duty. (shirk)
5. The cat on the chair just _____ at me. (blink)
6. Leo _____ for his car keys for over an hour. (search)

7. The college class _____ a tree in memory of their classmate. (plant)

8. The investor _____ only a small amount of money. (risk)

9. This morning, I _____ on the broken step. (stumble)

10. My dad _____ me enough money for the down payment. (loan)

Version B

1. The mama and papa quail and their nine newly hatched babies _____ across the lawn. (parade)

2. Andy _____ the broken fan belt in my car. (replace)

3. The surfer _____ to the beach to catch the high waves. (rush)

4. During my summer photography class, I _____ how to use a digital camera. (learn)

5. The athlete _____ weights to increase his upper-body strength. (lift)

6. The jacaranda tree _____ beautiful lavender blossoms. (produce)

7. During the rain, we _____ our picnic lunch with a plastic tarp. (cover)

8. After the rain, Joe _____ his truck. (wash)

9. Over the weekend, Frank _____ his favorite *Discovery* program. (watch)

10. At the St. Patrick's Day party, Brenda _____ corned beef and cabbage. (serve)

Exercise 18

In each blank, write the correct simple, past tense form of the verb in parentheses. These verbs are all **irregular.** If necessary, refer to the list of irregular verbs on pages 67–68.

Examples:

We ___*gave*___ our grandmother a new family portrait. (give)

Version A

1. Without planning ahead, I _____ to the grocery store. (go)

2. Before breakfast, Harry _____ three miles around the neighborhood. (run)

3. I _____ a birthday present for my brother. (buy)

4. The math class _____ on time every day. (begin)

5. The server _____ his best to please the customers. (do)

6. On my backyard fence, I _____ a pair of white-winged doves. (see)

7. My neighbor _____ my front door bell at dinnertime. (ring)

8. Laura _____ in the choir for five years. (sing)

9. The geraniums _____ in the raised flowerbed near my patio. (grow)

10. Last Tuesday, I _____ the bus to school. (ride)

Version B

1. The mischievous children _____ in whispers. (speak)

2. The refrigerator temperature was so high that the milk _____ . (freeze)

3. During the summers, we _____ in the lake. (swim)

4. In the winter, we _____ snowballs at each other. (throw)

5. I always _____ where to find my children. (know)

6. The airplane _____ dangerously close to the power lines. (fly)

7. As youngsters, my brother and I _____ the same childhood illnesses. (catch)

8. At the beach, we often _____ designs in the sand. (draw)

9. While working in the yard, we _____ over a gallon of water. (drink)

10. I slipped on the ice and _____ my leg. (break)

Exercise 19

Referring to the list of irregular verbs, write the correct present or past participle for the verb in parentheses.

Examples:

I have already __*given*__ to the United Way. (give)

Todd is __*reading*__ *The Dunes* for his literature class. (read)

Version A

1. Before lunch, I had _____ an apple. (eat)

2. Jack has _____ my car several times. (drive)

3. Have you _____ your suit for the wedding? (choose)

4. Nancy has _____ four e-mails to her staff. (write)

5. I was _____ my lunch break early. (take)

6. Terri has _____ the rent on her apartment. (pay)

7. The wasps had _____ me several times. (sting)

8. Michael is _____ a new Tahoe. (drive)

9. The sun has already _____ . (set)

10. At the symphony concert, we are _____ in the front row of the balcony. (sit)

Version B

1. Before Mom's birthday, I had _____ to save money for her present. (begin)

2. Until yesterday, Roy had not _____ about his son's injury. (know)

3. Before exercising, Kayla had _____ a liter of water. (drink)

4. Gayle is _____ orchids in the special greenhouse. (grow)

5. Alex is _____ to Virginia for his brother's wedding. (fly)

6. In court, Clark had _____ to tell the truth. (swear)

7. Aaron has _____ all his papers for the course. (do)

8. In the last month, Lee was _____ trouble with doctor appointments. (have)

9. Anita had _____ long and hard for the educational budget increase. (fight)

10. Kelli is _____ too much money out of her checking account each week. (draw)

Exercise 20

Write two sentences that contain one or more action verbs.

1. _____
   _____

2. _____
   _____

Write two sentences that contain one or more non-action verbs.

1. _____
   _____

2. _____
   _____

Write two sentences that contain one or more helping verbs.

1. _____
   _____

2. _____
   _____

Write two sentences that contain one or more simple verbs.

1. _____
   _____

2. _____
   _____

Write two sentences that contain one or more compound verbs.

1. _____
   _____

2. _____
   _____

 Summary

Being able to identify the eight parts of speech and understanding how they function in sentences helps you write grammatically correct sentences and paragraphs.

- A noun is the name of a person, place, or thing.

  A noun can be common or proper.

  A noun can be concrete or abstract.

  A noun can be a verb form.

- A pronoun is a word that takes the place of a noun.

  Some pronouns such as **I, we, us,** and **me** are called personal pronouns.

  Some personal pronouns such as **my** and **mine** are possessive and may be considered adjectives when coming before a noun.

  Some pronouns such as **each, few,** and **all** are indefinite, meaning they do not refer to a specific noun.

  Some pronouns that end in **-self** or **-selves** are reflexive or intensive. They usually refer to the subject of a sentence and add emphasis.

  Other pronouns are demonstrative and point out nearness or distance.

- A preposition is usually the first word in a prepositional phrase that ends with a noun or pronoun.

- A verb shows action, existence, or a state of being. It may be one word or several words.

  Verbs may be action or non-action words.

  Verbs may be simple or compound.

  Verbs may be one word or combined with helping verbs.

- An adjective describes a noun or pronoun.

- An adverb describes a verb, adjective, or another adverb.

- A conjunction joins words, phrases, clauses, or sentences.

- An interjection shows strong feeling.

Collaborative Activity

The following activity will give you practice in thinking about the individual words and phrases in your own sentences.

1. Working with a partner, write two or more sentences about going to a concert.
2. Then circle all the nouns in the sentences.
3. Find any pronouns that you used. Above each pronoun, write the noun or nouns that it replaces.
4. Then list the verbs in your sentences.
5. Identify your prepositional phrases.

Example:

                                                park   *John Hank*

(John) and (Hank) attended the (concert) at the (park). It was their favorite

                                 John Hank

(place) to hear a (band). Afterwards, they came (home) on the (bus) and talked about

John Hank

their favorite (songs).

Verbs: *attended   was   came   talked*
Prepositional phrases: *at the park, on the bus, about their favorite songs*

Sentences: _____

_____

_____

_____

Verbs: _____

_____

Prepositional phrases: _____

 ## Practice Test

Read the following paragraph, and then answer the questions that follow by circling the letter of the correct answer.

(1) For many children, having a cat or dog as a pet is a natural part of growing up, just as it was in my home. (2) However, my pet goat, Delilah, was my prized possession. (3) She felt like another member of the family, and she taught my dog to leap through the air. (4) They were quite a team as they half jumped, half floated, my goat always in front, leading. (5) A large persimmon tree grew at the far side of our yard, and Delilah always accompanied me there to enjoy the fruit. (6) She and I knew that unless the fruit was completely ripe, it was bitter. (7) As we neared the tree, we both sprinted, knowing the persimmons on the ground were sweet and juicy. (8) Many times she decided to be my shadow and followed me everywhere. (9) One day, I forgot she was behind me, and I walked down the block to get the mail. (10) She went with me, following more faithfully than any dog. (11) Delilah often rubbed the top of her head against me. (12) I always thought this was her way of being affectionate. (13) I, in turn, scratched the two little knobs that grew on top of her head. (14) When it was time to milk her, she walked into her stall and ate her supper as I squirted the warm milk into the bucket. (15) She was always patient with me even when I first learned to milk her. (16) Having Delilah for a long time made me marvel at her intelligence and loyalty.

1. Sentence #1: The pronoun "it" refers to
   a. children
   b. having a cat or dog
   c. growing up

2. Sentence #2: Identify the nouns.
   a. goat, Delilah, prized
   b. goat, prized, however
   c. goat, Delilah, possession

3. Sentence #3: Identify the verb form used as a noun.
   a. to leap
   b. through the air
   c. felt

4. Sentence #3: Identify the personal pronouns in this sentence.
   a. like, family, dog
   b. She, she, my
   c. and, taught, air

5. Sentence #4: **They** is used twice in this sentence. The pronoun **they** replaces what nouns?
   a. cat, dog
   b. children, home
   c. Delilah, dog

6. Sentence #5: Identify two main verbs.
   a. grew, to enjoy
   b. grew, accompanied
   c. accompanied, yard

7. Sentence #6: Identify the personal pronouns in this sentence.
   a. she, I, it
   b. and, I, the
   c. fruit, ripe, bitter

8. Sentence #6: What noun does **it** replace?
   a. she
   b. fruit
   c. bitter

9. Sentence #7: List the concrete nouns.
   a. tree, persimmons, ground
   b. we, sweet, tree
   c. sprinted, ground, juicy

10. Sentence #8: Identify the main verbs.
    a. to be, followed
    b. decided, followed
    c. to be, decided

11. Sentence #9: Identify the common nouns in this sentence.
    a. day, block, mail
    b. block, one, she
    c. forgot, down, mail

12. Sentence #9: Identify the prepositional phrases.
    a. I forgot, a few times
    b. she was, a few times
    c. behind me, down the block

13. Sentence #10: Identify the main verb.
    a. went
    b. following
    c. faithfully

14. Sentence #11: Identify the proper noun in this sentence.
    a. head
    b. top
    c. Delilah

15. Sentence #12: Identify the demonstrative pronoun in this sentence.
    a. I
    b. this
    c. her

16. Sentence #13: Identify the prepositional phrases.
    a. in turn, on top, of her head
    b. two little knobs, grew on, I scratched
    c. the two, top of, grew on

17. Sentence #14: Identify the action verbs in this sentence.
    a. was, walked
    b. walked, ate, squirted
    c. squirted, bucket, supper

18. Sentence #15: Identify the non-action verb in this sentence.
    a. learned
    b. patient
    c. was

19. Sentence #16: Identify the abstract nouns that summarize the important ideas about Delilah.
    a. Delilah, I
    b. intelligence, loyalty
    c. longer, realized

20. Sentence #16: Identify the –*ing* verb form used as a noun.
    a. Having
    b. Delilah
    c. intelligence

 ## Writing Assignment

Write a paragraph on one of the following topics. Be sure to brainstorm, freewrite, or talk with someone to find a main idea for your paragraph.

1. Favorite or least favorite holiday or event
2. Favorite or least favorite animal
3. What you like or dislike most about yourself
4. Why you respect one of the following people: nurse, firefighter, police officer, governor, president, teacher, doctor

Chapter 2

Developing Paragraphs with Examples and Details

The Paragraph

Objectives

- Identify and write strong topic sentences
  Distinguishing topic sentences from generalities
- Add support sentences
  Distinguishing topic sentences from facts
  Adding supporting examples
  Adding details
- Write strong concluding sentences

A paragraph is a group of related sentences that explain a distinct idea often expressed within a larger piece of work. Sometimes a paragraph consists of only one or two sentences, such as in a news story or in recorded conversation. Sometimes experienced writers use short paragraphs for emphasis or for other special purposes. This book, however, focuses on paragraphs that **develop or explain one main idea**, and paragraphs that serve this purpose are usually much longer than one, two, or even three sentences. These paragraphs often have eight, ten, or even more sentences to explain the main idea. A well-developed paragraph is usually organized into distinct parts: a topic sentence, ten to twelve supporting sentences, and a concluding sentence.

topic sentence

ten to twelve supporting sentences

a concluding sentence

Topic Sentences

In the prewriting step of the writing process, you saw how a direction for a paragraph emerged. This direction can become a **topic sentence**, the main idea that will be developed in the paragraph. Once you have identified this topic sentence, your job will be to develop this idea. *This main idea will be the most general statement in the paragraph. You can sometimes think of it as an opinion that the paragraph supports* because it usually contains a direction or general word that the paragraph will explain.

Sometimes you will choose your own topic, and other times your instructor will give you a topic and ask you to create a topic sentence that can be developed in one paragraph. Doing this requires some thinking skills that will become easier and easier as you do more writing. Developing a topic sentence involves the same type of activity you just learned about in prewriting. You will be taking a broad topic, brainstorming, freewriting, or talking to get supporting ideas, and then finding a way these smaller ideas fit together. As you learned previously, prewriting can help you develop a direction (topic sentence) for your paper. The first three exercises use brainstorming activities to help you see how this works.

Exercise 1—You will practice adding specific ideas that are examples of the general topic given (general to specific).

Exercise 2—Then, you will take specific ideas and decide how they fit together into a general topic (specific to general).

Exercise 3—You will work on both of these skills to see how prewriting can result in effective topic sentences with support ideas (general to specific and specific to general).

Finding Supporting Ideas

To help you practice the thinking skills needed to write effective topic sentences and support sentences, study the following broad ideas or topics that break into smaller topics or ideas.

General idea or topic	Supporting ideas or examples
eating fruit	eating an apple or an orange
buying furniture	buying a table, chair, or desk
playing a sport	playing football or golf
exercising	walking or lifting weights
sharing emotion	showing joy, love, or fear

Working through the following exercise will give you practice in telling the difference between general and specific ideas.

Exercise 1

In the following exercise that goes from general to specific, add two additional words or phrases to each group that add support or are examples of that idea.

Example:

Fishing in the ocean

> **lures**
> **pole**
> **bait**
> *bobber*
> *boat*

Version A

1. Browsing in a bookstore
   cookbooks
   novels
   mysteries
   _____
   _____

2. Kinds of travel
   car
   motorcycle
   boat
   _____
   _____

3. Services at a beauty salon
   haircut
   hair tint
   shampoo
   _____
   _____

4. Hobbies for children
   beading
   scrapbooking
   saving baseball cards
   _____
   _____

5. Ways to reduce stress
   listening to music
   gardening
   taking a walk
   _____
   _____

Version B

1. Being a safe driver
   obeying speed limits
   using turn signals
   obeying traffic signals
   _____
   _____

2. Unusual pets
   chinchillas
   pythons
   iguanas
   _____
   _____

3. Ways to show happiness
   laughing
   joking around
   humming
   _____
   _____

4. Ways to save money
   savings accounts
   bargain shopping
   eating at home
   _____
   _____

5. Leisure-time activities
   hiking
   taking pictures
   golfing
   _____
   _____

Fitting Supporting Ideas Together

The second step is to take these specific examples and find a general word that shows how these ideas are alike or fit together. For example, truck, boat, and trailer might make you think about equipment to take to the lake or ocean. On the other hand, truck, car, van, or jeep might be types of transportation. The next exercise helps you think about these groups or clusters.

Exercise 2

In this exercise, the words in the cluster are specific. Think of a general word that could include all the words in the group.

Example:

Specific example	**General topic**
sedan, convertible, truck	*motor vehicles*

Version A

Specific examples   General topic

1. carrots, green beans, potatoes _____
2. guitar, piano, violin _____
3. pants, shirts, socks _____
4. baseballs, tennis rackets, golf balls _____
5. *Arizona Republic, USA Today, New York Times* _____

Version B

Specific examples   General topic

1. 4th of July, Memorial Day, Labor Day _____
2. pepperoni, green peppers, olives _____
3. apple pie, strawberry shortcake, ice cream _____
4. mowing, trimming, edging _____
5. new clothes, vaccinations, registration _____

Now that you have practiced these thinking skills, try working through the next exercise, using the following ideas that might have come from a prewriting exercise. Once again, you will practice grouping like ideas together. Remember that these different ideas that fit together can become supporting ideas for the main idea or topic sentence.

Grouping Supporting Ideas Together

In the next exercise, supporting ideas have already been identified. You will want to think about how these small ideas fit together. Other supporting ideas could be added, or perhaps other clusters might be added. The important goal is to see how this process works in developing a topic sentence.

Version A

Work through both Parts 1 and 2 of Version A.

Part 1: Look at ideas or thoughts that were generated when using the broad topic "camping." Study the clusters. Part 2 shows "in what way" the words inside each of the five clusters are related to one another.

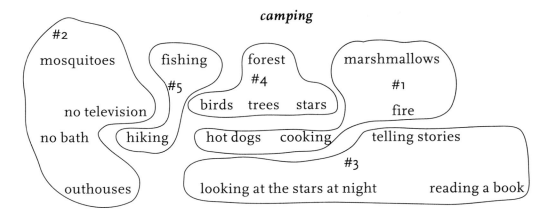

camping

Part 2: The clusters below are based on the above brainstorming. Using this material, **circle the letter of the idea that can be the best direction for a topic sentence.**

Cluster #1: Fire, cooking, marshmallows, and hot dogs fit together because they are all

Direction for a topic sentence:
a. part of cooking on an open fire.
b. fattening and unhealthy.
c. activities only children enjoy.

Cluster #2: Mosquitoes, no bath, no television, and outhouses fit together because they are all

Direction for a topic sentence:
a. harder on girls than guys.
b. negative parts of camping.
c. positive parts of camping.

Cluster #3: Telling stories, looking at the stars at night, and reading a book fit together because they are all

Direction for a topic sentence:
a. a relaxing part of camping.
b. activities to keep campers from going home.
c. boring parts of camping.

Cluster #4:   Trees, birds, forest, and stars fit together because they are all

Direction for a topic sentence:
a. activities only old people enjoy.
b. activities campers enjoy.
c. important elements of nature that campers enjoy.

Cluster #5:   Hiking and fishing fit together because they are both

Direction for a topic sentence:
a. activities only old people enjoy.
b. activities campers enjoy.
c. impossible in the city.

Version B

Work through both Parts 1 and 2 of Version B.

Part 1:   Look at ideas or thoughts that were generated when using the broad topic "dentist." Study the clusters. Part 2 below shows "in what way" the words inside each of the four clusters are related to one another.

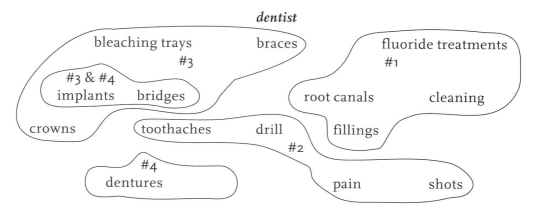

Part 2:   The clusters below are based on the above brainstorming. Using this material, **circle the letter of the idea that can be the best direction for a topic sentence.**

Cluster #1:   Fluoride treatments, cleaning, fillings, and root canals fit together because they are all

Direction for a topic sentence:
a. ways to preserve people's teeth
b. ways to amuse dentists.
c. ways to frighten patients.

Cluster #2:   Toothaches, drill, shots, and pain fit together because they are all

Direction for a topic sentence:
a. ways dentists create pain for patients.
b. reasons people with toothaches go to the dentist.
c. reasons shots keep patients from having toothaches.
d. things people dread about going to dentists.

Cluster #3: Braces, bleaching trays, implants, crowns, and bridges are all

Direction for a topic sentence:
a. cosmetic procedures people go through to make their teeth look better.
b. ways to make teeth stronger.
c. unnecessary procedures.

Cluster #4: Implants, bridges, and dentures fit together because they are all

Direction for a topic sentence:
a. types of implants.
b. unnecessary procedures.
c. ways to replace missing teeth for patients.

Identifying Topic and Direction

Now, look at the following topic sentences that contain both a topic and a direction. The direction should contain a general word or phrase that often serves as a clear opinion that the paragraph supports.

The little boy went on a rampage.

Topic: *the little boy*

Direction: *went on a rampage.*   (**Rampage** is the general word.)

The after-school program at Sunrise School provides a variety of activities for kids.

Topic: *the after-school program at Sunrise School*

Direction: *provides a variety of activities for kids.*   (**Variety of activities** is the general phrase.)

Work through the following exercise that gives you practice in identifying the topic and the direction in a topic sentence.

Exercise 4

Identify the topic and direction in the following sentences.

Example:

The tarantula made an excellent pet.

Topic: *The tarantula*

Direction: *made an excellent pet.*

Version A

1. Mary Elizabeth enjoys shopping for shoes.

Topic: _____

Direction: _____

2. Elderly patients in the doctor's waiting room appeared anxious.

   Topic: _____

   Direction: _____

3. The adult children showed appreciation for their parents.

   Topic: _____

   Direction: _____

4. The neighbors enjoyed living next door to the house with the beautiful garden.

   Topic: _____

   Direction: _____

5. The ceremonies featured the state's Native American people.

   Topic: _____

   Direction: _____

6. Jay Leno's sense of humor appeals to all varieties of people.

   Topic: _____

   Direction: _____

Version B

1. On the weekends, the children were resourceful at finding places to play.

   Topic: _____

   Direction: _____

2. The museum exhibit of ancient Chinese art was educational.

   Topic: _____

   Direction: _____

3. People are sometimes frustrated when buying a new car.

   Topic: _____

   Direction: _____

4. The mother and her young children were obviously prepared for the airplane trip.

   Topic: _____

   Direction: _____

5. The college president's office was a noisy, busy place.

   Topic: _____

   Direction: _____

6. The college art exhibit emphasized the tragedies surrounding abused children.

   Topic: _____

   Direction: _____

Distinguishing Topic Sentences from Support Sentences

As you just learned, topic sentences are general in nature. Support sentences, however, are specific. They can be examples of the topic, or they can even be facts. It is important for you to be able to tell the difference between topic sentences and supporting ideas.

Try working through the following exercise that will give you practice in distinguishing topic sentences from supporting ideas.

Exercise 5

Identify the topic sentence (TS). You will have one topic sentence and several supporting ideas.

Version A

1. Topic: Little League baseball
   _____ a. Part of playing Little League baseball means being with their friends.
   _____ b. Children look forward to celebrating after a game.
   _____ c. Little League baseball can be fun for children.
   _____ d. Team members enjoy wearing special uniforms.

2. Topic: rose garden
   _____ a. smelling the aroma of the roses brings pleasure.
   _____ b. A bouquet of roses can be gathered and brought into the house.
   _____ c. Admiring the many rose bushes brings satisfaction.
   _____ d. Having a rose garden can be rewarding.

3. Topic: petting zoos
   _____ a. Children enjoy feeding pellets to the goats.
   _____ b. They have the opportunity to learn about farm animals.
   _____ c. Youngsters can see how different animals live together.
   _____ d. Young people can learn how to be kind to animals.
   _____ e. Children can benefit by going to a petting zoo.
   _____ f. Children learn not to be afraid of animals.

4. Topic: homeless people
   _____ a. Homeless people sometimes collect aluminum cans to exchange for money.
   _____ b. Homeless people may look through dumpsters for discarded food.
   _____ c. Homeless people often do whatever is necessary to survive.
   _____ d. Homeless people may panhandle to buy food.
   _____ e. Homeless people may ask for handouts.

5. Topic: old houses
   _____ a. Old houses often provide spacious living conditions.
   _____ b. Old houses usually have large rooms.
   _____ c. Big backyards give children plenty of room to play.
   _____ d. Old houses have many rooms.

6. Topic: drivers

_____ a. Lighting a cigarette while driving takes one's attention from driving.

_____ b. Some distractions can be dangerous to drivers.

_____ c. Eating while driving takes the driver's mind off handling the car.

_____ d. Talking on cell telephones keeps them from concentrating on driving.

_____ e. Writing down telephone numbers or directions distracts drivers.

Version B

1. Topic: serious accidents

_____ a. People can recover from serious accidents.

_____ b. Hope gives them the determination they need.

_____ c. Perseverance keeps people from stopping even when life is hard.

_____ d. A positive attitude helps people focus on opportunity.

2. Topic: choosing college courses

_____ a. Before registering for classes, students should select classes carefully.

_____ b. Electives should count toward graduation.

_____ c. Courses should be compatible with a person's other schedules.

_____ d. Courses should fit into a chosen major.

3. Topic: professional athletes

_____ a. Professional athletes donate money for parks and playgrounds for youngsters.

_____ b. Professional athletes donate time and money to the community.

_____ c. Professional athletes read stories to promote literacy in young people.

_____ d. Professional athletes visit hospitals to cheer up sick kids.

_____ e. They teach athletic skills and sportsmanship at boys and girls' clubs.

4. Topic: wellness for children

_____ a. Parents make sure their children get exercise each day.

_____ b. Parents have their children immunized to avoid serious illnesses.

_____ c. Parents have an obligation to provide for the wellness of their children.

_____ d. Parents can provide nutritious, balanced meals.

_____ e. Parents provide a smoke-free and drug-free environment.

5. Topic: Business contributions

_____ a. Employees can serve as mentors to elementary school children.

_____ b. Some businesses give college scholarships to high schools.

_____ c. Corporations make important contributions to the local community.

_____ d. Businesses donate money to elementary schools for field trips.

_____ e. Employees volunteer at local food banks.

6. Topic: old age

_____ a. Vision can be impaired.

_____ b. Illnesses can destroy health.

_____ c. Old age can be unbearable.

_____ d. The ability to hear can decline.

_____ e. Mobility can be hampered.

_____ f. Losing family and friends can bring loneliness.

Remember, a topic sentence always has a topic and a direction, and that direction must be something that you can develop through prewriting activities such as freewriting, brainstorming, and talking.

Separating Facts from Topic Sentences

A sentence that is simply a fact and leaves no chance for development **cannot** be a topic sentence. For example, look at the following three statements.

My brother won a Presidential scholarship.	(fact)
My brother is enrolled in college.	(fact)
My brother is a good student.	(topic sentence)

Only one of these statements could be a topic sentence. When you say, "My brother won a Presidential scholarship," there is little else to say. Yes, he did; no, he did not. The same is true of the statement, "My brother is enrolled in college." Yes, he is; no, he is not. However, when you say, "My brother is a good student," you can show "in what way" he is a good student.

The topic sentence is an opinion that you prove by presenting specific evidence in the form of examples and details. Some support for being a good student might be: he won a Presidential scholarship; he makes all A's; he always is on time for class; he never misses class. This topic sentence could easily be developed into a paragraph.

The following exercise will give you practice in distinguishing simple facts from topic sentences.

Exercise 6

Identify the topic sentences (TS) and the simple facts (F).

Examples:

_TS_ **Playing ball in the streets can be dangerous.**

_F_ **The boys and girls played ball in the streets for two hours.**

Version A

_____ **1.** My cell phone fits into my pocket.

_____ **2.** My cell phone costs fifty dollars a month.

_____ **3.** My cell phone is quite convenient.

_____ **4.** My cell phone rang six times last night.

_____ **5.** Jeremy painted his house last week.

_____ **6.** Painting a house is expensive.

_____ **7.** My new computer is outstanding.

_____ **8.** My new computer cost me $1200.

_____ **9.** His ex-girlfriend is having lots of fun.

_____ **10.** The firefighters brought honor to the city.

Version B

_____ **1.** Traveling on a train can be great family fun.

_____ **2.** A herd of bison lives in Yellowstone National Park.

_____ **3.** The children made three snow people.

_____ **4.** The children had fun making snow people.

_____ **5.** My mother loves to cook holiday meals.

_____ **6.** My mother spent three hours cooking a meal.

_____ **7.** The expenses for my car are very low.

_____ **8.** Gas for my car costs 30 dollars a month.

_____ **9.** Maria's new glasses cost 375 dollars.

_____ **10.** Maria's glasses greatly improved her vision.

Avoiding Topic Sentences That Are Too Broad

Your topic sentence should have a strong direction so that it can be developed into a single paragraph. If your topic sentence is too broad, however, you will not be able to focus effectively on one idea. Restricting your idea, then, to a narrower topic is necessary. For example, the following topic sentence is broad.

Vacationing by car is enjoyed by thousands of people everywhere.   (broad)

If you try to write a paragraph using the above topic sentence, it will be difficult for you to focus on supporting details. You need to prewrite further to narrow your topic. A better topic sentence might be one of the following:

Traveling by car can help families bond.   (topic sentence)

Traveling by car can allow the family to see many interesting places.   (topic sentence)

Traveling by car can create stress for everyone in the family.   (topic sentence)

Whatever your topic and direction might be, it needs to be focused or narrow enough to be explained or developed in one paragraph. The following exercise will help you think about focused topic sentences.

In the following exercises, look at the topic, and then put a ✓ in the blank by the direction that creates a strong topic sentence.

Example:

Topic: **Buying a used car**

Direction: __✓__ requires some expert knowledge of cars.

                 _____ can be an overwhelming task.

Version A

1. Topic: Successfully recovering from surgery means
   Direction: _____ following the doctor's instructions carefully.
                _____ going home to get better.

2. Topic: Getting a house ready to be sold
   Direction: _____ means making the house look attractive.
                _____ can take months or even years.

3. Topic: Successful college students
   Direction: _____ achieve a lot in life.
                _____ have good study habits.

4. Topic: Children today
   Direction: _____ are tomorrow's future.
                _____ can learn love from their parents.

5. Topic: Living outside a city
   Direction: _____ is a major part of American life.
                _____ provides a quieter environment.

Version B

1. Topic: Stepparents
   Direction: _____ can provide security in children's lives.
                _____ can result in many complex relationships.

2. Topic: Communication
   Direction: _____ in my marriage is nonexistent.
                _____ in marriages is lacking everywhere in America.

3. Topic: Music
   Direction: _____ creates universal feelings.
                _____ helps people relax.

4. Topic: My boyfriend
   Direction: _____ enjoys spending time with me.
                _____ enjoys everything in life.

5. Topic: Photographers

Direction: _____ have always liked to record history.

_____ vividly recorded the September 11th events.

6. Topic: Visual effects

Direction: _____ in the new Star Wars movie were outstanding.

_____ in movies are becoming more and more sophisticated.

Writing Your Own Topic Sentences

Exercise 8

Write a topic sentence for each subject by adding a direction.

Example:

The special effects in the movie Spiderman _____*made it exciting.*_____

Version A

1. School _____
2. Potluck meals _____
3. Graduating from college _____
4. Blind dates _____
5. My cousin _____
6. Gardening _____
7. Snowboarding _____
8. Fishing at the lake _____
9. Listening to a CD _____
10. Martin Luther King _____

Version B

1. Training a puppy _____
2. My old car _____
3. Cable television _____
4. The college student's apartment _____
5. The cabdriver _____
6. The school bus _____
7. Playing soccer _____
8. The math class _____
9. My first job _____
10. The airplane flight _____

Supporting Ideas

Examples

Once you have a topic sentence, you will need several concrete illustrations to help you prove your topic idea. These illustrations are **examples that are specific references to events or to objects.** Strong examples provide strong support for your topic sentence. Look through your prewriting activities to gather a list of support material that you can use in writing your paragraph. You should be able to find several examples from your prewriting.

If you are using as your topic sentence, **I have wonderful memories of spending time with my grandmother,** you need to do some prewriting to generate examples that you can use to support this topic sentence. Look at the following examples, and see how they support this topic sentence.

Example #1: I especially remember my grandmother and me making a special cinnamon nut pastry for the holidays.

Example #2: I still remember the wonderful smell that filled her house as I entered.

Example #3: I always looked forward to taking her dog for a walk.

Example #4: Whenever I had homework to do, my grandmother sat and patiently helped me work through my assignments.

At the same time, adding an example that does not support the topic idea results in a paragraph that rambles and goes off focus, keeping your paragraph from being effective. Effective paragraphs are always unified. Just because an example is interesting does not mean that it should be included in the paragraph. Include only examples that support the topic sentence. Think back to the topic sentence, **I have wonderful memories of spending time with my grandmother,** and then examine the next example.

Example #5: I also remember the time my brother and I got in trouble for trying to dig a swimming pool next to the foundation of my grandmother's house.

Though you might vividly remember this event, you would **not** be able to use this example as support in your paragraph. It is a memory, but it is **not** one of the "wonderful memories" that you have. This would ruin the unity of the paragraph. This example could be used only if you write a paragraph that includes both the positive and negative memories of being at your grandmother's house.

Work through the following exercise to decide which examples can be used to support the topic sentence.

Exercise 9

Read each topic sentence, and then circle the letter of the example that does NOT support the topic sentence.

1. Topic Sentence: When I was a child, my older brother often played tricks on me.

   a. My father gave my brother and me three quarters to put in the offering plate at church. On the way to church, my brother talked me into putting two of my quarters into a gumball machine. My brother not only chewed one of the gumballs, but after church that day, he told my dad that I had not put my quarters in church because I wasted them on gum.

   b. When my brother and I got our Easter baskets, my brother talked me into sharing my candy with him and saving his for later, but he never got around to sharing his.

   c. Whenever my brother got candy or a cupcake at school, he saved it until he got home and shared it with me.

2. My neighbor stays active.

   a. At eighty-two years of age, she still mows and edges her grass.

   b. She likes to have a cup of tea before going to bed.

   c. Many weekends, she takes care of her great-grandchildren, taking them bowling.

   d. When she was diagnosed with arthritis, she began swimming every day to keep her body from getting stiff.

3. Children can learn kindness from examples set by adults.

   a. A mother helps an elderly lady at the mall find her car.

   b. A teacher tells his students how he saved an injured pet hit by a car.

   c. A father mows the lawn for a neighbor who is too ill to do the job.

   d. Parents discuss with their children how to save money.

   e. A busy neighbor drove her friend to the hospital.

4. Using the Internet helps people find valuable information.

   a. High school students find material about choosing a college.

   b. Youngsters in elementary school find ideas for school reports.

   c. Mothers and fathers find valuable information about children's health.

   d. Some people spend unlimited time in chat rooms.

5. Being the parent of young children gives parents many responsibilities.

   a. When a child gets hurt, the parents need to be able to perform first aid.

   b. The parents need to teach the children how to make brownies.

   c. The parents need to provide nutritious meals for the children.

   d. When parents are away from home, they need to be sure the children can reach them.

   e. The parents need to teach children how to share and get along with one another.

Details

At this point, it is valuable for you to practice distinguishing between examples and details. **Details** are facts and specific descriptive words that make an example more vivid, more believable. Examples, complete with details, will provide solid support for your paragraph.

> **Examples** are specific references to events or objects.
>
> **Details** are facts and specific descriptive words that make an example more vivid, more believable.

Once you decide on an example, you will want to go into detail about it. This means providing the specific information to help others visualize what you are saying. Suppose, for instance, in a paragraph about the wonderful memories you had at your grandmother's house when you were a child, you want to use the example of baking a dessert with your grandmother. Then, when sharing this with your reader, you need to supply specific details so that the reader feels as though he or she is there with you. Just as with examples, **include only details that are needed to make the example effective.** Study the following.

Topic sentence: I have wonderful memories of spending time with my grandmother.

Example #1: I especially remember my grandmother and me making a special cinnamon nut pastry for the holidays.

Details: We would make a wonderful pie crust from flour, shortening, and milk. Then we would roll the dough out on a special sheet of thick plastic that kept the dough from sticking to the countertop. Even when I was little, Grandma let me brush butter over the entire surface of the dough, and then we would make a special mixture of sugar and cinnamon that Grandma let me spread over the butter, making me feel important. She chopped pecans and then let me spread them over the cinnamon mixture. Grandma then brought one side up over the other, sealing the edges together. Just minutes after we put it into the oven, the smell of cinnamon filled the house, and I could hardly wait for us to sit down together with glasses of milk and our special creation.

Example #2: I still remember the wonderful smell that filled her house as I entered.

Details: Whenever I walked into my grandmother's house, I could smell the wonderful aroma of toasted tortillas drifting through the air, inviting me into her kitchen.

Example #3: I always looked forward to taking her dog for a walk.

Details: After lunch, we got out the bright, neon-pink leash for grandma's little white and tan Sheltie, Blazer, who immediately came to life, wagging her entire body and barking her approval. Grandma let me hold the leash, and I also felt the excitement as we headed out the door. No matter how fast or how slowly I walked, little Blazer followed my lead, holding her head high. Grandma walked next to me, and I felt proud that Grandma trusted me with her beautiful little dog.

Example #4: Whenever I had homework to do, my grandmother sat and patiently helped me work through my assignments.

Details: When I was a little boy in the first grade, I had a hard time learning to read, so Grandma had me sit next to her in her comfortable rocking chair, put her arm around me, and helped me sound out each word. If I missed a word, she just patted my arm and told me that I could do it if I didn't give up.

Remember that examples come from the prewriting that you do when you start thinking about your paragraph. The vivid details can also be in your prewriting. However, you may need to freewrite or brainstorm again to help you remember other specific details.

The following exercise will help you distinguish simple examples from examples with more details.

Exercise 10

Read each topic sentence, and then read both examples to see which one has the most details to support the topic sentence. Put the letter of the more detailed example in the blank.

Version A

___ **1.** Topic sentence: My neighbor's backyard is pleasant.

    a. As I sat on the deck of my home and looked around, I could see my neighbor's backyard. Several giant pine trees provided shade, and oleander bushes with pink and white blossoms grew as tall as the roof. Hibiscus shrubs with large, brightly colored red flowers grew on one side of the yard. A large prickly pear cactus grew along the back fence, giving an unusual but naturally attractive feeling. The lawn was nicely trimmed, and the pool was crystal clear.

    b. My neighbor's backyard is attractive. It has trees, flowers, and a swimming pool.

___ **2.** Topic sentence: I enjoyed sitting in my backyard.

    a. When I sat in my backyard, I could watch the hummingbirds near my house.

    b. I sat on the swing on the deck of my home, amazed at the size of the ficus tree that grew next door. It had grown large enough to hide my view of their house, but I could still see the beautiful orange trumpet-shaped flowers that drew the tiny hummingbirds. I watched one emerald green bird as it zipped around the flowers and then flew into the leaves of the enormous tree. As I looked closer, I could see a tiny nest almost hidden from view.

___ **3.** Topic sentence: The students in the ceramics classroom were very productive.
   a. Many of the students in the ceramics classroom were bent over their wheels. Their clay-coated hands shaped the grayish brown clay on the wheel that continued to rotate counterclockwise. With fingers locked together as one unit, their hands worked together. Some students were intent on bringing the sides of the clay up, and others were gently bringing the sides out, shaping the clay into a delicate bowl or pitcher.
   b. When I entered my ceramics classroom, I saw that the students were busy working on the wheels. Some were making bowls, and others were making pitchers.

___ **4.** Topic sentence: At the graduation ceremony at the university, the graduating students expressed their excitement.
   a. When each college was announced, the president walked to the microphone, and the students stood up and cheered.
   b. When the graduation began, students threw tortillas into the air, making them spin like Frisbees. Dozens of these small round flour and corn tortillas floated through the air simultaneously, crisscrossing one another. They landed on the excited graduates only to be airborne again at the next moment of celebration.

___ **5.** Topic sentence: Reading a newspaper before a primary election can help voters make decisions.
   a. All candidates for a particular office will let the newspaper know how they stand on issues like taxes, the environment, or education. If more money is needed to help with children's programs, the candidates will make clear their views on those topics.
   b. Columnists interview the candidates. Editorials analyze issues and may recommend how to vote.

Version B

___ **1.** Topic sentence: Even President Williams of the College of Education joined in the festivities.
   a. President Williams of the College of Education danced as his name was announced.
   b. President Williams of the College of Education, dressed in a blue robe adorned with black stripes on the sleeves and a colorful velvet cape, stood up, but instead of walking to the microphone, his stoic presence turned into wild and wonderful dance movements, including a back flip. The candidates for an education degree clapped and cheered, drowning out all other sounds.

___ **2.** Topic sentence: Using a cell phone while driving can be dangerous.
   a. Attempting to drive and punch in the telephone number at the same time is dangerous.
   b. One driver clutched her address book in her left hand and scanned the pages, looking for a telephone number. Only two fingers of her left hand touched the steering wheel. In her right hand, she held her cell phone, eager to punch in the correct numbers.

____ 3. Topic sentence: Transportation in cities is enhanced by sophisticated freeway systems.

     a. Many large cities have eight-lane highways that completely surround the city. This circle around the city has no lights, no stop signs, only on and off ramps. Transferring from one freeway to another is accomplished through moving onto sophisticated ramps that tower above the ground, allowing drivers to move from one freeway to another with unbelievable ease.

     b. Major freeways completely surround the city as well as run through them.

____ 4. Topic sentence: The baseball game was exciting.

     a. The home team was behind, but suddenly everything changed. After the home team center fielder caught a deep fly ball, he threw it on a straight line to third base to keep a run from scoring. In the home team's next inning, a player just off the disabled list hit a home run with two runners on base, and in the same game, he went on to hit two more home runs to help his team win. The excitement reached a peak when the visiting team's manager stormed onto the field, yelling uncontrollably at the home-plate umpire.

     b. The home team made many exciting plays, and the visiting manager was thrown out of the game.

____ 5. Topic sentence: A pet supermarket offers owners of cats many types of products.

     a. An entire aisle, 40 feet long, may contain many shelves of canned and dried food for healthy pets as well as for pets having health problems. Cans and vacuum-sealed pouches include such choices as roasted turkey in sauce or minced white fish to please feline companions. Other shelves offer rows and rows of both dry and canned foods for kittens. To keep kittens and cats happy and alert, many kinds of bouncing balls, pretend mice, and flying feathery objects on springs are always available. The shopper will also see special beds that reflect the pets' own body heat to keep them toasty warm. For cats that need extra nutrition, many kinds of vitamins fill the shelves.

     b. The shopper may have to consider many kinds of dry as well as canned food. Toys and beds will also seem in endless supply. Other necessities such as vitamins are also available.

Now, work through the next exercise, which will help you generate your own examples and details that could later be developed into a paragraph.

Think about each topic sentence and the specific examples given. Then, add details to support each example given.

Example:

The kitchen was messy.

sink:	*dried spaghetti covering yesterday's plates, cockroaches crawling around half-filled coffee cups and saucers and sampling the toast crumbs, forks plastered with dried cheese that had once been melted,*
table:	*newspapers piled one on top of another, unopened mail, a bottle of Tabasco sauce with a missing lid, a half-full can of Pepsi*
countertops:	*a half-empty package of spaghetti noodles, an empty can of tomato sauce still gooey around the edges, a stack of unopened magazines*

1. Sitting next to the lake provided a beautiful view.

    water _____

    _____

    trees _____

    _____

    mountains _____

    _____

2. The people at the open-air concert were enjoying themselves.

    talking _____

    _____

    dancing _____

    _____

    eating _____

    _____

The following exercise will help you practice writing topic sentences and listing examples and details that can be used in writing a paragraph.

Using the topic *working at a fast-food restaurant* or the topic for your next writing assignment, complete the following outline.

Topic: _____

Topic Sentence: _____

_____

Supporting Examples and Details

Example #1 _____

details _____

_____

Example #2 _____

details _____

_____

Example #3 _____

details _____

_____

Example #4 _____

details _____

_____

Note Refer to Chapter 1, pages 14–20, which discusses organizing support material by grouping in time or chronological order, grouping like ideas together, and grouping in order of importance.

Concluding Sentences

All paragraphs need concluding sentences to give them a sense of closure or completeness. After you have already written your topic sentence and support sentences, you should find it easy to write a concluding sentence. One thing you do want to remember is that you **never** want to end the paragraph with the same wording that you used in your topic sentence. For example, if your topic sentence is "Sitting next to the lake provided a beautiful view," you would **not** end the paragraph by saying, "This is why sitting next to the lake provided a beautiful view." This seems little more than a mechanical response. You want to be a bit more creative.

You do not want to spend all your time writing an effective paragraph only to end it without putting any thought into that last sentence. **The concluding sentence should go back to your topic idea without simply restating the topic sentence.** The concluding sentence is often a one-sentence summary of the paragraph. Other times it might be a commentary on what has been said in the paragraph, but it still must go back to the topic idea.

Look at the following paragraph, and then look at the possible concluding sentence.

> Having a baby is extremely expensive. Even before the baby is born, the parents need to purchase a baby bed. They will need to buy several sheets and mattress pads because once they bring the baby home from the hospital, they will probably need to change the sheets several times a day. Parents must also purchase other items, including a car seat, because they will need this item before they can even bring the baby home from the hospital. Of course, the hospital stay is not free, even for a simple birth. Once the baby comes home, however, the real expenses begin. Unless the baby is breastfed, the parents will need hundreds of bottles of formula. This means purchasing formula, bottles, bottle brushes, and even disposable liners for the bottles. Also, the baby will need eight to fifteen diapers a day, which can mount up over the weeks

and months before a baby is potty trained. However, babies need more than just formula and diapers. They also need such clothing as baby outfits, gowns, and little booties that they outgrow every few months. During the first year of a baby's life, the parents must take the child to the doctor for well visits to make sure the infant is developing correctly. If a baby becomes ill, then additional expenses mount up, including medicine, thermometers, vaporizers, and other medical expenses. Of course, all babies need toys to stimulate their minds and keep them occupied, so parents will need to purchase toys for all stages of a child's life. *The expenses do not taper off as the babies grow older, and usually these expenses continue until babies become adults.*

This is only one possible ending sentence. If you do not want to use the concluding sentence in the above paragraph, you could remove it and substitute one of the following concluding sentences.

Other Possible Concluding Sentences

- Before individuals decide to have children, they should be sure they can afford the expense.
- Having a baby seems like a wonderful thing to do, but many financial obligations come with the baby.
- All in all, having a baby involves thousands of dollars in expenses.

Of course, these are not the only concluding sentences that you could use, but you definitely DO NOT want to end with a weak sentence like the following.

- This is why having a baby is expensive.

If you have trouble writing a concluding sentence, just read through your paragraph one more time, and then think of an effective way to end it.

 Summary

Writing effective paragraphs means writing a paragraph that has a topic sentence, support sentences, and a concluding sentence.

- Topic Sentence—A topic sentence needs to have a topic (subject) and a direction but should not be a statement of fact or too broad to be developed in one paragraph. Remember, the topic sentence is the main idea of the paragraph and provides the direction for the paragraph.
- Support Sentences—The support sentences need to include examples and details that back up and verify the topic sentence.
- Concluding Sentence—The concluding sentence needs to recapture what was stated in the paragraph without simply restating the topic sentence or sounding dull. Always try to be creative.

As you continue to write stronger and stronger paragraphs, remember that writing an effective topic sentence and supporting it requires using specific examples and details that help the reader understand what you are saying.

Writing Assignment

Write a paragraph on one of the following topics.

1. A visit to the dentist
2. A favorite talk show or talk-show host
3. Current dress styles
4. A favorite restaurant
5. A favorite music group

Collaborative Activity

1. Working with another student, choose one of the above topics.
2. Talk and brainstorm together to generate a list of ideas and examples about your topic.
3. Still working together, sort through the ideas to see how they fit together for a possible direction for a paragraph.
4. Write down a possible topic sentence.
5. Working on your own, draft a paragraph that includes your topic sentence, support sentences, and a concluding sentence.

Practice Test

Read the following paragraph, and then answer the questions that follow by circling the letter of the correct answer.

(1) The high cost of prescription drugs in America forces a growing number of people with fixed incomes to find alternatives for this serious problem. (2) Some people need several expensive pills each day. (3) With drug costs constantly rising, they do whatever they can to stay supplied with these essential pills. (4) One choice is simply to cut down on the prescribed dosage so that their medications last longer. (5) Instead of two pills, they take only one, or they cut their pills in half to make them last twice as long. (6) Other times, they decide which drugs are the most important to their health and then simply fail to purchase the other ones. (7) They check all of their options. (8) During office visits, some people ask their doctors for free samples of the medications they use and, in this way, stretch their supply. (9) Ordering from mail-order companies or over the Internet can also help them pay less for these life-saving drugs. (10) A new trend is to purchase pharmaceuticals at a reduced price from Mexico or Canada. (11) For example, one bus line in Tucson, Arizona, has a "Prescription Express" to Mexico. (12) For only twenty dollars, people receive round-trip bus tickets to Mexico. (13) The buses also boast of having a licensed pharmacist on board to make sure patients buy the correct prescription, including dosage. (14) These pharmacists also

educate passengers as to which drugs can be purchased legally in Mexico. (15) In Maine, a group of senior citizens organize drug-shopping bus trips to Quebec. (16) There they can buy some medications for as little as one-fourth of their cost in the United States. (17) Limited resources and high drug prices force many American citizens to be resourceful in obtaining the drugs they so desperately need.

1. Sentence # 1 is the topic sentence for this paragraph. What is the topic?
   a. drugs in America
   b. high cost of prescription drugs in America
   c. serious problem

2. Sentence # 1 is the topic sentence for this paragraph. What is the direction?
   a. to find alternatives for this serious problem
   b. drugs in America
   c. high cost of prescription drugs

3. The first example is given in sentence #4. What is it?
   a. medications last longer
   b. one choice
   c. to cut down to the prescribed dosage

4. Details to clarify how people cut down on the prescribed dosage are in which two sentences?
   a. 5 and 6
   b. 4 and 5
   c. 6 and 7

5. Which words in sentence #8 support the topic idea?
   a. during office visits
   b. ask their doctors for free samples
   c. stretch their supply

6. In sentence #9, how does buying from mail-order companies or using the Internet support the topic idea?
   a. help them pay less
   b. life-saving drugs
   c. learn to use the Internet

7. Another example of an alternative is in sentence #10. What is this example?
   a. pharmaceuticals
   b. a new trend
   c. buying from Mexico or Canada

8. Which sentences contain details that support the example concerning Mexico?
   a. 10, 11, 12, and 13
   b. 11, 12, 13, and 14
   c. 12, 13, 14, and 15

9. Which sentences contain details that support the example concerning Canada?
   a. 10 and 13
   b. 9 and 10
   c. 15 and 16

10. In sentence #13, what detail supports the example of buying drugs in Mexico?
    a. having a licensed pharmacist on board
    b. the correct prescription
    c. avoid illegal drugs

11. In sentence #16, what specific detail supports the example that drugs cost less in Canada?
    a. in the United States
    b. buy some medication
    c. one-fourth of their cost in the United States

12. Sentence # 17 is the concluding sentence. It is linked to the topic sentence by key words. The key words **limited resources** refer to what words in the topic sentence?
    a. fixed incomes
    b. high drug prices
    c. to find alternatives

13. Sentence # 17 is the concluding sentence. It is linked to the topic sentence by key words. The key words **high drug prices** refer to what words in the topic sentence?
    a. fixed incomes
    b. high cost of prescription drugs
    c. to find alternatives

14. Sentence # 17 is the concluding sentence. It is linked to the topic sentence by key words. The key words **to be resourceful** refer to what words in the topic sentence?
    a. fixed incomes
    b. high drug prices
    c. to find alternatives

Something to Think About, Something to Write About

Professional Essay to Generate Ideas for Writing

It's Not How Smart You Are, It's How You're Smart!

Dr. René Díaz-Lefebvre, *Professor of Psychology at Glendale Community College*

1   Have you ever been told that you were not very smart or that you did not have much going for you? Has your self-confidence or self-esteem been affected by these notions and beliefs held by *others,* including teachers, counselors, friends? I am here to tell you **not** to believe any of it! Everybody has a special gift, a light to shine. I challenge you to find your special gifts and talents.

2   English is not my native language; however, I was born in the United States. My parents were fluently bilingual in Spanish and English, yet I was raised by my *nana* (grandmother) who spoke only Spanish. My *nana* was a wonderful person. I learned so much from her including being proud of my Mexican heritage. She would teach me different *dichos* or sayings. Two of my favorites,*"la educación abre puertas"* ("education opens doors") and *"saber es poder"*("knowledge is power"), gave me a foundation to continue my quest for learning even against great odds.

3   As a young boy, I struggled in a world called school. I would go to school, but since I did not understand English, I did not understand what the teacher was saying. I longed to be home with my *nana.* As I continued through school, I would speak (reluctantly, I might add) with an accent. I was self-conscious of not sounding like the rest of the kids. I did not do well in school, so I was placed in classes like shop and woodworking. I was told that I was not smart enough. When I was in high school, some of my friends were taking the ACT test, so I went in to sign up. My counselor told me, "You are going to fail it." I decided to take it anyhow because it seemed like the thing to do. I still remember walking into the testing room and looking at the test. The questions were about Mozart and Shakespeare, and I had no idea what to do. I glanced over at a friend who mouthed, "Eenie, meenie, miney, mo." That is what I did. I went through the test, guessing at every question. When the results came back in, my counselor called me into his office. He told me, "You have a wonderful family. Your mother makes great tamales for the fundraiser, and you are a great kid, but you just do not have it upstairs. College is out of the question. You need to go to trade school and become a mechanic. Be the best mechanic you can be." I listened and went to trade school, but instead of mechanics I ended up at a computer institute. I knew

college was not for me because that is what I had been taught all through school. There is nothing wrong with being a mechanic; it's just that I remembered what my grandmother had told me about education opening doors. I knew I was smart, but smart in ways that made sense to *me.*

4   Throughout grade school and high school, I was stuck in an environment that I did not like, but I decided that I better make the best of it! I was not "good" at taking tests or really anything having to do with school, but I did have an ability or talent for sports and music. These were two activities that were fun for me. I enjoyed them, and I was good at them, too. I spent my time playing baseball, and I became so efficient at the sport that I was rewarded by playing semi-pro baseball during my junior and senior year in high school. Also, I loved music, and playing the drums just came naturally for me. I became a jazz drummer and I played in various bands. My ability in music gave me a chance to express myself. It also supplemented my income for many years to come, including graduate school.

5   After I graduated from trade school, a new community college in Tucson, Arizona, was getting ready to open its doors, and I was hired to work as a student aide. I put my computer skills to good use and, along with two other students, developed a computer program for the college to register students. Somehow, on the first day of registration, after we had set up the computers, I was told to go ahead and register for classes. My friends pushed me in front of them, and I became the first student at Pima Community College. Thoughts raced through my mind. Was college just a dream, or could it be something I could attain? My goal was just to get into college. I would stay a couple of semesters and then work full-time. I needed to prove to myself and all the other people who thought I was "stupid" or *"muy burro"* (not bright or capable) that I could be "smart," that *Sí Se Puede* (It Can Be Done.)

6   Once I started taking classes, I was influenced by a special group of teachers and counselors. I remember Dr. Lee Scott, my humanities teacher, who made such an impact and impression on me that I model *my* teaching style after his. He challenged me to do the very best that I could, telling me that "knowledge is power!" He and other instructors such as Rudy Melone, Diego Navarrete, Liz González, and Miguel Méndez took me aside and told me "*Sí, lo tienes. Lo tienes adentro de ti, y no vamos a dejar ir el sueño que tenemos para ti.* (Yes, you have it. You have it inside of you and we're not going to let go of our dream for you.") They took me under their wings and pushed, supported, challenged me to be the best I could be. No one had ever taken the time to do this before. While there, I was elected to the board of trustees as a student, and I also was selected to give the graduation address. I was accepted at several universities including Stanford and Arizona State University, but was offered a full-ride academic scholarship to the University of Redlands. I accepted the scholarship to the University of Redlands where I studied under such scholars as Carl Rogers, Abraham Maslow, and Jacob Bronowski. I went on to earn master's and doctorate degrees, including post-doctorate work at Harvard University.

7   I returned to the community college to serve as a role model, to encourage other young people, to pass on what my *nana* taught me many years ago that *la educación abre puertas.* Today, I have had the privilege of

being a community college teacher for over 30 years. My whole life changed because of my experience that began at a Pima Community College where people believed in my potential as a student and as a person. More importantly, I *believed* in myself. I never let go of my dreams or my goals. You need to explore and find out the many ways that you are smart and begin applying them. I end with one last saying, "*Es el dolor de mi color, pero es me valor* (It's the pain of my color and who I am, but it's also my courage.)" Have the courage to get an education because it can never be taken from you. Remember, it is not how smart you are (you're already smart!); it's *how* (many different ways!) you're smart!

Understanding Words
Briefly define the following words as they are used in this selection.

1. heritage
2. quest

Writing Assignment

Write a paragraph on one of the following topics. Be sure to start with a strong topic sentence. Add specific examples and details for support, and end with a strong concluding sentence.

1. Describe a person who has helped you believe in yourself.
2. Describe a person who has tried to keep you from accomplishing your goals.
3. Write about some *dichos* (sayings) that have made an impact on your life.
4. Write about how an education can make a major change in a person's life.
5. Describe a special talent or ability you have.

Part 3

Student and Professional Paragraphs

Travel

Mark Bethke, *Student*

After school, I plan to travel the world. I have always wanted to drink beer in Germany, walk the streets of Rome, and climb the mountain ranges of Tibet. I want to see the Dalai Lama and ask about the mysteries of the universe and watch the Pope drive around in his bubble car as he waves his hand to bless me as he goes by. I will visit the ancient ruins of the great cities in Mexico and sip margaritas on the Gulf coast. It is not just other countries I want to visit. I would also enjoy traveling throughout the United States. I want to see New York City, climb skyscrapers that touch the sky, and then scream, "I'm on top of the world!" when I reach the top. These are dreams now, but dreams do come true. First, I have to get through school, an adventure of its own.

Questions on Form

1. What is the topic sentence?

2. What are some examples that support the topic sentence?

3. What word in the concluding sentence ties together the whole travel experience?

Questions on Content

1. What details add to the effectiveness of seeing the Pope?

2. Where in the United States does the author wish to visit?

3. What does he plan to do before he travels?

Phoenix

Joshua Sewell, *Student*

Even though I have come to like living in Phoenix, when I first moved here, the negative aspects of the city overwhelmed me. My first impression of Phoenix was that it was a very boring city. It has many chain stores and restaurants, but few specialty stores. To me, this seems quite boring. There are very few places where I can get things like Mediterranean food, and the first Trader Joe's wasn't built here until about five years ago. In the past eight years, I have come to find many stores and restaurants that appeal to my taste; however, I am still irritated by the fact that I have to drive so far to get to them. When I first moved to Phoenix, the summer weather was unbearable. However, I have now become acclimated to the summer heat, but I still hate the amount of driving I do on a daily basis. In fact, the closest good record store is a twenty-five-minute drive from my house, and I have to drive all the way to Tempe to find the majority of rare music that interests me. I used to live in southern California where there is a very active local music scene. Until I became more familiar with the local music scene in Phoenix, I was under the impression that there wasn't one. In the last few years, however, I have found enticing coffee houses where local guitarists and musical groups perform regularly to enthusiastic audiences. In spite of these complaints and the many others I have not mentioned, I have come to like living in Phoenix and consider it to be my home.

Understanding Words
Briefly define the following word as it is used in the selection.

acclimated

Questions on Form
1. What is the author's topic idea?

2. What specific details does the author give about music groups?

3. What time words does the author use to introduce the summer weather?

Questions on Content
1. How has his attitude about Phoenix changed?

2. What three examples does the author discuss?

3. What has the author concluded about Arizona?

Learning to Be Responsible

Kalli Mussetter, *Student*

When I was a young teenager, owning and breeding my own flock of sheep for a 4-H project helped me learn how to be responsible and accountable. I always had to get up very early, especially in the spring when the ewes were giving birth, often referred to as dropping lambs or lambing out like crazy. At six a.m., I could hear the footsteps of my father as he came downstairs headed for my room. "Get up," he would bellow. "You have to go to work." I rolled out of bed and began putting my iodine-stained coveralls over my pajamas, putting my hair up in a tight lump on the back of my head, while looking for the thickest stockings I could find to go under the worn, very smelly boots that I shuffled out to the barn with. As I scuffled through a brand new layer of snow, which fell overnight, sometimes even more was falling on my burning face, still warm from the pillow and then seconds later in shock from the cold air. I entered the barn to find I had two more lambs starting on their first legs of life. With my sheep project, early mornings and late nights spent feeding bum lambs were common in the spring when ewes were lambing out. In summer, I spent hot afternoons shoveling sheep manure out from in front of their feeder, into the back of the trailer of my riding lawn mower, only to shovel it again out into my front pasture. Feeding took a big part of my time, always having to make time before going to school. In addition, there was always something to clean, especially because I found my father to be a very picky man. I was always having to sweep out and tidy up the stalls. With this responsibility, I was in care of lives. They were not human, but they were living. Because I took my responsibilities seriously, I know I will be better off in the future as I face challenges in my family life and in my jobs to come.

Understanding Words
Briefly define the following words as they are used in the selection.

1. ewes
2. scuffled

Questions on Form

1. What is the direction for the topic of owning and breeding a flock of sheep?

2. Name one example that supports the direction.

3. What is the key word in the concluding sentence that leads back to the topic sentence?

Questions on Content

1. What was the special project?

2. How did she describe her boots?

3. What does the author think she could face later in life?

Excerpt from THEFWORD, How to Survive Your Family

Louie Anderson with Carl Kurlander

1   Underneath the jokes, my dad was a complicated figure. We never really know who our parents are. In researching *Dear Dad,* I discovered that Dad had a soft side that was pretty much invisible by the time I came along. I found love letters he'd written to my mother in which he endearingly called her "Toy." I also discovered one of the reasons he'd been so harsh to us all those years. When he was young, he was sent off to live with a cold foster family who treated him as a farm slave and worked him all the time. He was made to sleep in the unheated attic. When they passed the food around at dinner, my father wasn't allowed to have seconds unless everyone else in the family had eaten as much as each one wanted. But in looking further into his background for this book, I've discovered even more about him.

2   . . . My mother's side of the family was a little more stable. She grew up well-to-do. Her father owned a fleet of gas stations. He was a kind man who so loved children that he made the windows on their house lower so that his little kids could look out the front windows and see everything. During the Great Depression, when everyone was hit hard, he extended credit to all his customers who couldn't pay for gas. But when the Depression was over, no one paid him back. He never got over that. My mother always said he died of a broken heart.

3   My mother's ancestors, the Windsors, dated all the way back to the Pilgrims. They came over on the *Mayflower* and were probably there for the first Thanksgiving. You think that Thanksgiving was any different from the ones we have today? I can just see my mom's great-great-great grandmother pushing her favorite dishes on those Native Americans. "Oh, come on, chief, try a little of my sweet potatoes. They've got marshmallows on top." . . . .

Questions on Form

1. What example did the author use to show his dad's soft side?

2. What is the topic sentence in the first paragraph?

3. What is the topic sentence in the second paragraph?

Questions on Content

1. What did his mother's father own?

2. How did his mother say her father died?

3. What would an ancestor probably have done at the first Thanksgiving?

Excerpt from Angela's Ashes

Frank McCourt

In fine weather men sit outside smoking their cigarettes if they have them, looking at the world and watching us play. Women stand with their arms folded, chatting. They don't sit because all they do is stay at home, take care of the children, clean the house and cook a bit, and the men need the chairs. The men sit because they're worn out from walking to the Labour Exchange every morning to sign for the dole, discussing the world's problems and wondering what to do with the rest of the day. Some stop at the bookie to study the form and place a shilling or two on a sure thing. Some spend hours in the Carnegie Library reading English and Irish newspapers. A man on the dole needs to keep up with things because all the other men on the dole are experts on what's going on in the world. A man on the dole must be ready in case another man on the dole brings up Hitler or Mussolini or the terrible state of the Chinese millions. A man on the dole goes home after a day with the bookie or the newspaper, and his wife will not begrudge him a few minutes with the ease and peace of his cigarette and his tea and time to sit in his chair and think of the world.

Understanding Words
Briefly define the following words as they are used in the selection.

1. dole
2. shilling
3. begrudge

Questions on Form

1. What is the topic idea?

2. What words in the concluding sentence link back to key words in the topic sentence?

3. What makes the paragraph interesting to read?

Questions on Content

1. How do the women stay busy?

2. What wears out the men so they need the chairs?

3. What time of day do the men sign for the dole?

Part 4

Understanding Grammar
Adjectives and Adverbs

Objectives

- Identify adjectives
- Use correct adjective forms in sentences
- Identify adverbs
- Use correct adverb forms in sentences
- Understand how adjectives and adverbs add necessary details to sentences

As you have already learned, all sentences must have at least one main subject and at least one main verb. Adding stronger details and additional information to your sentences can be done in different ways, including using adjectives and adverbs. This not only makes your sentences stronger but also allows you to communicate more effectively with your reader. Instead of just saying, "The children played," you might say, "The excited children played endlessly each day."

Reading through the following information and completing the exercises will help you understand adjectives and adverbs. It will also help you feel more comfortable when you add details to your own sentences.

Adjectives

As you learned previously, adjectives describe or modify nouns and pronouns. Adjectives may tell **what kind, how many,** or **which one.** Usually, these words come before nouns.

Adjectives may tell **what kind, size, color,** or **shape:**

Carol admired the **large** house.

Sue bought the **red** car.

Nikki bought the **round** cushion.

I bought **finishing** nails to use on the porch.

We enjoyed the **roasted** turkey.

Adjectives may tell **how many**:

Jason needs **two** boxes for the papers.

Irene bought **four** yards of cotton fabric for the sewing project.

Many roads need to be repaired.

Some adjectives **point out a particular noun**.

Let's go into **this** store to buy **that** book.

Hang **these** pictures on **those** walls.

Sometimes an adjective comes after the verb and, therefore, after the noun or pronoun it describes. To see how this works, study the following examples.

Carol's house was **large**.

Sue's car was **red**.

Nikki's cushion was **round**.

Sometimes two or more adjectives in a row can modify the same **noun**.

The disgruntled, bitter man left the store.

Francisco left the old, stale, moldy sandwich on the table.

Note Remember that a word can be a noun in one sentence and an adjective in another sentence, depending on how the word is used. For example:

noun
Winter brings relief from hot summer weather.

adjective
Winter weather brings relief from hot summers.

Identifying Adjectives

Exercise 1

Underline the adjectives in each sentence. Remember, **a, an,** and **the** are articles used as adjectives, but you do not need to mark them in these sentences.

Example:

The _twisted_ vines wrapped around the _old_ house.

Version A

1. The strong wind blew the rain into the new carport.
2. The fierce competition wore out the young contestants.
3. Summer weather in Phoenix is usually hot.
4. The parade featured the largest band in the state.
5. Up on the mountain, the anxious skiers waited to fly down the steep slope.
6. I lost my fuzzy green sweater yesterday.
7. Kay wanted new blinds in the living room.
8. Seventy people waited in line in the stifling heat.
9. James bought flowering shrubs for the front yard.
10. Yesterday, Katrina walked for thirty minutes.

Version B

1. Inside the brown box in the attic, Carol found sixteen letters.
2. The struggling hikers walked along the narrow trail.
3. The chef put the large steak onto the hot grill.
4. Before leaving, Mandy wrote an extensive shopping list.
5. The six legal pads fit into the side pocket of the briefcase.
6. The wheels on the rolling chair caught on the torn carpet.
7. I saw those broken cups on the kitchen floor.
8. The smiling young mother hung three pictures in the cheerful nursery.
9. From the cool patio, the savory aroma from the gas grill floated through the neighborhood.
10. After lunch, I worked on a paragraph for two hours.

Sentence Combining with Adjectives

Many times you will be able to eliminate extra words that add little to your sentences. You can do this by combining two or more short sentences into one strong sentence. There is no need to say, "My dog is my friend. He is sable and white," when you could simply say, "My sable and white dog is my friend."

Exercise 2

Combine the two short sentences into one clear sentence.

Example:

Dennis read the book first. The book was interesting.

Dennis read the interesting book first.

Version A

1. The rug needed to be cleaned. It was dirty.

2. The fans enjoyed the game. The fans were cheering.

_____

3. The pine needles crunched under my feet. They had fallen from the tree.

_____

4. The microwave made a strange sound. The sound was like a buzzing.

_____

5. I spilled my milkshake. The milkshake was chocolate.

_____

6. The flood came during the summer. It was devastating.

_____

7. We went to the concert. It was the last concert.

_____

8. Laura admired the bikes. They were mountain bikes.

_____

9. I worked at the Burger King. It was new.

_____

10. My umbrella would not open. My umbrella was red.

_____

Version B
1. The weather kept us from going on vacation. The weather was cold.

_____

2. The law was unpopular. The law was new.

_____

3. Floyd had the treatment at the hospital. The treatment was for cancer.

_____

4. Susan's class toured the factory. It was a potato chip factory.

_____

5. Anita went to the video store. She went to the nearest one.

_____

6. The bolt of lightning hit the tree. It hit the tallest tree.

_____

7. Water churned around me. The water was black.

_____

8. They fixed my car and returned the keys. They were the wrong keys.

_____

9. I drove my car through the tunnel. The tunnel was long and dark.

_____

10. The newspapers were a fire hazard. They were scattered everywhere.

_____

Exercise 3

Combine the following sentences into one clear sentence.

Example:

The parents were young.

Their baby was new.

They were proud of their baby.

The young parents were proud of their new baby.

Version A

1. The gardeners set out the plants.
They set out tomato plants.
The gardeners were proud.
The plants were healthy.

_____

2. The tourists gazed into the canyon.
The tourists were silent.
The canyon was deep.

_____

3. The white rhino has a tumor on his front leg.
He is old.
The tumor is cancerous.

_____

4. I drove to my parents' cabin.
The cabin was small.
The cabin was cozy.

_____

5. The weather required us to use fans.
The weather was hot.
We used all our fans.

_____

6. We drove on the mountain road.
The road was narrow.
We drove our new truck.

_____

7. Madison started a restaurant.
It was a pizza restaurant.
It was well planned.

_____

8. I withdrew money from my checking account.
The money was hard earned.
My checking account was shrinking.

_____

9. Rosa applied for a job.
It was a new job.
It was an exciting job.

_____

10. The trees were covered with blossoms.
They were peach trees.
The blossoms were pink.
The blossoms were fragrant.

_____

Version B

1. His eyes caught my attention.
   His eyes were big.
   His eyes were vacant.

   _____

2. My sister ate all the pie.
   My sister was selfish.
   The pie was pumpkin.

   _____

3. Tony wanted to test-drive the car.
   It was a sports car.
   It was red.

   _____

4. The cars quickly filled the parking lot.
   The cars were old.
   The parking lot was small.

   _____

5. We fed the bread to the pigeons.
   The bread was stale.
   The pigeons were hungry.

   _____

6. Clare went to the store to buy fruit.
   It was a neighborhood store.
   She wanted fresh fruit.

   _____

7. The tortoises were from the Galápagos Islands.
   The tortoises were ancient.
   They were also huge.

   _____

8. I can still hear my mother's words.
They are now famous.
My mother is wise.

_____

9. The speaker was the candidate for mayor.
The speaker was educated.
The speaker was the most qualified.

_____

10. The doctor prescribed exercises for Linda.
The doctor was understanding.
The exercises were simple.

_____

Exercise 4

Make a clear sentence out of each group of scrambled words. Remember to start the sentence with a capital letter and end the sentence with a period. Be sure to use all the words.

Example:

the pizza the family homemade enjoyed

The family enjoyed the homemade pizza.
_____

Version A

1. bookstore to students buy to went books their campus

_____

2. town into bears hungry cubs young and their came

_____

3. their neighbors the are roof old new replacing

_____

4. flee wildfire people their made homes the anxious

_____

5. two jam lasted hours traffic the for

_____

Version B

1. planned picnic a we quiet

_____

2. often informed to listen the news people

_____

3. rented couple honeymoon the beach the house

_____

4. character story the is main worker the a factory in

_____

5. twenty was nearest the away miles town

_____

Using Adjectives to Show Comparisons

Comparing Two Nouns or Pronouns, Using -er

As you learned earlier, adjectives modify or describe nouns and pronouns. Using carefully selected adjectives will help make your writing more interesting and, perhaps, more accurate. In addition, one of your commitments to better writing should also be to use the language that is appropriate in school and in the business world. Making comparisons correctly is a writing skill you will be expected to have.

Look at the following pairs of sentences, paying close attention to the adjectives that are in bold type. In the first sentence of each pair, the adjective is the basic form. In the second sentence of each pair, the adjective shows the comparison.

The first movie was **short**. It was **shorter** than the second one.

In the morning light, the curtains appeared **green**. They looked **greener** than the tree leaves outside the window.

In the above sentences, notice that adding **-er** to the basic form shows the comparison. For example, **short** becomes **shorter** and **green** becomes **greener**. The exercise below will help you practice using these comparisons.

Exercise 5

Add -er to each adjective below to show the correct form for a comparison. Write the correct form in the blank.

Examples:

short _____ _shorter_ _____

small _____ _smaller_ _____

Version A

1. quick   _____
2. tall   _____
3. full   _____
4. straight   _____
5. cool   _____
6. long   _____
7. kind   _____
8. deep   _____
9. great   _____
10. clean   _____

Version B

1. clear   _____
2. hard   _____
3. black   _____
4. few   _____
5. brown   _____
6. soft   _____
7. near   _____
8. plain   _____
9. light   _____
10. dark   _____

Using the Word *More* to Show Comparisons

When you want to use a longer adjective to compare two nouns or pronouns, just adding *-er* might make the adjective too awkward to say or read. In that case, another way to make the comparison is by using the word **more**. For example, look at the following:

beautiful	more beautiful	(not "beautifuler")
honest	more honest	(not "honester")

Exercise 6

Write the correct comparisons below by using the word **more**.

Examples:

valuable   _____ *more valuable* _____

workable   _____ *more workable* _____

Version A

1. surprising   _____
2. wonderful   _____
3. suitable   _____
4. expensive   _____
5. tragic   _____
6. attractive   _____
7. dangerous   _____
8. normal   _____
9. talkative   _____
10. grateful   _____

Version B

1. talented   _____
2. hideous   _____
3. alert   _____
4. active   _____
5. distant   _____
6. energetic   _____
7. vicious   _____
8. patient   _____
9. capable   _____
10. competent   _____

More About Using Adjectives—Using *-ier*

Sometimes when you are comparing two nouns or pronouns, you will need to **change the spelling** of the basic form. If the word ends in **-y**, change it to an **-i** before adding **-er.** Study the following sentences.

Mariah was **happy.** She was **happier** than her sister.

My room was **messy.** It was **messier** than my brother's.

Practice this change by working through the following exercise.

Exercise 7

Change the following basic forms into the comparison forms.

Examples:

creamy   _____ *creamier* _____

tricky   _____ *trickier* _____

Version A

1. spongy   _____
2. busy   _____
3. sooty   _____
4. nasty   _____
5. crafty   _____
6. bossy   _____
7. easy   _____
8. rocky   _____
9. classy   _____
10. nifty   _____

Version B

1. leafy   _____
2. boxy   _____
3. showy   _____
4. silly   _____
5. wealthy   _____
6. holy   _____
7. choppy   _____
8. shiny   _____
9. cozy   _____
10. tiny   _____

Comparing More Than Two Nouns or Pronouns—Using -est

Often you will need to compare more than two objects or people. This time, you will use the ending **-est**.

The first movie was **short**. It was the **shortest** one of the three. (three or more)

We took a **long** car trip. It was the **longest** one I had ever experienced. (many trips being compared)

Work through the exercise below to practice making these kinds of comparisons.

Exercise 8

Complete the following comparisons by using **-est**.

Examples:

short   _____*shortest*_____

small   _____*smallest*_____

Version A

1. quick   _____

2. tall   _____

3. full   _____

4. straight   _____

5. cool   _____

6. long   _____

7. kind   _____

8. deep   _____

9. great   _____

10. clean   _____

Version B

1. clear   _____

2. hard   _____

3. black   _____

4. few   _____

5. brown   _____

6. soft   _____

7. near   _____

8. plain   _____

9. light   _____

10. dark   _____

Using the Word *Most* to Compare Three or More Items

You learned earlier to use **more** when you were using a longer adjective to show a comparison between two things. When you need to compare three or more people or objects and the adjective would be too hard to pronounce, use the word **most**. Study the following:

beautiful	most beautiful	(not "beautifulest")
honest	most honest	(not "honestest")

Exercise 9

Complete the following comparisons by using the word **most**.

Examples:

valuable _____*most valuable*_____

workable _____*most workable*_____

Version A

1. surprising _____

2. wonderful _____

3. suitable _____

4. expensive _____

5. tragic _____

6. attractive _____

7. dangerous _____

8. normal _____

9. talkative _____

10. grateful _____

Version B

1. talented _____

2. hideous _____

3. alert _____

4. active _____

5. distant _____

6. energetic _____

7. vicious _____

8. patient _____

9. capable _____

10. competent _____

More About Using Adjectives—Using *-iest*

You learned above to change the spelling of some adjectives before you could add the **-er** ending. You also need to make the same change for these words when you add the **-est** ending. If the word ends in **-y**, change it to an **-i** before adding the **-est**.

Mariah was **happy**. She was the **happiest** person in her family.

My bedroom was **messy**. It was the **messiest** one in the whole house.

To help you understand this change, work through the following exercise with the same words that you used before.

Exercise 10

Change the following basic forms into the comparison forms that would be used for three or more things.

Examples:

creamy _____*creamiest*_____

tricky _____*trickiest*_____

Version A

1. spongy _____

2. busy _____

3. sooty   _____

4. nasty   _____

5. crafty   _____

6. bossy   _____

7. easy   _____

8. rocky   _____

9. classy   _____

10. nifty   _____

Version B

1. leafy   _____

2. boxy   _____

3. showy   _____

4. silly   _____

5. wealthy   _____

6. holy   _____

7. choppy   _____

8. shiny   _____

9. cozy   _____

10. tiny   _____

Adverbs

Using adverbs can be fun because they give you a chance to describe **how, when,** or **where** events happen. You can describe **to what extent** actions are true. Adverbs modify verbs, adjectives, or other adverbs. This might not mean much to you right now, but after practicing using adverbs, you can see how they also can add interest and precise meaning to your sentences. In addition, just like adjectives, adverbs should be placed near or even next to the words(s) they modify.

Adverbs Describing Verbs

Study the following sentences that contain adverbs (in bold) that modify or describe verbs. Notice that they all end in **-ly.** This is the most common signal for an adverb.

The children ran **quickly** to the water slide.

The manager **hesitantly** opened the door to the store.

Sometimes, for emphasis, adverbs can be placed at the beginning of the sentence. In each sentence below, the adverbs still describe the verb.

Hesitantly, the manager opened the door to the store.

Fortunately, we found our tickets.

The adverbs above add additional meaning to these sentences. They all tell how something happened. Different adverbs would add different meanings, but they would still tell how something happened.

The children ran **slowly** to the water slide.

The manager **blindly** opened the door to the store.

Adverbs can be as important as adjectives to help you express your ideas not only clearly but creatively.

Work through the following exercise to help you learn to identify adverbs.

Exercise 11

Underline the adverbs in the following sentences.

Example:

The trees _barely_ moved in the wind.

Version A
1. The parents proudly watched the ceremony.
2. Reluctantly, she paid the large water bill.
3. The winter weather repeatedly cracked the pavement.
4. The attorney formally presented the motion to the judge.
5. Quietly, the springer spaniel waited by the front door.
6. The dancer moved gracefully.
7. The child waited patiently for her breakfast.
8. Instantly, the police officer turned on the siren.

Version B
1. The stranded motorist desperately waved for help.
2. We definitely want to travel this summer.
3. Cautiously, the infantry soldier crossed the minefield.
4. That was an unusually interesting movie.
5. Matthew listened intently to the music.
6. Unfortunately, I was unable to attend her wedding.
7. Susan worked intently on the art project.
8. They waited impatiently for the mail carrier to arrive.

Other frequently used adverbs, though, do not have an **-ly** ending. Study the following sentences, all related to each other. These adverbs tell **how, when,** or **where** something happened.

Yazzie tried **hard** to get a job, and **then** he found one at the local gas station.

On payday, he **always** put part of his money in the bank.

He left it **there** without spending it.

Soon, he had enough money saved to take a class in college.

He registered **yesterday** for a course in art.

To keep the meaning clear, you should put the adverbs close to the words they modify, in this case, the verbs. Perhaps one should be placed right before the verb. Another may not make good sense unless it comes after the verb. Look at the third sentence above. The adverb "there" could only be where it is or at the beginning of the sentence. Just use your common sense to put ideas in logical order. Notice, also, how the adverbs above help keep the events in clear order. Using adverbs in this way is an important part of making ideas flow smoothly.

Sometimes, a word becomes an adverb simply because it functions like one. A word may seem to be a noun, for example, but if it describes a verb, it becomes an adverb.

Luke sprinted **home** in the rain.

"Home" is ordinarily a noun, but because it tells **where** Luke went, it becomes an adverb.

Being able to identify a word as an "adverb" is not the most important skill you can have. Rather, the important idea to remember is that words in English are very flexible and can serve as different parts of speech. They should help you express your ideas clearly and accurately.

Exercise 12

Add a detail to each of the following sentences by adding an adverb that tells more about the verb. Try to use different adverbs from the following list.

accurately	quietly	carefully	efficiently	energetically	correctly
strangely	swiftly	quickly	unexpectedly	modestly	capably
randomly	oddly	slowly			

Example:

The climbers moved _swiftly_ **to the top of the cliff.**

Version A

1. We looked _____ at the new furniture before buying any.

2. Alexis worked _____ at her new job.

3. _____ , the new puppy ran around the living room.

4. The journalist _____ reported the events to the television audience.

5. The ceiling fan did not turn as _____ as we had hoped.

Version B

1. People sat _____ in the doctor's waiting room.

2. The woman was _____ drawn to the light.

3. We were _____ chosen to register for class.

4. The little boy ran _____ from the barking dog.

5. Every year the freeway traffic moves more _____ .

Adverbs Describing Adjectives

Many times, you may have written a sentence that sounds all right in the first draft. However, during revision you may want to add an idea to a sentence to make it more real or more interesting to your reader. For example, look at the following:

Harriet seemed to be a **bright** child. (adjective)

Matt wrote a **fine** essay. (adjective)

Perhaps you want to add a detail to make the adjectives express more of what you were really thinking.

Harriet seemed to be a **remarkably** bright child.

Matt wrote a **surprisingly** fine essay.

Each additional word is an adverb because it modifies the adjective in each sentence. The important point to remember is that when you add details to your writing, you will be able to use the words correctly when you know how the word functions or works—whether it modifies a verb or an adjective. Still, when you are writing a draft, just put in the details as you need them. During the time for revision and editing, you can figure out if you have the right form.

Sometimes you will want to emphasize an adjective to tell to what extent something is true. For example, if you say, "I ate some delicious pie today for lunch," you might want to add more power to "delicious." Probably you would say, "I ate some **very** delicious pie today for lunch. The word "very" is an adverb simply because it modifies the adjective "delicious." In fact, "very" is always an adverb. You will learn a little later that "very" is the correct form to use here because it modifies an adjective.

Exercise 13

Add an appropriate adverb that modifies the adjective.

Example:

This is ___*incredibly*___ **good cake.**

Version A

1. My paper was _____ easy to write. (extreme)

2. This paper is _____ different from my other one. (slight)

3. The exhibits were _____ well done. (equal)

4. He likes to study in the _____ lighted library. (bright)

5. His _____ spoken words upset me. (harsh)

Version B

1. The _____ painted house overwhelmed me. (colorful)

2. The father-to-be waited in the _____ silent room. (unexpected)

3. My roll had a _____ spread layer of peanut butter. (thick)

4. Jason was _____ optimistic about the race. (fair)

5. The lemon pie turned out to be _____ good. (uncommon)

Exercise 14

Add an appropriate adverb to each sentence. Use a different word for each sentence. Remember that adverbs tell *how, when, where,* and *to what extent.* Answers will vary.

Example

stiffly

The gentleman walked up the steps into his house.

∧

Version A

1. The mother spoke to her daughter.

2. We arrived at the airport.

3. Before lunch, Heather sat down in the snack bar.

4. Ernie uses his bicycle to go to work.

5. Jose joined the band at school.

6. Katie went shopping in the morning.

7. Jim bought a red convertible.

8. The golfers strolled down the fairway.

Version B

1. At the ballpark, the crowds of people walked to their seats.

2. The puppies ran around the backyard.

3. Jeremy played soccer.

4. Tom went to his brother's wedding.

5. The paramedics arrived at the scene of the accident.

6. Nancy arranged the pictures on the wall.

7. My favorite house plant needs water.

8. We walked through the neighborhood.

Writing Adjectives and Adverbs Correctly

Sometimes in writing, an adjective is used by mistake where an adverb should be used. For example, to say "Jack ran slow" is incorrect. The correct way to describe how Jack ran would be "slowly." "Jack ran slowly." "Slow" should be used to describe Jack. "Jack was slow."

Exercise 15

Choose the correct word to describe the verb in each sentence.

Example:

He played the piano just _____*beautifully*_____. **(beautiful, beautifully)**

Version A

1. The directions were not written very _____. (clear, clearly)

2. The buttercream frosting was spread _____ between the cake layers. (thick, thickly)

3. Our football team is not a _____ ranked team. (national, nationally)

4. The traffic moved _____ through the fog. (slow, slowly)

5. Our vacation went _____ last summer. (quick, quickly)

6. The meeting moved along _____ . (smooth, smoothly)

Version B

1. The wheat flour was ground _____ for the bread. (coarse, coarsely)

2. She came down the stairs _____ . (graceful, gracefully)

3. The church service was _____ uplifting. (spiritual, spiritually)

4. Katie _____ started her new business last year. (success, successfully)

5. My mother beamed at my _____ made bed. (fresh, freshly)

6. He _____ sang our national anthem. (enthusiastic, enthusiastically)

Exercise 16

Add the correct adjective or adverb in each blank. The adjective form is given, so you will need to change the form when it is used as an adverb.

Example:

Jerry was _____*quick*_____ **to answer the phone. (quick)**

Jerry ran _____*quickly*_____ **to answer the phone.**

Version A

1. The child sat _____ in the car. (quiet)

   The child was _____ in the car.

2. I was _____ about my schoolwork. (serious)

   I _____ studied for all my exams.

3. My friend Beth was never a _____ person. (patient)

   My friend Beth waited _____ for her friends.

4. Harry felt _____ after his surgery. (helpless)

   He stood _____ by his hospital bed and waited for a nurse.

5. Candice _____ walked up the stairs for her diploma. (courageous)

   Walking up the stairs to get her diploma, Candice looked _____ .

6. Very _____, the mother picked up her new baby. (careful)

   Picking up her new baby, the mother was very _____ .

7. David was prepared for the _____ job ahead of him. (mental)

   David was _____ prepared for the job.

8. The driver was frowning _____. (angry)

   The frowning driver was clearly _____.

9. The children played _____ together. (nice)

   The children were _____ to each other.

10. _____, the flowers did not cause an allergy attack. (fortunate)

    I was _____ not to have an allergy attack.

Version B

1. The announcement _____ surprised me. (complete)

   The announcement was a _____ surprise to me.

2. The twins were _____ to try the new video game. (eager)

   The twins _____ tried out their new video game.

3. Carrie spoke _____ to her parents. (rude)

   Carrie's conversation with her parents was _____.

4. Patrina was _____ committed to her job. (absolute)

   Patrina's commitment to her job was _____.

5. We wanted to be _____ about dividing the money. (fair)

   We wanted to divide the money _____ .

6. Jason's portrait of his wife was _____ painted. (beautiful)

   Jason painted a _____ portrait of his wife.

7. Henry _____ earned his college degree. (easy)

   Earning a college degree was _____ for Henry.

8. Spending less was _____ the way to solve his financial problems. (obvious)

   The _____ solution to his financial problems was to spend less.

9. The thief's response to the police officer was a _____ lie. (blatant)

   The thief _____ lied to the police officer.

10. Marti's _____ future was secure. (financial)

    Marti's future was _____ secure.

Using *Good* and *Well*

Sometimes you may be unsure whether to use *good* or *well* in a sentence. Study the following examples, and then work through the exercises.

> *Good* is always an adjective.

>> Mario is a *good* cook.

> *Well* is usually an adverb.

>> Mario cooked the steak *well* for his friends.

> *Well,* however, is used when you are describing someone's health.

>> Mario did not feel *well.*

>> After being sick, Mario did not look *well.*

Exercise 17

Use *good* or *well* correctly in the following sentences.

Example:

The band performed __*well*__ on Saturday.

Version A

1. I did _____ on the test.

2. We saw a _____ movie over the weekend.

3. Anita is always a _____ friend when I need one.

4. My dog Lucy plays _____ with the neighborhood children.

5. Anne's students follow instructions _____ .

6. Her students are _____ at following instructions.

7. After surgery, Matt did not look _____ for a week.

8. Shelly wanted to look _____ for her interview.

Version B

1. Tom is a _____ person to have around in an emergency.
2. Christine carved the turkey _____.
3. I wanted to make a really _____ pumpkin pie.
4. The doctor knew his patients _____.
5. The handyman repaired the sprinkling system _____.
6. I needed to buy a _____ pair of hiking shoes.
7. Carol looks _____ in her new blue dress.
8. After having the flu, Roy did not look _____ for days.

Using *Bad* and *Badly*

Another question you may encounter in your writing is when to use *bad* and when to use *badly*. You will be expected to use them correctly in both your academic and your business writing.

> *Bad* is always an adjective.
>
> > Mario is a *bad* cook.
>
> *Badly* is usually an adverb.
>
> > Mario cooked the steak *badly* for his friends.
> > My back hurts *badly*.

When you use verbs that refer to emotions or the senses, such as feeling or smelling, use the adjective *bad* instead of the adverb *badly*.

> > I feel bad (*not* badly).
> > The flowers smell bad (*not* badly).

Exercise 18

Use *bad* or *badly* correctly in the following sentences.

Example:

The baseball team played _badly_ on Saturday.

Version A

1. I felt _____ about missing my mother's wedding.
2. His description of the accident was _____.
3. The food from the sidewalk vendor tasted _____.
4. My little puppy limped _____ on her front leg.
5. On the night I saw the play, it was _____.
6. Harriet performed _____ in the interview.

Version B

1. The Valentine cookies my boyfriend made tasted _____.
2. The service I received was _____.
3. The team felt _____ about losing three games in a row.

4. The violinist played _____ because he was ill.

5. The child felt _____ about lying to his mother.

6. The water in the polluted lake smelled _____ .

Summary

- Adjectives modify nouns and pronouns.

  Adjectives use **-er, -ier,** and **more** to show comparisons between two people or objects.

  Adjectives use **-est, -iest,** and **most** to show comparisons among three or more people or objects.

  Vivid, exact adjectives add details to sentences.

- Adverbs modify verbs, adjectives, or other adverbs.

  Vivid, exact adverbs add details to sentences.

Practice Test

Read the following paragraph, and then answer the questions that follow by circling the letter of the correct answer.

(1) When my childhood went away, it took pleasures but left memories to fill the empty spaces. (2) At one time, I had three bantam hens and a bantam rooster. (3) I often enjoyed watching them bobbing around in a large pen, picking and pecking with the bigger chickens. (4) More than once, the bantams escaped. (5) I chased them down the dusty alley behind our house and managed to bring them back one by one. (6) Each small, warm body quivered in my even smaller hands until we reached our back fence. (7) I could barely give them a little boost into the backyard. (8) They hopped and half flew a few feet into the pen, waiting, I was sure, for another good chance to fly away. (9) I was protective of them, and I did not want them to have clipped wings. (10) I also remember that during the spring, our neighborhood was a haven for many wild birds. (11) My mother's favorite soon became mine, a single, amazingly bright, male cardinal. (12) My mother patiently helped me identify the cardinal by his "chip, chip." (13) When I heard it, I hurried outside to spot the dash of red in our palo verde tree. (14) Another special memory includes the darting, red-winged blackbirds, clustering near the sprinklers on the front lawn. (15) Their red wings glistened from the spray flying around them. (16) When the water quickly pooled on the grass, the birds carefully high-stepped through it, on the watch for the tastiest insects. (17) These birds had an even more distinctive call than the cardinal's. (18) To this day, I can hear their haunting, two-note sound, echoing across the yard. (19) On our Sunday afternoon drives, I heard the red-winged blackbirds calling loudly and watched them swooping in the irrigated fields outside the city. (20) As the years passed, the city grew, spreading out through the valley. (21) The bantams and wild birds disappeared altogether yet still live in my mind's eye.

1. In sentence #1, what adjective describes the spaces?
   a. away
   b. empty
   c. memories

2. In sentence #2, what two adjectives describe the hens?
   a. three, bantam
   b. one, bantam
   c. bantam, rooster

3. In sentence #3, what adverb tells when the hens and rooster were watched?
   a. around
   b. often
   c. bigger

4. In sentence #5, what concrete nouns show where the hens and rooster ran?
   a. them, chased
   b. chased, down
   c. alley, house

5. In sentence #5, what adjective describes the alley behind the house?
   a. dusty
   b. behind
   c. them

6. In sentence #6, what adjective shows a comparison?
   a. warm
   b. smaller
   c. back

7. In sentence #7, identify the adverb.
   a. boost
   b. little
   c. barely

8. In sentence #8, identify the four adjectives.
   a. few, another, good, sure
   b. pen, waiting, chance, sure
   c. fly, hopped, flew, away

9. In sentence #9, what is the adjective that modifies I?
   a. want
   b. clipped
   c. protective

10. In sentence #9, what is the adjective that modifies wings?
    a. want
    b. clipped
    c. protective

11. In sentence #10, what two adjectives describe the birds?
    a. many wild
    b. the spring
    c. our neighborhood

12. In sentence #11, how was the bird described?
    a. bright, male
    b. single, bright, male
    c. single, amazingly

13. In sentence #11, what adverb tells how bright the male cardinal was?
    a. amazingly
    b. favorite
    c. male
14. In sentence #12, what adverb describes how the mother helped the child?
    a. identify
    b. patiently
    c. beautiful
15. In sentence #13, what adverb tells where the child hurried?
    a. dash
    b. spot
    c. outside
16. In sentence #14, what adjectives described the blackbirds?
    a. darting, red-winged
    b. special, clustering
    c. sprinklers, front
17. In sentence #16, what adverb describes how the birds high-stepped through the water?
    a. quickly
    b. tasty
    c. carefully
18. In sentence #17, what adjective describes the bird's call?
    a. more
    b. distinctive
    c. cardinals
19. In sentence #18, what two adjectives describe the sound the birds made?
    a. haunting, two-note
    b. their, haunting
    c. sound, echoing
20. In sentence #19, what adverb tells how the birds called?
    a. swooping
    b. loudly
    c. irrigated

 ## Writing Assignment

Write a paragraph on one of the following topics. Be sure to start with a topic sentence. Then add support sentences, and end with a concluding sentence.
1. A favorite talk show or talk-show host
2. Current dress styles
3. A favorite restaurant
4. A favorite music group
5. Working in a fast-food restaurant

Chapter **3**

Building Better Paragraphs,
One Sentence at a Time

Part 1

Writing Correct and Interesting Simple Sentences

Objectives

- Identify and write basic simple sentence patterns
- Add additional details to create more interesting simple sentences

    Using carefully selected adjectives

    Using precise adverbs

    Using prepositional phrases

    Using concrete nouns

    Using strong verbs

- Improve word choice to create more interesting simple sentences

    Using active rather than passive voice

    Avoiding clichés

Writing effective sentences and understanding why they are effective is important in writing paragraphs and even longer papers. Just remember, putting words together in a way that makes sense to others and helps you write strong sentences helps you communicate your ideas to others. When you write, it is important to be grammatically correct as well as to use sentences that are interesting and creative. In this chapter, you will first look at basic simple sentence patterns. Then you will look at ways to make those sentences more interesting and appealing.

Identifying and Writing Simple Sentences

A simple sentence, often referred to as an independent clause, is a group of words that contain both a subject (noun or pronoun) and a verb (action or non-action) and express a complete thought. Just because a sentence is labeled a simple sentence does not mean that the sentence lacks sophistication or is inferior. Rather, "simple" refers to the grammatical classification of the sentence. Once you study compound and complex sentences, you will be able to distinguish among the different types. Some simple sentences may be only one or two words, but most simple sentences have many more words. You do not want all of your sentences to be only two words in length, but as long as you have a subject and a verb, you can expand, building different sentence patterns. Sentence variety should be your goal. The following patterns will be covered:

- One subject and one verb S V
- Two subjects and one verb S S V
- Two subjects and two verbs S S V V
- Subject, verb, direct object S V DO
- Subject, verb, complement S V C

One subject and one verb S V

A simple sentence may have only one subject and one verb. Look at the following sentence.

$$\overset{S}{Nancy}\ \overset{V}{sings}.$$

The subject is Nancy and answers the question of who or what the sentence is about. The verb is **sings**, an action verb. It says what Nancy does. Once you know the verb, you can ask who sings. Nancy sings, so **Nancy** is the subject.

Now look at other simple sentences that have more than two words yet still have only one subject and one verb.

$$\overset{S}{Josh}\ \overset{V}{works}\ on\ cars.$$

$$\overset{S}{He}\ \overset{V}{works}\ every\ Saturday.$$

$$Before\ leaving,\ \overset{S}{Jarod}\ \overset{V}{finished}\ his\ work.$$

"-ing" Verb (Gerund)

As you have already seen, a word can function as more than one part of speech. For instance, a word that is often thought of as a verb can also function as a noun. **The -ing form of a verb used as a noun is called a gerund.** When you use the **-ing** form of a verb, it cannot be the main verb in a sentence unless it is preceded by a form of the verb **be**. The **-ing** verb form can be a noun and, therefore, may be the subject of a sentence.

$$\overset{S}{Nancy}\ \overset{V}{is\ singing}.\ (\text{-ing verb form preceded by a form of the verb } \mathbf{be})$$

$$\overset{S}{Singing}\ often\ \overset{V}{relaxes}\ Nancy.\ (\text{-ing verb form used as the subject})$$

Note that in the above sentence, "singing" is the subject of the sentence, and "relaxes" is the verb. Including this type of simple sentence in your writing allows you to vary your sentence pattern. Now look at two other sentences that also have an **-ing** form used as the subject of the sentence.

$$\overset{S}{Crossing}\ the\ street\ in\ a\ big\ city\ \overset{V}{can\ be}\ dangerous.$$

$$\overset{S}{Going}\ on\ a\ picnic\ \overset{V}{brings}\ excitement\ to\ all.$$

The -ing verb form that is used as the subject may be only one word, such as "singing," or it may be the first word in a group of words such as "crossing the street" or "going on a picnic." These are phrases that may be used as nouns. A phrase that begins with an -ing verb can be the subject of a sentence. (Remember, an -ing verb form can only be the main verb in a sentence when it is preceded by a form of the verb be.)

As you work through the exercises that contain -ing verb forms used as nouns, you may mark the one word that is the subject, or you may mark the entire phrase as the subject. Look at the following sentences.

Training at the gym can be addictive.

Training at the gym can be addictive.

Going to a Krispy Creme doughnut factory is educational.

Going to a Krispy Creme doughnut factory is educational.

Investing in the stock market is often risky.

Investing in the stock market is often risky.

"To" Before a Verb (Infinitive)

Another verb form that can function as the subject of a sentence is an **infinitive**, which is a verb form starting with the word **"to."** Just as the -ing form of a verb, when used alone, cannot be the main verb in a sentence, the infinitive form cannot be the main verb in a sentence. It can, however, function as a noun, and as such may be the subject of a sentence. Note that in the following sentence, the infinitive **to sing** is the subject of the sentence and **relaxes** is the main verb.

Just as with the -ing verb forms used as subjects, **to** before a verb may also have other words that complete the phrase that is the subject.

     S   V

To sing <u>relaxes</u> Nancy.

To sing in the morning <u>makes</u> the day enjoyable.

To sing in the morning <u>makes</u> the day enjoyable.

To score high on a test <u>brings</u> satisfaction.

To score high on a test <u>brings</u> satisfaction.

To ride a bull for ten minutes <u>can make</u> me stiff.

To ride a bull for ten minutes <u>can make</u> me stiff.

Remember A verb form used as a noun can be the subject of the sentence:

    -ing verb form used as a noun

    Kicking a football skillfully takes practice.

    Kicking a football skillfully takes practice.

    to before a verb used as a noun

    To kick a football skillfully takes practice.

    To kick a football skillfully takes practice.

As you write your sentences, be sure to include some of these different types of nouns that add variety to your writing. Try to be as creative as possible, but be sure you always have a complete sentence.

Exercise 1

Identify the simple subjects and simple verbs in the following sentences. Underline the subjects once and the verbs twice.

Example:

Carol waited for the plumber for an hour.

Version A

1. Booking airline tickets over the Internet saves money.
2. The rose bushes bloom in the spring.
3. They produce healthy stems with beautiful yellow roses.
4. To listen to children's problems and concerns is important.
5. Jasper played the piano beautifully.
6. Twelve of the students completed all of the work on time.
7. Balancing a checkbook at the beginning of the month is a worthwhile habit.
8. The museum was busy during the summer.
9. The dog in the yard dug under the fence.
10. Tony bought tickets to the soccer game.

Version B

1. To eat at Grandmother's house comforts me.
2. An eagle symbolizes freedom.
3. Jeremy paid his cable television bill.
4. Jayda discovered many treasures in the basement.
5. The microphone fell off the lectern.
6. Colleges provide many educational opportunities.
7. The loud music annoyed the neighbors.
8. They complained to the police.
9. Children learn from their parents' example.
10. Snowboarding is an Olympic sport.

Exercise 2

Write five simple sentences, each with a single subject and a single verb. Be creative.

1. _____
2. _____
3. _____
4. _____
5. _____

Simple sentences may have more than one subject. Now look at the next pattern.

Two subjects and one verb S S V

S   S   V
Nancy and *Pervin* sing.

The sentence is about Nancy and Pervin, so the sentence contains two subjects.

Exercise 3

Identify the two subjects and the one verb in the following simple sentences. Underline the subjects once and the verbs twice.

Example:

Sugar and cream spilled on the table.

Version A
1. The tourists and their guide became friends.
2. Swimming and snowboarding are healthful activities.
3. Rain and sleet fell for several hours.
4. The boys and girls played hopscotch on the sidewalk.
5. Firefighters and police officers often work together.
6. Laughing and crying reduce stress.
7. My brother and sister left for school together.
8. Wind and rain blew into the house.
9. To plant seeds and to see growth excited the children.
10. The onions and celery in the tuna taste super.

Version B
1. The toy engine and box cars flew around the track.
2. Heather's energy and determination never falter.
3. My uncle and aunt visit us often.
4. Skating and jogging keep him fit.
5. To be loyal and to care about others are important.
6. Flowers and green vines grew outside the windows.
7. Sitting and crying about the problem are useless.
8. Her loyalty and honesty are steadfast.
9. My frog and turtle live by the pond in my backyard.
10. To work and to accomplish many things make me happy.

Exercise 4

Write five simple sentences, each with two subjects and one verb. Be creative.

1. _____
2. _____
3. _____
4. _____
5. _____

Now look at the next pattern.

One subject and two verbs S V V

$$\text{S} \quad \text{V} \quad \text{V}$$
Nancy sings and dances.

The sentence now contains one subject but two verbs.

Exercise 5

Identify one subject and two verbs in the following sentences. Underline the subject once and the verbs twice.

Example:

The neighbor rang the bell and waited patiently.

Version A

1. We played in the snow and made snowmen.
2. Avoiding bankruptcy keeps businesses alive and helps the economy.
3. The old car rattled and rumbled down the street.
4. Stock prices fell in the morning but then rose in the afternoon.
5. The chef whistled and hummed in the kitchen.
6. After practice, they walked and jogged back to the gym.
7. Every morning Alan exercised with his son and then read to him at bedtime.
8. The traffic moved a little and then stopped completely.
9. Reading that book relaxed me and helped me sleep.
10. Big red fire ants invaded my house and devoured the cat food.

Version B

1. The birds nested in the trees and laid eggs.
2. Henry opened his wallet and found his credit card.
3. His medical expenses increased and created a hardship.
4. Frank works hard and takes care of his family.
5. Juggling school and work creates difficulties but builds character.
6. The man ran into the building and rushed to his office.

7. The trees grew around the house and sheltered it from the wind.

8. My favorite ceramic bowl fell to the floor and shattered.

9. My retired uncle makes wooden bowls and presents them as gifts.

10. His attorney worked hard and won the lawsuit.

Exercise 6

Write five simple sentences, each with one subject and two verbs. Be creative.

1. _____

2. _____

3. _____

4. _____

5. _____

A simple sentence can also have two or more subjects as well as two or more verbs.

Two subjects and two verbs S S V V

      S   S   V   V

Nancy and Pervin sing and dance.

The sentence now contains two subjects and two verbs, but it is still a simple sentence. Work through the following exercise.

Exercise 7

Identify the two subjects and two verbs in the following sentences. Underline the subjects once and the verbs twice.

Example:

The potatoes and onions bubbled and boiled on the stove.

Version A

1. My daughters and I went to the library and read the books until 6:00 P.M.

2. My dog and bird often play and then sleep side by side.

3. Yowling and barking came from the backyard and woke Elijah.

4. Marie and Mary went to the car show and ate hot dogs.

5. Natasha and her mother laughed and cried together.

6. Paula and Sue listened to the music and then went home.

7. Mike and his friend walked slowly and chatted in low voices.

8. The attorney and her client talked quickly and then went into the courtroom.

9. Laughing and crying can relieve stress and can erase bad feelings.

10. Coughing and sneezing spread germs and may make others sick.

Version B

1. The books and folders fell from the table and scattered across the carpet.
2. Writing songs and singing them brought satisfaction and made others happy.
3. Kevin and Kim whistled and sang.
4. The boys and girls swam at the lake and dove off the rocks.
5. My mother and father went inside and whispered for hours.
6. Paul and Liz packed that night and left in the morning.
7. Sitting on the swing and listening to the wind relaxed me and almost put me to sleep.
8. My friend and her brother called and invited me to their house.
9. To pound on the walls and to play music loudly annoyed the neighbors and made enemies.
10. Waking early and fixing breakfast upsets me and ruins my day.

Exercise 8

Write five simple sentences, each with two subjects and two verbs. Be creative.

1. _____
2. _____
3. _____
4. _____
5. _____

Direct Objects and Complements

All of your sentences must have a subject and a verb; however, they may also have additional words, including direct objects and complements. Think of them as words that complete the meaning of the subject or the verb. Action verbs may have direct objects, and non-action verbs may have complements, though not all sentences have direct objects or complements. Study the following information that explains direct objects and complements.

Direct Objects

Direct objects can make sentences more informative and interesting. Action verbs are sometimes followed by a noun or pronoun called a **direct object, which tells "who" (a person) or "what" (a thing) receives the action of the verb.** A verb may have one or more direct objects.

- **One subject, one verb, one direct object S V DO**

  Nancy sings beautiful (songs) (noun that answers *what*)

  Singing relaxes (me) (pronoun that answers *who*)

  Nancy wants (to sing) (infinitive that answers *what*)

Note   In the previous sentence, "to sing" is a verb form (infinitive) used as a noun.

- **One subject, two verbs, each with a direct object S V DO V DO**

Nancy sings beautiful (songs) and dances the (tango).

In the above sentence, the word "songs" receives the action of "sings," and the word "tango" receives the action of "dances."

- **One subject, one verb, two direct objects S V DO DO**

In the next sentence, the **-ing** forms of the verbs used as nouns are direct objects.

Students enjoy (reading) books and (talking) about movies.   (enjoy what?)

James plays the (guitar) and the (drums).   (plays what?)

Note   The noun or pronoun in a prepositional phrase cannot be the subject of a sentence. In the same way, the noun or pronoun in a prepositional phrase cannot be a direct object. For example, in the following sentence, "fence" is the object of a preposition, so it cannot be the subject or the direct object.

My nephew painted the (boards) in the fence.

Work through the following exercise that will give you practice identifying direct objects in sentences.

Exercise 9

In the following sentences, underline the subject once and the verb twice, and circle the direct object.

Example:

The driver stopped the (taxi) at the curb.

Version A
1. They flew their kites in the afternoon.
2. The hungry elephants stripped the trees.
3. The strong wind pushed the child along the street.
4. The safety guard unlocked the schoolrooms.
5. The fruit trees withstood the freezing temperatures.
6. The cat heard his owner at the front door.
7. The coach and her students enjoyed their trip to the tournament.
8. The cat and her kittens ate the food hungrily.
9. The pitchers and catchers met the deadline for training camp.
10. The doctor and the nurse encouraged the patient.

Version B

1. The owner and the trainer cheered the horse across the finish line.
2. Seeing the banners and hearing the crowd overwhelmed the team.
3. Tiff loves children and animals.
4. Rose spent ten years as a foster child.
5. April planted six trees in her backyard.
6. Andrew tossed the coins in the fountain.
7. Tanner pushed the swing for his sister.
8. Casey dropped the carton of eggs on the floor.
9. Carmen created outstanding pieces of pottery.
10. Henry and Albert fixed my car for me.

Complements

Another way to complete the meaning of a sentence is by adding **complements, words that describe or rename the subject of the sentence.** Complements follow non-action verbs and may be nouns, pronouns, or adjectives. The important thing to remember is that these words either describe the subject or rename the subject. Look at the following sentences, all of which have a complement.

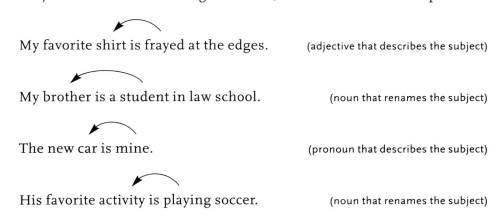

My favorite shirt is frayed at the edges.   (adjective that describes the subject)

My brother is a student in law school.   (noun that renames the subject)

The new car is mine.   (pronoun that describes the subject)

His favorite activity is playing soccer.   (noun that renames the subject)

You have learned that sentences may have one or more subjects and one or more verbs. Sentences may also have one or more complements. Just remember that a complement comes after the verb. Look at two possible combinations.

- **One subject, one verb, one complement S V C**

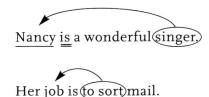

Nancy is a wonderful singer.

Her job is to sort mail.

- **One subject, one verb, two complements S V C C**

Nancy is a wonderful singer and dancer.

Now work through the following exercise that will help you identify subjects, verbs, and complements.

Identify the subjects, verbs, and complements in the following sentences. Underline the subject once and the verb twice, and circle the complement.

Example:

The children seem happy with their new books.

Version A

1. The freshest apples were red.
2. At the concert, sitting in the expensive seats was exciting.
3. My childhood dream was to play professional golf.
4. In Florida my favorite pastime was to collect shells.
5. To play in the NBA All-Star Game is rare and profitable.
6. The new painter was an expert at his job.
7. He always felt proud of his work.
8. The sky looks dark and threatening today.
9. The pumpkin pie tastes delicious.
10. The water in my swimming pool is cold.

Version B

1. Jerry is a member of the wrestling team.
2. The chocolate pie remains uneaten.
3. Brett Wallace is an actor and model.
4. Our instructor seemed eager to grade the tests over the weekend.
5. Jennifer Lopez's second husband was Chris Judd.
6. To play the piano at the age of four is unusual.
7. Playing in the band is his favorite job and pastime.
8. Bianca's new dress is stunning.
9. My ranch has been home for many stray kittens.
10. The dead branches on the tree are a fire hazard.

Creating More Interesting Simple Sentences

Though writing sentences that are grammatically correct is extremely important, building sentences that create interest and say exactly what you mean to say can be equally important. Doing this takes practice, but if you are willing to take the time to edit your papers carefully, you will be pleased with the results. Some ways to do this are explained next.

- Adding additional information
    - Adding adjectives for more vivid or precise details
    - Adding adverbs for more vivid or precise details
    - Adding prepositional phrases
- Improving word choices
    - Using concrete nouns
    - Using stronger verbs
    - Using active rather than passive verbs
    - Avoiding clichés

Adding Adjectives for More Vivid or Precise Details

In the previous chapter, you learned about using effective adjectives and adverbs to create more interesting sentences. As you recall, these words not only add more detailed information but often help you eliminate unnecessary and repetitive wording. (See more detailed information about adjectives and adverbs in Chapter 2.)

Look at the following sentence that includes a subject, a verb, and a direct object. Then watch as the adjectives **neighborhood, crack-of-dawn**, and **serious** are added.

The yard sale attracted bargain seekers. (simple sentence)

The **neighborhood** yard sale attracted **serious, crack-of-dawn** bargain seekers.

The **neighborhood, crack-of-dawn** yard sale attracted **serious** bargain seekers.

Note Two or more adjectives in a row that modify the same noun use commas to separate them.

Both of the above sentences are correct, so looking at these sentences in the context of a paragraph determines which sentence provides the best meaning. Are you talking about "crack-of-dawn" yard sales or "crack-of-dawn" bargain seekers? As the writer, you will know what you want to say and which words fit most smoothly. However, you can see how adding precise adjectives results in stronger sentences.

Just as important, you do not want to use adjectives just to add words to your sentences. Rather, you add adjectives because they provide the exact details that you need to communicate your ideas to others. For example, if you say, "The little boy clutched his big, hairy, old, misshapen teddy bear tightly," you might not need all of those adjectives. You might just say, "The little boy clutched his misshapen teddy bear tightly," especially if you just want to show how much the little boy loved his teddy bear.

Adding Adverbs for More Vivid or Precise Details

Adding adverbs can also help you build better sentences by adding needed details to your sentences. You could add the adverb **unexpectedly** to the earlier sentence to add even more detail.

The neighborhood yard sale **unexpectedly** attracted serious, crack-of-dawn bargain seekers.

Try practicing using adjectives and adverbs to add more detail and exact meaning to sentences.

Exercise 11

Revise the following sentences by adding the adjectives and adverbs given.

Example:

Add the words "narrow," "hospital," "rolled-up," and "bony" to the following sentence.

> *narrow hospital   rolled-up   bony*
> **The nurse put Amy on the bed and slid towels under her knees.**

Version A

1. Add: black and white, yellow, tennis

   The kittens wanted to play with the balls.

2. Add: gently, heavy, carved, quickly

   She opened the door and slipped away.

3. Add: quietly, worn, wooden

   We sat at the desks.

4. Add: elderly, carefully

   The saleswoman looked at me.

5. Add: frisky, tumbling, roughly,

   The kittens played with each other.

6. Add: well-trained, routine

   The police officer made a traffic stop.

7. Add: busy, chattering, excited

   The airport was filled with people.

8. Add: new, silk, closest

   Jennifer took her blouse to the cleaners.

9. Add: cornbread, homemade, vegetable

   He dropped the crumbs into his soup.

10. Add: constantly, fresh

    The outside faucet dripped water into the cat's dish.

Version B

1. Add: fiery, new, green-gray

   The sparks jumped from the fireplace and landed on the rug.

2. Add: tight, white

   Her shorts attracted everyone's attention.

3. Add: frowning, careless

   The waitress had to clean up after her customers.

4. Add: bumper-to-bumper, freeway, usually

   The traffic created stress.

5. Add: construction, dangerously

   The crew worked close to the edge of the building.

6. Add: fresh, somewhat, slightly

   The kettle corn was both salty and sweet.

7. Add: hungry, dried, bread

   The pigeons devoured all the crumbs.

8. Add: tiny, purple, continuously

   The flowers in my front yard bloomed.

9. Add: teenage, television, correctly

   The contestants on the game show answered the questions.

10. Add: apple, entire, spicy

    The pies in the oven filled the house with tempting aromas.

Using Prepositional Phrases

Prepositional phrases can also add detailed information to your sentences. As you have already learned, prepositional phrases can show location, identify particular people or things, indicate time, and show exclusion. (Read more about prepositional phrases in Chapter 1.) Sometimes prepositional phrases can help you avoid wordiness in your sentences and paragraphs. Look at the following sentences.

> Philip planted most of the seeds. He planted them in his
> raised flowerbeds.   (repetitive)

> Philip planted most of the seeds in his raised flowerbeds.   (avoids wordiness)

The second sentence above contains the same information as the first one; however, there is no need to use the word "planted" twice.

Other times, prepositional phrases add information necessary to make your meaning clear to the reader.

He taught me a lot. (with no prepositional phrase)

He taught me a lot **about love.** (prepositional phrase that adds clarity)

He taught me a lot about the love **of a real family.** (prepositional phrase with more concrete information)

The above sentences show how prepositional phrases can help build a simple idea into a sentence with a clearer, more precise meaning. The first sentence, "He taught me a lot," has grown from a vague idea into a sentence with a definite meaning that might even be a topic sentence for a paragraph. This sentence could be edited further, but looking at these changes can help you see how to strengthen your own sentences. You will want to revise your own sentences until your meaning is clear. If you take the time to do this and stay committed to revision and editing, you will be able to create better sentences.

Now work through the following exercise.

Exercise 12

Combine the following sentences to use prepositional phrases to help you avoid wordiness.

Example:

Jonah enjoys going to the zoo. He enjoys going in the springtime.
Jonah enjoys going to the zoo in the springtime.

Version A

1. Tori practiced her guitar lessons. She practiced them after school.

2. I took my truck through the car wash. I took it on Saturday.

3. Joseph and Ron planned a fishing trip. They planned to go to Lake Pleasant.

4. We found the meowing, hungry kittens. They were in the backyard.

5. The young driver ran into the parked truck. The truck was near the fence.

Version B

1. Trish jogged each morning. Her dog went with her.

   _____

   _____

2. For Thanksgiving, we made special desserts. They were for the family.

   _____

   _____

3. The vet was serious about the surgery. The surgery was for Nugget.

   _____

   _____

4. Paul told the best story. He was at the party.

   _____

   _____

5. Roger opened an auto repair shop. It was the one on Hatcher Road.

   _____

   _____

Using Concrete Nouns

Earlier, you learned to write strong paragraphs by prewriting so that you have examples to support your main idea. You also learned that as you use examples, you need to add details. In this chapter so far, you have practiced several ways to build upon and improve simple sentences by adding details.

Another way to strengthen the sentences in your paragraphs is to use as many concrete nouns as possible. Previously you discovered the difference between abstract and concrete nouns. For example, "accepting responsibility" is abstract, but "paying the electric bill on time" is concrete. You also studied the difference between general and specific words. In the same sense, "accepting responsibility" is general, but "paying the electric bill on time" is specific. Think of abstract and general words as being almost the same and specific and concrete words as being similar. The important part to remember is that you want to be accurate and convincing in your writing. Use general words when necessary, but always support them with concrete and specific words.

Study the following sentences to see how concrete words have been used to clarify and strengthen each general sentence.

Lou **played sports** in **high school.** (general)

Lou played **quarterback on the football team** for **Arcadia High School.** (concrete)

The concrete nouns in the second sentence above give more specific, accurate information to the reader.

Work through the following exercise to practice revising sentences so they include more concrete nouns.

Study each sentence given. Replace the general noun in parentheses with a more concrete noun.

Example:

Lisa eats (snack food) _potato chips and candy bars._ _____

Version A

1. My family wants to buy a new (car). _____
2. Bart enjoys (outdoor activities). _____
3. My best friend loves (music). _____
4. Trin bought (country western) CDs. _____
5. My sister's (clothes) fit me nicely. _____
6. Leslie loves to bake (desserts) on holidays. _____
7. The classroom has many (resources) for students to use. _____
8. (The television celebrity) supported the charity golf tournament. _____
9. The new (appliance) in the kitchen did not work. _____
10. My neighbors want to plant (trees) in their yard. _____

Version B

1. Family (celebrations) became fond memories for Giovanna.

   _____

2. My sister's (pet) has his own house on the patio. _____
3. Steven enjoyed the (large animals) at the Phoenix Zoo. _____
4. My teacher Mr. Hudson encouraged us to read the (newspaper).

   _____

5. Every week, Karina watched (her favorite television show). _____
6. I went to buy (winter clothes) at Golden West Mall.

   _____

7. I wanted to spend the summer in (the East). _____
8. Jack likes to play (card games) on Saturdays. _____
9. At age ten, Henry wanted to take (music) lessons. _____
10. No one liked the (Italian food) my brother made. _____

Using Stronger Verbs

The verbs you choose for your sentences can make them more exact or accurate. They can even completely change the meaning of what you write. For example, look at the difference in meaning in the following sentences.

He **left** his first wife for someone younger. (In this sentence, using "left" as the verb makes the information in the sentence seem quite matter of fact.)

He **dumped** his first wife for someone younger. (In this sentence, "dumped" is a stronger word, suggesting that he did not care for his first wife at all.)

The elderly saleswoman **looked** at me. (The saleswoman seems willing to be helpful.)

The elderly saleswoman **eyed** me carefully. (The saleswoman seems to think that the customer might be a shoplifter.)

Using different verbs will give your sentences slightly different meanings. Take the time during revision to find the verb that will say what you really mean in the context of your paragraph. Look at the following five sentences. They are exactly the same except for the verbs. Think about the meaning that each sentence carries.

She flicked him on the top of the head.

She thumped him on the top of the head.

She tapped him on the top of the head.

She smacked him on the top of the head.

She patted him on the top of the head.

As you write your sentences, pay attention to your verbs to see if they say exactly what you mean. The following exercise will make you aware of all the different verbs that can be used to get your idea across.

Exercise 14

Add as many differerent verbs as you can to complete the meaning of the following sentences. Think about how each verb gives the sentence a slightly different meaning.

Version A

1. She _____ her hot chocolate.

2. I _____ my finger with a hammer.

3. The grocery cart _____ my car.

4. Paul _____ that he was wrong.

5. I _____ my schoolbooks onto the large wooden table.

Version B

1. The dogs _____ through the doggie door.

2. He _____ all his tools into the back of his car.

3. The baseball players _____ to the dugout.

4. Sadie _____ through the hospital corridor.

5. The boulders _____ to the highway from the cliff above.

Using Active Rather Than Passive Voice

Your writing will have stronger sentences if you avoid passive verbs. In the following sentence, the verb is **passive, meaning that the subject does not do anything.**

> The lemon pie was made by my aunt.

In the sentence above, the verb is passive because the subject is not doing the action. In other words, the "lemon pie" is not doing anything. In strong sentences, the verb should be active so that the subject is the doer, not the receiver. Here is how this sentence should be revised.

> My aunt made the lemon pie.

In this sentence, the subject is active. The aunt made the pie. Remember that when the verb is **active, the subject does something.** When the verb is passive, the subject is acted upon.

Now look at the following pairs of sentences that move from passive to active.

Passive	Active
All the food was eaten by the stray cats.	The stray cats ate all the food.
This job has been done before by the painter.	The painter has done this job before.
My paper was completed early.	I completed my paper early.

Using passive voice is not wrong, but it should be done sparingly. For instance, if you simply want to emphasize an event like a wedding, but you do not necessarily want to emphasize the person planning the wedding, you might say, "The wedding was well planned." For the most part, however, you will want to avoid using passive voice in your papers.

Exercise 15

Revise each sentence so that it has an active verb. Each passive verb is underlined.

Example:

The good news <u>was received</u> by the family from the doctor.

Active verb: *The family received the good news from the doctor.*

Version A

1. The mobile home <u>was damaged</u> by the rainstorm.

---

2. The seasoning for the pumpkin pie <u>was changed</u> by the chef.

_____

3. The magazines <u>were stacked</u> by the librarian.

_____

4. The garbage barrels <u>were emptied</u> by a mechanical arm on the trash truck.

_____

5. A sheriff <u>was flagged</u> down by the desperate motorist.

_____

6. The lawn <u>was mowed</u> by the boy next door.

_____

7. The wedding pictures <u>were taken</u> by my brother.

_____

8. Her car <u>was repaired</u> by Vivian's son.

_____

9. The shoplifter <u>was sentenced</u> to two years of probation by the judge.

_____

10. After the rain, the mud <u>was tracked</u> onto the carpet by the children.

_____

Version B

1. The cabin <u>was ransacked</u> by vandals.

_____

2. The holiday cookies <u>were decorated</u> by the children themselves.

_____

3. The children's costumes <u>were made</u> by the mothers.

_____

4. The forests <u>were cleared</u> of undergrowth by high school volunteers.

_____

5. The Atlanta Braves <u>were defeated</u> by the San Francisco Giants.

_____

6. The house <u>was painted</u> by the new owners.

_____

7. The tickets to the Boston Pops concert <u>were purchased</u> by Honeywell.

_____

8. The moving poem about terminal illness <u>was written</u> by a nine-year-old child.

_____

9. The grades <u>were posted</u> by the teacher.

_____

10. The orange-blossom honey <u>was made</u> by the bees.

_____

Avoiding Clichés

The English language is filled with **clichés, words or ideas that are often considered overused**, though the first time someone used them, they were original, precise, and insightful. These clichés often originated many years ago, but some are more recent. For example, referring to someone as a "sponge" dates back to Shakespeare. Other phrases are more current, such as Flip Wilson saying, "What you see is what you get," or Forrest Gump saying, "Life is like a box of chocolates. You never know what you are going to get."

Overused expressions such as "Don't even go there" or "You have hit the wall" are easily understood but do not provide details about what really happened. They have become generalities that apply in almost any situation. Some clichés such as "dropped the ball" and "sky high" originated with sports but have transferred to other areas of life. When someone at work does not do the job, others might say, "He dropped the ball," meaning he did not carry through with the job, but saying precisely what happened is more effective if you want to prove the point you are making in a topic sentence. For example, you could say that clichés are "old hat," but you could more effectively explain why a particular cliché is "old hat."

Clichés may be quite acceptable in conversation, but in writing they are simply taking other people's ideas for your own. You want to be more original and provide specific examples and details to develop your idea.

If everyone is familiar with the way a sentence ends, the information is probably overused and a cliché.

Exercise 16

Complete the following clichés.

Example:

She saw everything through _rose-colored glasses_ .

Version A

1. This is easy as _____ .

2. She took me under her _____ .

3. He was last but not _____ .

4. He lived to a ripe _____ .

5. You are worth your weight in _____ .

Version B

1. Let's go for _____ .
2. He was hot under the _____ .
3. I was thrown for a _____ .
4. She is on a _____ .
5. This is right up my _____ .

Exercise 17

Read the following sentences that include well-known clichés, and then rewrite each sentence, substituting more exact, concrete, and original wording for the cliché.

Example:

He took to water like a duck.

He discovered he was a natural swimmer who loved being in the water.

Version A

1. Don't put all your eggs in one basket.

   _____

2. I was glad you came on board.

   _____

3. We are in a holding pattern.

   _____

4. He has ice water in his veins.

   _____

5. I can't see the forest for the trees.

   _____

Version B

1. This was a red-letter day.

   _____

2. I talked until I was blue in the face.

   _____

3. He hit the nail on the head.

   _____

4. This takes the cake.

   _____

5. It was a slam dunk.

   _____

Once you write sentences that go beyond just identifying subjects and verbs, you begin to have a feel for sentences that include details that will add your own voice to your writing. You are no longer writing generic sentences—you are writing something that is uniquely yours.

Summary

Learning how to put together strong simple sentences is the foundation you need to help you write sentences that are not fragmented or difficult to understand. When you understand the fine points that make a sentence strong, you are on your way to recognizing and writing effective simple sentences.

- All of your sentences must have one or more subjects and one or more verbs.

    Sentences may also have one or more direct objects.

    Sentences may also have one or more complements.

- Using different sentence patterns will help create sentence variety.

    Use **-ing** phrases as subjects.

    Use infinitive phrases (**to** plus a verb) as subjects.

- Adding other parts of speech can help you build simple sentences that are more interesting, precise, and detailed.

    Effective adjectives can make your writing more exact and can avoid unnecessary wordiness.

    Adverbs can make your sentences more detailed.

    Prepositional phrases can help prevent repetitiveness in sentences as well as add necessary information.

    Concrete nouns can make your writing more accurate.

    Stronger verbs can make your meaning more exact.

- Using active rather than passive voice makes the meaning more direct.

- Avoiding clichés keeps your writing fresher, free of generalities.

Practice Test

Read the following paragraph, and then answer the questions by circling the letter of the correct answer.

(1) From the beginning whistle to the ending buzzer of a basketball game, five players from each team are constantly moving. (2) The initial tipoff is the beginning of the action. (3) Sometimes the point guard, the team director, catches the tipped basketball and begins dribbling up the court. (4) His teammates are watching for his play signal and are running into their positions. (5) Other times, another member of the team catches the basketball and in a flash passes it to the point guard. (6) To keep the ball moving demands everyone's attention. (7) At the same time, the other team tries to get the ball away from them. (8) Most of the action, however, happens around the basket. (9) Setting up the play allows the point guard to pass immediately to a teammate. (10) This

teammate may either shoot or pass the ball to another player. (11) He may break to the basket for a layup. (12) At this quick pace, the players try to hit the open man for a good shot. (13) After a basket, a player from the other team throws the ball in bounds to one of his teammates. (14) This player dribbles up the court and passes the ball quickly to one of his teammates. (15) They pound down the court toward their basket but work in harmony. (16) Passes and quick movements are made back and forth by all five players. (17) Instantly, the players from the other team guard them closely and look for a chance to steal the ball. (18) Team members also persistently move their hands in front of their opponents' faces and block their vision. (19) Sometimes a player can lob the ball precisely over the rim of the basket. (20) At the same time, another teammate jumps up, catches the ball, and slams it into the net. (21) The players continually transfer the ball from player to player, from team to team, and hope to score more points. (22) These kinds of plays continue throughout the game.

1. In sentence 14, what are the two verbs that describe precisely what the player is doing?
   a. court, quickly
   b. dribbles, passes
   c. player, ball

2. In sentence 18, what adverb adds strength to the verb "move"?
   a. persistently
   b. hands
   c. block

3. In sentence 15, identify the nouns.
   a. court, basket, harmony
   b. they, work, harmony
   c. pound, toward, court

4. In sentence 10, what simple sentence pattern is used?
   a. S V V DO
   b. S S V
   c. S S V V

5. In sentence 22, identify the subject.
   a. games
   b. plays
   c. kinds

6. Which sentence has three verbs for an S V V V pattern?
   a. sentence 4
   b. sentence 12
   c. sentence 20

7. Which sentence has two subjects for an S S V pattern?
   a. sentence 16
   b. sentence 2
   c. sentence 22

8. Which sentence has a complement for an S V C pattern?
   a. sentence 4
   b. sentence 18
   c. sentence 2

9. Which sentence has two adverbs?
   a. sentence 17
   b. sentence 1
   c. sentence 2

10. Which sentence has four prepositional phrases?
    a. sentence 19
    b. sentence 10
    c. sentence 1

11. Which sentence has a direct object for an S V DO pattern?
    a. sentence 8
    b. sentence 19
    c. sentence 22

12. Which sentence has a prepositional phrase that shows location?
    a. sentence 2
    b. sentence 8
    c. sentence 6

13. Which sentence uses one **-ing** form of the verb as the subject?
    a. sentence 4
    b. sentence 3
    c. sentence 9

14. Which sentence uses "to" before a verb as the subject?
    a. sentence 12
    b. sentence 6
    c. sentence 7

15. Which sentence contains a cliché?
    a. sentence 8
    b. sentence 5
    c. sentence 21

16. Which sentence uses passive voice?
    a. sentence 1
    b. sentence 11
    c. sentence 16

 ## Writing Assignment

a. Now, write a simple sentence that describes the most wonderful person or the most terrible person you remember as a child. Within your sentence, you need to include the name of the person and the one word you could use to describe the person.

_____

_____

b. Now draft a paragraph that shows "in what way" this person was wonderful or terrible.

Part 2

Something to Think About, Something to Write About

Professional Essay to Generate Ideas for Writing

An Addiction That Never Goes Away

Kathy Sins, *Artist and Teacher*

1   An addiction never goes away. I know that now. When I was eleven years old and obese, I did not know that. I only knew that I wanted to be accepted by others, not disappoint them. I remember being five years old and being excited because my kindergarten teacher said we were going to have a play, but the excitement was short lived when I found out that I had been cast as the elephant. I cried; I did not want to go to school. A year later when we had a Christmas play, the teacher selected the two fattest girls to be the elves. Once again, I was mortified in front of everyone. When I was eleven, I had to have an emergency appendectomy, and as I awoke from the anesthesia, I heard anger and irritation in the surgeon's voice as he told me, "Your incision is three times bigger than it should be because you are so fat." He would not let me leave the hospital until I had lost ten pounds. I was just a little girl, but I was ashamed. I soon learned how to be thin, to be like everyone else, but I did not know that what I learned would afflict me for the rest of my life.

2   I tried hard to be good, to please my teachers, my doctors, my mother. I needed to control my eating, but my obsession to food would not go away. I hid cookies under my bed, in my dresser drawers where I knew my mother would never look. One day I found a box of cake mix, and when I was sure no one could see me, I took it in my room, locked the door, and ate the entire box of powdered mix, spoonful by spoonful. When I had eaten the last bite, I was horrified at what I had done, but it was too late. Just as impulsively, I ran into the bathroom and made myself throw it up. No harm had been done, or so I thought because I had gotten rid of the crime. Through my teen years, I alternated between binge eating then throwing up and simply not eating at all. I became quite efficient at purging. Two or three times a day, I emptied my stomach of the poison I had put there. Today, I am better, yet I am still disappointed when I do this every couple of months or so. I am angry at myself for losing control.

3   Though my mind had long since rejected the thoughts of eating food, my body still craved it. I tried to make my body happy by spending hours in the kitchen cooking elaborate dishes that I could never permit myself to eat or even taste. I denied myself food, yet I sat up at night reading cheese cake

recipes, my specialty. I found new recipes, and the next day I would try them out. My favorite was peanut butter cheesecake. I became an accomplished cook, using only the best, richest ingredients. I expanded to cookies. I literally made every cookie recipe in the *Joy of Cooking* book. I made dozens and dozens of peanut butter, raisin, chocolate chip, and ginger cookies. I made rich baklava with honey and sesame seeds. I gave everything to friends, neighbors, family, everyone except me. I created every imaginable dessert. My boyfriend loved homemade bread, so I set out to master this, too. I learned to make delicious sweet bread, egg bread, wheat bread. My boyfriend had homemade bread twice a week, but I never took even one bite. The smell and his praise were my reward. I started teaching art and was assistant chair, so I volunteered to bring refreshments to our monthly planning meetings. I spent the entire month cooking desserts, putting them in the freezer, asking others to put them in their freezer. I always made excuses, saying my freezer was too small. Everyone raved over my goodies, so I made sure they took home the leftovers. I realized I was obsessed with cooking food for others, but I could not stop.

4   Today, I get no pleasure from eating. I never get hungry, but I never get full either. Other people look forward to the holidays, filled with parties and unsurpassed food. They anticipate tables that are overflowing with incredibly delicious food. I, on the other hand, dread parties, potluck meals, and family get-togethers. I find excuses not to attend these festive affairs, but when there is no way out, when I am obligated to attend something, I look for excuses to explain why I cannot eat. I cook gourmet dishes that I could never eat, and I put them out for others. I watch as my family and friends indulge in irresistible dishes, laughing, having a good time. I feel uncomfortable as my eyes quickly scan the table, looking for the carrot sticks, celery, anything to munch on so I do not look so conspicuous. I fear that someone will walk over to me and say, "Kathy, have you tried the Kahlua cake I made?" I become irritated, and I want to yell out, "No, no, I have not. Just leave me alone," but I can't do that. It would be rude. Instead, I smile and comment on how fantastic it smells.

5   Sometimes my addiction still takes over. On these occasions, I eat alone. I take one bite, and I have lost the battle. I can best explain this as an out-of-body experience. I move to the corner of the room and watch myself as I stuff one thing after another into my mouth. I do not taste anything, but I keep eating, unable to stop. When I can eat no more, I panic. Then I watch myself as I go into the bathroom and throw everything up. It is easy. I have done it thousands of time. Then and only then am I allowed to return to myself. I feel as though I have been an observer; I have been unable to control my own actions. Then I think about others who enjoy their food, savor the taste, eat together.

6   My loss of control over food has left its mark on my health. My first dose of reality came when I was admitted to the hospital emergency room because I was throwing up blood. The doctors told me my esophagus was badly scraped, was raw, a direct result of the acid in my mouth, a byproduct of purging. If the irritation to my esophagus got any worse, it could break and I

could easily die. This was the first time anyone had ever taken my addiction seriously. They told me I was suffering from malnutrition and starvation. My weight had dropped to 95 pounds though I stood five feet nine inches tall. They gave me names of programs that could help me. My body stopped having periods—for fifteen years—until my weight increased to 115 pounds. From my ankles up to my knees, my legs were covered with splotches, dark like leopard's spots and visible enough to be seen from across the street. I had a tumor on my thyroid, so I had part of my thyroid removed, and currently I have too much calcium in my urine. That means that my kidneys are casting off the precious calcium that I need for my bones. I have been left with chronic heartburn that will probably never go away. Now it is triggered by anything I eat, even cottage cheese. The doctors suspect that these problems are a direct result of my eating disorder, but they cannot be positive.

7   When I was in my early 30s, I was accidentally hit in the jaw, and a couple of months later I woke one morning to find that all of my upper teeth were so loose they were ready to fall out. Frantically, I went in to see my dentist who sent me to a specialist. I had advanced osteoporosis, most probably caused by starvation. All of my upper teeth had to be removed, along with bone fragments from my jaw that had been shattered in the blow to my jaw because the osteoporosis had left all my bones brittle. I was in so much pain that I just wanted my teeth out. Up until my 23rd birthday, I had never had a cavity in my life and now this. Over the next few years, osteoporosis and acid from purging brought destruction to my remaining teeth. My bottom teeth have become a constant focus for dentists. I have had cavities, root canals, double root canals, infections. The pain that I suffered from this, however, was nothing compared to the two biopsies done on my tongue. The constant purging left blistery bumps on my tongue that were further irritated by the acid. They hardened and remained painful, but not nearly so painful as the biopsies done to determine if they were cancerous. Two times I was subjected to biopsies, each resulting in 10 stitches in my tongue. There is not a painkiller on the planet that could numb the pain I felt. Today, I have scar tissue that serves as a constant reminder.

8   I have seen counselors, doctors, psychiatrists, so I understand the nature of an addiction. When I started at age eleven, I did not understand the consequences. Today, at 49, I do. No matter how much I know, no matter what I do, I will always be addicted to food. It would be easier if I were addicted to alcohol or to heroin because I could spend time in a rehabilitation center, and I could wean my body from its toxic remains, but it is impossible to wean myself from food. My body must have nourishment to survive, but once I start eating, I fear that I will be unable to stop. I have no oven in my house. I have no elaborate foods, no deadly stuff. I do have a refrigerator that contains cottage cheese, carrot sticks, and celery, but mostly it contains my art supplies and photography chemicals that need to be kept cold. I still fear that I will lose control, that once I start eating I will be unable to stop.

Understanding Words

Briefly define the following words as they are used in the selection.

1. obese
2. mortified
3. binge eating
4. purging
5. baklava
6. esophagus
7. osteoporosis
8. malnutrition
9. biopsies

 Writing Assignment

Write a paragraph on one of the following topics. Be sure to start with a strong topic sentence. Add specific examples and details for support, and end with a strong concluding sentence.

1. What is the biggest challenge you or someone you know has overcome?
2. Is there something you wish you could change about yourself?
3. What is the reason people try to please others?
4. What can help children become more fit without making them self-conscious?
5. What are the pressures that cause youngsters to want to be thin?
6. Give an example of what someone might do to be accepted by others.

Part 3

Student and Professional Paragraphs

Least Favorite Animal

Tarya Tjernagel, *Student*

My least favorite animals are the *cucarachas*.* They are disgusting. They are gross to look at with their little eyes staring at me. Cucarachas are everywhere. They are in my refrigerator, television, microwave, and many other places. When I go to sleep, they crawl all over me. They get in my ears, my nose, and my mouth. I swear I could almost taste them. Sometimes they get in my backpack and follow me to school. They are nasty dirty little things, and I wish I did not have them. I try to get rid of them, but they keep coming back. They move from apartment to apartment, and no matter where I move, they always find me. One time I threw a party, and when I took out the food, the cucarachas came out and everyone left. No wonder they are my least favorite animals, and I wish they would die.

*cucarachas: cockroaches

Questions on Form
1. How does the topic sentence make the main idea more humorous?

2. What detail does she use to describe the physical appearance of the cucarachas?

3. Identify some specific examples she uses.

Questions on Content
1. What are cucarachas?

2. What is her closing example?

3. What does she wish would happen to the cucarachas?

California

Ashleigh Wolfe, *Student*

Every year without fail, I go to California to visit my aunt, uncle, and four-year-old cousin, and I hate every minute of it. Whenever I go there and it is time for a meal, I am not allowed to eat the food the way that I like it. If I put soy sauce on rice or dressing on a salad, they tell me I am disrespectful and do not like their cooking. I notice though that they have both soy sauce and salad dressing in their refrigerator. They also have a dog that produces so much slobber and leaves so much hair behind, I cannot walk two feet in front of myself without stepping in something. When I go out there, I like to see some of the sights whether it is going to the beach, to a museum, or to other places, yet I hardly get to see these sights because my cousin does not want to go there or because my aunt and uncle want to go somewhere else and they "just assumed I was going to baby sit." When I go there once a year, I like to see some of my friends and maybe try to see some of the sights with them, but this is a serious taboo. The household's bedtime is at eight-thirty, so that means the television, lights, headphones, telephone, cell phone, and kitchen are all off limits to everyone. Because I hate this yearly visit to California, maybe this year I can stay home with my own family.

Questions on Form

1. What is the main idea in the paragraph?

2. Name some examples that support this idea.

3. What does the concluding sentence add to the paragraph?

Questions on Content

1. Where does the author hate to go?

2. What does the author not like about meals?

3. What would the author like to do on her own in California?

September 11, 2001

Travis Mays, *Student*

I believe the impact of September eleventh was enormous. I personally watched on television as the Twin Towers came crashing down into a pile of rubble. At the time, I remember thinking, who would do this terrible crime? In the midst of the September tragedy, I saw the people in our country pull together. Before my eyes, I watched heroic firefighters and police officers give everything they had to save lives. I watched President Bush stand tall as the leader of the United States of America. I saw people donate blood and supplies around the nation to help the victims. I witnessed Congress standing together and giving full support to President Bush in his decisions regarding the tragedy. I personally witnessed patriotism come from almost every American. September eleventh brought this country closer together and showed the world what we were made of. Along with the rest of the nation, I learned that we cannot ignore terrorism and its supporters. I will always remember more than ever how lucky I felt to live in this great country of the United States of America. I will always remember September 11, 2001, and what happened that tragic day.

Questions on Form

1. What is the topic sentence?

2. What concrete words are effective in sentence 2?

3. Underline four sentences that begin with a prepositional phrase.

Questions on Content

1. What did the author see the American people doing after the tragedy of September 11?

2. What national leaders did the author see on television?

3. What did the author learn about terrorism and its supporters?

Excerpt from A Long Way from Home

Tom Brokaw

My parents and their friends were members of the "waste not, want not" generation. They measured everything from food to wrapping paper to soap for its potential secondary value. No scrap of food was summarily disposed of without first getting an evaluation from Mother on its leftover possibilities. Sunday's leftover mashed potatoes became Monday night's fried potato patties. Gifts were opened carefully, and the wrapping paper was folded and put away for another gift later on. When bars of soap became so small they hardly seemed worth saving, they were pressed onto other bars in the same condition. Worn-out T-shirts became dust rags. Nails pulled out of boards were hammered back into shape and stored in an empty coffee can. A friend's father could never get used to the idea of paper towels. He used them carefully and dried them for another time. . . . Theirs was a generation whose members were so conditioned by the economic perils of their upbringing that they sometimes carried caution and frugality to a fault. At a stage in their lives when they could easily afford personal indulgences, they were still reluctant to spend money on anything that wasn't practical. For a long time, they refused to believe that the Great Depression was a once-in-a-lifetime event.

Understanding Words
Briefly define the following words as they are used in this selection.

1. summarily

2. perils

3. frugality

4. indulgences

Questions on Form

1. What is the topic sentence?

2. What examples and details support the topic idea?

3. How is the material in this excerpt concluded?

4. Underline the eight simple sentences, including the topic sentence.

Questions on Content

1. What does "waste not, want not" mean?

2. How was everything measured?

3. What did his parents refuse to forget about the Great Depression?

Excerpt from If I Die in a Combat Zone, Box Me Up and Ship Me Home

Tim O'Brien

I thought about a girl. After thinking, she became a woman, only months too late. I spent time comparing her hair to the color of sand just as dusk, that sort of thing. I counted the number of soldiers I would trade for her. I memorized. I memorized details of her smell. I memorized her letters, whole letters. Memorizing was a way to remember and a way to forget, a way to remember a stranger, only a visitor at Fort Lewis. I memorized a poem she sent me. It was a poem by Auden, and marching for shots and haircuts and clothing issue, I recited the poem, forging Auden's words with thoughts I pretended to be here. I lied about her, pretending that she wrote the poem herself, for me. I compared her to characters out of books by Hemingway and Maugham. In her letters she claimed I created her out of the mind. The mind, she said, can make wonderful changes in the real stuff. So I hid from the drill sergeants, turned my back on the barracks, and wrote back to her.

Questions on Form

1. What is the topic sentence?

2. Why is it effective to use a form of "memorize" five times in one paragraph?

Questions on Content

1. What did he do to forget he was in war?

2. Whose poem did he memorize?

3. How did he lie about the girl?

Part 4

Using Verbs Correctly

Objectives

- Understand subject–verb agreement in sentences and paragraphs

    Edit to make subjects and verbs either both singular or both plural
- Understand verb tense in sentences and paragraphs

    Keep a consistent verb tense

    Shift verb tense when necessary

Earlier in this chapter, you learned to identify subjects and verbs and use them in sentences. You learned that all simple sentences must be **independent clauses.** This means that **they must have a subject and a verb as well as make sense when written by themselves.** The material in this part of the chapter focuses on using the correct verbs in your sentences and paragraphs.

The first part will focus on making the subjects and verbs in your sentences **agree in number, meaning that both the subject and the verb will be singular or both will be plural.**

The second part will focus on **consistent verb tense,** which means **keeping the same verb tense throughout your paragraphs.**

Subject–Verb Agreement

Using verbs correctly in your college writing and in your job shows that you understand subject–verb agreement. Once again, this means that **singular subjects have singular verbs and plural subjects have plural verbs.** Look at the following examples.

The event starts at 6:00 tonight.	(correct—singular subject and singular verb)
The events start at 6:00 tonight.	(correct—plural subject and plural verb)
The event start at 6:00 tonight.	(incorrect—singular subject and plural verb)
The events starts at 6:00 tonight.	(incorrect—plural subject and singular verb)

When the subject is singular, the verb must be singular. When the subject is plural, the verb must be plural. Mixing singular and plural is an error that is unacceptable in your college writing as well as at work. If English is your second language, look at the chart that simplifies the singular and plural forms of nouns and verbs.

ESL Reminder Adding **s** to a noun makes the word plural. However, adding **s** to a verb makes the word singular.

	Singular	Plural
Noun	no **s** (event)	add **s** (events)
Verb	add **s** (starts)	no **s** (start)

Do the following exercise for practice.

Exercise 1

Choose the verb that agrees with each subject.

Example:

My uncle __*visits*__ us almost every summer. (visit, visits)

Version A

1. The dogs _____ their dinner right away. (want, wants)
2. Jason _____ at least two books a month. (read, reads)
3. Each Saturday, Marta _____ forward to working in her yard. (look, looks)
4. The portraits _____ hung on the wall in the den. (were, was)
5. Carita and her sister _____ to travel in the city on the new subway. (like, likes)
6. Every weekend Antonio _____ to a football game with his brother. (go, goes)
7. Jogging slowly and humming quietly _____ Sandy forget her problems. (help, helps)
8. The tires and the battery _____ checked at the dealer's. (were, was)
9. Coming upon stray dogs or cats always _____ Veronica. (bother, bothers)
10. Veterinary bills _____ a big part of Jean's budget. (consume, consumes)

Version B

1. The children _____ hot chocolate in the evening. (enjoy, enjoys)
2. One cheerleader _____ higher than all the others. (jump, jumps)
3. Spaghetti and ravioli _____ my family's favorite pasta. (are, is)
4. Angry parents _____ their children. (upset, upsets)
5. During the holidays, brand new bikes and skates _____ in almost every neighborhood. (appear, appears)
6. In their cage, the hamsters _____ running on their exercise wheels. (are, is)
7. An investor _____ to monitor accounts regularly. (need, needs)
8. In the winter in the Midwest, rain and snow _____ traffic. (affect, affects)
9. Clay bowls not completely dry _____ when they are in the kiln. (explode, explodes)
10. The heavy truck traffic near my house _____ my dishes to vibrate. (cause, causes)

Sometimes choosing the correct verb can be a problem if the sentence has a prepositional phrase right between the subject and the verb. To find the subject more easily, mark through the prepositional phrases. Then find the subject and verb of the sentence. Study the following examples.

One ~~of the candles~~ were flickering weakly. (incorrect)

One ~~of the candles~~ was flickering weakly. (correct)

My hunch ~~about the answers~~ was wrong. (correct)

His reasons ~~for his choice of vacation~~ were not clear. (correct)

Remember that the noun or pronoun in the prepositional phrase cannot be the subject.

Work through the following exercise to help you use verbs correctly.

Exercise 2

Mark through each prepositional phrase, and then choose the correct verb to agree with the subject.

Example:

One ~~of the dishes~~ _was_ cracked. (was, were)

Version A

1. The loaves of bread _____ hot and delicious. (was, were)
2. Singing at national events _____ not her favorite activity. (was, were)
3. His notes for the test _____ soaked in the downpour. (was, were)
4. The records for his tax returns _____ always in good order. (is, are)
5. Her regret over the forgotten lunch dates _____ to be genuine. (seems, seem)
6. Signing up for new classes _____ not an option for me at this time. (is, are)
7. CDs under the bed _____ dust. (collects, collect)
8. Buying on the Internet _____ now relatively safe. (is, are)
9. The income of the cooperating countries _____ risen recently. (has, have)
10. The good fortune of my sister's children _____ all of us. (surprises, surprise)

Version B

1. Six boxes of books _____ stored in the garage. (were, was)
2. Often in a restaurant, the sound of a cell phone _____ our dinner. (interrupt, interrupts)
3. During a parade, the rhythm of the marching bands _____ toes to tapping. (set, sets)
4. The food at the concession stands _____ the fans. (tempt, tempts)

5. The violin players in the high school orchestra _____ like professionals. (sound, sounds)

6. The box of chocolates _____ melting in the sun. (is, are)

7. The aroma of hamburgers cooking on the grill _____ the whole family. (attract, attracts)

8. The precision of the Army skydivers _____ me every time. (impress, impresses)

9. The excitement of good college bowl games usually _____ the fans. (exhaust, exhausts)

10. Fires in the national forest _____ a problem every summer. (are, is)

Sometimes making subjects and verbs agree can also be a problem when certain pronouns are subjects. In this case, you have to look at the meaning of the noun in the prepositional phrase. Is it something in separate parts that can be counted one by one? Or is it something in a single amount that cannot be counted one by one? Study the following examples.

Some of the rocks are broken.   (plural subject; plural verb)

The word **some** stands for two or more rocks and is, therefore, a plural subject.

Some of the sand is wet.   (singular subject; singular verb)

This time, the word **some** stands for part of a single amount that you cannot count one by one. How would you explain the following sentences?

Some of the rocks are covered with trash.

Some of the rocky shoreline is covered with trash.

The pronouns below may sometimes be singular and sometimes plural, depending upon the noun they replace.

all				
any	more	most	some	

S   V
Some of the rocks are broken.   (correct because **rocks** is plural)

S   V
Some of the sand is wet.   (correct because **sand** is singular)

Work through the following exercise to help you use verbs correctly.

Exercise 3

Mark through each prepositional phrase, and then choose the correct verb to agree with the subject.

Example:

One ~~of the shirts~~ _*was*_ torn. (was, were)

Version A

1. Most of my neighbors _____ on vacation in June. (go, goes)
2. Some of the guests _____ coming from Texas. (are, is)
3. Some of them _____ related to me. (is, are)
4. Most of my friends _____ college. (attend, attends)
5. Some of it _____ missing. (are, is).
6. Some of the questions _____ very difficult. (are, is)
7. One of us _____ to go to the store. (have, has)
8. Any of that band's music _____ good to me. (sound, sounds)
9. All of the desserts _____ delicious. (look, looks)
10. Most of the animals _____ been fed. (have, has)

Version B

1. Some of the money _____ missing. (are, is)
2. Some of the bicycles _____ stolen from the racks in front of the dorm. (were, was)
3. All of my lunch _____ spoiled. (are, is)
4. All of the cake _____ eaten yesterday. (were, was)
5. One of the meals _____ to be vegetarian. (have, has)
6. Some of the milk in the refrigerator _____ gone sour. (have, has)
7. Most of the paint _____ gone. (are, is)
8. Any of his suggestions _____ acceptable. (are, is)
9. Most of the newly planted flowers _____ ruined by the hailstorm. (were, was)
10. Some of my mail _____ put into my neighbor's mailbox. (were, was)

The following exercise will give you more practice in subject and verb agreement.

Exercise 4

Choose the correct verb to agree with each subject.

Example:

They_____*were*_____waiting in the will-call line at the theater. (were, was)

Version A

1. We _____ just hanging out at the mall. (were, was)
2. Several of the children _____ not had any breakfast. (has, have)
3. She _____ not want to go with us tonight. (do, does)
4. The waves on the ocean _____ rough. (seem, seems)
5. I _____ not the one to do this job. (is, am)
6. Avoiding the puddles _____ hard in the spring. (is, are)

7. Studying for exams _____ always easy for Sam. (was, were)

8. To know you have done well _____ a satisfying thought. (is, are)

9. He _____ the best on his math test. (do, does)

10. Young girls in some cultures _____ sold into marriages. (is, are)

Version B

1. Jim's mother always _____ his sack lunch before school. (pack, packs)

2. My friend and her son _____ time shooting baskets in the evenings. (spend, spends)

3. Many heroes from September 11 _____ still remembered. (is, are)

4. In the mornings, Tessa and her dog _____ through the silent neighborhood. (walk, walks)

5. The new dinner theater _____ next month. (open, opens)

6. Many people in our society_____ participating in yoga classes. (is, are)

7. Returning to college _____ many challenges to students. (offer, offers)

8. RV parks _____ of many new kinds of benefits. (boast, boasts)

9. Young children _____ to use computers quite easily. (learn, learns)

10. Many of my favorite restaurants _____ good appetizers. (serve, serves)

Writing correct sentences includes editing for subject–verb agreement. As you put your sentences together into paragraphs, you will want to be sure that you stay in either the present or the past tense, often referred to as consistent verb tense.

Consistent Verb Tense

An important part of using verbs correctly is using the same tense throughout your paragraphs. Present tense means that the events in your paragraph are going on right now; past tense means the events happened earlier; and future tense means the events will happen some time in the future. However, the tenses used most often are the present and the past tense. Mixing present tense with past tense can confuse your reader. Watch what happens in the following paragraph:

> Visiting the pond **is** very peaceful. The noise of the city **fades,** and the soothing sounds around the pond **make** it quiet and relaxing. Even the soft clacking of the ducks **blended** with the regular sounds of the paddle boats on the water. Occasionally children **laughed** and **giggled** as they **interrupted** the silence.

inconsistent verb tense

After three verbs in the present tense—**is, fades,** and **make**—the writer shifts to the past tense with **blended, laughed, giggled,** and **interrupted.** Notice the difference when consistent tense is maintained.

Visiting the pond **is** very peaceful. The noise of the city **fades,** and the soothing sounds around the pond **make** it quiet and relaxing. Even the soft clacking of the ducks **blends** with the regular sounds of the paddle boats on the water. Occasionally children **laugh** and **giggle** as they **interrupt** the silence.

consistent verb tense

The most important part of verb tense may be awareness of time. Most of the time you will want to maintain the same tense, so you need to work through the following exercises that give practice in being consistent in time.

Exercise 5

Identify the tense in the first sentence as either past or present. Then change the remaining verbs so that they are consistent with that tense.

Example:

past **Parking on campus last semester turned out to be a real problem.**
                        arrived   _got_
However, if I ~~arrive~~ **between classes, I often** ~~get~~ **a good spot.**

Version A

_____ 1. We moved into a new apartment last month. It is a good move because it brings me closer to my job.

_____ 2. Every day the cats eat several cans of food. I spent more than twenty dollars a week on pet food.

_____ 3. The throat lozenges soothe my scratchy throat. I liked their assorted citrus flavors.

_____ 4. Last year, I traveled to Oakland for the winter holidays. I really enjoy making that trip because I fly over the Sierras.

_____ 5. In January in Arizona, the sun shines almost every day. Some out-of-state travelers came to visit and ended up staying a month or two.

_____ 6. The city-wide ban on smoking irritates some restaurant owners. Customers, however, really supported the new ordinance.

_____ 7. Two of the goldfish grew too large for the tank. We have to buy a new tank for them.

_____ **8.** I spent many hours making a green lap quilt for my father. He asks for a new one because his old quilt falls apart.

_____ **9.** Yesterday, the weather caused a ten-car pileup on the freeway. Traffic is backed up for two miles.

_____ **10.** Our family rented an additional refrigerator for the holidays. We store all the extra desserts and other special food in it.

Version B

_____ **1.** Today, many people drink bottled water. Local water supplies seemed to taste bad or seemed to be unsafe.

_____ **2.** Violent crimes against defenseless children saddened the community. They pass laws to aid in stopping further crimes.

_____ **3.** The real estate agent was honest and dependable. He receives the outstanding-realtor-of-the month award.

_____ **4.** Over two thousand young men and women applied for the job of firefighter. Because of a hiring freeze, only five people are hired.

_____ **5.** Many people look forward to weekends. They spent time at home with their families and relaxed.

_____ **6.** People received many unwanted advertisements over their fax machines. They frequently turn off their machines.

_____ **7.** Lance enjoyed watching old western movies in his free time. He especially likes to watch John Wayne movies.

_____ **8.** At the beginning of a new year, many people resolve to make changes in their lives. They worked harder, ate less, and exercised more.

_____ **9.** Having parents as coaches can mean a lot to children. They grew

closer to their parents and respected them more.

_____ **10.** Prepaid phone cards make using long distance easy and inexpensive.

They were available at almost any supermarket or discount store.

Once you are aware of verb tense and are careful to keep the same tense throughout your writing, you will be able to make a shift in verb tense when necessary. Read carefully through the following information.

Necessary Shift in Verb Tense

Sometimes it is necessary to shift your verb tense to indicate that there is a time difference. For example, in the first sentence below, tense has gone from past (*started*) to present (*feel*) to future (*will do*). These are necessary shifts, but most of the time, you will want to keep a consistent past or present tense in your paragraphs. The first sentence in your paragraph establishes the time that you will want to maintain in your paragraph.

When college **started**, I **was** nervous, but now, a few weeks later, I **feel** confident that I will do well.   (necessary shift in tense)

When I **was** in high school, I **started** classes at 8:00 every morning. Now that I **am** in college, my classes **do** not **start** until 10:00.   (necessary shift in tense)

Summary

Writing sentences and paragraphs that are effective and communicate your ideas to others involves using verbs correctly. You will want to edit your writing for subject–verb agreement and consistent verb tense.

- Subject–verb agreement means that singular subjects have singular verbs and plural subjects have plural verbs.
- Consistent verb tense means using the same tense throughout your paragraphs. The most commonly used tenses are present and past.
- Shifting verb tense may be necessary to show a difference in time.

Practice Test

In the following paragraph, sentence #1 establishes the past tense that needs to be used throughout the paragraph. In sentence #2, a necessary shift occurs because the author *is* remembering, in the present, something that happened in the past. All other sentences have at least one mistake in either subject–verb agreement or consistent verb tense. Find these mistakes, and correct them by writing the correct verb form above the word.

(1) In the 1950s, my brother and I grew up poor, but we learned to be resourceful, and we made the best of what we had. (2) I can still remember the excitement when we pulled into a gas station. (3) Beautiful glasses, bowls, china dishes, and variegated pink and amber piggy banks was loaded on the tables between the gas pumps. (4) When my dad filled up the gas tank in our car, we get our choice of one of these items. (5) One day I get to pick my treasured piggy bank. (6) Together we found another way to get prizes, and that were with Blue Horse school paper. (7) My dad, who was a teacher, have us all cut out and save the pictures of the horse printed on the outside. (8) Everyone use this brand of paper in school, but most kids just threw their wrappers into the trash can. (9) We, on the other hand, retrieve them, count them, and save them in a shoe box. (10) We often scanned the list of free prizes to see how many of the Blue Horses we need for each prize. (11) One day, we have enough for a bicycle, and we excitedly sent in the coupons and waited for the bicycle. (12) My dad were as proud as we was a few weeks later when we opened the big carton and took out the shiny blue bicycle that had been shipped to us. (13) Sometimes we wanted money to buy other things, so we walk around town looking for empty glass pop bottles that we redeemed for two cents each at the grocery store. (14) I bought the biggest piece of candy I could for the money, and it were a peanut butter "chicken leg" that cost five cents, but it was worth every penny. (15) My brother loved to save baseball cards, so he use his money to earn baseball cards. (16) Dad took him to a wholesale candy store where he buy a whole box of baseball cards at a discount. (17) He then sells them for a penny each. (18) After he had gotten back all the money that he had paid for the cards, he still have cards left over for himself. (19) He also have enough money to buy another box of cards. (20) These and many other bargains keep us happy.

Writing Assignment

Write a paragraph on one of the following topics. Be sure to start with a topic sentence. Then add support sentences, and end with a concluding sentence.

1. Living with an unusual pet
2. First impressions on hearing about a particular tragic event
3. Most important quality of a valuable friend
4. Most important quality of a valuable employee
5. Main advantage of being home-schooled
6. Biggest disadvantage of being home-schooled

Chapter 4

Combining Sentences for Effective Writing

Part 1

Compound Sentences

Objectives

- Distinguish between simple and compound sentences
- Combine simple sentences into compound sentences

    Use a comma and an appropriate coordinate conjunction

    Use a semicolon

    Use a semicolon, an appropriate conjunctive adverb, and a comma

Now that you have practiced simple sentences, you are ready to study compound sentences. A compound sentence is simply two or more simple sentences joined together, either with a word or words or with punctuation.

Distinguishing Between Simple and Compound Sentences

You need to be aware that compound sentences are not the same as simple sentences having either two subjects or two verbs. A compound sentence is made up of two complete sentences, each having one or more subjects and one or more verbs. You need to be able to distinguish between simple sentences and compound sentences.

Now look at the following sentence. It is a simple sentence, but it has two verbs. (This type of sentence does not need any punctuation to separate the verbs unless it has three main verbs.)

    S   V   V
Jake **went** to the lake and **launched** his boat.   (SVV = simple sentence)

    S   V   V   V
Jake **went** to the lake, **launched** his boat, and **relaxed**
on the water.   (SVVV= simple sentence)

Look at the next sentence. It is a compound sentence because it consists of two simple sentences joined by a coordinate conjunction and a comma.

    S   V   S   V
Jake **went** to the lake, *and* he **launched** his boat.   (SV SV = compound sentence)

Work through the following exercise to distinguish simple sentences from compound sentences.

Identify the simple sentences and the compound sentences. Put an "S" in the blank by each simple sentence and a "C" in the blank by each compound sentence. Add a comma correctly to each compound sentence. Identify the subjects and verbs in each sentence.

Examples:

               S   V   V

_S_ 1. Jake drove to California and visited his grandparents at their farm.

               S   V   S   V

_C_ 2. Jake drove to California, and he visited his grandparents at their farm.

Version A

_____ 1. Kyle played baseball in college and won most of the games.

_____ 2. Swimming keeps my sister in good condition and it makes her happy.

_____ 3. Brett drove to school and parked his car in the north lot.

_____ 4. Alex's girlfriend met him after class and she offered to buy him lunch.

_____ 5. The firefighter proudly carried the flag in the memorial service and held it throughout the ceremony.

_____ 6. Before going home, Evelyn went to the computer lab and accessed the library.

_____ 7. Sandra drove to the mall and spent the afternoon window shopping.

_____ 8. The lizards lived in the backyard and they kept the plants insect free.

_____ 9. Josh played on the college baseball team and he hit several home runs.

_____ 10. The pomegranate tree produced beautiful fruit and many hummingbirds sat on the branches.

Version B

_____ 1. Yesterday, Rebecca bought a new laptop computer and hooked it up to the Internet.

_____ 2. Competing in the Olympic Games is a great honor yet winning a gold, silver, or bronze metal is the dream of many athletes.

_____ 3. Working hard is important but enjoying life is even more important.

_____ 4. The snow on the mountains melted and, as a result, filled the rivers with water.

_____ 5. Four hundred men and women applied for the job but only ten were hired.

_____ 6. Big snowflakes fell from the sky and covered the trees.

_____ 7. He remodeled his home and then invited his friends over for a party.

_____ 8. We went to our favorite restaurant but it was closed.

_____ 9. Trish loved all of her children but she also enjoyed doing things by herself.

_____ 10. My brother had a vivid imagination and invented new games for us to play.

Combining Simple Sentences into Compound Sentences

Simple sentences may be joined into compound sentences in three ways. These include adding:

- a comma and a coordinate conjunction
- a semicolon
- a semicolon, a conjunctive adverb, and a comma

Using Coordinate Conjunctions

Two or more sentences joined by connecting words called coordinate conjunctions become a compound sentence. Remembering the words "fan boys" can help you memorize the list of coordinate conjunctions.

Coordinate Conjunctions	
for	but
and	or
nor	yet
	so

Note The first letters of the conjunctions in the above box spell "fan boys."

Now, look at the two simple sentences below.

The wind blew.

The rain began to fall.

Notice how the two simple sentences are combined into one compound sentence by using the coordinate conjunction **and** plus a comma.

The wind blew, **and** the rain began to fall.

The wind is blowing, **and** the rain is starting to fall.

Each of these coordinate conjunctions has definite meaning:

For (joins two sentences when the second sentence gives a reason for the first sentence)

The dogs started barking. The doorbell rang.

The dogs started barking, **for** the doorbell rang.

And (joins two sentences of equal importance)

The doorbell rang. The dogs barked at the sound.

The doorbell rang, **and** the dogs barked at the sound.

Nor (joins two sentences, both of which are negative ideas)

The dogs were not housebroken. They could not stay alone without tearing up the house.

The dogs were not housebroken, **nor** could they stay alone without tearing up the house.

But (joins two sentences that show a contrast)

The doorbell rang. The dogs did not bark at the sound.

The doorbell rang, **but** the dogs did not bark at the sound.

Or (joins two sentences that give a choice between two ideas)

The dogs need to eat less. They will become fat.

The dogs need to eat less, **or** they will become fat.

Yet (joins two sentences that show a contrast)

The puppies want to explore the yard. They do not want to leave their mother.

The puppies want to explore the yard, **yet** they do not want to leave their mother.

So (joins two sentences that show a result)

The baby puppies made a pitiful sound. The mother ran to them.

The baby puppies made a pitiful sound, **so** their mother ran to them.

When you write your compound sentences, you will want to try to find the coordinate conjunction that connects the two simple sentences in the most logical way. Work through the following exercise to practice using coordinate conjunctions.

Combine each pair of simple sentences into one compound sentence, using a comma and a coordinate conjunction. Look back at the list, and decide which connecting word is logical. Use all of the conjunctions at least once.

Example

I water my yard often. The afternoon heat turns it brown anyway.

I water my yard often, but the afternoon heat turns it brown anyway.

Version A

1. Jason studied for his math exam. He passed it easily.

   _____

2. The restaurant was open for business. It had no customers.

   _____

3. Kyle and Josh wore their raincoats. They knew it was going to rain.

   _____

4. The Cubs scored only one run. They won the game.

   _____

5. The patient needs to take the doctor's advice. The illness will not be cured.

   _____

6. My girlfriend does not like my shirt. She does not like my haircut.

   _____

7. Americans showed respect for their country. They flew their flags.

   _____

8. I did all my assignments and prepared for my exam. My instructor did not show up for class.

   _____

9. Sandra gathered a bouquet of flowers from her garden. She wanted to decorate her dining room table.

   _____

10. The little boy's grandmother bought him a train. She bought him a book about trains.

    _____

Version B

1. Sharon bought new batteries. The radio still would not run.

   _____

2. To sit in the nonsmoking section was not an option in that restaurant. We chose to eat elsewhere.

_____

3. Passenger lines at airports are now very common. People do not object to the delays.

_____

4. Hearing the fire engine sirens startled me. I quickly moved over to the right and stopped.

_____

5. The frail woman walked slowly down the street. She was clearly enjoying the day.

_____

6. The tiny green frog sat on the lily pad. She caught insects as they came her way.

_____

7. After forty years of marriage, the woman lost her husband. She stayed busy.

_____

8. The students at the university were used to harsh winters. They walked in underground tunnels to get from class to class.

_____

9. The basketball team lost in double overtime. Some of the players cried in disappointment.

_____

10. The papers scattered on the floor. We rushed to pick them up.

_____

Using Semicolons

Another way to combine simple sentences into a compound sentence is to use a semicolon. When combining sentences in this way, you need to remember not to capitalize the first word after the semicolon unless it is a proper noun.

If a semicolon is used, it is used to join short, related sentences. Most of the time, a period can replace the semicolon.

The editor read the story. He liked it.
The editor read the story; he liked it.

Exercise 3

Combine the two simple sentences into one compound sentence by using a semicolon.

Example:

The storm hit after midnight. All my clocks stopped.

The storm hit after midnight; all my clocks stopped.

Version A

1. Heather made brownies. They were delicious.

2. Kurt practiced his tennis serve. It was clocked at 100 miles per hour.

3. The United States and Russia developed the International Space Station. They now share responsibility for it.

4. Richard and Helen went to the theater. They saw a Shakespearean play.

5. The quarterback threw four touchdown passes. His team won the game.

6. In parts of the world, everyday life is hard. In other parts, life is easy.

7. The pizza delivery driver took his time. He made his deliveries safely.

8. Felicia wanted to paint her house. She talked to an interior designer.

9. Some college expenses can be as high as $25,000 a year. Financial aid can help ease the burden.

10. The ceramics class includes students of all ages. They help each other with their projects.

Version B

1. The main waterline burst at the intersection. Traffic had to detour to another street.

2. The mascot at the baseball game scared the little girl. She burst into tears.

_____

3. My Uncle Hector came over to our house. He cooked steaks on the grill.

_____

4. The oatmeal macadamia nut cookies stayed in the oven too long. We ate them anyway.

_____

5. The chef's specialty was shrimp stir-fry. He always featured it on Friday.

_____

6. The halogen lamps were banned from the dorm rooms. The bulbs became dangerously hot.

_____

7. The hikers encountered quicksand. They struggled to get through it.

_____

8. The burglar alarm went off in the office building. The potential thieves quickly fled.

_____

9. The frumpy old man boarded the airplane. He proudly sat in the first-class section.

_____

10. I heard a crunch as I backed out of the driveway. I had hit the curb again.

_____

Using Conjunctive Adverbs

Another way to combine simple sentences into compound sentences is to use a semicolon and a transitional word called a conjunctive adverb. Below is a list of conjunctive adverbs.

Conjunctive Adverbs		
moreover	otherwise	consequently
in addition	furthermore	however
therefore		in fact
thus		nevertheless
		as a result

Note The conjunctive adverbs in the previous box are arranged so that their first letters spell "mitt of China."

When two simple sentences are joined with a conjunctive adverb, use a semicolon after the first sentence and a comma after the conjunctive adverb. Look at the following example.

> The earthquake rocked the city.
>
> Little damage occurred.
>
> The earthquake rocked the city; however, little damage occurred.

In the above sentence, the punctuation is logical because what you are really doing is joining the sentences with a semicolon and setting off the conjunctive adverb with a comma. In the following sentence, the semicolon still joins the simple sentences, but the transitional word *however* is in the middle of the second sentence and needs to be set off with commas.

> The earthquake rocked the city; little damage, however, occurred.

Just as the coordinate conjunctions have definite meaning, the conjunctive adverbs also have a definite meaning.

Moreover (adds an equally important idea)

> The dogs need to eat less. They need to get more exercise.
>
> The dogs need to eat less; moreover, they need to get more exercise.

In addition (also adds an equally important idea)

> The dogs need to eat less. They need to get more exercise.
>
> The dogs need to eat less; in addition, they need to get more exercise.

Thus (shows a result)

> David gave his dog too many treats. She became fat.
>
> David gave his dog too many treats; thus, she became fat.

Therefore (also shows a result)

> The swarm of bees landed in a tree. The owner called the fire department.
>
> The swarm of bees landed in a tree; therefore, the owner called the fire department.

Otherwise (shows a result if the idea in the first sentence does not happen)

> Barbara needs to get a job. She will not be able to pay her rent.
>
> Barbara needs to get a job; otherwise, she will not be able to pay her rent.

Furthermore (adds an additional idea)

> Ben plans to get a college degree. He wants to start his own business.
>
> Ben plans to get a college degree; furthermore, he wants to start his own business.

Consequently (shows a result)

> Sharon wanted to buy a horse. She bought property with horse privileges.

> Sharon wanted to buy a horse; consequently, she bought property with horse privileges.

However (shows a contrast)

> Rodrigo wanted to customize his car. He needed more money.

> Rodrigo wanted to customize his car; however, he needed more money.

In fact (adds information for emphasis)

> Sergio wanted to make his car look better. He wanted to customize it.

> Sergio wanted to make his car look better; in fact, he wanted to customize it.

Nevertheless (shows a contrast)

> Sara was nervous about going to the park. She wanted to walk her dog.

> Sara was nervous about going to the park; nevertheless, she wanted to walk her dog.

As a result (shows a consequence)

> Keith installed dual exhaust pipes on his car. Everyone could hear him coming.

> Keith installed dual exhaust pipes on his car; as a result, everyone could hear him coming.

> Choosing the best conjunctive adverb is important when writing compound sentences. One good rule to remember is not to use the same conjunctive adverb more than once in the same paragraph.

Exercise 4

Using a conjunctive adverb from the above list, combine each pair of simple sentences into a compound sentence. Remember to use a semicolon and a comma. Use as many different conjunctive adverbs as possible. Refer to the above examples if necessary.

Example:

Jim wanted to buy a new motorcycle. He needed to save more money.

Jim wanted to buy a new motorcycle; however, he needed to save more money.

Jim wanted to buy a new motorcycle; consequently, he needed to save more money.

Version A

1. Mr. Lewis is open-minded. He is likely to succeed as a manager.

2. Susan had tickets for the game. She could not go.

_____

3. Fatima had saved enough money to buy a new stereo. She wanted to wait for a sale.

_____

4. Christian put his income tax refund check into the bank. His brother used his for a vacation.

_____

5. All the gate receipts were donated to charity. Even more pledges came from television viewers.

_____

6. Doug reads the newspaper every morning. He watches television news programs in the evening.

_____

7. Tony fertilized the tomato plants. The tomatoes grew to be large and flavorful.

_____

8. Ninety percent of the students drive cars to school. Finding a parking space is really difficult.

_____

9. Anthony just lost his job. He still has to make his house and car payments.

_____

10. Overnight, the snow piled up on the roads. The snowplows cleared the roads as soon as possible.

_____

Version B

1. Putting down new kitchen tile pleased the potential home buyers. They did not buy the house.

_____

2. To prepare for the birthday party took extra time and effort. Everybody helped.

_____

3. The smells from the beauty salon floated into the mall. Most shoppers paid no attention.

_____

4. The teenagers were extremely hungry. They raided the refrigerator.

_____

5. Justin was in love with his girlfriend. He asked her to marry him on Valentine's Day.

_____

6. I really wanted to make an A in my class. I spent extra time editing my papers.

_____

7. We spent the weekend camping. We were able to watch the fireflies light up in the evening.

_____

8. Juanita created unique silver earrings. She had a supply on hand to use them as gifts.

_____

9. I ran out of protein bars. I bought one at the gym.

_____

10. I wanted to go to Fort Lauderdale for spring break. I had to write a research paper.

_____

Exercise 5

Now write your own compound sentences. If you have trouble, write two simple sentences, and then combine them into one compound sentence.

1. Write three compound sentences, using a different coordinate conjunction in each sentence.

a. _____

_____

b. _____

_____

c. _____

_____

2. Write three compound sentences, using a semicolon.

a. _____

_____

b. _____

_____

c. _____

_____

3. Write three compound sentences, using a different conjunctive adverb in each sentence.

a. _____

_____

b. _____

_____

c. _____

_____

Summary

You have learned that effective paragraphs have a variety of different types of sentences. Being able to write simple sentences and then combine them into effective compound sentences is one way to achieve sentence variety in your paragraphs.

- Combining simple sentences into compound sentences

   Use a comma and a coordinate conjunction.

   Use a semicolon.

   Use a semicolon, a conjunctive adverb, and a comma.

Practice Test

Read the following paragraph, which contains only simple and compound sentences. Identify the simple sentences (S) and the compound sentences (C) and fill in the correct answer in the blanks.

(1) My thoughts of my grandmother bring wonderful memories. (2) As a little girl, I learned early to count on my grandmother. (3) My mother sent me to preschool, but some days I did not want to go. (4) On those days, my grandmother let me stay at home with her. (5) In grade school, sometimes I got sick, so my grandmother always let me stay at her house. (6) On these special days, she fixed lemon tea and chicken

noodle soup. (7) My grandmother spent hours patiently helping me learn my schoolwork. (8) Many afternoons, she listened to me read, and then she helped me practice my multiplication tables. (9) Before long, my grades came up. (10) Also, my family did not have a lot of money, so I did not have as many clothes as the other children. (11) My grandmother noticed, and she often surprised me with a trip to the store. (12) She bought me clothes and pretty ribbons for my hair. (13) I was proud of my clothes and my grandmother. (14) In my family, I was the only girl, so I had to do all the chores. (15) Every day, it was my job to wash all the dishes. (16) My grandmother noticed and told my mother to have everyone help. (17) I liked having someone stand up for me. (18) At seventeen, I got my first job. (19) I could not drive, so my grandmother took me to work. (20) I met a cute boy there, and I told my grandmother all about him. (21) She convinced my mother to let me go on a picnic with him and his family. (22) Over the years, my grandmother and I spent many hours together and shared many secrets. (23) I will always love her.

(1) _____ (7) _____ (13) _____ (19) _____
(2) _____ (8) _____ (14) _____ (20) _____
(3) _____ (9) _____ (15) _____ (21) _____
(4) _____ (10) _____ (16) _____ (22) _____
(5) _____ (11) _____ (17) _____ (23) _____
(6) _____ (12) _____ (18) _____

Writing Assignment

Write a single paragraph on one of the following subjects. Decide on a direction for your paragraph. Be sure to have a topic sentence, support sentences, and a concluding sentence. Be sure to include both simple and compound sentences.

1. Car race
2. Farmers' market
3. Swap meet
4. Crafts fair
5. Carnival
6. Public hiking trail
7. Bookstore like Barnes & Noble

Part 2

Something to Think About, Something to Write About

Professional Essay to Generate Ideas for Writing

Who Said Women Don't Make Good Soldiers?

Shyrl Elizabeth Emhoff, *Lt. Col., USAR, Retired*

1   "Eight active, twenty-one reserve, and four years of school," is still my response when anyone asks me about my stint in the Army. The daughter of a lieutenant colonel, I grew up as an Army brat, loving the life. I remember my sister and me living in a very disciplined household, and I thrived in that environment. As I think about my early years, I realize it was perfectly natural for me to want a career in the Army.

2   I got my first taste of serving my country during World War II when I was only twenty-one years old. After enlisting in January of 1943, I went through basic training at three different Army bases before going overseas. Our official designation was the First Separate Battalion of the Women's Army Auxiliary Corps (WAAC), later known as the Women's Army Corps (WAC). We were the first Army women to go overseas, and my troop left New York, traveling by ship to London. I noticed that every few miles our ship changed direction, and I soon found out why. For the entire trip as we moved toward our destination, we zigzagged so that German submarines could not line us up and fire off a torpedo at us. One other vivid recollection of this trip overseas that is embedded forever in my mind is having just one helmet full of water each day to wash up. That was it. I could have no water to wash my clothes, only water to drink, and so began my Army war experiences.

3   Once we arrived in England and settled in at 8th Army Headquarters at High Wycombe, twenty-eight miles outside of London, my routine was quite predictable. Every morning was the same. We got up at 6:00 and stood reveille. This meant that we all stood with our hands to our backs until the commanding officer said, "Attend-HUT," the Army version of attention. Without a second's hesitation, we all snapped to and waited for our names to be called. When I heard Emhoff called, I immediately saluted and responded with, "Here, Mam." Some days, after this initial inspection, we went inside, and the commanding officer checked everything. When she walked up to me, I immediately went back into the formal "attention" stance. I waited while she looked me over again from head to toe to make sure she hadn't missed anything earlier. Quickly her eyes encompassed my living area. Not missing anything, she made an extra effort to make sure the corners of my bedding

were square. Some days she dropped a quarter in the middle of the bed, and if it didn't bounce high enough, boy, was I in trouble. After every name was called and every salute was made, we heard the word we were waiting for, "Dismissed." That meant we could head for the chow line at the mess hall.

4   After breakfast, I reported to my job in Research and Development. From eight to five every day, seven days a week, I worked with a team of other soldiers to analyze the results of the bombing runs over Germany. We had to determine the precise moment our pilots were to drop their bombs so they could hit the target without putting our soldiers' lives in danger. As the American airplanes neared their targets, enemy bombs exploded in the air, and shreds of metal called flak burst into the air and sliced the American airplanes. To avoid this, our soldiers had to get in, drop their bombs, and get out as efficiently as possible. Some days we would get off work just to be called back because pilots had submitted new information that needed to be interpreted. When I first started analyzing data, the men were skeptical of my ability because I was the only woman, but they soon learned that I had graduated from Cass Technical High School in Detroit, Michigan, had attended Purdue University, and I made exact calculations. When we were at work, we put everything aside except the safety of our pilots who were risking their lives on bombing missions. Many a night, we worked until after 11:00 P.M., and it seemed that I no sooner got to bed than it was 6:00 A.M., time to start all over again.

5   In the midst of war and surrounded by bombing, I found ways to escape the harshness of war. I lived in the women's dormitory at High Wycombe, but because we were so crowded, five or six of us discovered the basement one day, and we gradually moved down there. We took our bunks, cleaned the place so it was spotless, including an old stone fireplace. England can get extremely cold in the winter, and the fireplace helped keep us warm. Of course, we were enlisted soldiers, so we had to keep our quarters and ourselves in perfect order so we could pass inspection. When we had to use the bathroom, we had to go upstairs. Also, we had to do our laundry upstairs in the bathtub or down in the basement using buckets. When we were downstairs, we could still hear the bombers, but we felt a little bit safer there, a little bit like we were somewhere else. I also loved music, so on my day off, I went into town and took piano lessons. One day coming back to quarters, I found a half starving dog, and I found some food for him. After that, at every meal, I saved some of my food for him. He was a big brown friendly guy, and when the temperature was freezing outside, I hid him in the basement a couple of times until my superior found out. I probably could have gotten into more trouble, maybe even court-martialed, but instead, she sharply reprimanded me, "Get rid of that dog, SOMEHOW." I knew she meant business, so I left him with the lady where I had been taking piano lessons. During this time, I experienced inconveniences, but I never really minded the hardships so much; rather I learned to make the most of the situation.

6   Before the war was over, I had earned the rank of Sergeant, but I continued to serve in the Army Reserve. Over the years, I climbed the ranks, but the one promotion that I will never forget was when I was called in by my commanding officer. Without changing her expression, she ordered, "Sit

down, Sergeant." I sat down, thinking I was probably in trouble. Instead, she said, "Stand up, Lieutenant." I didn't know what to say because I had moved from sergeant to lieutenant, bypassing the intervening ranks. Like I said, I continued to serve in the Army for many more years, totaling thirty-three. Would I do it again? Yes, I would, in a heartbeat.

Understanding Words
Briefly define the following words as they are used in the selection.

1. auxiliary
2. reveille
3. snapped to
4. court-martialed

 Writing Assignment

Write a paragraph on one of the following topics. Be sure to start with a strong topic sentence. Add specific examples and details for support, and end with a strong concluding sentence.

1. Describe someone you know who has made a sacrifice for his or her country.
2. Biggest advantage of serving in the military
3. Biggest disadvantage of serving in the military
4. Reasons people need to work as a team
5. How someone influenced you to work toward a certain career
6. What can people do to be accepted as a new employee

Part 3

Student and Professional Paragraphs

My Father

Christian Kelly, *Student*

My father was an amazing man. He always took the time out of his day to listen to me. I can remember a time when I was eight years old, and my mother had accused me of stealing money out of her purse. My father, on the other hand, was not ready to jump to any irrational accusations. Instead, he was willing to listen to my side of the story and help me to find where the lost money had gone. Eventually, the money that had disappeared was found, and I was allowed to go outside. I will never forget that moment of trust that my father had shown me. When I was ten, my father was the coach of my soccer team. Some of the other players believed that because I was the coach's son I would receive special treatment. One of my teammates who was fighting for the same position accused my father of favoritism because he did not take me out even though I played very poorly for three straight games. My father was faced with a hard decision to demote his son to the bench. Before deciding, he gave me an opportunity to talk about my performance on the field. I explained to him that I could not get my mind off losing my dog earlier that week. My dad said that we would put up signs around the block, and if that did not work, he would buy me a new dog. After hearing that, I scored a goal in the next game and had two assists and was named player of the game. Listening to what I had to say before making any decisions is what I love most about my dad.

Questions on Form

1. What is the main idea of the paragraph?

2. What are his examples?

3. How does the conclusion tie the paragraph together?

Questions on Content

1. What sport did his dad coach?

2. Why was the son not playing well?

3. What did his father offer to do to help the situation?

Downfalls of Censoring Public Art

Joseph Ronald Fahoome, *Student*

Censoring public art shows has some serious downfalls. Most importantly, it denies people their Constitutional right to freely and openly express their own thoughts and feelings without being judged as "wrong." For example, Julie Glaze created a sculpture "Mother Earth," and entered it in a community college student art show. In this piece of art, Glaze expressed her feelings and perceptions of a black woman whom she rode with on an Atlanta city bus, but several students were enraged with this piece and demanded that the art show be closed. Rather than remove the piece, the art department elected to close the show. This denial of Glaze's piece in the art show was a denial of her right to openly and freely express her thoughts and feelings suggested in the art. It also robbed viewers of the chance to experience or see something through someone else's eyes. They were stripped of the chance to encounter the thoughts and feelings of a piece as well as the opportunity to observe or feel something in a way they never had before. For instance, students who viewed the piece experienced Julie's feelings and got to view her perspective of the black woman as "Mother Earth." Although it enraged a couple of students, it challenged their perspectives, values, and beliefs, and got them thinking, which is at the very heart of learning and growing. No conversation would take place, and nothing would be gained if the piece were not admitted. Another shortcoming of censoring public art is the message that it sends. The removal of Glaze's sculpture and the closing of the art show sent a message to Julie and others that certain thoughts and feelings which are a part of their very being are unacceptable, and this, in turn, may cause her and other students to block out and ignore certain feelings or ideas that make up who they are. Censoring public art shows denies people the opportunity and experience to grow.

Questions on Form

1. What is the direction in the topic sentence?

2. Is the topic sentence a simple or a compound sentence?

3. Is the concluding sentence a simple or a compound sentence?

Questions on Content

1. Where had the art show been held?

2. What is a major downfall to censoring public art shows?

3. What did the art department choose to do?

My Children

Joshua Sewell, *Student*

There are definitely two things in my life that fill me with pride; their names are Ian and Lainey. Ian is my two-year-old son, and Lainey is my three-and-a-half year old daughter. Like every parent, I, too, think that my kids are the cutest and the smartest children ever born. Ian turned two in February; he already has quite a good sense of humor. My daughter has such clear speech and such a large vocabulary that she often makes me forget that she is so young. The thing that I am most proud of is the relationship the kids have with each other and with my wife and me. When these two little brains start to work together toward a common goal, they are almost unstoppable. At times, they are so effective that I do not even realize what they are trying to get away with, and sometimes I am so impressed by their ingenuity and teamwork that I let them get away with their schemes. Both of my kids look after each other and try to help each other out, and they are always looking for ways to help us out. If my son falls asleep in the car, my daughter will open doors and help carry things in so I can hold her baby brother. I love my kids more than anything in the world, and even when they are acting like little monsters, I am proud of them.

Understanding Words
Briefly define the following word as it is used in this selection.

ingenuity

Questions on Form

1. What is the topic sentence?

2. What makes the conclusion effective?

3. What could be done to develop the paragraph further?

Questions on Content

1. How many children does the author have?

2. What is the one thing about his children that makes him the proudest?

3. What makes him forget how old his daughter is?

Excerpt from A Walk Through the Year

Edwin Way Teale

Always when we have an opportunity to watch a litter of young wild animals [three young bear cubs], we are fascinated by the differences in attitudes and character exhibited by the different individuals. One of the three cubs is the most trusting, the boldest. Another is considerably more wary. And the third is the shyest, the most timid of all. It sits beside the plums, ready for a quick retreat into the tangle. It watches its more daring companions ranging over the yard in a search for food that carries them as far as the terrace and the apple tree. But it remains where it is until one of the foragers discovers a good-sized piece of suet. As it comes trotting back across the grass with this prize in its jaws, the timid cub comes to life. It gives chase, trying to hijack the food in transit. The two disappear, racing away down the path toward the brook. A little later, returning from its unsuccessful sally as a freebooter, the shy fox—as shy as ever—takes up the same position again, sitting facing out over the yard, its back protected by the maze of the wild plums behind it.

Understanding Words
Briefly define the following words as they are used in this selection.

1. wary
2. tangle
3. foragers
4. suet
5. hijack
6. sally
7. freebooter
8. maze

Questions on Form

1. What is the topic sentence?

2. What details does Teale use to develop the example of the bear cubs?

Questions on Content

1. How many bear cubs does he observe?

2. How does the shyest cub try to get food?

3. Underline several concrete nouns in the passage.

Excerpt from Or Perish in the Attempt: Wilderness Medicine in the Lewis & Clark Expedition

David J. Peck, *D.O.*

The leader would need numerous talents and abilities. For starters, the commander [of the Lewis & Clark expedition] must be able to make scientific observations and accurately record what he witnessed. The area would need to be mapped, so the leader would have to be able to calculate latitude and longitude. He would then have to draw accurate maps of the areas through which he traveled. He would have to describe in a scientific manner any biological discoveries. The leader would have to know a great deal about the flora and fauna in the eastern United States so that he would be able to identify which plants and animals were new to science in the western region. His mind would have to be inquisitive and his eye remarkably observant. . . . He would have to be knowledgeable about mineralogy and geology. He needed diplomatic abilities for meeting Indian tribes and French and British nationals along the Missouri. All would have to be effectively, firmly, but respectfully dealt with, and informed that they were now operating within United States territory. The leader would also be responsible for the physical welfare of the men who accompanied him on the trip.

Understanding Words
Briefly define the following words as they are used in this selection.

1. latitude

2. longitude

3. flora

4. fauna

5. mineralogy

6. geology

7. inquisitive

Questions on Form

1. What is the topic sentence?

2. Of the more than a dozen examples in the paragraph, identify five.

Questions on Content

1. What will the commander have to be able to calculate?

2. What does he need to know before he goes on the expedition?

3. Why does he have to have diplomatic abilities?

Part 4

Run-on Sentences and Comma Splices

Objectives

- Identify run-on sentences and comma splices
- Correct run-on sentences and comma splices
  - Add a period at the end of each complete thought
  - Use a comma and a coordinate conjunction
  - Use a semicolon
  - Use a semicolon, a conjunctive adverb, and a comma

As you write your sentences, you will want to avoid run-on sentences and comma splices. These are serious errors because your reader may not be able to follow your ideas if your sentences are run together or are not separated with the correct punctuation. You can avoid such errors by writing simple sentences that have a subject and a verb and make sense by themselves. Then you can build on these simple sentences to make them more interesting.

Run-on Sentences

Sometimes you may be afraid to separate sentences because you think your individual sentences would be too short; however, a sentence cannot be determined by the number of words it contains. Rather it is determined by whether or not it has a subject and a verb and makes sense by itself. For example, "Jenny keeps excellent records" has only four words, but it has a subject and a verb, and it makes sense on its own. If you attempt to make it longer by adding another sentence, you might have something like, "Jenny keeps excellent records she has good math skills." This is not correct because you now have two sentences run together. "She has good math skills" also has a subject and a verb and makes sense on its own. Your goal is not to have long or short sentences. Your goal is to understand what a complete sentence is and then add details to develop it more fully.

A **run-on sentence is two or more sentences (independent clauses) that are punctuated as though they are one sentence.** For example, look at the following simple sentences that have been punctuated as only one sentence.

Animals become more than pets they become
companions.   (run-on sentences)

Animals become more than pets. They become
companions.   (punctuated correctly)

Running two sentences together like this can cause confusion for readers. Look at the following sentences that have been merged together. It is difficult to decide where one sentence ends and the other begins. Notice how changes in punctuation create different meanings in the corrected sentences.

Finding a job is very difficult on holidays employers
want people to work overtime.   (run-on sentence)

Finding a job is very difficult on holidays. Employers
want people to work overtime.   (1st correction)

The above sentence says that it is difficult to find a job on holidays. On the other hand, the sentence below, punctuated differently, says that employers want their employees to work overtime on holidays.

Finding a job is very difficult. On holidays, employers
want people to work overtime.   (2nd correction)

Look at one more example, and notice the change in meaning when the punctuation changes.

People's attitudes change during their lifetime then
they must make many choices.   (run-on sentence)

People's attitudes change. During their lifetime, then,
they must make many choices.   (1st correction)

People's attitudes change during their lifetime. Then,
they must make many choices.   (2nd correction)

As you can see, you must punctuate your sentences correctly so that your reader will know what you really mean. As a writer, you know what you want to say, but your reader may be confused and hope for some clarification through commas and periods.

Comma Splices

Another error to avoid is comma splices. Sometimes you realize that some punctuation is missing, but you are not sure what to do about it, so you just add a comma. However, using a comma to connect two sentences is the error known as a comma splice. A **comma splice is simply two or more sentences (independent clauses) that are joined with only a comma.** Look at the following sentences:

They rented a movie, they also ordered in a pepperoni pizza. (comma splice)

The comma in the above sentences offers no solution. The simplest way to correct this comma splice is to put a period at the end of the first sentence and capitalize the first word in the second sentence. Your sentences will be short, but they will be grammatically correct.

If you have problems with run-on sentences or comma splices in your writing, you might find it helpful to be aware of some signals that often mean you are starting a new sentence. Most effective, however, is to write simple sentences that you know are independent or can stand alone and then build on them by adding important information. With understanding, you can then combine them to form compound sentences.

Identifying Run-on Sentences and Comma Splices

There is absolutely no list of words that signal the beginning of a new sentence, but there are some words and phrases that are often used to begin a sentence. The following list may be helpful.

Words that often but not always start a new sentence

- phrases
  - in fact
  - for instance
  - for example
  - in some cases

- other words
  - this
  - that

- contractions
  - it's
  - there's
  - that's

- subject pronouns
  - I
  - you
  - she, he, it
  - we
  - they

- adverbs
  - then
  - there
  - now

I would catch up on one bill then the baby needed diapers.

(run-on—incorrect)

I would catch up on one bill, then the baby needed diapers.

(comma splice—incorrect)

I would catch up on one bill. Then the baby needed diapers.

(two sentences punctuated correctly)

In the first two examples above, **then** is not a word that can connect two sentences by itself. Look at the following sentences. Reading them aloud and identifying subjects and verbs is the only certain way to know if you have two sentences.

Traveling to other countries has a lot of advantages people enjoy themselves.

(run-on)

Traveling to other countries has a lot of advantages, people enjoy themselves.

(comma splice)

Traveling to other countries has a lot of advantages. People enjoy themselves.

(correct)

Returning to college can be a challenge making good grades is tough.

(run-on)

Returning to college can be a challenge, making good grades is tough.

(comma splice)

Returning to college can be a challenge. Making good grades is tough.

(correct)

The most important thing you can do is practice finding where one sentence ends and another one begins. Be patient with yourself; eventually doing this will seem simple.

Exercise 1

Read the following sentences that have been punctuated as one sentence. Then circle the word or phrase that begins the second sentence.

Examples:

I thought about her words (now) I understand.

In many cases, anger causes physical violence, (in some cases), it can even cause a fatality.

Version A

1. There is always plenty of food there are many types of main dishes and desserts.
2. My sister often took me with her this made me happy.
3. I like the park extremely well I can see the birds fly free.
4. The school police officer came in he asked if I needed any help.
5. Making mistakes is a part of life that's why children learn from their mistakes.
6. I admired the rookie basketball player he spent an hour working hard.
7. The players need to receive cheers for example, they will respond by playing well.
8. Smoking is harmful to people's health in fact, it can cause cancer.
9. Seeing a doctor can be expensive in some cases, many ill people cannot pay their medical bills.
10. I believe my father is right there would be more laziness in the world.
11. Teenage girls are not mature they do not know how to be good parents.
12. Young people need to learn that this is real life there is no turning back.
13. Eddie called her on the telephone then he asked her for a date.
14. The answer is simple we wanted to show our neighbors our patriotic spirit.
15. Parents buy pets for their children this is a great way to keep an only child company.
16. Playing in the snow was fun for everyone the children loved to make snow angels.
17. The nicotine in tobacco is addictive people just cannot seem to stop smoking.
18. The university has thousands of students many are on scholarships.

Version B

1. I painted my mother's house now it looks beautiful.
2. My bills never end I never seem to have enough money.
3. Communication is important to a group in fact, it is vital to working well together.
4. New parents need to have patience being a parent does get easier as time goes on.
5. In the evenings, he told me about the country store I listened very carefully.
6. In some countries, corruption keeps governments from caring for children then children start living in the streets.
7. People love to see movies they're relaxing.
8. We bought chips and salsa then we settled in and watched the ball game.
9. Having fun is a major part of a teenager's life in some cases, going out has to stop.
10. Pets do not come with manners they have to be taught.
11. Many people overcharge on their credit cards this happens quite often.
12. Finding a place to live can be difficult for teenage parents they might not have the money to move into an apartment.
13. For example, a young mother might be in a gang in most cases, she is not going to want to raise her child in this environment.
14. Dogs can help people stay in good health for instance, dogs can help lower blood pressure.
15. Living in a large city is an advantage that's what attracts new residents.
16. Edith and Francisco had twin boys both of the babies are doing well.
17. Randy worked many hours each week he wanted to provide for his family.
18. Missing a final exam results in a failing grade there are few exceptions to the rule.

Correcting Run-on Sentences and Comma Splices

The way to avoid run-ons and comma splices is to identify the spot where one sentence ends and the next one begins. Once you can identify an **independent clause, a group of words that stand alone or make sense when written alone,** you will find it easy to correct them. There are several ways to revise these sentences. Use a variety of correction methods to add interest to your writing.

Ways to Correct Run-on Sentences and Comma Splices

- Add a period at the end of each complete thought.
- Use a comma and a coordinate conjunction.
- Use a semicolon.
- Use a semicolon, a conjunctive adverb, and a comma.

Add a Period at the End of Each Complete Thought

The first and perhaps simplest step in correcting run-ons and comma splices is to punctuate each sentence one at a time. This means ending each sentence with a period and starting the next sentence with a capital letter. Practice doing this in the next exercise as well as in your own writing.

Exercise 2

Read the following sentences that have been punctuated as one sentence. Determine where one sentence ends and the next sentence begins. End the first sentence with a period, and begin the second sentence with a capital letter.

Example:

difficult. Growing

Having a baby at a young age is difficult, growing up fast is hard.

Version A

1. Jessie fell behind on the assignments she worked hard to catch up.

2. I often went to the gym every day now I go only three times a week.

3. I enjoy spending time with my family in fact, we plan to go on vacation together.

4. Going to college is important graduating is even more important.

5. I will finish all my assignments then I will have a good chance to pass my classes.

6. Gerard is a good friend he is always willing to help me out.

7. William hopes to graduate from college soon he has only four more classes to complete.

8. Rob loved the breathtaking view of the mountains he also felt the warmth of the sun.

9. Alex wanted to rest after work he turned off his cell phone.

10. At six A.M., the radio came on she did not want to start the day.

Version B

1. My little girl loves to draw pictures in fact, she even draws them on the walls.

2. Julio spent ten years doing drugs he does not touch them today.

3. I enjoy working at Costco the benefits are quite good.

4. After our first date, she told me she was married that changed everything.

5. We ordered hot wings and pizza then we rented a couple of movies.

6. Caffeine increases people's metabolism it helps them lose weight.

7. Throughout the world, many people are logging on to computers it is exciting.

8. My son finds the zoo very interesting he likes to go whenever possible.

9. Heather confronted challenges she did not just try to escape them.

10. Too much salt aggravates high blood pressure it can also cause loss of calcium.

Use a Comma and a Coordinate Conjunction

Another simple way to correct run-ons and comma splices is to make them into one compound sentence by adding a comma and a coordinate conjunction. Remember that coordinate means equal, so coordinate conjunctions can join two or more simple sentences. Work through the following exercise so you can practice doing this.

Note Refer to the following list if necessary.

Coordinate Conjunctions

for	but
and	or
nor	yet
	so

Exercise 3

Correct the following sentence-structure errors by adding a comma and a coordinate conjunction or just a coordinate conjunction if the comma is there.

Examples:

, for
My friends often go out to eat they enjoy each other's company.

for
My friends often go out to eat, they enjoy each other's company.

Version A

1. The military pays for my tuition and books I do not have to pay for anything.

2. People need to do the job well it's okay if it takes them a few minutes longer.

3. My wife is excited we are going to be parents.

4. The weather is turning warm that's great news.

5. Mariah received a puppy for her birthday she loves him very much.

6. Going to preschool can help children learn they often miss their parents.

7. Thirty years ago, picking up a hitchhiker was not unusual it's very dangerous today.

8. The leaves all fell from the tree that made it easier to see the mountains.

9. They needed to earn money for the band tour they did not have enough time.

10. Steven will have to pass all his classes he cannot play baseball.

Version B

1. I threw away all of my graded exams it's too late to find them now.

2. Growing up, my sister always teased me now we are best friends.

3. On the weekends, we often went to the lake we had a cookout under the stars.

4. Someone stole my wallet with all my credit cards this made me mad.

5. My friends talked me into going to the party then they did not go themselves.

6. Staying busy was just part of growing up then I grew up and had little extra time.

7. My children wanted to go outside they kept asking to play in the snow.

8. The sales associates at the store were sick in some cases, they even had to go home early.

9. We spent the weekend skiing that's what we really enjoy.

10. We needed to paint the inside of the house we would not be able to sell it.

Use a Semicolon

Another way to correct these sentence-structure errors is simply to use a semi-colon. Remember that most of the time when you use a semicolon, you could use a period. When you use a semicolon, the two sentences you are joining are often short.

Exercise 4

Correct the following sentence-structure errors by adding a semicolon. Do not capitalize the first word in the second sentence.

Example:

Police officers need to be very sharp⹁they have to outthink criminals.

Version A

1. Sara applied for the nursing program she wanted to change careers.

2. I enjoyed working in the science lab that helped me understand the course material.

3. Temptations were everywhere he refused to buy any drugs.

4. Liz could not study the radio was too loud.

5. Kurt saw the bus coming he sprinted down the street.

6. Airport security has improved inspectors are better trained.

7. The old bridge withstood the flood the newer one washed away.

8. Pigeons roosted on the power line no trees grew in the yard.

Version B

1. The governor was sworn into office her inaugural speech was optimistic.

2. Plant bulbs in the fall then they will bloom in the spring.

3. Rafe went to New York for six months he stayed for ten years.

4. The weather turned hot in Arizona wildfires erupted in the forests.

5. My cat Pinky loves his igloo home on the porch he sleeps there every night.

6. The car's engine sputtered twice then it stopped altogether.

7. They loved everything about the house for example, they liked the carpeting.

8. The furnace kept the house warm it ran day and night.

Use a Semicolon, a Conjunctive Adverb, and a Comma

Another good way for you to practice correcting these sentence-structure errors is to use a semicolon, a conjunctive adverb, and a comma. The punctuation is logical because what you are really doing is joining the sentences with a semicolon and setting off the conjunctive adverb with a comma. Remember that a conjunctive adverb is an adverb that functions as a transitional word between two or more simple sentences. Look at the following sentences.

The baby kittens were abandoned outside Petsmart they were soon found by employees. (run-on sentences)

The baby kittens were abandoned outside Petsmart; however, they were soon found by employees. (correct)

The run-on sentence is corrected by adding a semicolon and a conjunctive adverb. If the conjunctive adverb had been located somewhere else in the sentence, it still would have been set off by a comma. Look at the following sentence.

The baby kittens were abandoned in front of Petsmart; they were, however, soon found by employees. (correct)

Just remember that when a conjunctive adverb comes between two complete sentences (independent clauses), a semicolon comes at the end of the first sentence, and a comma follows the conjunctive adverb. Look at the following sentences that follow the same logic for punctuation.

My computer ran slowly I had high-speed Internet installed. (run-on sentences)

My computer ran slowly, as a result, I had high-speed Internet installed. (comma splice)

My computer ran slowly; as a result, I had high-speed Internet installed. (correct)

My computer ran slowly; I, as a result, had high-speed Internet installed. (correct)

Note Refer to the following list if necessary.

Frequently Used Conjunctive Adverbs

moreover	consequently
in addition	however
therefore	in fact
thus	nevertheless
	as a result
otherwise	
furthermore	

Now work through the following exercises that give you practice in correcting sentence-structure errors.

Exercise 5

Correct the sentence-structure errors in the following sentences by adding a semicolon, a conjunctive adverb, and a comma. More than one conjunctive adverb may be correct.

Example:

; therefore, **or** *;consequently,*
; as a result,
Martin lost his job␣he fell behind on all of his bills.

Version A

1. I got caught up on all of my bills then my car stopped running.

2. He ate the entire pie he was still hungry.

3. Being thirty pounds overweight is harmful it can cut years off a person's life.

4. I locked my keys in my car I had to call a locksmith.

5. Paddling the kayak proved to be dangerous he almost drowned.

6. Norm is a very considerate person he is a good friend.

7. Tanya quit her job she had to drop out of school.

8. Finding the best major can be a challenge completing the courses takes dedication.

Version B

1. Eating homemade chicken soup is healthy it can even reduce symptoms of a cold.

2. The young man became ill he called the doctor.

3. Cathy is a talented potter she even gathers her own clay.

4. Doing crossword puzzles kept her mind alert she became an expert at doing them.

5. Denise had a beautiful baby girl she decided never to do drugs again.

6. Dan was sent to prison he earned college credits.

7. The Amish are excellent cooks they're known for their apple pies.

8. The college students spent many hours studying now they are ready to graduate.

You will want to correct your run-on sentences and comma splices using all of these methods. Use variety. The most important building block you can have is to be able to identify simple sentences, punctuate them correctly, and then move on to other types of sentences.

 ## Summary

Writing simple and compound sentences without making serious errors such as run-ons and comma splices is extremely important in communicating your ideas to others. Identifying these sentence-structure errors and correcting them can give you the confidence and knowledge you need to move on to more complicated sentences. To summarize the tips given in this chapter on how to avoid errors in sentence structure:

- Identify the place where one sentence ends and the next sentence begins.
- Correctly punctuate these sentences using the following methods:

  Add a period at the end of each complete sentence, and begin the next sentence with a capital letter.

  Use a comma and a coordinate conjunction to link each complete sentence.

  Use a semicolon between each complete sentence.

  Use a semicolon, a conjunctive adverb, and a comma between each complete sentence.

Practice Test

Read the following paragraph that has many sentence-structure errors. Then take the test that follows by circling the best correction for each sentence.

(1) Our family camping trip to the Mogollon Rim provided a week of healthy, refreshing enjoyment. (2) Smog had blanketed the city, here smog was replaced with blue skies and white clouds. (3) We no longer had to fight for space on the crowded freeways and city streets we parked our camper under huge pine trees and walked wherever we wished. (4) We soon discovered a small stream it was just fifty feet from our campground. (5) The clear, crisp water flowed steadily, gently sprayed the nearby plants, and soothed our feet we walked upstream right through the middle of the creek. (6) The creek was too small for fishing, we soon discovered newly hatched, half-dollar-sized turtles. (7) We welcomed simply sitting on a rock next to the creek there in the warm sunshine we watched the baby turtles slowly walk by the edge of the water. (8) On the second day, we found blackberry bushes covered with ripe berries, one taste, and we decided to pick some to take back to camp. (9) That evening, we cooked them over the open campfire, the smell of the berries bubbling in the pan filled the air and blended with the sweet smell of pine trees. (10) We wrapped our thickened berries in tortillas and toasted them over the heat nothing had ever tasted so delicious. (11) The last day before heading home, we hiked several miles to the fire lookout tower, after climbing to the top, we were rewarded with the never-ending view of tall pine trees, oak trees, and exceptionally beautiful blue skies. (12) The next morning, we packed up our belongings and headed back to the city but at that moment we vowed to return again as soon as possible.

Circle the best correction for each sentence in the above paragraph.

1. a. correct as written
   b. healthy; refreshing
   c. healthy, and

2. a. correct as written
   b. city, but here
   c. city here

3. a. streets; so
   b. streets, so
   c. streets; so,

4. a. stream, it
   b. stream; it
   c. correct as written

5. a. feet, therefore, we
   b. feet, we
   c. feet; therefore, we

6. a. fishing; however, we
   b. fishing, we
   c. fishing, however, we

7. a. creek; and there
   b. creek, and there
   c. creek, there

8. a. berries; One
   b. correct as written
   c. berries. One

9. a. campfire, and
   b. campfire; and,
   c. campfire and the

10. a. heat, nothing
    b. heat, however,
    c. heat. Nothing

11. a. tower after
    b. tower, and after
    c. tower and after

12. a. city, but
    b. city; but
    c. city, but,

Writing Assignment

Write a single paragraph on one of the following subjects. Be sure to have a topic sentence, support sentences, and a concluding sentence. Be sure to avoid any sentence-structure errors.

1. Your biggest fear
2. Your greatest source of pride
3. Favorite or least favorite place to go on a date
4. Favorite season of the year
5. The most irritating person or thing you know
6. Your best or worst quality

Chapter 5

Using Sentence Variety for Better Paragraphs

Part 1

Complex Sentences

Objectives

- Understand complex sentences.

    Identify independent clauses.

    Identify dependent clauses.

- Combine simple sentences into one complex sentence.
- Punctuate complex sentences correctly.
- Compose effective complex sentences.

Previously, you learned to identify and write both simple and compound sentences. As you become more experienced in writing, you will want to use still other kinds of sentences to express your ideas. Learning to use other patterns will help you achieve more variety in and respect for your writing. A third major sentence pattern is called a **complex** sentence. The word "complex" does not mean that the sentence is harder to understand or more sophisticated. It just refers to the number of independent and dependent clauses a sentence has. The following will help you understand complex sentences.

Independent Clauses

To understand a complex sentence, you need to understand **independent clauses.** All complex sentences must have one independent clause that has a subject and a verb and can stand by itself.

Alexandra Demetrian

As you look at the above illustration, try to imagine a train roaring down the railroad tracks. The engine is pulling several boxcars behind it. If for some reason the engine and boxcars become disconnected, the engine will continue to move down the tracks. However, the boxcars will not move anywhere by themselves because they are dependent on the engine to move them from place to place. Working together, however, the engine and boxcars form an effective means of transportation. The independent clause (simple sentence) and engine are similar because they both function independently. A dependent clause (fragmented sentence) is like a boxcar because it must be linked to an independent clause (complete sentence). Independent and dependent clauses work together to form effective sentences. Study the following examples:

S   V
I took a nap.   One independent clause
                                                     (simple sentence)

        S   V
The Mustang stopped quickly.   One independent clause
                                                     (simple sentence)

        S   V
Swimming after work is refreshing for me.   One independent clause
                                                     (simple sentence)

        S   V
To earn an A in this class is my goal.   One independent clause
                                                     (simple sentence)

Dependent Clauses

A dependent clause also has a subject and a verb, but because it begins with a subordinator, it is like a boxcar. It cannot function by itself.

Frequently used subordinators:

after	because	since
although	before	though
as	even though	unless
as if	if	until
as long as	once	when

A dependent clause is only part of a sentence because it leaves the reader hanging, expecting another idea to complete the sentence. The dependent clause has to be linked to an independent clause (sentence) to make it complete. Study the following example:

One dependent clause (incomplete sentence)

When I finished planting my garden

Now combine this dependent clause with the independent clause (complete sentence) "I took a nap."

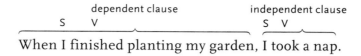

When I finished planting my garden, I took a nap.

The two clauses have been combined to make a **complex** sentence: **one independent** clause and at least **one dependent** clause. For a sentence to be labeled "complex" in grammar terms, it must have only one independent clause and at least one dependent clause. Notice how each of the independent clauses below can be combined with a dependent clause to make a **complex** sentence. Different combinations are possible.

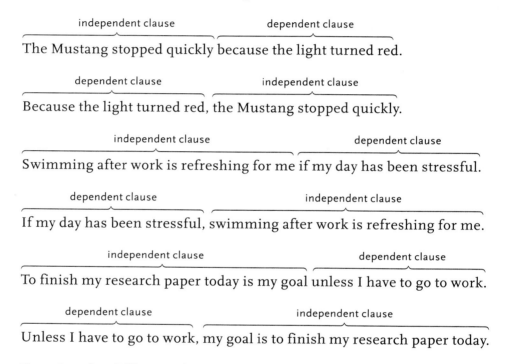

Knowing the difference between independent clauses (sentences) and dependent clauses (fragments) is very important. Fragments are sentence-structure errors. One important goal for you to reach in your writing is to write without using fragments. The next exercise will help you practice identifying complete sentences and fragments.

Exercise 1

Some of the following groups of words are sentences (independent clauses), and some are fragments (dependent clauses). Label the following clauses as sentences (S) or fragments (F).

Example:

   _F_   Because the ants are invading my house.

   _S_   The ants are invading my house.

Version A

_____ **1.** After we watch both of the movies.
_____ **2.** Jon and Jose worked hard all afternoon.
_____ **3.** Seventeen times he locked and unlocked the door.
_____ **4.** As long as he keeps locking and unlocking the door.
_____ **5.** One of my favorite teams will be playing a game this afternoon.
_____ **6.** If Americans stand together as "one nation under God."
_____ **7.** The tourists provide needed income for the small town.
_____ **8.** Because Luther plays football.
_____ **9.** Caring parents protect their children.
_____ **10.** As soon as you finish your homework.

Version B

_____ **1.** To earn money is every teenager's goal.
_____ **2.** Even though it is snowing outside.
_____ **3.** After I bought the tickets to the play.
_____ **4.** More and more people are visiting their relatives.
_____ **5.** When I finish my lunch.
_____ **6.** Because the recycle truck came early.
_____ **7.** Before the game, many fans have tailgate parties.
_____ **8.** Before I leave for my trip.
_____ **9.** If you want to go to the concert.
_____ **10.** Jared spent the summer with his grandfather.

Now you will want to look at some complex sentences so that you can identify which clauses are independent (can stand alone) and which clauses are dependent (cannot stand alone).

Exercise 2

Read the following complex sentences carefully, and in the space above each grouping, identify the independent and dependent parts of the sentence. Add a comma if the dependent clause comes first.

Example:

dependent

Because the teenagers were hungry∧

independent

they decided to send for two extra-large pizzas.

Version A

1. Once I have eaten my lunch I will have time to work in my garden.

2. I should try to get all of my assignments completed before I get too far behind.

3. While people ran down the stairs to escape the fire

firefighters went upstairs to fight the fire.

4. I will need to water my lawn if it does not rain today.

5. I do not wish to go to the concert unless you come with me.

6. Rick stayed at his friend's house until his mother came home from work.

7. After the World Trade Center was destroyed

Americans became more aware of their freedom.

8. Jim jumped back as the car veered into the gutter.

9. Even though Barb was late she showed up for class.

10. Fred bought a house after he moved to Dallas.

Version B

1. Chris spent the afternoon with his girlfriend

although he had a paper due on Monday.

2. Unless I get tickets for the game I will not be able to go.

3. Chelsea bought her books after she picked up her paycheck.

4. As the traffic came to a stop I worried about being late for work.

5. Rudy worked on the computer as long as he could concentrate.

6. When the puppy is hungry she sits patiently by her bowl.

7. My microwave oven made a buzzing sound before it went out.

8. Todd worked out for two hours

even though he was leaving for vacation the next day.

9. Once I turned in my paper I relaxed and watched a movie.

10. When you see the doctor perhaps he will give you a new prescription.

Using sentence variety is one of the keys to effective writing, so consciously altering your sentence patterns can result in more sentence variety. The previous exercises in this section gave you practice in recognizing dependent clauses in complex sentences. To have variety in your sentences means you must be able to use dependent clauses in different ways. The following examples are simple sentences.

Living in America gives me a sense of pride. People are free.

To vary your sentences, you might combine them into a complex sentence. For instance, you can simply make "people are free" a dependent clause by using "because." "**Because** people are free" is then combined with the first sentence. The resulting complex sentences follow:

Living in America gives me a sense of pride because people are free.

Because people are free, living in America gives me a sense of pride.

Combine the two simple sentences into one complex sentence by using the subordinator given. Use a comma after the dependent clause if it comes at the beginning of the sentence. Do not use a comma if the dependent clause comes at the end of the sentence.

Example:

I visited the Oregon coastline last year. I locked my keys in my car. (when)

When I visited the Oregon coastline last year, I locked my keys in my car.

I locked my keys in my car when I visited the Oregon coastline last year.

Version A

1. I was hungry and short on time. I went to a fast-food restaurant. (because)

2. The cell phone rang. I went outside to answer the call. (when)

3. We will eat in the cafeteria. The food is good. (as long as)

4. Sara helps her students. They were her own children. (as if)

5. Josh and Tara have separate checking accounts. They are married. (even though)

6. I will work on my research paper. I feel it is well written. (until)

7. I have a headache. I need to take the test. (although)

8. The weather clears up. The airplane will be grounded. (unless)

_____

_____

9. Justin attends college. He can stay on his parents' insurance. (as long as)

_____

_____

10. She sends another rude e-mail. I will tell her she is offending me. (if)

_____

_____

Version B

1. I complete the sale. I will close the shop. (once)

_____

_____

2. We go on vacation. We must pay our bills. (before)

_____

_____

3. We will practice our sentence patterns. They are outstanding. (until)

_____

_____

4. I will do it this way. You have a different idea. (unless)

_____

_____

5. I cut my finger. I needed more time to type my paper. (because)

_____

_____

6. We moved into our new house. We have had to repair the roof. (since)

_____

_____

7. We arrived at the gate. We heard the announcement to board our airplane. (as)

_____

_____

8. The homemade bread is done. We will enjoy it. (after)

_____

_____

9. Lydia buys the car. She can go see her father in Florida. (if)

_____

_____

10. The fish tank needed to be cleaned. We left for the weekend. (before)

_____

_____

Other Kinds of Dependent Clauses

Many complex sentences have another kind of dependent clause that can help you write with more variety. These dependent clauses begin with **other common subordinators.**

that	which	whose
where	who	

Study the dependent and independent clauses in the following sentences. You will notice that these types of sentences are already familiar to you.

> independent   dependent
> I read the book that I checked out of the library.

> independent   dependent
> Jason knows the directions which need to be changed.

> independent   dependent
> Carrie admired the players who started the game.

> independent   dependent
> David put his money in the same bank where his ex-wife banks.

> independent   dependent
> I met the artist whose painting hung in the main office.

Exercise 4

Underline the dependent clauses in the following sentences.

Example:

I really enjoyed the meal _that you cooked._

Version A

1. I have paid for the magazines that we delivered.

2. Please talk to the police officer whose patrol dog saved his life.

3. Harry wanted to watch the concert that was in the park.

4. You need to talk to the nurse who is taking care of your mother.

5. I took the pictures of the dog that won the ribbons.

6. Henry loves the park where he walks his dog.

7. We met in the building which had no windows.

8. They fined the man whose dog roamed the streets.

Version B

1. I gave you the questions that you need to study for the test.

2. I sent a letter to my cousin who lives in Bosnia.

3. We want to buy a new car that gets good gas mileage.

4. The manufacturer recalled all the cars that had defective brakes.

5. The parents liked the director who ran the daycare center.

6. I brought the blueprints that you ordered.

7. Shawn respected the neighbor whose lawn flourished.

8. Kentucky Fried Chicken is next to the building where I work.

Embedded Clauses

Sometimes dependent clauses that begin with **that, where, which, who,** or **whose** do not always end the sentence; rather, they can be embedded within a sentence. Remember the two previous sentences:

Living in America gives me a sense of pride. People are free.

Instead of using the subordinator "because," you can change the sentence "People are free" into "**where** people are free." A new complex sentence emerges.

Living in America, **where people are free,** gives me a sense of pride.

It is imperative to remember that the dependent clause must be placed right after the noun it explains. You could not say:

Living in America gives me a sense of pride where people are free.

(Incorrect)

It is not the **pride where people are free,** but rather it is **America where people are free.** Another pair of sentences can also show you how dependent clauses must be used correctly.

The captain and crew made it to their destination. They believed in themselves.

Combine the two sentences by subordinating "They believed in themselves" into "**who** believed in themselves." Two possible combinations follow, but only one is correct.

The captain and crew *who believed in themselves* made it to their destination. (Correct)

The captain and crew made it to their destination **who** believed in themselves. (Incorrect)

Obviously, only the first sentence is correct because the captain and crew, not the destination, believed in themselves.

Exercise 5

Now work through the following sentences, and determine which complex sentences contain material that is embedded correctly. Draw an arrow from the dependent clause to the noun it modifies. Circle the letter of the correct sentence.

Example:

The fish pond is in my backyard. I made the fish pond.

   a.   **The fish pond is in my backyard that I made.**

   (b.) **The fish pond that I made is in my backyard.**

Version A

1. The park becomes eerie and scary late at night. We play at that park during the day.

   a. The park becomes eerie and scary late at night where we play during the day.

   b. The park where we play during the day becomes eerie and scary late at night.

2. All items were put into the kiln to be fired. She made the items.

   a. All items were put into the kiln that she made to be fired.

   b. All items that she made were put into the kiln to be fired.

   c. All items were put into the kiln to be fired that she made.

3. Several students did their research in Spain. They were ready to write their papers.

   a. Several students did their research in Spain who were ready to write their papers.

   b. Several students who were ready to write their papers did their research in Spain.

4. Hercules is the best-known hero in Greek mythology. Hercules is the son of Zeus.

   a. Hercules, who is the son of Zeus, is the best-known hero in Greek mythology.

   b. Hercules is the best-known hero who is the son of Zeus in Greek mythology.

   c. Hercules is the best-known hero in Greek mythology who is the son of Zeus.

5. The little girl laughed at the silly clowns. Her mother took her to the circus.

   a. The little girl laughed at the silly clowns whose mother took her to the circus.

   b. The little girl whose mother took her to the circus laughed at the silly clowns.

6. The house won second place in the competition. It used energy-efficient appliances.

   a. The house won second place in the competition which used energy-efficient appliances.

   b. The house which used energy-efficient appliances won second place in the competition.

   c. The house won second place which used energy-efficient appliances in the competition.

7. I drove my sister's car to the shopping center. The shopping center was an hour away.

   a. I drove my sister's car that was an hour away to the shopping center.

   b. I drove my sister's car to the shopping center that was an hour away.

8. The neighborhood was filled with wonderful people from different ethnic backgrounds. I lived in that neighborhood.

   a. The neighborhood was filled with wonderful people where I lived from different ethnic backgrounds.

   b. The neighborhood where I lived was filled with wonderful people from different ethnic backgrounds.

   c. The neighborhood was filled with wonderful people from different ethnic backgrounds where I lived.

9. The residents of the care center adopted the baby kittens. Their mother had died.

    a. The residents of the care center whose mother had died adopted the baby kittens.

    b. The residents whose mother had died of the care center adopted the baby kittens.

    c. The residents of the care center adopted the baby kittens whose mother had died.

10. The baseball team welcomed the new pitcher. He had played in Mexico.

    a. The baseball team who had played in Mexico welcomed the new pitcher.

    b. The baseball team welcomed the new pitcher who had played in Mexico.

Version B

1. The applications for me and my twins are enclosed. The applications are in the envelope.

    a. The applications for me and my twins that are in the envelope are enclosed.

    b. The applications that are in the envelope for me and my twins are enclosed.

    c. The applications that are enclosed in the envelope are for me and my twins.

2. The desert plants did not bloom this spring. They did not receive any winter rain.

    a. The desert plants that did not receive any winter rain did not bloom this spring.

    b. The desert plants did not bloom this spring that did not receive any winter rain.

3. The storm rattled the windows. The storm came suddenly.

    a. The storm that came suddenly rattled the windows.

    b. The storm rattled the windows that came suddenly.

4. The children collected stickers. The stickers were colorful.

    a. The children that were colorful collected stickers.

    b. The children collected stickers that were colorful.

5. The fish were grown on a farm in Michigan. They were tasty.

    a. The fish were grown on a farm in Michigan that was tasty.

    b. The fish were grown on a farm that was tasty in Michigan.

    c. The fish that were tasty were grown on a farm in Michigan.

6. The strawberry plants needed to be replaced. They grew in my backyard.

    a. The strawberry plants that grew in my backyard needed to be replaced.

    b. The strawberry plants needed to be replaced that grew in my backyard.

7. The doctor ordered penicillin for Michael. The doctor was on call.

    a. The doctor ordered penicillin for Michael who was on call.

    b. The doctor who was on call ordered penicillin for Michael.

    c. The doctor ordered penicillin who was on call for Michael.

8. My neighbor often works in the yard. He is retired.

    a. My neighbor who is retired often works in the yard.

    b. My neighbor often works in the yard who is retired.

    c. My neighbor often works who is retired in the yard.

9. Snow fell on the ski runs. The snow enabled the resorts to open.

    a. The snow enabled the resort to open that fell on the ski runs.

    b. Snow fell on the ski runs that enabled the resort to open.

    c. The snow that fell on the ski runs enabled the resort to open.

10. The young writer's book was published. She received an award.

    a. The young writer whose book was published received an award.

    b. The young writer received an award whose book was published.

    c. The young writer's book was published who received an award.

Using Commas Correctly in Dependent Clauses

One more very important point you need to remember is that when you embed material into an independent clause (a sentence), you need to use commas correctly. If the material is needed to identify the noun in the sentence, you do not use commas.

I bought the puppy **that walked up to me and licked my hand.**

However, if the information is **NOT** necessary to identify the noun in the sentence, it is set off with commas.

My poodle, **who greets me at the door every afternoon,** is fed right away.

When a common noun is used, you have to decide if that information is important in identifying the noun. On the other hand, if *the noun is a proper noun, one that requires a capital letter, you will need to use commas.* Look at the sentence that uses "America," a proper noun.

Living in America, where people are free, gives me a sense of pride.

In the above sentence, America is a proper noun, so you do not need "where people are free" to identify America. Therefore, commas are necessary.

However, if the dependent clause is needed to identify the noun, you do not use commas. Study the following sentence.

Living in a country **where people are free** gives me a sense of pride.

This sentence does not require commas because living in just any country does not result in a sense of pride. It is only living in a country that is free that gives the writer a sense of pride.

Exercise 6

Read the following sentences, and add commas when needed.

Examples:

The plant that is wilting needs to be watered.

A Dream of Passion, **which the class watched, is a rare video.**

Version A

1. My cousin Leo who likes to swim spent his summer at the lake.
2. We fed the ducks the stale, leftover pretzels that were in the car.
3. David who had taken his friends for granted went to a movie by himself.
4. The young man who had taken his friends for granted went to a movie by himself.
5. My youngest sister who wanted to repay a favor gave me a present.
6. The man whose car was stolen was angry.
7. Richard whose car was stolen was angry.
8. I bought a painting which was quite expensive.
9. My clothes dryer which was only one year old needed to be repaired.
10. My brother bought a new truck that runs on alternative fuel.

Version B

1. My mother's house which had just been painted was damaged by the hailstorm.
2. Jenny bought David a shirt that was extremely expensive.
3. We often go to the secluded lake where we built our vacation cabin.
4. I have only one alarm clock that works.
5. Our 2003 family reunion which took place in New Mexico was the high point of my mother's summer.
6. The old shoe that my dog found belonged to my neighbor.
7. The test that was given to new employees was fair.
8. The clothes that were on sale were of good quality.
9. The Chevy truck that was in the wreck was in the repair shop.
10. Mack who was in the hospital was injured slightly in a car wreck.

Combine each pair of sentences into a complex sentence. You may have to omit a word or two in your new sentence. You will also probably have to add some words. Try to use a variety of subordinators from the earlier list on pages 225 and 232.

Example:

The young applicant was hired. He succeeded in the interview.

The young applicant who succeeded in the interview was hired.

Because the young applicant succeeded in the interview, he was hired.

The young applicant was hired because he succeeded in the interview.

Version A

1. We bought the hand lotion. It was on sale.

2. The salesperson will get a bonus. The salesperson pleases the customers.

3. Jim wants to buy a new car. The car must get good gas mileage.

4. The Siamese cat roams the neighborhood. The Siamese cat has a moody disposition.

5. Andrea invested money in Enron. The company went bankrupt.

6. Jimmy loved the peanut butter sandwiches. He ate them for lunch every day.

7. The bookmobile needed volunteers. It traveled to isolated little communities.

8. In the fall, the bright yellow aspen leaves fall to the ground. The ground is often covered with snow.

_____

_____

9. The letter was in the mailbox. He was waiting for the letter.

_____

_____

10. The clowns fell off the wheelbarrow. They were laughing hard.

_____

_____

Version B

1. A band member gave an outstanding performance. He played the snare drums.

_____

_____

2. My neighbor made a coconut pie. It was unbelievably delicious.

_____

_____

3. The folding tables fit into the trunk of my car. We could get them home.

_____

_____

4. The state quarters are educational. Many people save them.

_____

_____

5. The couple planned their wedding for April. They both had a vacation then.

_____

_____

6. Eric can make the team. He works hard.

_____

_____

7. The phone call came from the hospital. It was upsetting.

_____

_____

8. I always loved my mother's hot chocolate. She never used a ready-made mix.

_____

_____

9. The telephone drove everyone crazy. It rang seven times while we were eating.

_____

_____

10. The geese enjoyed the pond. They were from the frozen north country.

_____

_____

Exercise 8

Create a complex sentence by adding a dependent clause to each simple sentence.

Example:

The smoked oysters were delicious.
that we had for a snack
The smoked oysters ⌄were delicious.

Version A

1. The students passed the test.

2. Mark bought a new car.

3. Yesterday, Kevin mailed all the letters.

4. Maria applied for the job.

5. The mountain goats climbed to the top of the peak.

Version B

1. My neighbor hopes to have surgery.

2. The flood waters destroyed many homes.

3. James seldom missed a class.

4. The basketball game went into overtime.

5. The builders removed all the big beautiful trees.

Exercise 9

Now write your own complex sentences. Remember, you need one independent clause and one or more dependent clauses.

1. _____
   _____

2. _____
   _____

3. _____
   _____

4. _____
   _____

5. _____
   _____

 ## Summary

Using sentence variety in your writing means using simple, compound, and complex sentences. Complex sentences have one independent clause and one or more dependent clauses.

An independent clause, which is a simple sentence by itself, is a group of words that has a subject and a verb and can stand alone.

A dependent clause has a subject and a verb but cannot stand alone because it depends on more information to be a complete thought.

 ## Practice Test

Part A

The following paragraph contains only simple sentences. To make the paragraph more effective, you will want to use some sentence variety by combining simple sentences into compound or complex sentences. Follow the directions, and make your revisions in the actual paragraph. Then rewrite the revised paragraph in the space provided.

1. Join sentences #1 and 2 into one compound sentence using **and.**

2. Join sentences # 4 and 5 into one complex sentence by using **until** between the two sentences.

3. Join sentences #6 and 7 into one complex sentence by putting **As** before sentence 6.

4. Join sentences #8 and 9 into one compound sentence by using **so** between the two sentences.

5. Join sentences #10 and 11 into one complex sentence by putting **while** between the two sentences.

6. Combine sentences #13 and 14 into one sentence by using **and.**

7. Join sentences #15 and 16 into a compound sentence by using **but**.
8. Join sentences #17 and 18 into a compound sentence by using **however** between the two sentences. (Use a semicolon before **however** and a comma after it.)
9. Join sentences #19 and 20 into a complex sentence by using **after** before the first sentence.

(1) I kept my granddaughter's three-month-old boxer puppy for a full month. (2) He was a constant challenge. (3) His entire body was constantly in motion. (4) He never stopped. (5) He dropped on the floor and fell asleep within seconds. (6) He slept. (7) His limp tongue hung out of his mouth and onto the floor. (8) One time he noticed the open front door. (9) He instantly charged outside toward the busy street. (10) He was obviously enjoying himself. (11) Eight of us were trying to lure him back into the house. (12) We were frantic. (13) He teased us. (14) He came close enough for me to touch him. (15) He sprinted off. (16) Finally, we tempted him back with food. (17) He had exhausted us. (18) We had saved him from the traffic. (19) We got him back in the house. (20) We watched his every move.

Rewritten paragraph

_____

_____

_____

_____

_____

_____

_____

_____

_____

_____

_____

_____

_____

_____

Part B

Now look at the following paragraph, which contains only simple sentences. Combine them however you wish into compound and complex sentences. Make your revisions on the page. Pay close attention to punctuation.

Horace also found a way to torment my dogs. The doggie door was a mystery to him. He watched the other dogs going in and out. He stood there puzzled. He cocked his ears. He stood at attention. He watched the other dogs disappear through the block wall. The other dogs headed in the direction of the doggie door. He beat them there. He sat in front of the door. He blocked them. He sat there pleased with himself. I fed the dogs. Horace was an only dog at home. He thought all the food was for him. Horace went from dish to dish. He ate from every bowl. The other dogs were small. They could not stop Horace. He seemed to enjoy making their lives miserable.

 Writing Assignment

Select one of the following topics. Be sure to start with a strong topic sentence. Then add support sentences, and end with a concluding sentence. Edit carefully. Use sentence variety.

1. Favorite sport
2. Favorite athlete
3. Best job I have ever had
4. Body tattooing
5. Body piercings
6. Favorite food
7. Internet relationships

Part 2

Something to Think About, Something to Write About

Professional Essay to Generate Ideas for Writing

Just One Drop

Jim Reed, *Professor of Communication, Glendale Community College*

1   Hi, my name is Jim Reed. I'm Black from my father, White from my mother, **and** Jewish from my Russian grandmother. I look like any ordinary White guy, probably, although people would no doubt wonder where I got such a nice tan and where I had my lips done. (I guess it's my year!) Although a few drops of Black blood will qualify someone as Black, we ordinarily don't think of Black folks as being White because of the slight amount of white they may have inherited from some slave master's evening visit to the quarters "out back." Interesting, don't you think?

2   My grandfather and grandmother met each other in the middle 1890s. She (Rose) had just come here from Russia, and he (Emanuel) was given the task of teaching her to speak English. My grandfather used to joke about this, saying, "All I taught her how to say was 'I do.'" Mixed marriages in 19th century America were not really in vogue. I mean he wasn't an NBA player, a Hollywood entertainer, or anything like that, so they split for Montana where my granddad Emanuel opened up Reed's Tonsorial Parlor. In 1897, Rose gave birth to Fred Ward Reed, my father. At about the time he was learning to walk, his mother (my grandmother) Rose passed, leaving him and an older brother LeRoy (wouldn't you know it) totally in Emanuel's care.

3   Before too many years had gone by, my great-grandmother Catherine came out west to help her son Emanuel raise his children. I mention this only because I grew up in this exact same neighborhood and, yes, same house as well. Is it even possible for anyone to begin to understand this? Catherine was born into slavery, gave birth to Emanuel, held him on her shoulders in Wheeling, West Virginia, so he could see Abraham Lincoln parading by, and then years later she came out west to help Emanuel take care of Fred (my dad) down on the south side of Billings, Montana, in a little three-room home, the place that would someday be *my* home.

4   My father Fred decided to seek his fortune early in life. He quit school in the seventh grade, took off for Denver, and began a career in the boxing ring. He became a second—that's the guy who wipes the boxer off and catches his spit between rounds. After doing this for a couple of years, he lied his way into the Navy so he could defend his country and help with the WWI effort.

He became a cook because a black man at that time could only serve in the kitchen or in a hot dirty engine room. He also excelled in the ring, almost becoming the lightweight champion of the Navy. I have since found out what a great accomplishment that really was. We won the war, and my dad emerged as the "Dixie Kid." I still have his fight pictures to show that few of his offspring have ever looked as fit.

5   During the next few years, my dad collected stories that would be told to us until the day he died. I remember going home with a tape recorder one summer just so we could spend a week talking about his life. Full of my newfound "Black pride," I asked him what it was like growing up as a "Black" man. He immediately corrected me and said, "You show some respect. The word is 'colored.'" My mind shot back to the time when I had unsuspectingly called someone "boy," and he, overhearing my shrill voice, collared me with his strong hands, furrowed his brow, and ever so sternly pursed his lips and growled, "Don't you ever use that word around here again!" I never did.

6   I guess I might say that he taught me quite a bit. He became a preacher in the early 1920s, went back to college in Los Angeles, plastered houses, and held street meetings. I will forever remember his honesty. He often remarked that he "would never want a shoe string that belonged to someone else." I also remember his listening to the radio, to the news, and to how a Negro had driven his car at a high rate of speed into a Ku Klux Klan meeting. He threw his head back, laughed, and delightedly exclaimed, "Amen, hallelujah!" Sometimes we would go to the baseball game in the evening and sit up there in the cigar smoke and the smell of beer. Dad used to holler, "Get the water hot" or "You bums, go take a shower!" He would whisper to me to root for that colored player over at shortstop. (His name was Pablo Bernard. We yelled for another Dominican, Chico Fernandez, as well.) One time a man sitting next to us muttered gruffly, "God damn it anyway." Although I remember reacting by looking away, dad quickly put his arm around the gentleman, looked him straight in the eye, and said, "You're talking about the best friend I have."

7   My dad lived his belief in God. I could begin my dad virtually anywhere in the Bible, and he could quote until the last willing listener retired or requested he stop, but he never preached at anything except small fundamentalist evangelical churches on the bad side of town. Sometimes he would start with a drunk on the street, telling him how Jesus had died for him, and that would begin a church. The African Methodist Episcopal church wanted him to come aboard and be a headliner, but he stayed with a predominantly White denomination. Today, I truly believe that he thought our family would gain acceptance and someday even *be* White. I've learned, however, that Sunday remains the most segregated day of America's week.

8   I spent a lot of time with my dad, and I watched his interaction with other people. However, it wasn't until later that I realized that watching people and events as I matured definitely influenced how I would come to view the world. Today I use the word phenomenology to explain how each of us sees and participates in a totally separate reality. My father preached forgiveness on the one hand, but then on the other, he taught me to defend myself and even went so far as to give me a bulldog—Gus—for protection when I entered the

first grade. Gus went with me everywhere, and there were few Mexicans or Whites on my block who had not dealt with or seen his rage. I remained safe until he succumbed to a very strong poison after spending years as my loyal companion and constant bodyguard.

9   I really did not like to fight, but my dad erected a punching bag in the basement, an additional room my brothers and sisters had dug out as our family expanded. He told me I didn't have to run from anyone or be called names—ever—as he made that bag whiz so fast that it disappeared into a blur. I grew to hate being called "Nigger." I remember one time especially when a kid named Eddie Lucas followed me home from school and chanted in a sing-song manner the words "Nigger, nigger, nigger." As he rode his bike by mine, I placed a relatively sturdy stick in his front spokes. I could not believe what I had set in motion. There was little need to turn around and see his misfortune as the racket from the pavement said it all. I have never ridden so furiously in my life. Upon my arrival at home, the phone immediately rang, and my mom called out, "Fred." I cringed in the next room—knowing the pain that could come from his hands. I recall him asking Eddie's mom what he had done to me. A long silence followed as the distraught mother explained—I'm sure—Eddie's remarks and his ensuing encounter with the asphalt. Dad did not say much, not even a "We're sorry." He simply hung up the phone. No, we never ever talked about it again, not once.

10   My mom experienced a little different world. She hated it when I brought things home from school that asked for "race." She would always complain and mumble, "None of their business," and then she would write "American." I guess she taught me not to talk about *it,* and so I never really did, except in times of crisis. A few years ago, I looked down in my father's casket, and I couldn't believe *it*–he really was Black. I never really saw him that way when I hugged him or cursed him (always to myself and at a safe distance). My brother Fred (another Dr. Reed) even talked about *it* during the funeral when he gave the eulogy. He spoke of how proud dad was, how he always stood up for principles, and how some of them may not have always made the most sense. My mom grumbled words under her breath to the effect of, "I knew he'd have to bring *that* up," but then mom always made sure her White friends over at the nicest church in town heard through the grapevine that one of us had recently received a doctorate or done well in business, or her grandchildren had done this or that, and there has been a lot of this or that, God knows.

11   These special circumstances, compelling me to offer up this invisible information, seemed to occur almost daily, even flowing over to my relationships with women. I remember telling a girl on the first date (if she did not know my family) that I was part black. (Thinking, of course, that she could be The One.) Today I'd probably say something smart like, "Do you want to know which part?" As a teenager, such disclosure presented tense moments and, I have since learned, left me quite vulnerable. I remember sharing this information with an attractive young white girl whom I would later marry. She replied, "That's not a problem, but don't ever tell anyone in my family." Well, I've always said, "Bad news doesn't get better with time." Before my parents had signed an under-age consent form for me to marry, *it*

began germinating into a formidable, if not insurmountable, block in the relationship. I recall that years later she looked at me and said, "I can't believe *it*. Sometimes you're black. I mean *really* black!" It must have been tremendously frustrating for her. At various points during the relationship, she would grow angry with my discussing race and intercultural issues and explode with, "Jim, does everyone have to know?"

12   When people look at this golden brown face and arms, nice full lips, and graying black hair, they have no idea what I'm about. No one can even begin to understand some of my feelings or actions because my siblings and I remain more than a bit confused ourselves. Today I'm pissed at White people because at a grievance hearing yesterday I defended a marginalized colleague from the dominant culture. However, tomorrow I'll probably nail this black kid in my class because he could have done two grades higher but chose to be hip instead. I arrived at a Southwestern community college as a "White" sixteen years ago but soon changed to "Black" and even became the Black Student Union advisor. At my brother's university, he wrote down "Jewish" because, as he explains, he gets several more holidays. He also believes himself to be an absolute genetic miracle, a member of the Black/Jewish power movement if you will. My other brother screams at people on the Los Angeles freeway calling them "fucking niggers." He and his very white wife will never forgive me for spilling *the beans* to his five children several years ago. One sister has asked me not to tell her husband—number three or four. (I'm not sure, but it doesn't matter anyway. They just divorced.) The other sister's former husband says, "Your brothers and sister may be niggers, but my kid's mom isn't."

13   Last year a census worker came up to me in the yard—since I had refused to send the form back—and asked if I would agree to answer a few questions. I felt like giving her the line from the movie "A Few Good Men" when Jack Nicholson explodes with "You can't handle the truth." Well, I refrained. She came to the part where she asked "race," and I stood there straight-faced and said, "African American." She didn't have any idea what to do. There were, no doubt, fewer categories in her mind than on that form. Her dumbfounded reaction told me she simply had nowhere to place me; our brief interaction would nonetheless be a source of interesting comment later around her dinner table as she recounted the day's activities.

14   If I could today change anything about my life, especially the early years, it would not be the actual events as much as my reactions to them. When my mom, who was older than the other parents, came to visit school without make-up or a wedding ring, and with her beautiful long hair gathered into that tight "Christian" roll around the back of her head, I was embarrassed. Today, however I would beam with pride, run to her, and hold her tight. Other times, my friends, who waited for me to emerge from my house and walk to school, looked through the kitchen window and saw my family kneeling around the breakfast table praying. When they asked me what we were doing, I laughed off their comments and provided no answers for their disturbing questions. Today, I would tell them, "Not only that, but we pray before we eat, after we eat, before we go to bed at night, and whenever someone needs healing." Quite frankly, I would revel in their stares of amazement.

15   The family pictures in my father's top drawer found little or no explanation either. Today, I wish that all of us—even mom and dad—could have shared our peculiar circumstance of color, this lifelong bond, and come to some awareness and acceptance, maybe even a partial understanding of how we should cope. I spent some of my early life unwittingly wishing I was someone else, maybe with younger, more understanding parents, a nicer home in a better part of town, a newer car, and money, yes, money. I wanted anything but what fortune had thrown my direction. These experiences, however, have made me the person I am today, grateful for everything I went through with my mom and dad even though I did not realize at the time how these events would impact my life and fill me with pride for everything—especially *that one drop.*

Understanding Words

Briefly define the following words as they are used in this selection.

1. vogue
2. phenomenology
3. succumbed
4. evangelical
5. eulogy

Writing Assignment

After reading through this selection, think about your own childhood and upbringing. As you work on this writing assignment, think about the events in your life that make you the person you are today. Writing about real events will give you the specific examples and details that you need to develop an interesting, believable paragraph.

Write a well-developed paragraph. Be sure to start with a topic sentence, include 8 to 12 support sentences, and end with a concluding sentence.

1. What makes your family unique from other families?
2. What makes you proud or ashamed of your mother or father?
3. What one person influenced you the most in your life?
4. How would you describe your ethnicity?
5. What do you like or dislike most about yourself?
6. How would you describe one person who played an important role in raising you?
7. If you could change one thing about your childhood, what would it be?
8. As a child, what did you do to defend yourself from others?

Part 3

Student and Professional Paragraphs

A Pregnancy That Changed My Life

Valerie Lewis, *Student*

When my daughter was born on September 17, 1987, she made a change in my life that I thought would never happen. When she was born, I was on drugs, and she was born with drugs in her system. The night that I delivered her, I had just gotten finished doing drugs before going home. I went into labor, and when I went to the hospital and the nurse asked all the important questions about my history and about drugs, I never lied, and I told her what kind and the last time I used. When the doctor was called in and was told what I had done, he sat at the end of the table with his nurses, and during the delivery, he let me do all the work as a punishment, and only when he saw her head did he get up and help. I visited my baby every day she was in the nursery, wishing I could just hold her. I felt so bad that I had fed her drugs for nine months of her life. I prayed to God to ask Him to guide me and help me to overcome this because my child needed me, her mother. She was fine with everything she should have to live: fingers, toes, hands, eyes, mouth, and ears. I continued to make some major mistakes. When the Department of Children and Family Services stepped into our lives, I thought that would be the end of me. I tried to end my life because I did not know how to stop, but looking at her made me realize that she had no one else, and this made me try harder. She was the reason I decided to continue to live and try everything that was remotely possible to change my life around. I remember the night that she began to cry, and nothing would stop her. I did not know what to do, but I remember the doctor telling me, "She is fine for now, but later on in life remember what you fed her for nine months." Today she is a straight A student, and now 14 years later, I am drug free. I wonder where I would be if it had not been for her.

Questions on Form

1. What is the main idea in the paragraph?

2. What details support the idea in the topic sentence?

3. How does the last sentence provide a sense of closure?

Questions on Content

1. What was the mother doing while she was pregnant?

2. What did the doctor and nurse do during the first part of the delivery?

3. What was the major change in the author's life after the birth of her child?

4. How does the author feel about her daughter now?

Proud to Be a Woman

Patrina Begay, *Student*

In my Navajo culture, being a woman is a very special and valuable gift. It shows that we are strong enough to take on the world because we give birth, nourish, and comfort our future generations. We can overcome any obstacles because we've experienced pain, happiness, and sacrifices from our daily lives. We as women deal with many obstacles in our daily lives, so we soon learn how to deal with our problems and solve them. Doing that makes us stronger. By knowing how to cook or to deal with our emotions and by getting respect, we can walk down a street on any given day and just be happy and proud for who we are and what we know. When we move out on our own, we really have nothing to worry about because we know the basics. Just knowing how to cook is a huge thing, especially to my native people. My people say, "You are not a woman until you know how to provide for yourself."

Questions on Form

1. In the topic sentence, what is the topic? What is the direction?

2. Underline two complex sentences.

3. How does the author effectively conclude the paragraph?

Questions on Content

1. What makes the author proud to be a woman?

2. Why is moving out no big deal for women in her culture?

3. Why can women overcome obstacles?

4. What is the author's ethnic background?

My Life

Benny Alvarez, *Student*

The thing that I dislike most about my life is that I did not take advantage of my educational opportunities when I was younger. The only things I cared about in high school were parties, girls, and being a tough guy. All I did was hang around a bunch of knuckleheads that liked to do drugs and get into trouble. I think I was the only one who actually carried books home and did homework, but I did all of that just to pass my classes. I could have excelled in school if I had not wasted my time. I was very angry with myself when I saw that my high school grade point average was only a 2.17. However, during my first semester at a local community college, I received an average of 3.25. At least I knew that I was not a complete idiot. My only problem now is choosing a major. There are not many disciplines that are appealing to me. The only thing that I have ever wanted to do is to be a police officer. If I had cared more about my education as a teenager, my life would be a lot easier now. I think, though, that if I can graduate from college, I eventually will be able to meet my goal of being a police officer.

Questions on Form

1. What is the topic sentence?

2. How does the author support this idea?

3. In the next-to-last sentence, what key words link back to the topic sentence?

Questions on Content

1. What did the author care about when he was in high school?

2. What is his biggest problem today?

3. What is his major goal?

Excerpt from Mother Tongue

Amy Tan

Recently, I was made keenly aware of the different Englishes I do use. I was giving a talk to a large group of people, the same talk I had already given to half a dozen other groups. The nature of the talk was about my writing, my life, and my book, *The Joy Luck Club*. The talk was going along well enough until I remembered one major difference that made the whole talk sound wrong. My mother was in the room, and it was perhaps the first time she had heard me give a lengthy speech, using the kind of English I have never used with her. I was saying things like, "The intersection of memory upon imagination" and "There is an aspect of my fiction that relates to thus-and-thus"—a speech filled with carefully wrought grammatical phrases, burdened, it suddenly seemed to me, with nominalized forms, past perfect tenses, conditional phrases, all the forms of standard English that I had learned in school and through books, the forms of English I did not use at home with my mother.

Understanding Words

Briefly define the following words as they are used in this selection.

1. nominalized forms

2. past perfect tenses

3. conditional phrases

Questions on Form

1. What is the main idea of this paragraph?

2. How does Tan support this main idea?

Questions on Content

1. What made Tan feel self-conscious when she was giving her speech?

2. What does she realize about the "Englishes" she uses?

3. What was her talk about?

Excerpt from The Seasons of a Man's Life

Daniel J. Levinson

The process of separation from parents continues over the entire life course [of a child's life]. It is never completed. It is thus more accurate to speak not of separation but of changes in the degree and kind of attachment in various key periods. During the first two or three years of life, the child establishes the distinction between self and non-self. This brings about an initial separation from the mother, though the attachment remains very strong, and she provides an external centering for his life. At age five or six, with the shift from early to middle childhood, the boundaries of the child's life expand beyond the household to include new relationships and institutions. An adolescent's world is more complex, but it is still primarily a pre-adult world, centered in the family and in peer groups. Adults figure as authorities, teachers, helpers and enemies but not as peers. The boy may at times enter their world, but he is not of it.

Questions on Form

1. What is the main idea of the paragraph?

2. In what order is the material presented?

3. In the last sentence, the author says that the boy may enter the adult world but "he is not of it." How does this relate to the topic idea?

Questions on Content

1. What separates the two- to three-year-old from the mother?

2. According to the author, when does middle childhood begin?

3. How does the adolescent's world become more complex?

Part 4

Fragments

Objectives

- To identify and correct fragments that lack a subject or a complete verb.
- To identify and correct fragments that have a subject and verb but do not make sense on their own.

As you have already learned, sentences must have both a subject and a verb and must make sense on their own. A fragment, on the other hand, is missing one of these parts and, therefore, is incomplete. In this section of the text, you will first look at fragments that lack a subject or a verb, and then you will look at fragments that have a subject and a verb but do not make sense on their own.

Fragment That Lacks a Subject or a Complete Verb

Verb but No Subject

Correcting the following fragments is easy. You simply need to **add a subject** that tells **who** "told" or **what** "fell."

Told many wonderful stories	(fragment with no subject)
Maria told many wonderful stories.	(The word **Maria** tells who told the stories.)
Fell to the floor	(fragment with no subject)
The book fell to the floor.	(The word **book** tells what fell to the floor.)

In the next sentence, you also need to say who was skating on the ice, but with an **-ing** verb form, you must also include some form of the verb **be** (*is, am, are, was,* or *were*). Also, see the example below where "skating on the ice" becomes the subject.)

Skating on the ice	(fragment with no subject)
Maria was skating on the ice.	(The word **Maria** tells who was skating on the ice.)

Subject but No Complete Verb

Correcting the following fragments means **adding a verb** that shows what the subject does or explains the subject.

In the next sentence, you simply need to add a verb to show what the unfinished project did.

The unfinished project   (fragment with no verb)

The unfinished project lay untouched.   (**Lay** tells what the project did.)

In the next sentence, **skating** is used as a noun. The **-ing** form of a verb can function as a noun and as such becomes the subject in the next sentence.

Skating on the ice   (fragment with no verb)

Skating on the ice made the children happy.   (**Made** shows what skating did.)

In the next example, **to** is used before a verb. **To** before a verb signals an infinitive, and an infinitive cannot function as a verb in the sentence. Rather, it is a verb form that can function as a noun and thus can be the subject of the sentence.

To skate on the ice   (fragment with no verb)

To skate on the ice was difficult.   (**Was** explains that skating on the ice was difficult.)

To correct these last two types of fragments (verb forms with an **-ing** verb or **to** before the verb), you can simply link the fragment to a complete sentence. The **-ing** verb form, however, must refer to the subject that follows it.

Skating on the ice, Tamika often thought about her future goals.

To skate on the ice, Tamika had to buy warmer clothes.

It is very difficult to correct fragments unless they are written within a larger piece of work. Look at the following word groups and see if you can determine why each group of words in bold is a fragment. Then notice how sentences are formed by adding a subject or a verb.

Example #1

Rick goes to school in the mornings. **Then goes to work in the afternoons.**

An easy way to correct this is to **add a subject.**

Rick goes to school in the mornings. Then he goes to work in the afternoons.

Example #2

There are some things that good parents have to do every day. **Fix nutritious food for their children.**

One way to correct this is to **add a subject** to the fragment.

There are some things that good parents have to do every day. **They** fix nutritious food for their children.

Example #3

My employer wanted me to work overtime. **To clean the tables after everyone left.** He offered to pay me overtime.

One way to correct this is to **add a verb and other words if needed** to the fragment.

My employer wanted me to work overtime. To clean the tables after everyone left **would take several hours.** He offered to pay me overtime.

Note You might also combine the last two sentences. The combined sentence might read, "To clean the tables after everyone left would take several hours, but he offered to pay me overtime."

Example #4

Often, when you are writing your paragraphs, you will want to edit to eliminate fragments. For example, if you found the following fragment, "Doing something fun," you could correct it by adding a verb, but if the verb is already there in your writing, you might just make the **-ing** verb the subject of the next sentence. Doing this eliminates an unneeded "it" and forms a stronger sentence.

Doing something fun. It is a way to reduce stress.

Doing something fun is a way to reduce stress.

Example #5

Sometimes you will want to correct the **-ing**-verb-form fragments and the **to-**before-the-verb fragments by linking them to a complete sentence.

Rearranging the furniture, Tasha slipped on a rug and twisted her knee.

In the morning outside the lumberyard, the unemployed men stood patiently, **waiting for jobs.**

The only way to avoid fragments in your writing is to write continually and to edit over and over again. The most important thing to remember is that there is no single way to correct fragments. It is up to you to find the most effective method. Sometimes having someone point out certain patterns that you have in your sentences can help you the most. There can be no substitute, however, for learning to write effective simple sentences and then combining them into strong compound and complex sentences.

Exercise 1

Now look through the following sentences and fragments, and decide which one is a fragment because it lacks a subject or a verb. Then underline the fragment, and think about possible corrections. After you do this, look below to see some possible corrections.

Part 1

1. Answering cell phones in public restaurants. This can be annoying.
2. To watch football games on the weekend. This kept him from getting exercise.
3. I loved to listen to my professor. Talk about Greek gods and their many adventures.

4. The job seemed simple. All I had to do was answer the telephone and schedule routes for the driver. On Fridays received a paycheck.

5. The Fire Museum had many displays. Antique ladder trucks and horse-drawn fire trucks. We enjoyed them all.

6. The new high-speed Internet cables sat in the box. Wondered if they would ever be connected. I was paying for the service, but my husband and I had not had time to put the package together.

7. Oatmeal is healthy for the heart. Eating it every morning. Esther reduced her bad cholesterol by twenty points.

Part 2

Study the following corrections to the above exercise.

1. Answering cell phones in public restaurants. ~~This~~ can be annoying.

2. To watch football games on the weekend. ~~This~~ kept him from getting exercise.

3. I loved to listen to my professor. ~~Talk~~ *talk* about Greek gods and their many adventures.

4. The job seemed simple. All I had to do was answer the telephone and schedule routes for the drivers. On Fridays, ∧*I* received a paycheck.

5. The Fire Museum had many displays. Antique ladder trucks and horse-drawn fire trucks∧. *were beautiful* We enjoyed them all.

6. The new high-speed Internet cables sat in the box. *I w*~~W~~ondered if they would ever be connected. I was paying for the service, but my husband and I had not had time to put the package together.

7. Oatmeal is healthy for the heart. Eating it every morning∧. *, Esther* ~~Esther~~ reduced her bad cholesterol by twenty points.

Now, you will want to practice correcting some fragments yourself. Try working through the next exercise.

Exercise 2

Underline the fragment in each grouping, and then correct it by adding a subject or a verb, or correct it by joining it with another sentence.

Version A

1. Keeping track of receipts. It is important when doing income tax. Being prepared makes the job easier.

2. Sam and Marilyn quickly came into the room. They had found the information everyone was anxiously anticipating. Then began making phone calls.

3. Andrew spoke about the harmful results of violence. Said violence can only lead to trouble.

4. To register for classes. Brittany had to talk to an advisor. She was looking forward to the semester.

5. Every summer, the children went to the Boys and Girls Club. By summer's end, they had planted and nurtured their vegetable garden. Picking the tomatoes, corn, carrots, and green beans had been fun. Then made soup.

6. The little boy was afraid of the buzzing creatures outside. The big yellow and black bumblebees. They especially scared him.

7. I am thankful for many things. Sometimes I think about how little others own. To have a warm house and loving family. That makes me feel secure.

8. My neighbors were always doing nice things for my family. They took care of our dogs when we went on vacation. Also kept an eye on our house so that burglars did not break into our home.

9. Everyone looks forward to going on vacation. Going on cruises or going camping. It can be exciting.

10. Jeong wanted to visit her uncle in Canada. Leaving her family behind. She boarded the airplane in New York.

Version B

1. Ward wanted to impress his girlfriend. Took her flowers.

2. To build up his resume. This would help him get a good job. Volunteering at the hospital would be his first step.

3. The children loved going to the zoo. Liked watching the gorillas and crocodiles, and they also loved to feed the animals in the petting zoo.

4. Every day Elmer worked out at the gym. Even worked out on holidays. Nothing could keep him away from the weights.

5. Sara started going to the gym with Elmer. Swimming laps in the pool after a workout. It was the best part.

6. Paul has a job interview on Thursday. Needs to be sure he is dressed appropriately.

7. I am not rich myself, but I will donate every bit of clothing and all the canned foods that I can for the homeless. I hope to make their day somewhat better. Having warm clothes to wear. It is important for everyone.

8. Frances loved her job as a medical doctor. She did not even mind being on call during the weekends. During the week, making sick children well. It made her realize she was doing something special.

9. Buying lunch in the cafeteria every day. That ended up being expensive.

10. Trying to outrun the police, the suspects stole a car and crashed it into a bridge. The vehicle burst into flames. The crash was fatal. Killed them instantly.

Fragment That Has a Subject and a Verb but Does Not Make Sense on Its Own

Sometimes a clause has a subject and a verb, but it does not make sense on its own, making it a fragment. It is a fragment because the thought is left unfinished. These sentences start with one of the same subordinators that you learned when you studied complex sentences.

after	because	since
although	before	though
as	even though	unless
as if	if	until
as long as	once	when

As you recall, you joined these unfinished thoughts with complete sentences, forming complex sentences. Also, note that a dependent clause (fragmented thought) sometimes goes at the beginning of a sentence and sometimes goes at the end.

Before you fill the birdfeeder	(fragment)
Before you fill the birdfeeder, you should clean it.	(linked with sentence)
You should clean the birdfeeder before you fill it.	(linked with sentence)

Because an earthquake erupted. (fragment)

Because an earthquake erupted, people had to leave the city. (linked with sentence)

People had to leave the city because an earthquake erupted. (linked with sentence)

Note If the idea with the subordinator introduces the sentence, it is followed by a comma. If the idea with the subordinator ends the sentence, no comma is needed.

Someone might have taught you simply to drop the subordinator, but this solution just leaves you with simple sentences and takes away the variety you can achieve by using dependent clauses.

Some subordinators may be used as the subject of a sentence and may be correct if the sentence is asking a question.

that	which	whose
where	who	

Unless the sentence is a question, however, you still have a fragment. Look at the following example.

I came with a friend. **Who left the party early.** (fragment)

Who left the party early is not meant as a question, so it needs to be combined with the first sentence or made into a sentence by itself.

I came with a friend who left the party early. (linked with a sentence)

I came with a friend. He left the party early. (substituted a pronoun)

I told him that I did not want to go. **That I was busy.** (fragment)

I told him that I did not want to go, that I was busy. (linked with sentence)

These examples show that often you can easily combine the dependent clause with a complete sentence. Other times, you will want to replace the subordinator with a noun or pronoun.

Exercise 3

Correct the fragments in the following exercise by joining a fragment to a complete sentence or by replacing a subordinator with a noun or pronoun.

Example:

She drank the carrot juice. ~~That~~ *that* was in the refrigerator.

She drank the carrot juice. ~~That~~ *It* was in the refrigerator.

Version A

1. If you are away from other people and you need help. A cell phone could save your life.

2. While Wes was driving the bus. He slammed on the brakes. Thankfully, no one was hurt.

3. Wal-Mart built a new shopping center. Which was just down the street from me. I finally shopped there last weekend.

4. My instructor gave us two tests. Which were very hard. I am in college, though, to learn as much as possible.

5. Going out and having a good time is important to many people. Who spend many hours at their jobs. This way, they can relax and return to work refreshed.

6. If I had the ideal job. I would have plenty of money to spend on my family and myself. First, I would buy a new home with green grass in the backyard.

7. After one year of marriage, they talked about buying a house. That was outside the city. For the next year, they saved as much money as they could for a down payment.

8. Before the winter is over. I get to celebrate Valentine's Day with the ones I love the most. We often go out to eat and then watch a movie.

9. I told him that I did not want to go. That I was busy. He understood and thanked me for being truthful with him.

10. During recess, the little boy bought two Popsicles. He ate one and kept the other one in his back pocket. Until it began to drip onto the floor.

Version B

1. Danielle made banana bread and took it to work. Because she did not bring a knife. She did not have any way to slice the bread.

2. I get to travel across the country. Which is absolutely beautiful.

3. I did not understand what my mother meant. Until I listened to everything she had to say. Then I slowly realized how much I appreciated her.

4. When I was a teenager, spending time with my family was sometimes a chore. After I grew up. I realized how much those times meant to me.

5. Jim was an expert at upholstering furniture. He often showed me some of his little secrets. Who also taught me how to make beaded vests.

6. I sympathize with my neighbors. Whose dog is missing. They are not sure how he got out.

7. Sometimes we did not have anything important to do. On those days, we packed up the kids and went to the beach. Which always seemed like an exciting place to go.

8. After I get out of the doctor's office. I will still have time to do my errands.

9. Many people have stress in their lives. Doing something they like to do. It is an ideal way to reduce stress.

10. I will always remember the stream of water and the small green and blue fish. That swam in the water. Squirrels lived in the trees and jumped from branch to branch. It was like a mini forest.

Summary

As you edit your sentences and paragraphs, you will want to eliminate fragments because they often keep your meaning from being clear. As you write, be aware of groups of words that lack a subject or a verb as well as groups of words that have both a subject and a verb but do not make sense on their own. Correcting these fragments often means adding a subject or a verb or combining them with other sentences.

Practice Test

Read the following paragraph carefully, and then answer the questions below.

(1) Working as a team. (2) The Phoenix Zoo has tried hard to recreate the natural environment that their animals would experience in the wild. (3) For example, one exhibit has a large grassy area or savannah. (4) As it is called in Africa. (5) Even the trees are similar to the ones that grow in Africa. (6) Because the giraffes eat the leaves as high up on the trees as their long necks can reach. (7) The zookeepers actually tie freshly cut leafy branches to the bottoms of these trees. (8) The wild giraffes roam there along with the other similar animals. (9) Including sleek gazelles and waterbucks. (10) These animals graze on the thick grass. (11) That is

green year round. (12) Compatible animals such as vultures and ostriches. (13) They are also in this savannah, living together as they would in Africa. (14) Their water supply is a small man-made stream. (15) Running through this three- to four-acre piece of land. (16) A small, chain-link fence separates them from the zebras. (17) Whose home extends the grassy area. (18) Not too far away, in another part of the zoo, a large multi-acre, untouched area covered with hills, valleys, and rocks has been set aside for the bighorn sheep. (19) Their natural rocks are similar to small rocky hills, some as high as fifty to one hundred feet. (20) The rocks are so large that the sheep are difficult to spot without binoculars. (21) On a good day, can be seen literally on top of these huge rocks. (22) Just stand and gaze out over the zoo as though they are the keepers of the other animals. (23) They live as naturally as possible and are protected from harm by hunters or other wild animals. (24) These and many other animals are benefiting from the zoo's efforts. (25) To provide the best possible place for their wildlife to live.

1. Identify the sentences (S) and fragments (F) in the above paragraph.

   (1) _____   (6) _____   (11) _____   (16) _____   (21) _____
   (2) _____   (7) _____   (12) _____   (17) _____   (22) _____
   (3) _____   (8) _____   (13) _____   (18) _____   (23) _____
   (4) _____   (9) _____   (14) _____   (19) _____   (24) _____
   (5) _____   (10) _____   (15) _____   (20) _____   (25) _____

2. Correct the fragments you have found by combining the numbers as follows.
   1 & 2, 3 & 4, 6 & 7, 8 & 9, 10 & 11, 12 & 13, 14 & 15, 16 & 17, 24 & 25

3. Add a subject to numbers 21 and 22.

 ## *Writing Assignment*

Write a paragraph on one of the following topics. Be sure to start with a topic sentence. Then add support sentences, and end with a concluding sentence.

1. Effective communication with a particular person such as a boss, neighbor, family member, teacher
2. Reasons sharing a car, a room, or an apartment is difficult
3. Adding a new family member
4. Family vacations
5. Helpful or frustrating study group

Chapter 6

Improving Writing

Part 1

Using Pronouns Correctly

Objectives

- Use subject and object pronouns correctly.
- Have pronouns agree with the nouns they refer to or replace.
- Maintain a consistent point of view in sentences and paragraphs.

Subject and Object Pronouns

You previously learned how to identify different kinds of pronouns. Because personal pronouns appear so often in both speaking and writing, you need to be able to use them correctly. One form of a pronoun is used when the pronoun is the subject of the sentence, and a different form is used when the pronoun is an object.

Personal Pronouns as Subjects		Personal Pronouns as Objects	
I	we	me	us
you	you	you	you
she, he, it	they	her, him	them

Personal Pronouns Used as Subjects

The subject pronoun is used only when a personal pronoun is the subject of the sentence or when it renames the subject.

I left my book on the table.	(**I** is the subject of the sentence.)
He likes to play baseball.	(**He** is the subject of the sentence.)
This is **she.**	(**She** renames the subject, **this.**)
My cousin is **he.**	(**He** renames the subject, **cousin.**)

When a word renames the subject, you can usually turn the sentence around and make the personal pronoun the subject of the sentence. For instance, instead of "My cousin is he," you could say, "He is my cousin."

The real confusion, however, comes when your sentences have two subjects, one or both of which are pronouns. Look at the following sentences.

I went to the game.

Jack and **I** went to the game.   (correct)

Jack and **me** went to the game.   (incorrect)

In the first sentence, it is easy to realize that you should use **I** rather than **me**. The second sentence is not so easy. However, a simple way to help you know which pronoun to use is to read each personal pronoun directly in front of the verb one at a time. For example, to hear which pronoun is the correct one to use, you need to say, "Me went to the game." Then say, " I went to the game." You can easily see that you would not say, "Me went to the game." Therefore, you would not say, "Jack and **me** went to the game." The pronoun **me** is never the subject of a sentence. In fact, these pronouns are never subjects: **me, him, her, us, them.**

Note When two personal pronouns are used and one refers to yourself, you always put the other person first just to be polite. You should not say, "I and Jack went to the game."

The next exercise will give you practice in using subject pronouns correctly. If this is a particular problem for you, be sure to read through all the choices to decide which pronoun is correct.

Exercise 1

In the following sentences, look at the personal pronouns used as subjects. Decide which pronoun in parentheses is correct. Then write the correct pronoun in the sentence as indicated.

Example:

Carol **and him saved money for school. (he, him)**

He **saved money for school. (correct? yes)**

Him **saved money for school. (correct? no)**

Carol and ____*he*____ **saved money for school.**

1. **Leo** and me love to play soccer. (I, me)

   I love to play soccer.

   Me love to play soccer.

   Leo and _____ love to play soccer.

2. **Them** and their **grandchildren** liked the movie. (they, them)

   They liked the movie.

   Them liked the movie.

   _____ and their grandchildren liked the movie.

3. **Marsha** and **me** saw the yard sale sign. (I, me)

   I saw the yard sale sign.

   Me saw the yard sale sign.

   Marsha and _____ saw the yard sale sign.

4. **Him** and his **dog** walked up the trail. (he, him)

   He walked up the trail.

   Him walked up the trail.

   _____ and his dog walked up the trail.

5. **Her** and **me** went to the video store. (she, her / I, me)

   She went to the video store.

   Her went to the video store.

   I went to the video store.

   Me went to the video store.

   _____ and _____ went to the video store.

Exercise 2

Mentally, follow the same steps that you did in Exercise 1 to decide which subject pronoun to use.

Example:

Rhonda and ____*I*____ helped set up the display. (I, me)

Version A

1. The girls and _____ spent many hours practicing with the band. (he, him)

2. _____ and his wife liked baseball games. (He, Him)

3. _____ and _____ both decided to go to church. (her, she / I, me)

4. _____ and her parents went to the alumni basketball game. (Her, She)

5. My cat and _____ lounged on the sofa in front of the fire. (I, me)

Version B

1. Brenda and _____ all got jobs working in the math department at school. (they, them)

2. My sister and _____ watched the parade. (I, me)

3. Tyrone and _____ had fun bowling with their friends. (she, her)

4. My children and _____ went to the skating rink. (he, him)

5. Our neighbors and _____ plan to spend the weekend at the lake. (we, us)

Personal Pronouns Used as Objects

Look again at this list of personal pronouns.

Personal Pronouns as Subjects		Personal Pronouns as Objects	
I	we	me	us
you	you	you	you
she, he, it	they	her, him	them

Any time you use one of the above pronouns, you are going to be using either the subject form or the object form. If the pronoun is not the subject of the sentence or does not rename the subject, it is the object form that you need to use. An object pronoun is used as the object of a preposition or the object of a verb. Read the next two sentences. To decide which pronoun is correct, all you have to do is ask yourself, "Is it the subject? Does it rename the subject?" If the answer is no, it is the object form.

The coach threw the ball to **I**.   (incorrect)

The coach threw the ball to **me**.   (correct)

Again, the confusion comes when your sentence has two objects and one is a pronoun.

Jack saw Susan and **I**.   (incorrect)

Just as you learned to say subject pronouns one at a time, you will want to do the same with two objects. Read the sentence and leave out the second object. Then read it again and leave out the first object. To decide which pronoun is correct, say, "Jack saw I." Then say, "Jack saw me." You would normally say, "Jack saw me." In this way, you can hear which pronoun is correct.

The following exercise will give you practice in using object pronouns correctly. Again, if this is a particular problem for you, be sure to read through all the choices.

Exercise 3

In the following sentences, look at the personal pronouns used as objects. Decide which pronoun in parentheses is correct. Then write the correct pronoun in the sentence as indicated.

Example:

Ken saved some pie for Mike **and** I. **(I, me)**

Ken saved some pie for I. **(correct? no)**

Ken saved some pie for me. **(correct? yes)**

Ken saved some pie for Mike **and** ___*me*___.

1. Mom bought my **sister** and **I** some new school shoes. (I, me)

   Mom bought I some new school shoes.

   Mom bought me some new school shoes.

   Mom bought my sister and _____ some new school shoes.

2. Music from the steel drums appealed to **him** and **I**. (he, him / I, me)

Music from the steel drums appealed to he.

Music from the steel drums appealed to him.

Music from the steel drums appealed to I.

Music from the steel drums appealed to me.

Music from the steel drums appealed to _____ and _____.

3. The wind seemed to blow right through **her** and **I**. (she, her / I, me)

The wind seemed to blow right through she.

The wind seemed to blow right through her.

The wind seemed to blow right through I.

The wind seemed to blow right through me.

The wind seemed to blow right through _____ and _____.

4. The librarian asked my **friends** and **I** to go outside to talk. (I, me)

The librarian asked I to go outside to talk.

The librarian asked me to go outside to talk.

The librarian asked my friends and _____ to go outside to talk.

5. Mario gave tickets to **they** and **us**. (they, them / we, us)

Mario gave tickets to they.

Mario gave tickets to them.

Mario gave tickets to we.

Mario gave tickets to us.

Mario gave tickets to _____ and _____.

Exercise 4

Mentally, follow the same steps that you did in Exercise 3 to decide which object pronoun to use.

Example:

Many weekends Jade and ___*I*___ hike the mountains. (I, me)

Version A

1. My neighbor offered Paul and _____ a summer job. (I, me)

2. Our professor gave Claire and _____ good grades on that test. (I, me)

3. She had a wonderful surprise for Zach and _____. (I, me)

4. The biggest challenge for _____ and _____ is to get to class on time. (she, her / he, him)

5. Sam was pleasantly surprised when the city honored _____ and Jake. (he, him)

Version B

1. Retirement gave Bob and _____ a chance to travel across the country. (I, me)
2. Graduating from college made it possible for my friends and _____ to get a job. (I, me)
3. The message to you and _____ as students is to do our best in everything we do. (I, me)
4. My mother is waiting for you and _____ to come home to visit. (I, me)
5. I was happy when my neighbor brought my children and _____ a lemon meringue pie. (I, me)

The following exercise requires you to decide which sentence uses the personal pronouns correctly. This time both subject and object pronouns are used. Put the letter of the correct answer in the blank.

Exercise 5

In the following sentences, select the sentence that uses the correct pronoun.

Example:

___b___ a. **Shawna gave Karen and I tickets to the concert.**

b. **Shawna gave Karen and me tickets to the concert.**

Version A

_____ 1. a. Steven read the story to him and I.
b. Steven read the story to him and me.

_____ 2. a. My parents and me were proud of my test grade.
b. My parents and I were proud of my test grade.

_____ 3. a. Hiking the canyon was a thrill for her and me.
b. Hiking the canyon was a thrill for her and I.

_____ 4. a. Him and his father went trout fishing.
b. He and his father went trout fishing.

_____ 5. a. The wasps at the picnic stung both my brother and me.
b. The wasps at the picnic stung both my brother and I.

_____ 6. a. My fiancé and I sent out wedding invitations to her and her brother.
b. My fiancé and I sent out wedding invitations to she and her brother.

_____ 7. a. My teacher urged my parents and me to plan for college.
b. My teacher urged my parents and I to plan for college.

_____ 8. a. Several stores sent advertisements to them and we.
b. Several stores sent advertisements to them and us.

_____ 9. a. The surgeon explained the operation to he and I.

b. The surgeon explained the operation to him and me.

_____ 10. a. Their bank balance shocked them and their children into spending less money.

b. Their bank balance shocked they and their children into spending less money.

Version B

_____ 1. a. You and I can clean the kitchen fast.

b. You and me can clean the kitchen fast.

_____ 2. a. The bus left she and I standing at the corner.

b. The bus left her and me standing at the corner.

_____ 3. a. On their walk, the snow began to fall on she and her dog.

b. On their walk, the snow began to fall on her and her dog.

_____ 4. a. We received e-mails from him as well as his sister.

b. We received e-mails from he as well as his sister.

_____ 5. a. As we waited for the delivery, my boss and I chatted.

b. As we waited for the delivery, my boss and me chatted.

_____ 6. a. There is a lot of work for you and me to do.

b. There is a lot of work for you and I to do.

_____ 7. a. The art department invited they and their parents to the open house.

b. The art department invited them and their parents to the open house.

_____ 8. a. My dad taught my sister and me to change the oil in our cars.

b. My dad taught my sister and I to change the oil in our cars.

_____ 9. a. Habitat for Humanity invited professionals and us to build a new home.

b. Habitat for Humanity invited professionals and we to build a new home.

_____ 10. a. The new store gave samples to Jackie and I.

b. The new store gave samples to Jackie and me.

Pronoun Agreement

So far, you have learned to use pronouns as subjects and objects. Another important point to remember is that pronouns have to agree in number with the noun or nouns they refer to or replace. This means that if the noun is singular, the pronoun has to be singular. If the noun is plural, the pronoun has to be plural. Even if the pronoun replaces or refers to another pronoun, they both have to be singular or both plural. Study the following sentences.

Jim and **Mark** went shopping with **their** mother. (Nouns referred to are plural.)

Sam exercises to keep **his** muscles in tone. (Noun referred to is singular.)

Sue and **I** read different books for **our** English class. (Words referred to are plural.)

I made **appointments** with the doctor but later cancelled **them**. (Word referred to is plural.)

For the most part, you will not make mistakes in these kinds of sentences, but there are a few instances in which you might have to think carefully to choose the correct pronoun in your writing. These types of errors can occur when you are using third-person singular and plural pronouns and when you are using pronouns that are always singular.

3rd Person Singular (he, him; she, her; his, her) and Plural (they, them, their)

Third-person pronouns are a big challenge when a noun can be either male or female. For instance, you might have the following sentence.

Eventually, a child reaches the age when they are accountable for their actions. (incorrect)

To be grammatically correct, you would need to use both **he** and **she** as well as **his** and **her** pronouns, or you would need to make the noun plural.

Eventually, a child reaches the age when **he** or **she** is accountable for **his** or **her** actions. (correct)

Eventually, children reach the age when **they** are accountable for **their** actions. (correct)

Even though using **he** and **she** over and over again is correct, it can be wordy and very boring. Think about your options. As the above examples show, you can correct this pronoun agreement error in two possible ways.

1) Use both singular forms of the 3rd person pronoun.
2) Change to a plural noun.

Try working through the following exercise to use 3rd person singular and plural pronouns.

Read each sentence carefully, and edit it first by using singular (both the male and female) pronouns and second by changing the noun to plural. Change other words to the plural when necessary.

Example:

a. **Use singular pronouns.**

    his or her

    A teenager wants ~~their~~ own car.

b. **Use a plural noun.**

    Teenagers   *cars*

    ~~A teenager wants~~ their own ~~car~~.

Version A

1. a. Revise the sentence to use singular pronouns.

        When a student arrives on campus, they will need to attend orientation.

    b. Revise the sentence to use a plural noun.

        When a student arrives on campus, they will need to attend orientation.

2. a. Revise the sentence to use singular pronouns.

        The manager gave their employees Friday off.

    b. Revise the sentence to use a plural noun and a plural pronoun.

        The manager gave their employees Friday off.

3. a. Revise the sentence to use singular pronouns.

        A good nurse wants their patients to feel comfortable while in the hospital.

    b. Revise the sentence to use a plural noun.

        A good nurse wants their patients to feel comfortable while in the hospital.

4. a. Revise the sentence to use singular pronouns.

        A taxi driver usually takes their passengers as close to the door as possible.

    b. Revise the sentence to use a plural noun.

        A taxi driver usually takes their passengers as close to the door as possible.

5. a. Revise the sentence to use singular pronouns.

        A teenager often sees their younger brothers and sisters as needing a lot of guidance.

    b. Revise the sentence to use a plural noun.

        A teenager often sees their younger brothers and sisters as needing a lot of guidance.

6. a. Revise the sentence to use singular pronouns.

A parent spends many hours teaching their children to survive in society.

b. Revise the sentence to use a plural noun.

A parent spends many hours teaching their children to survive in society.

7. a. Revise the sentence to use singular pronouns.

A child may need friends, but they do not know how to make them.

b. Revise the sentence to use a plural noun.

A child may need friends, but they do not know how to make them.

8. a. Revise the sentence to use singular pronouns.

An efficient construction worker follows their supervisor's orders.

b. Revise the sentence to use a plural noun.

An efficient construction worker follows their supervisor's orders.

9. a. Revise the sentence to use singular pronouns.

A doctor may not realize that their patients do not have insurance.

b. Revise the sentence to use a plural noun.

A doctor may not realize that their patients do not have insurance.

10. a. Revise the sentence to use singular pronouns.

A firefighter has to pass their engineering test before they can drive the truck.

b. Revise the sentence to use a plural noun.

A firefighter has to pass their engineering test before they can drive the truck.

Version B

1. a. Revise the sentence to use singular pronouns.

When a car owner needs to get their oil changed, they go to a local shop.

b. Revise the sentence to use a plural noun.

When a car owner needs to get their oil changed, they go to a local shop.

2. a. Revise the sentence to use singular pronouns.

During a drought, a suburban home owner might find a thirsty black bear in their yard.

b. Revise the sentence to use a plural noun.

During a drought, a suburban home owner might find a thirsty black bear in their yard.

3. a. Revise the sentence to use singular pronouns.

A bus passenger dropped their sunflower seed shells along with their other trash all over the floor.

b. Revise the sentence to use a plural noun.

A bus passenger dropped their sunflower seed shells along with their other trash all over the floor.

4. a. Revise the sentence to use singular pronouns.

An airplane pilot usually cautions their passengers to fasten their safety belts.

b. Revise the sentence to use a plural noun.

An airplane pilot usually cautions their passengers to fasten their safety belts.

5. a. Revise the sentence to use singular pronouns.

A volunteer soldier trains hard so they can be ready for combat.

b. Revise the sentence to use a plural noun.

A volunteer soldier trains hard so they can be ready for combat.

6. a. Revise the sentence to use singular pronouns.

An artist usually wants their work to be shown in public.

b. Revise the sentence to use a plural noun.

An artist usually wants their work to be shown in public.

7. a. Revise the sentence to use singular pronouns.

The telemarketer would not leave their number on the answering machine.

b. Revise the sentence to use a plural noun.

The telemarketer would not leave their number on the answering machine.

8. a. Revise the sentence to use singular pronouns.

A college student has to budget their time carefully.

b. Revise the sentence to use a plural noun.

A college student has to budget their time carefully.

9. a. Revise the sentence to use singular pronouns.

A grandparent looks forward to seeing their grandchildren.

b. Revise the sentence to use a plural noun.

A grandparent looks forward to seeing their grandchildren.

10. a. Revise the sentence to use singular pronouns.

A television repair person treats their customers courteously.

b. Revise the sentence to use a plural noun.

A television repair person treats their customers courteously.

Pronouns That Are Always Singular

Some pronouns are always singular, but sometimes in popular speech you will hear them being used as plural. The words **everyone** and **everybody** fall into this category. For example, you will hear, "Everybody bought **their** ticket." To be grammatically correct, however, you would have to say, "Everybody bought **his** ticket." What if the group included both males and females? You would have to say, "Everybody bought **his or her** ticket." This would be grammatically correct because the pronouns would agree, but using them over and over in a paragraph could become awkward and clumsy.

Perhaps the best solution would be the one you previously learned. Be as specific as possible in your writing, and revise these sentences to be plural. Depending on the main idea of your paragraph, you might say, "All the **students** bought **their** tickets" or "All of my **friends** bought **their** tickets." When you revise your sentences and paragraphs to make the ideas plural, you will eliminate these pronouns.

Here are the pronouns that are always singular:

anyone	anybody	neither	either
everyone	everybody	each	one
someone	somebody		

Study the following sentences:

Each of the male dogs ate **his** dinner.   (The dogs are all males.)

Neither of the mothers enrolled **her** child in Saturday classes.

(Mothers are female.)

Everyone turned in **his or her** homework.   (A mixed group of males and females.)

Anyone can file **his or her** tax returns early.   (A mixed group of males and females.)

Practice using these singular pronouns in the following exercise.

Exercise 7

Choose the pronoun that agrees with the word in bold. Put the correct pronoun in the blank.

Example:

Everybody **needed** _his or her_ flu shot. (their, his or her)

Version A

1. **Everyone** on the men's basketball team earned _____ letter. (their, his)

2. **Neither** of the girls put _____ name into the database. (their, her)

3. **Each** of the teachers volunteered _____ time after school. (their, his or her)

4. **Anyone** can turn in _____ essay early. (their, his or her)

5. **Everyone** put _____ best effort into the class project. (their, his or her)

Version B

1. **Anybody** can improve _____ skills by practicing. (their, his or her)

2. **Someone** called but would not leave _____ name. (their, his or her)

3. **Somebody** parked _____ car in front of the fire hydrant. (their, his or her)

4. **Everybody** at the crafts fair had _____ best items for sale. (their, his or her)

5. **One** of the girls brought _____ parents to the open house. (their, her)

Sometimes using one of these pronouns correctly might not sound right to you because you have heard it used incorrectly so often. If this is true, then try to use the word correctly in a sentence as many times as possible in one day. Soon it will sound correct to you, and that is important.

Consistent Point of View

So far, you have read about and practiced what you need to do to write effective sentences and paragraphs that will be acceptable in your college writing and on your job. Another important skill for you to study is to keep a consistent point of view in your sentences and paragraphs. **Consistent point of view means not shifting from one person to another.** For example, you do not want to start a thought with **I** and then end that thought with **you** or **he** unless that is really what you mean. Think about the meaning in the following sentences.

In case I have an emergency, you can use a cell phone to get help. ⎫ different
  ⎬ meanings
In case I have an emergency, I can use a cell phone to get help. ⎭

The first sentence above leaves the impression that the person speaking is depending on the **you (someone else)** to call for help in an emergency. In the second sentence, the person speaking is justifying having a cell phone so that he or she can use it in an emergency.

Now look at the next sentence.

When Stacy and Jesus were on their honeymoon in California,
you could just relax and walk on the beach. (incorrect)

The information is probably not correct unless Stacy and Jesus took **you** along on **their** honeymoon.

A shift in point of view is sometimes necessary, but when you do shift, you need to do it for a reason. Most writing requires a consistent point of view, so learning to keep the point of view consistent is important. The first step in having a consistent point of view is being able to identify point of view.

Identifying Point of View

Study the following list that tells you which pronouns are used to indicate the 1st, 2nd, and 3rd person point of view and gives you the singular and plural forms for each person:

	Singular	Plural
1st person	I, me, my, mine	we, us, our, ours
2nd person	you, your, yours	you, your, yours
3rd person	she, her, hers; he, his; it, its	they, them, their, theirs

Now think through each pronoun, using the above list. This will make it easier to determine point of view in your writing.

The word **I**	is	1st person	singular.
The word **me**	is	1st person	singular.
The word **us**	is	1st person	plural.
The word **you**	is	2nd person	singular or plural.
The word **your**	is	2nd person	singular or plural.
The word **she**	is	3rd person	singular.
The word **they**	is	3rd person	plural.

To help you identify the point of view in a sentence or paragraph, just remember that all nouns are 3rd person. Of course, some are singular and some are plural. Singular nouns are replaced with 3rd person singular pronouns, and plural nouns are replaced with 3rd person plural pronouns. If you are not sure what point of view you have used, ask yourself what personal pronoun can be used to replace the subject in the first sentence. Then, study the following examples. As you think through each one, look back at the lists above to help you become more familiar with 3rd person pronouns. Notice that the pronoun/s at the end of each sentence are the correct ones to replace the noun/s in each sentence.

The noun **book**	is	3rd person	singular.	(it, its)
The noun **books**	is	3rd person	plural.	(they, them, their)
The noun **Jerry**	is	3rd person	singular.	(he, him, his)
The nouns **Jerry** and **Walt**	are	3rd person	plural.	(they, them, their)
As a noun, **walking**	is	3rd person	singular.	(it)
As a noun, **fearing**	is	3rd person	singular.	(it)
As a noun, **to sing**	is	3rd person	singular.	(it)

Exercise 8

Identify person for the following pronouns in bold. Then decide if the pronoun (person) is singular or plural. Write the answer in the blank at the left. Remember, the pronoun **you** can be either singular or plural. Use the lists above to help you.

Example:

1st person plural **We** wanted to travel to Canada last summer.

Version A

_____ 1. Students, **you** will find out about **your** books on the first day of class.

_____ 2. **He** did not want to miss **his** appointment with the doctor.

_____ 3. **She** is really enjoying **her** new high-speed Internet modem.

_____ 4. **They** investigated the possibility of boarding **their** dogs for a day.

_____ 5. **We** asked **our** neighbor to take in **our** mail.

Version B

_____ 1. **Your** car is in excellent condition.

_____ 2. **Her** personal identity was stolen last year.

_____ 3. **They** moved to a new location.

_____ 4. **It** is fun to travel to many new places.

_____ 5. **They** closed the restaurant after fifty years of quality service.

Keeping Point of View Consistent

Once you have decided to use **I, you,** or **he** (1st, 2nd, or 3rd) point of view, you will want to keep that same point of view throughout your paragraph. Keeping a consistent point of view means keeping the same person throughout your sentences or paragraphs.

Having a consistent point of view also means that you do not shift without good reason from one person to another. Look at this needless shift in person or point of view:

They wanted to go to a campus bookstore where **you** can buy all **your** books.

This shift is from **they** to **you** and **your**, which is a shift from 3rd person to 2nd person. To eliminate this shift, you could revise the sentence to read,

They wanted to go to the campus bookstore where **they** can buy all **their** books.

This time, the sentence starts with 3rd person and stays with 3rd person.

Exercise 9

Revise the following sentences to maintain the point of view that begins the sentence. You may have more than one change.

Example:

Having a little fun will not hurt students because ~~you~~ can often relieve some of ~~your~~ everyday stress.

they above *you*
their above *your*

Version A

1. When students miss school, you miss out on a lot of important things.

2. I love going to the gym. Exercising is important to me because you burn up energy.

3. Young people like the thrill of driving fast. However, driving fast is scary because you are in a chunk of metal going at high speeds.

4. When you get a new puppy, it will be a good friend to me.

5. I realized that I do not need to know your major to enroll in college.

6. Your most important goals are to pass my classes.

7. At a party, people have a chance to meet new friends. You can even dance with new people.

8. When the dog is over at my house, you cannot describe how I feel.

9. Hikers are usually very polite. As you pass each other, you exchange greetings.

10. I work as a certified nursing assistant. The nurses look down on you and make you do most of the messy jobs.

Version B

1. I do not plan on being a millionaire because you cannot. You just hope that everything goes well for me.

2. Living in a large city is an advantage for people because you can get medical care quickly.

3. After my daughter was born, my friends became a thing of the past because they did not want to be burdened with your baby.

4. Some shows make me cry because you learn that entertainers are human, too.

5. I like to go to Barnes & Noble because in one section you can read books with your children.

6. When you get up every morning, I have to get my kids ready for school and feed the dogs.

7. Jack discusses all of his options before making up my mind.

8. When people are around the cage, the little animals actually sit still and look at you.

9. At the gym, personal trainers help members identify the best machines to use for your particular workout goal.

10. At the day-care center, the workers ask for identification if the parents have someone else pick up your child.

If you are not sure about what point of view you used in a paragraph, read the first sentence in the paragraph. Then ask yourself,

Did I use a **you** or **your** in the first sentence?

If the answer is yes, then you have established 2nd person (*you*) point of view and will want to maintain it throughout the paragraph. If not, ask yourself,

Did I use **I, me, we,** or **us** in the first sentence?

If the answer is yes, then you have established 1st person (*I*) point of view and will want to maintain it throughout the paragraph.

If your sentence does **not** have 2nd person (*you*) or 1st person (*I, me, we, or us*), you have established 3rd person (*he, it, they*) point of view. Because all nouns are either 3rd person singular or 3rd person plural, you may not have a 3rd person pronoun (*it, he, she, they*) in the sentence. For example, look at the following sentence in 3rd person point of view.

Sitting on the fence and looking in all directions, the hummingbird guarded the feeder.

One other bit of information that you want to keep in mind is that even when you use 1st or 2nd person point of view, you will have other pronouns in the paragraph. They are there because they replace a noun, not because the paragraph is written from that point of view. For example, look at the following sentences that are written in 1st person point of view, but the **her** refers to "my little girl."

I enjoyed fishing from the bank of the river when my little girl was with me. I loved teaching her how to watch the bobber for signs that a fish was biting.

Your primary goal is to keep a consistent point of view in your writing. However, most of your writing will be in 1st person or 3rd person rather than 2nd person. In other words, you will want to avoid using **you** in most of your papers.

In your writing, you will often use 3rd person point of view for your research papers and essays. You will use 1st person for your personal writing, such as letters and journals. You will use 2nd person point of view for directions and how-to types of papers.

Look at the following groups of related sentences. The point of view is given for each group.

Mixed Point of View

Because the point of view in the following passage is mixed, it distracts from the overall effectiveness of its content.

The pigeons built a nest under the eaves on the roof just above the front door. They gathered pine needles, leaves, and twigs from branches to build their nest. I could hear their cooing in the early mornings and late evenings. Soon, you could see tiny little birds that made their own sounds as they waited for their meals. I loved watching the birds, but they left an unbelievable amount of mess on your tile roof. Before long, even the tile path to my front door was splattered with their droppings. As soon as the babies were able to fly free, I had to close off their home and bid them farewell.

3rd Person Point of View

This same passage, rewritten in 3rd person point of view, is more informative or objective in content. Most of your writing for college will be in 3rd person.

The pigeons built a nest under the eaves on the tile roof just above the front door. They gathered pine needles, leaves, and twigs from branches to build their nest. They cooed in the early mornings and late evenings. Soon, tiny little birds made their own sounds as they waited for their meals. Though people might have enjoyed watching them, they left an unbelievable amount of mess on the roof. They even splattered the tile path to the front door with their droppings. As soon as the babies were able to fly free, the owner of the home closed off their nesting area to prevent further problems.

2nd Person Point of View

This passage, now in 2nd person point of view, is written directly to readers so that they will understand that something must be done to change the situation described.

> Everywhere in the city, you see pigeons building nests under the eaves of the roofs. You can watch as they gather pine needles, leaves, and twigs from branches to build their nests. You can hear their cooing in the early mornings and late evenings. Soon you can see tiny little birds that make their own sounds as they wait for their meals. You can also see an unbelievable amount of mess on the roofs of the buildings and even droppings on the sidewalks below. When you can no longer stand the mess, you must close off these places so the birds will move on somewhere else.

1st Person Point of View

Putting the passage in 1st person point of view adds more personal feeling to the content.

> I watched the pigeons build a nest under the eaves on my roof just above my front door. I observed as they gathered pine needles, leaves, and twigs from branches to build their nest. I could hear their cooing in the early mornings and late evenings. Soon, I could see tiny little birds that made their own sounds as they waited for their meals. I loved watching the birds, but they left an unbelievable amount of mess on my tile roof. Before long, even the tile path to my front door was splattered with their droppings. I had to close off their home and bid them farewell as soon as the babies were able to fly free.

As you have just seen, the overall point of view in writing depends on the purpose of your writing and the people who will read the material. Learning to write with a consistent point of view is important in your papers to add clarity and meaning.

Exercise 10

Look at the following groups of related sentences. The point of view shifts throughout the material. Revise for the point of view indicated.

A. Revise the following sentences, using a consistent 1st person point of view in each sentence.

Every morning, I get up and read the newspaper so you can get information on different events in the city. You can read about all the violence happening in schools, communities, and homes. It seems as though every day you read about a child drowning in a swimming pool or in a freezing lake. One morning, people read about a computer virus that hits the banks, and you are not able to make withdrawals from many banks, including the Bank of America ATMs. Another morning, I read about a drug bust where police seize a thousand pounds of marijuana.

B. **Revise the following sentences, using a consistent 2ⁿᵈ person point of view in each sentence.**

Every morning, I get up and read the newspaper so you can get information on different events in the city. You can read about all the violence happening in schools, communities, and homes. It seems as though every day you read about a child drowning in a swimming pool or in a freezing lake. One morning, people read about a virus that hits the banks, and I am not able to make withdrawals from many banks, including the Bank of America ATMs. Another morning, I read about a drug bust where police seize a thousand pounds of marijuana.

C. **Revise the following sentences, using a consistent 3ʳᵈ person plural point of view in each sentence.**

Every morning, Americans get up and read the newspaper so you can get information on different events in the city. You can read about all the violence happening in schools, communities, and homes. It seems as though every day you read about a child drowning in a swimming pool or in a freezing lake. One morning, people read about a virus that hits the banks, and I am not able to make withdrawals from many banks, including the Bank of America ATMs. Another morning, I read about a drug bust where police seize a thousand pounds of marijuana.

 Summary

Understanding personal pronouns and using them correctly in your writing is important because it can help you communicate more clearly with your reader.

- Subject pronouns are used when the pronoun is the subject of a sentence or when the pronoun renames the subject of the sentence.
- Object pronouns are used when the pronoun is not the subject of a sentence or if it does not rename the subject. They are used as objects of prepositions and objects of verbs.

- Pronouns must agree in number with the noun or nouns they replace. This means that the noun and the pronoun will both be singular or both be plural.
- Keeping a consistent point of view in your sentences and paragraphs means that you do not shift from one person to another.

Practice Test

In this practice test, you are given three versions of one paragraph: one with subject and object pronoun errors, one with pronoun agreement errors, and one with inconsistent point of view. Work through each paragraph.

A. Subject and Object Pronouns
In the following paragraph, some of the subject and object personal pronouns are used incorrectly. Edit the paragraph by putting in the correct personal pronouns.

Finding pleasure in life seemed so simple when my little sister Anne and I were young. Her and I delighted in mixing soap and water together and then blowing bubbles that gently floated in the air. We spent hours together. I blew them to her, and then her and me caught them, only to watch the bubbles suddenly disappear in front of our eyes. Other times, when her and me were given paper, crayons, and scissors, we created our own pieces of art that we proudly showed our parents. In the winter, when snow fell, her and I saw it as a chance to bundle up and feel the soft touch of the light flakes landing on our faces. On an experimental day, Anne and me even opened our mouths and tried to catch snowflakes on our tongues. Excitedly, we scrambled to see who could build the biggest or the best snowman. As her and me grew older, we viewed an empty field as a place to play a baseball game with our friends or just to hang out. Even rain did not make any difference in our enthusiasm as it gave she and I a chance to walk through rain puddles and splash each other. Nothing could take Anne and I from these adventures except the smell of popcorn or the offer to try some chocolate chip or peanut butter cookies that our mother had just taken out of the oven. The newness of these wonderful and adventurous events seemed to fade as Anne and me grew into adulthood but surfaced once more as her and me raised our own children.

B. Pronoun Agreement

In this version of the same paragraph, not all singular nouns are replaced with singular pronouns, nor are all plural nouns replaced with plural pronouns. Correct these errors by using the plural noun **children** in the first sentence and throughout the paragraph. Use plural pronouns when they replace **children**. (In some sentences, you will need to change the verbs to match.)

Finding pleasure in life seems so simple when a child is young. They delight in mixing soap and water together and blowing bubbles that gently float in the air. He or she can spend hours catching them, only to watch the bubbles suddenly disappear in front of their eyes. Other times, when a child is given papers, crayons, and scissors, they can create their own pieces of art that they proudly show their parents. In the winter, when snow falls, a child sees it as a chance to bundle up and feel the soft touch of the light flakes landing on her face. On an experimental day, he or she might even open their mouths and try to catch snowflakes on their tongues. Excitedly, they may scramble to see who can build the biggest or the best snowman. As a child grows older, an empty field might be viewed as a place to play a baseball game with their friends or just to hang out. Even rain does not make any difference in a child's enthusiasm as it gives them a chance to walk through rain puddles and splash each other. Nothing can take him from these adventures except the smell of popcorn or the offer to try some chocolate chip or peanut butter cookies that his or her mothers have just taken from the oven. The newness of these wonderful and adventurous events seems to fade as a young person grows into adulthood but surfaces once more as they raise their own children.

C. Point of View

This version of the paragraph is written with a mixed point of view. Edit it to have a consistent 3rd person point of view. Change any 1st or 2nd person pronouns to 3rd person. (This means that you need to change all forms of **you** or **I** to the 3rd person.)

Finding pleasure in life seems so simple when children are young.

You delight in mixing soap and water together and blowing bubbles that gently float in the air. Children can spend hours catching them only to watch the bubbles suddenly disappear in front of your eyes. Other times, when children are given papers, crayons, and scissors, you can create your own pieces of art that you proudly show your parents. In the winter, when snow falls, I see it as a chance to bundle up and feel the soft touch of the light flakes landing on my face. On an experimental day, youngsters might even open their mouths and try to catch snowflakes on your tongue. Excitedly, you may scramble to see who can build the biggest or the best snowman. As they grow older, an empty field might be viewed as a place to play a baseball game with your friends or just to hang out. Even rain does not make any difference in their enthusiasm as it gives you a chance to walk through rain puddles and splash each other. Nothing can take you from these adventures except the smell of popcorn or the offer to try some chocolate chip or peanut butter cookies that have just come from the oven. The newness of these wonderful and adventurous events seems to fade as I grow into adulthood but surfaces once more as I raise my own children.

 ## Writing Assignment

Write a single paragraph on one of the following subjects. Be sure to have a topic sentence, support sentences, and a concluding sentence. Be sure to avoid any pronoun errors.

1. Playing in the rain or snow
2. Playing a favorite board game
3. Watching a football game on television
4. Driving in the city
5. A pregnancy that changed your life (self, sibling, child, friend, relative)
6. A local food bank, shelter, or jail
7. A local or national monument

Something to Think About, Something to Write About

Professional Essay to Generate Ideas for Writing

Navigating Without a Compass

Elizabeth Minnich, *Case Manager and Teacher*

1   As young people grow into adulthood, it is important for them to become independent from their parents, yet their parents remain as a natural compass to point them in the right direction throughout their lives. The loss of both of my parents—my father when I was six and my mother when I was seventeen—left me without this compass, so I had to learn quickly how to maneuver through life by myself, something that touches my life even today. Finding my way through college and my first job, developing relationships with others, and looking toward the future all have been reminders that my parents are gone.

2   When I had questions about difficult situations, I painfully felt the lack of parental support and unconditional love. No one will ever love me as my parents did. Without this safety net, situations were more crippling and had much higher stakes. Though I am thirty-three years old today, I still remember being seventeen and having to find an apartment right after my mother died, but I felt lost without my parents to guide me. Eventually I went off to college and lived in the dorm, but little things still made it hard. For example, I noticed everyone carrying around buckets of what I thought was Kentucky Fried Chicken, and I wondered why. Later that day, I found out that all parents had been able to purchase care packages for their kids, but since my parents were gone, I was left out. This incident served as a reminder that I no longer had my parents to guide me. Following college, I found my first job and an apartment. After only six months, job cuts were being made and most employees were threatened with losing their jobs, including me. Many of my coworkers discussed their options. Most of the options related to their parents, including borrowing money from their parents until they found another job or moving back home for a while. I obviously did not have these options, and I couldn't even ask my parents for advice on what to do. To my relief, my job was not cut, but these situations are always a possibility I will have to face.

3   My relationships with others also have been affected by not having my parents in my life. Even today, people do not know how to react. There is no easy way to answer a question about my parents. People have become very

uncomfortable when I tell them that my parents are dead, reacting startled and then becoming quiet and apologizing. This difference has become glaringly apparent as my fiancé and I meet with people to make plans for our wedding. People from the church, the reception halls, and even the dress shops often pose questions to me and my fiancé about parental involvement in our wedding. When talking to the priest at the church, he asked about my parents' participation in my wedding, and I had to explain that my parents had passed away. This also became a critical issue when they asked me to produce religious records I did not possess, records that became misplaced when my mother passed away. This issue will continue as I have to approach the church that I was baptized in. I will have to explain that I need copies of these records because my parents are dead and I cannot ask them for the papers I need. Reception halls and dress shops all asked about the financial involvement of my parents, and again I had to offer the explanation of their deaths. I miss having my parents to direct me as I prepare for my wedding, but I am thankful for the short time I did have them.

4   I look forward to what many other people do, with one little difference. With each step I take into my future—getting married, having children—I take a step back into the past with the reminders that I have no parents. I will not be able to share my joy and ask questions of my parents in any of these future events. Holidays will never be celebrated with my parents, and traditions will not be passed down from my parents to their grandchildren. My past and my future have been and will continue to become disconnected in some way because my parents aren't there to make that link between them.

5   The loss of my parents has affected my life in so many ways, and trying to live life can sometimes feel like an overwhelming task. At times I can only compare it to trying to do something that I am not able to do, like trying to sky dive and do my taxes at the same time. I think a coworker of mine said it best when she told me, "Losing your parents is like becoming a member of a club that no one wants to join." Today, I have completed college and have a successful career, but it would have been and would continue to be a lot easier if I had my parents to help me navigate through life.

Understanding Words
Briefly define the following words as they are used in the selection.

1. maneuver
2. unconditional
3. baptized

Writing Assignment

Think about your own parents or someone who has served as a parent to you, or think about a friend's parents and then write a paragraph on one of the following topics. Be sure to start with a strong topic sentence. Add specific examples and details for support, and end with a strong concluding sentence.

1. Describe one important thing parents or parent figures do to guide their children.
2. How do parents help their adult children?
3. What do children resent most about their parents?
4. What do children appreciate most about their parents?
5. What quality do you wish your parents had?
6. What is the most important quality you hope to teach your children?
7. What is your strongest or weakest quality as a parent?

Part 3

Student and Professional Paragraphs

Grandmother's

Patrina Begay, *Student*

My favorite place to visit is my grandmother's home on the Navajo Reservation. The ladies cook mutton stew with vegetables, toss fry bread under the tree, and the men do as they please. The young ones ride horses, climb the mountains, or horse around themselves. As for myself, I sit under the tree listening to the beauty of the Navajo language. I hardly understand my own feeling for the beauty of the words coming from the women, the sweet tongue-twisting words. I always like to lie down on the bare sand, looking through the tree branches, staring up into the sky and listening to the tone of voices. Just lying there and listening could hypnotize me, leaving me feeling weightless, above all careless. This feeling would last for the longest time of all, actually until the smell or sight of food brought me back to consciousness. My aunt's cooking is the best of all. Her bread pure gold, veggies boiling in hot water, the sight of food leaves my mouth watery, craving the taste of it. The food sends a sweet aroma around, making everyone impatient. Then it is time to eat. Everyone gathers around and one-by-one gets his or her own plate. We all sit by one another, reminiscing about yesterday, sharing goals for tomorrow. It all ends, but not until the food is all gone. After that, we clean up, say our goodbyes, and head off to our own lives again.

Understanding Words

Briefly define the following words as they are used in this selection.

1. mutton

2. reminiscing

Questions on Form

1. What is the main idea of the paragraph?

2. Name some concrete details that support the topic sentence.

3. How does the conclusion tie the ideas together?

Questions on Content

1. Where is the grandmother's home?

2. What does the author especially like to do before the food is ready?

3. What do they all do as they are enjoying the food?

My Grandfather

Josh Seyfert, *Student*

Since the day I came into this stellar world, my grandpa was there to be my best bud, especially when we went camping. The great outdoors was my grandfather's favorite place to be, so it is no wonder that it soon became mine, too. Because this is where we spent most of our time together, it became the place of teaching, the teachings of life. He taught me to respect nature by having me every night pick up camp so our trash would not whorl away in the nightly winds, cluttering the forest floor as if a hurricane had hit the city dump. He also told me before and after all of my hunting trips that hunting is a privilege and a sport that can be taken away, so I needed to respect the animals by only killing what I would eat. He used to tell me, "You kill it. You eat it." The lesson he taught me was not to hunt for the pure thrill of the kill or for the prize rack or pelt but for the love of the sport and for the love of the animal. My grandfather's teaching helped me become respectful of all life.

Understanding Words
Briefly define the following words as they are used in this selection.
1. stellar
2. whorl

Questions on Form

1. What is the topic idea in this paragraph?

2. Name several examples that make the paragraph effective.

3. From what point of view is this paragraph written?

Questions on Content

1. What did the author's grandfather have him do each night while camping?

2. What did the author and his grandfather love to do?

3. What was his grandfather's rule about killing animals?

Basketball

Veronica Carmelo, *Student*

My ideal weekend activity is playing basketball on Sundays. For me, playing basketball has a lot to do with relieving stress, getting a physical workout, and meeting new people. Working forty hours a week and attending school at the same time can be quite hectic. I do not have much time for myself, so when I go play, I can release a lot of stress and tension built up through the week. Perhaps most importantly of all, I do not get a lot of exercise during the week. When I do play, I am getting a great workout. I am constantly running, jumping, and moving around. This is good for me because I am getting my workout without going to a gym. In addition, playing on Sundays has been a great way to meet new people. I now know so many people there that I did not think it was possible to have so many guy friends who love to play sports. The only rule to meeting new people is basically approaching a person and making sure I smile and am friendly. We have a lot in common because of basketball. It is simply a great sport that keeps me busy on the weekends.

Understanding Words
Briefly define the following word as it is used in this selection.

hectic

Questions on Form
1. From what point of view is this paragraph written?

2. What pronoun in the first sentence establishes this point of view?

3. How does the last sentence provide a sense of closure?

Questions on Content
1. What movements allow the author to get a good workout playing basketball?
2. What is another reason for playing basketball?
3. When does she play basketball?

Excerpt from Walden, "The Ponds"

Henry David Thoreau

Nevertheless, of all the characters I have known, perhaps Walden wears best, and best preserves its purity. Many men have been likened to it, but few deserve that honor. Though the woodchoppers have laid bare first this shore and then that, and the Irish have built their sties by it, and the railroad has infringed on its border, and the ice-men have skimmed it once, it is itself unchanged, the same water which my youthful eyes fell on; all the change is in me. It has not acquired one permanent wrinkle after all its ripples. It is perennially young, and I may stand and see a swallow dip apparently to pick an insect from its surface as of yore. It struck me again tonight, as if I had not seen it almost daily for more than twenty years—Why, here is Walden, the same woodland lake that I discovered so many years ago; where a forest was cut down last winter another is springing up by its shore as lustily as ever; the same thought is welling up to its surface that was then; it is the same liquid joy and happiness to itself and its Maker, ay, and it *may* be to me. It is the work of a brave man surely, in whom there was no guile! He rounded this water with his hand, deepened and clarified it in his thought, and in his will bequeathed it to Concord. I see by its face that it is visited by the same reflection; and I can almost say, Walden, is it you?

Understanding Words

Briefly define the following words as they are used in this selection.

1. sties
2. yore
3. infringed
4. guile
5. perennially
6. swallow
7. lustily
8. bequeathed

Questions on Form

1. What are the specific examples used to show change around Walden?

2. What is Thoreau's topic idea in this paragraph?

3. What makes the concluding sentence effective?

Questions on Content

1. What is Walden?

2. How often has the author seen it in the last twenty years?

3. Though this place has not changed in the author's eyes, what around it has changed?

Part 4

Improving Sentences

Objectives

- Identify parallel form:

    words

    phrases

    other forms

    Correct parts of sentences that are not parallel.

    Use repetition of parallel form for emphasis.
- Use modifying phrases correctly.

    Improve sentences by avoiding dangling modifiers.

    Improve sentences by avoiding misplaced modifiers.
- Identify parallel form in the context of a paragraph.
- Identify dangling and misplaced modifiers in the context of a paragraph.

Parallel Form

In this text, you have learned skills to help you write stronger and more interesting paragraphs. This section will help you build sentences in a more effective way. As you add details to a paragraph, you will have a chance to improve your sentences by using parallel form. **Parallel form means that parts of speech or phrases are written in the same way.** For example, parallel form should be used in sentences that have two or more ideas that are equal to each other.

Two words of equal importance: nouns, verbs, adjectives, adverbs

Prepositional phrases

Other forms

   -ing verb forms

   to-plus-the-verb forms

Two Nouns or Two Verbs in Parallel Form

Tony bought **pants** and **shirts**.   (two nouns in parallel form)

Tony bought two kinds of things, but they are of equal importance, so the same kinds of words are used to show this, two nouns.

If you want to add more information, such as a detail, to one noun, you also must add a detail to the other to keep the parts the same.

Tony bought **blue** pants and **white** shirts.   (two parts still in parallel form)

Here is another example, this time using two verbs.

Ben **mopped** and **vacuumed**.   (two verbs in parallel form)

Ben did two things, both of equal importance, so the same kinds of words are used, two verbs.

Just as before, if you add a detail to one part of the parallel form, you need to add one to the second part as well.

Ben **mopped the kitchen floor** and **vacuumed the carpet**.

              (parts still in parallel form)

The above sentences have been made stronger because details were added in an effective way. The details keep the parts parallel.

As you see, the conjunction **and** is often used in parallel form. If you need to show a contrast, you can use **but** or **yet** and still keep parts in parallel form. For example, the following sentences show contrasting ideas in parallel form, using adjectives or adverbs.

Sara looked **pretty** but **sad** today.   (two adjectives in parallel form)

The parents were **worried** yet **confident**.   (two adjectives in parallel form)

The cat jumped **quickly** but **quietly**.   (two adverbs in parallel form)

Sometimes, you may want to use the conjunction **or** to show contrast. For example,

I could not decide if he was **angry** or **tired**.   (two adjectives in parallel form)

For dessert, I wanted **apple pie** or **chocolate cake**.   (two adjective-noun forms in parallel form)

Now work through the following exercise to help you understand basic parallel form.

Exercise 1

Underline the words in parallel form in the following sentences. Look for the parts connected by **and, but, yet,** or **or**.

Example:

On the table, we saw _yellow pansies_ and _red carnations_.

Version A

1. The buffet featured blueberry muffins and bread pudding.

2. We saw perky dogs and friendly cats at the no-kill shelter.

3. The players were nervous but happy before the game.

4. To get ready for vacation, we made reservations and packed luggage.

5. Jim saved money and followed a budget.

6. The women in the beauty salon were lively and talkative under the driers.

7. At the drugstore, Tim bought toothpaste and shaving gel.

8. The shirts were attractive yet expensive.

9. The chef rapidly but efficiently prepared the entree.

10. Now touring the United States, *The Producers* is a clever but sarcastic play.

Version B

1. Brenda coughed and sneezed repeatedly.

2. Rosalind bought new denim pants and a red flannel shirt.

3. While at the child-care center, the little girls giggled frequently and happily.

4. We stayed up late but slept in the next morning.

5. The little calico kitten's fur was long and silky.

6. During the weekend, I often fertilize the plants or pinch off dead leaves.

7. My mother raised five children by herself yet completed a college degree at the same time.

8. When a call came in, the firefighters' half-eaten meal and unfinished drinks were left behind.

9. When taking a test, the students work quickly but carefully.

10. After going on a long hike, we were tired yet relaxed.

Exercise 2

Write 5 sentences containing parallel nouns, verbs, adjectives, or adverbs. In your sentences, underline the words in parallel form.

1. _____

   _____

2. _____

   _____

3. _____

   _____

4. _____

   _____

5. _____

   _____

Prepositional Phrases in Parallel Form

In addition to using single words in effective parallel patterns, you can also improve your sentences by putting prepositional phrases into parallel form. Study the following examples. Each sentence below contains two phrases written in parallel form (marked in bold). Each uses **and** to connect the parallel parts. Remember, you are looking for ideas of equal importance that are put into the same kind of wording.

The dogs ran **into the backyard** and **beyond the rose garden.**

(two prepositional phrases in parallel form)

The cooking aromas drifted **through the house** and **out the door.**

(two prepositional phrases in parallel form)

Now notice the same phrases connected by **but:**

The dogs ran **into the backyard** but **not beyond the rose garden.**

The cooking aromas drifted **through the house** but **not out the door.**

This time, to make the meaning clear, the word **not** had to be used, but it does not spoil the parallel form.

As you learned earlier, you can also show parallel form by using **or.**

Every day, Tonya goes to the gym **in the morning** or **before dinner.**

An important point to understand now is how to use the preposition **to** in parallel form. When you have a sentence like the following one, you may use the word **to** in front of both parts of the parallel structure: "We went **to dinner** and **to a show,**" or you may also drop the second **to:** "We went **to dinner** and **a show.**" (Later in this section, you will learn how to use **to** when you have more than two prepositional phrases in parallel form.) For example, you may also use the preposition **for** in the same way.

If you repeat these prepositions several times in a row, they can become monotonous and actually detract from the effectiveness of your writing. Other times, using **for** twice could be done for emphasis. For example, you might want to emphasize that you went to the store both **for fresh fruit** and **for ground beef.**

I went to the grocery store **for fresh fruit** and **ground beef.**

I went to the grocery store **for fresh fruit** and **for ground beef.**

Another important point to remember is that the parts of the parallel wording should always match. They should be the same kind of words. At this point, try to get a feel for the rhythm established by ideas in parallel form. The human mind responds to patterns like these and even expects the patterns to occur.

Work through the following exercise to help you practice using parallel form.

Underline the parallel form in each sentence below. Look for the parts connected by **and**, **but**, **yet**, or **or**.

Example:

We wandered *along the path* and *into the wood*.

Version A

1. The sun shone through the window and onto the carpet.
2. We watched the gulls fly slowly above the waves and across the sand.
3. Across the street and down the alley, his voice carried unbelievably far.
4. We scattered crumbs for the birds and for the chipmunks.
5. We walked underneath the bridge and around the lagoon to reach the picnic area.
6. My professor told us we could get help from the writing center or from the library.
7. Whenever I have a little extra time in the spring, I hike over the bridge and through the beautiful meadow.
8. The kids loved to camp in the trailer but not in the tent.
9. We need to put the groceries in the refrigerator but not on the counter.
10. In a real estate sale, repairs need to be done after the walkthrough yet before the closing.

Version B

1. I love to hike over the mountain and into the valley.
2. The speeding car flew over the cliff and down the mountain.
3. Every evening Sheila puts out food and water for the hungry cats as well as for the stray dogs.
4. When it is raining, I seldom get wet because I use the underground tunnels to get to my classes and to the lab.
5. I had to look for a small loan or for a second job.
6. When I complete my education, I will work for the state or for the federal government.
7. On the weekends the children love to go to the ballgames or to the movies.
8. When I visit California, I plan to fish off the pier, not in a boat.
9. Wherever we go on vacation, we plan ahead for unusual dining and for interesting museums.
10. To make sure she does well in her classes, Carla relies on serious study groups as well as on complete notes.

Other Kinds of Parallel Form

-ing Verb Forms

You can also use **-ing** verb forms in parallel patterns to improve your sentences. For example, to use an earlier sentence, you could say,

> Ben spent half the day **mopping the kitchen floor** and **vacuuming the carpet.**

> **Mopping the kitchen floor** and **vacuuming the carpet** took half the day.

The two jobs were of equal importance and are in the same kind of wording.

To-plus-the Verb

Previously, you learned to recognize and use infinitives—**to**-plus-the-verb. These verb forms can also be used in effective parallel form. Read the following example:

> **To show progress** and **to give encouragement,** the instructor posted midterm grades.

The two reasons for posting midterm grades are written in parallel form to show that they are of equal importance. The sentence could also be written without the second **to,** depending on the meaning in your paragraph.

> **To show progress** and **give encouragement,** the instructor posted midterm grades.

Remember that one **to** will be enough. If you use only one, put the **to** before the first word in the parallel form.

All the above sentences use **and** to connect the parts of the parallel form, but as you learned earlier, you can also use **but** or **or** to make parts parallel.

> **Fishing** but not **catching** anything can be disappointing.

> Alex considered **leasing a new car** or **buying a used one.**

> Next week, Jeff plans **to go to a concert** or **(to) work on his car.**

The following exercise will help you practice recognizing these kinds of parallel form.

Exercise 4

Underline the parallel form in each sentence. Look for **-ing** verb forms and **to**-plus-the-verb forms.

Example:

I enjoyed *raking the yard* and *planting the flowers.*

Version A

1. The puppy seemed happy just chewing on toys and sleeping in the sun.

2. Shoveling the snow and salting the walkways kept the custodians busy every winter.

3. Marilyn liked filling the feeder and watching the hummingbirds.

4. A major part of the dean's job was evaluating teachers and informing the community.

5. Chewing tobacco and smoking cigarettes will lead to major health problems.

6. Clara wanted to tour the museum and to visit the gift shop.

7. Seeing the lightning and hearing the thunder upset the young children.

8. When starting on a writing assignment, Aimee likes brainstorming or freewriting.

9. Eating but not overeating can be a challenge for some people.

10. Encouraging athletes to perform on the field and to succeed in the classroom requires outstanding coaching.

Version B

1. The student enjoyed going to class but not doing homework.

2. When working on his psychology paper, Al had time to get information but not to write the paper.

3. Using the Internet at home or driving to the library at school were both options.

4. Many families today must decide whether to eat in or to dine out.

5. While preparing for the best and guarding against the worst, the family felt secure.

6. Kevin likes going to the gym and working out with his friends.

7. Every weekend, Iris spends Saturday morning buying groceries and cooking meals.

8. Whether practicing with each other or playing against each other in tournaments, the Williams sisters are exciting to watch.

9. I wanted to fly to Denver and to tour the U.S. Mint.

10. The student government plans to protest the increase in tuition and to discuss their concerns with the college president.

Three or More Parts in Parallel Form

Now that you have seen how parallel form works with two ideas put into words or phrases that are alike, you are ready to move on to other kinds of parallel form. As you are drafting a sentence or paragraph, you may have several details you want to use to make your point. Very effective sentences may have **three or more** words or phrases in parallel form. Here are earlier examples of sentences, now with a third detail added to each.

Tony bought **blue pants, white shirts,** and **black shoes.**

Ben **mopped the kitchen floor, vacuumed the carpet,** and **washed the windows.**

Ben spent half the day **mopping the kitchen floor, vacuuming the carpet,** and **washing the windows.**

The cooking aromas drifted **through the house, out the door,** and **down the street.**

Work through the following exercise. All the kinds of parallel form that you have just studied are included in this exercise.

Exercise 5

Underline the parallel form in each sentence.

Example:

The student athletes _studied hard_, _practiced carefully_, and _trained regularly_.

Version A

1. Jodi spent her Saturday mornings playing CDs, doing laundry, and cleaning her room.
2. We went to the hardware store, the bank, and the dry cleaners.
3. My mother asked for a blue scarf, a red jacket, and a white hat.
4. The chocolate candy was filled with stale nuts, rubbery caramels, and hard raisins.
5. The innocent, sweet, but impish little girl stole everyone's heart.
6. Many college students spend the summers working, volunteering, and relaxing.
7. The strong winds battered the power lines, splintered the oak tree, and destroyed the roof.
8. After the children went home, I found bubble gum on the carpet, in the trash can, and under the coffee table.
9. The robbers entered the bank quietly, swiftly, but dangerously.
10. Last week at the gym, Leo bench pressed 225 pounds, curled 135 pounds, and squatted 315 pounds.

Version B

1. Frank was tall, thin, but strong.
2. Carefully, precisely, and courageously, the soldiers prepared for war.
3. Jenny practiced swimming, running, and biking so she could enter the triathlon.
4. When I am at the lake, I hope to swim, jet-ski, and fish.

5. Before going on our trip to Canada, we bought calling cards, road maps, and snacks.

6. Lisa's dog, Cricket, bounded up the stairs eagerly, quickly, and easily.

7. I wrote a short, undeveloped, but promising paragraph.

8. I bought a spa to soothe my back, ease my stiff joints, and relax my whole body.

9. We hid the Easter eggs in the grass, on the tree branches, and under the leaves.

10. Darrel wanted to test-drive a Hummer II, an Escalade, and an Expedition.

Work through the following exercise to see if you can complete the parallel form in each sentence. Try to get a feel for the parallel pattern that words can have.

Exercise 6

Fill in an appropriate word or words from the list to complete the parallel form in each sentence. Each answer is used only once.

Example:

List of words:

ate soup   **eating the homemade soup**

During lunch today, we enjoyed discussing the school news and
eating the homemade soup .

Version A

List of Words for Version A:

| difficult | pleased | washed | walked to our seats | avoiding mistakes |
| filled | entertains | unpacked | in the desk drawer | to avoid mistakes |

1. We opened the box and _____ the books.

2. Fred _____ his car and then waxed it.

3. The water covered the yard and _____ the flower beds.

4. Harrison looked tired but _____ after finishing the race.

5. We found the golf course _____ but beautiful.

6. Our most important goals are organizing activities and _____.

7. We sensed the excitement of the concert as we came into the theater and

_____.

8. _____ and to be fair, the teachers used an outside judge.

9. We put the directions on the computer file and _____ .

10. Old Faithful erupts every hour and _____ the visitors.

Version B

List of Words for Version B:

stringing beads	counting their blessings	repainted	admired	softly
reed baskets	playing catch	efficient	charged	ate

1. _____ and gently the father picked up his baby daughter.

2. Karen replaced the carpeting and _____ the walls.

3. _____ and celebrating their victory made everyone even more excited.

4. We saw the sunset and _____ the colors.

5. We watched the team running sprints and _____ .

6. At the art exhibit we saw silver jewelry, _____ , and clay pottery.

7. The national park _____ admission and limited visitors.

8. The man was _____ and organized.

9. We watched the movie and _____ popcorn.

10. _____ and making quilts are part of my family tradition.

Using Pairs of Connecting Words in Parallel Form

Certain pairs of connecting words require parallel form.

> either . . . or
> neither . . . nor
> both . . . and
> not only . . . but   *or*   not only . . . but also

You will want to be careful when you use these connecting words to be sure that your parallel words and phrases are always in similar wording. For example, read the following sentences:

Tanita wanted to borrow **either** the car **or** the truck.

The same kind of word (a noun) follows each connecting word.

Neither Bob **nor** his brother made the basketball team in high school.

Again, the same kind of word (a noun) follows each connecting word.

Here is another example that is a bit more complex:

Mark wanted **both** <u>to go to school</u> **and** <u>to wait for the mail</u>.

This sentence may sound more formal to you, but it is a good example of being precise in wording. This time, **both** and **and** are followed by a **to-**plus-the-verb form and a prepositional phrase. Mark wanted to do **two** things: *go to school* and *wait for the mail*. This sets up the parallel form. Because he could not do both of these things, using **both . . . and** helps to make these contrasting ideas clearer.

To help you line up the parallel pattern, you might want to put the parts on parallel lines.

Mark wanted   **both** <u>to go to school</u>   (*to*+verb and prepositional phrase)

             and <u>to wait for the mail</u>   (*to*+verb and prepositional phrase)

You could also use **not only . . . but also:**

Mark wanted   **not only** <u>to go to school</u>

             but also <u>to wait for the mail</u>

This type of parallel form will work whether you use two words, two phrases, or two whole sentences. (Putting the parts on parallel lines will work especially well with three or more items.)

Note   The main point for you to remember here is that when you are using these pairs of connecting words, whatever type of wording comes after the first connecting word must also come after the second connecting word.

Using Pairs of Connecting Words with Complete Sentences

Study the examples below to see how parallel form is used with whole sentences. Because you are writing sentences now, you should be careful to use a subject and a complete verb in each part.

Either <u>Sue will buy the computer,</u>	(one sentence)
or <u>she will rent one.</u>	(one sentence)
Either <u>the author was too tired to give autographs,</u>	(one sentence)
or <u>she just did not want to stay.</u>	(one sentence)
Neither <u>did I read the book,</u>	(one sentence)
nor <u>did I see the movie.</u>	(one sentence)
Not only <u>did I want to meet the author,</u>	(one sentence)
but <u>I wanted to get her autograph.</u>	(one sentence)

These sentences help you understand that you can use the connecting words to show how ideas relate to each other. The ideas balance each other or contrast to each other.

The next section shows you how to revise poorly worded sentences and use parallel form to make them clearer and stronger.

Revising to Maintain Parallel Form

Study the following sentences and the corrections. Be sure you understand the corrections.

Yvette bought ten gallons of gas and oil for her car.

In the above sentence, the parts are not parallel; did she buy ten gallons of oil for her car? The sentence needs more details about the oil to make it match the details about the gas. Look at the revised sentence.

Yvette bought <u>ten gallons of gas</u>

and <u>five quarts of oil</u> for her car.

Now look at the next sentence that needs to be revised to make the sentence stronger.

Andy was upset about losing his tickets

and could not buy more.   (needs revision)

The above sentence is not in parallel form. Put the two things Andy was upset about in the same kind of wording—two **-ing** verb forms.

Andy was upset about <u>losing his tickets</u>

and <u>not being able to buy more.</u>   (revised with parallel form)

The above sentence is now in parallel form because the second idea is worded like the first one—with an **-ing** verb.

Now look at one more sentence that needs revision. (Remember, to be parallel, **either . . . or** means that the same type of wording comes after each word.)

Either we will paint our house

or sell it as is.   (needs revision)

The above sentence is not in parallel form. The information that follows the word **either** is a complete sentence, but the information that follows the word **or** is not a complete sentence. You can either revise the second part of the sentence to match the first part of the sentence, or you can revise the first part of the sentence to match the second part of the sentence. Both revisions are correct.

Revise the second part to be like the first part:

We will **either** <u>paint our house</u>

or <u>sell it as is.</u>

Or revise the first part to be like the second part:

Either <u>we will paint our house,</u>

or <u>we will sell it as is.</u>

Work through the following exercises to help you use parallel form correctly.

Rewrite each sentence, and correct the non-parallel parts.

Example:

Bill either paid the bill, or he forgot to pay it.

Bill either paid the bill or forgot to pay it.

Revise to make the second part match the first part.

Version A

1. Either the dog needs to stay outside or needs to get a bath.

_____

Revise to make the second part match the first part.

2. I not only went back to college, but I made excellent grades.

_____

Revise to make the second part match the first part.

3. He missed neither a meal nor did he miss a conference.

_____

Revise to make the second part match the first part.

4. I will either take my child to daycare, or I will get a babysitter.

_____

Revise to make the second part match the first part.

5. The car not only had a flat tire but a damaged fender.

_____

Revise to make the second part match the first part.

Version B

1. At the store, I bought neither fresh fruit nor did I buy canned vegetables.

_____

Revise to make the second part match the first part.

2. She not only was late for class, but she also forgot her book.

_____

Revise to make the second part match the first part.

3. Sharon wanted both to go on vacation, and she wanted to stay at home.

_____

Revise to make the second part match the first part.

4. I hoped to put in either a swimming pool or install a spa.

_____

Revise to make the second part match the first part.

5. The storm was not only devastating but it was also frightening.

_____

Revise to make the second part match the first part.

Repetition of Parallel Form for Emphasis

Sometimes parallel form is used to emphasize ideas that carry strong feelings. Deliberately repeating these ideas for emphasis underlines these feelings. The most memorable speeches and writings have examples of parallels that have become famous. For example, think about Martin Luther King Jr.'s words in "I Have a Dream": "Go back to Mississippi, go back to Alabama, go back to Georgia, go back to Louisiana, go back to the slums and ghettos of our northern cities, knowing that somehow this situation can and will be changed." He repeats "go back" five times because he wants his listeners to know that the problem is widespread.

Lincoln's *Gettysburg Address* is another famous speech that contains phrases that many Americans know by heart:

". . . that government **of the people, by the people, for the people** shall not perish from the earth."

More recently, the cover of *People* magazine (Feb. 17, 2003) featured a picture of the crew from *Columbia,* the space shuttle that broke apart during reentry from outer space. Under the picture is a caption that reads,

"Family and friends recall *Columbia's* crew—the lives they made and the lives they touched."

Because of the emotions surrounding this accident, this parallel phrasing has a way of reaching out to the reader and drawing attention to the article.

Just as overusing a word can be boring and monotonous, repeating a key idea or word can be effective.

Using Modifying Phrases Correctly

Another way to improve your sentences is to use modifying phrases correctly. Two common errors that occur are dangling modifiers and misplaced modifiers.

- A dangling modifier has nothing to modify because the subject is missing from the sentence.
- A misplaced modifier creates confusion in a sentence because it is not placed next to the noun or pronoun that it modifies.

Improving Sentences by Avoiding Dangling Modifiers

When writing sentences, your main concern is to write clearly and effectively so you can communicate your ideas to other people. Dangling modifiers keep your ideas from being clear.

A dangling modifier is a phrase that comes at the beginning of a sentence but has no noun or pronoun to modify because there is no subject to which it is logically connected. When you begin a sentence with a phrase such as "riding my bike along the trail," the information that tells who is riding the bike needs to be identified in the subject of the sentence. Putting in a correct subject will eliminate this confusion. Look at the following two sentences. In the first sentence, there is no subject to identify who is riding the bicycle.

Riding my bike along the trail, a coyote surprised me.   (rider not identified)

Riding my bike along the trail, I was surprised by a coyote.   (rider identified)

Most likely, the coyote was not riding the bicycle; rather, the person riding the bike needs to be identified as the subject of the sentence. These types of misunderstandings can be avoided if you make the subject of the sentence the one who was doing something.

Look at the following sentences to see if you can see why they are not clear.

Sentences with dangling modifiers	Correct sentences
Driven by greed, many old people were cheated out of their savings.	Driven by greed, the attorney cheated many old people out of their savings.
Climbing up the rope, my mother had to take me to the emergency room.	Climbing up the rope, I tore the skin from my hands and had to be taken to the emergency room.
Climbing up the rope, my hands were bleeding.	Climbing up the rope I made my hands bleed.
Hit by a strong storm, I saw an uprooted tree.	Hit by a strong storm, the tree was uprooted by the force of the wind.
Bitten by a snake, I had to take my dog to the vet.	Bitten by a snake, my dog almost died.
To stop the bleeding, a bandage was put on.	To stop the bleeding, a nurse put on a bandage.

After you become familiar with these types of errors, you will want to try to spot these types of mistakes as well as correct them. Work through the following exercises for practice.

Exercise 8

Choose the correct sentence from each pair of sentences below. Circle the letter of the correct answer.

Example:

a. **Visiting California in the wintertime, the weather was pleasant.**

b. **Visiting California in the wintertime, I enjoyed pleasant weather.**

Version A

1. a. Being very spicy, we enjoyed the hot Mexican food.

    b. Being very spicy, the hot Mexican food was delicious.

2. a. Stumbling on the broken sidewalk, my new shoes were scratched.

    b. Stumbling on the broken sidewalk, I scratched my new shoes.

3. a. Built in 1800, the house had to be restored.

    b. Built in 1800, we had to restore the house.

4. a. After parking the bus, the driver invited the passengers to go shopping.

    b. After parking the bus, the passengers went shopping.

5. a. After having a second serving of spaghetti, the dog ate the leftovers.

    b. After having a second serving of spaghetti, the man fed his dog leftover spaghetti.

6. a. At the age of three, I went to a horse show with my father.

    b. At the age of three, my father took me to the horse show.

7. a. Making a routine traffic check, ten bags of marijuana were confiscated.

    b. Making a routine traffic check, the police officer confiscated ten bags of marijuana.

8. a. Nudged out of the nest, the baby bird flew a few feet.

    b. Nudged out of the nest, I watched the baby bird fly a few feet.

9. a. To save money, a budget was carefully planned.

    b. To save money, the company carefully planned a budget.

10. a. Picking apples, the buckets filled fast.

    b. Picking apples, we filled the buckets fast.

Version B

1. a. To find the owner of the bulldog, an ad ran in the paper.

    b. To find the owner of the bulldog, my mom ran an ad in the paper.

2. a. Using honey-lemon cough drops, my coughing stopped.

    b. Using honey-lemon cough drops, I stopped coughing.

3. a. Left out in the snow, the letter remained buried for months.

    b. Left out in the snow, I found the letter months later.

4. a. Waiting for the bus, the rain drenched us all.

    b. Waiting for the bus, we were all drenched by the rain.

5. a. Eating pizza on Monday night, I dropped the cheese on the floor.

    b. Eating pizza on Monday night, the cheese fell on the floor.

6. a. Cruising down the street in my new Mustang, I had a flat tire that ruined my fun.

    b. Cruising down the street in my new Mustang, a flat tire ruined my fun.

7. a. To sell the house at a good price, the refrigerator was included.

   b. To sell the house at a good price, I included the refrigerator in the price.

8. a. Left without a date, my new dress hung unworn in the closet.

   b. Left without a date, I hung my new unworn dress in the closet.

9. a. Practicing the piano, I heard the ice cream man drive down the street.

   b. Practicing the piano, the ice cream man drove down the street.

10. a. Running out of time, I had to get an extension on my income tax.

    b. Running out of time, my income tax was going to be late.

___

Exercise 9

Complete the following sentences by adding a complete sentence to the phrases. Be sure that the subject of the sentence refers to the phrase. (Notice that a comma comes after the introductory phrase.)

Example:

Running through the house, *the children knocked over the lamp* .

Version A

1. Lost for two days, _____

   _____

2. Caught in the backyard, _____

   _____

3. Painted with bright colors, _____

   _____

4. Walking through the mall, _____

   _____

5. Brushing my dog, _____

   _____

6. Landscaping my back yard, _____

   _____

7. Arranging the food on the picnic table, _____

   _____

8. Discovering the mistake in my checking account, _____

   _____

9. Enjoying the sale, _____

   _____

10. Cooked thoroughly, _____

    _____

Version B

1. Reading the newspaper, _____
   _____

2. Bitten by the dog, _____
   _____

3. Chatting over the Internet, _____
   _____

4. Stopping to mail the letters at the post office, _____
   _____

5. Putting my books back on the bookshelf, _____
   _____

6. Purchased at the discount store, _____
   _____

7. Bottled in Maine, _____
   _____

8. Standing in a long line at the box office, _____
   _____

9. Chatting on a cell phone, _____
   _____

10. Speeding on the interstate, _____
    _____

Improving Sentences by Avoiding Misplaced Modifiers

Other times, a phrase that modifies a noun or pronoun is so far from the noun or pronoun that the reader is confused. These are called misplaced modifiers. In the following sentence, the phrase "without a helmet" seems to modify "bike" because it comes right after it. You need to ask yourself, "Did the bike have a helmet, or did the child have a helmet?" Of course, the child, not the bike, had the helmet. To correct the mistake, you simply need to put the phrase next to "child," the noun that it modifies.

A child was riding a bike without a helmet.   (phrase placed incorrectly)

A child without a helmet was riding a bike .   (phrase placed correctly)

Sentences with misplaced modifiers	Correct sentences
A dog was limping down the street with a sore paw.	A dog with a sore paw was limping down the street.
The letter was sealed in the envelope with the correct information.	The letter with the correct information was sealed in the envelope.

Choose the correct sentence from the pair of sentences below. Circle the letter of the correct answer.

Example:

   (a.) **The kitchen with the built-in microwave was ideal for my family.**

   b. **The kitchen was ideal for my family with the built-in microwave.**

Version A

1. a. The children were outside playing on the swings with happy faces.
    b. The children with happy faces were outside playing on the swings.
2. a. The man walking along the street carried a brightly wrapped package.
    b. The man carried a brightly wrapped package walking along the street.
3. a. The house burned to the ground with the three-car garage.
    b. The house with the three-car garage burned to the ground.
4. a. The dog won the championship trophy trained by an expert handler.
    b. The dog trained by an expert handler won the championship trophy.
5. a. The singer winning the Grammy Award declined an interview.
    b. The singer declined an interview winning the Grammy Award.
6. a. The race car starting in the first row went fast into the turn.
    b. The race car went fast into the turn starting in the first row.
7. a. The movie won an Academy Award made on location in the Rockies.
    b. The movie made on location in the Rockies won an Academy Award.
8. a. The car with the leaking radiator was abandoned on a country road.
    b. The car was abandoned on a country road with the leaking radiator.
9. a. The young couple getting married in Las Vegas planned a Hawaiian honeymoon.
    b. The young couple planned a Hawaiian honeymoon getting married in Las Vegas.
10. a. A young man knocked on the front door carrying a big bouquet of roses.
    b. A young man carrying a big bouquet of roses knocked on the front door.

Version B

1. a. I bought a picture at a yard sale without a frame.
    b. At a yard sale, I bought a picture without a frame.
2. a. The greyhound with the gentle disposition learned to walk on a leash.
    b. The greyhound learned to walk on a leash with the gentle disposition.
3. a. A customer looking at a Blazer decided to test-drive a Corvette.
    b. A customer decided to test-drive a Corvette looking at a Blazer.
4. a. In the late afternoon, the children went to a movie together on my street.
    b. In the late afternoon, the children on my street went to a movie together.

5. a. The candidate running for office made campaign trips on a private bus.

   b. The candidate made campaign trips on a private bus running for office.

6. a. The newspaper called it a disaster analyzing the Senate bill.

   b. The newspaper analyzing the Senate bill called it a disaster.

7. a. The youngster played the trumpet with the hearing aids.

   b. The youngster with the hearing aids played the trumpet.

8. a. The NASCAR race shortened by the storm was won by a rookie.

   b. The NASCAR race was won by a rookie shortened by the storm.

9. a. The scruffy-looking cat chased butterflies with three kittens.

   b. The scruffy-looking cat with three kittens chased butterflies.

10. a. The young man with distinct tattoos on his shoulder was playing basketball.

    b. The young man was playing basketball with distinct tattoos on his shoulder.

 ## *Summary*

You can improve your writing by paying careful attention to your writing and by editing carefully. Knowing how to use effective parallel form and repetition for emphasis can help you strengthen your sentences and paragraphs. You also need to be aware of errors such as dangling modifiers and misplaced modifiers. As you edit your paragraphs, look for these types of revisions.

- Parallel form means that parts of speech or phrases are written in the same way. Using parallel form can not only strengthen your sentences but make your sentences clearer to your reader.

    Two or more equal parts of a sentence need to be written using the same form.

    Connecting words like *either . . . or* are used in pairs to keep complete sentences in parallel form.

    Repetition of parallel form can be used when you wish to emphasize a point that carries strong feelings.

- Using modifiers correctly can also improve sentences.

    A dangling modifier is a phrase that comes at the beginning of the sentence but has no noun or pronoun to modify because the subject is not logically connected to the phrase.

    A misplaced modifier is a phrase that modifies a noun or pronoun that is so far away that the reader may be confused about the meaning of the sentence.

Practice Test

Complete **both** Part 1 and Part 2 of this practice test. Part 1 contains parallel form, and Part 2 contains dangling and misplaced modifiers.

A. Parallel Form

Read the following paragraph, and then answer the questions that follow. Circle the letter of the correct answer.

(1) Watching the nonstop, well-organized action at the Papa John's Pizza restaurant was enough to make anyone tired. (2) Two employees quickly but efficiently answered the telephones that rang with no break. (3) Between calls, they took orders from people who came in to place an order or to pick up an order they had already called in. (4) The workers then passed the orders to another employee who carefully and skillfully was throwing pizza dough in the air, catching it with both hands, and shaping it into a perfect circle. (5) At this point, another young man took over as he scooped the spicy, thick sauce onto the dough. (6) He then covered the sauce with cheese, added pepperoni, onions, or other ingredients, and then put each pizza into the oven. (7) Another person, on the other side of the oven, took each pizza from the oven, cut it into pie-shaped pieces, slid it into the prepared boxes, and stacked it on a shelf. (8) If no pizza was coming out of the oven, he joined the other person who was magically and gracefully tossing the dough. (9) Just as quickly, drivers grabbed an order and started a delivery. (10) No one stopped for even one minute, but the young people stayed cheerful and kept working.

1. In sentence #1, what two adjectives are parallel?
   a. watching, well-organized
   b. nonstop, action
   c. nonstop, well-organized

2. In sentence #2, what two adverbs are parallel?
   a. quickly, efficiently
   b. employees, answered
   c. efficiently, with no break

3. In sentence #3, what two phrases are parallel?
   a. between calls, from people
   b. from people, who came in
   c. to place an order, to pick up an order

4. In sentence #4, what two adverbs are parallel?
   a. then, shaping
   b. carefully, skillfully
   c. workers, employee

5. In sentence #4, what three verb forms are parallel?
   a. throwing pizza dough in the air, catching it with both hands, shaping it into a perfect circle
   b. passed the orders, carefully, skillfully
   c. workers, employee, orders

6. In sentence #5, what two adjectives are parallel?
   a. dough, spicy
   b. young, spicy
   c. spicy, thick

7. In sentence #6, what are the parallel verbs?
   a. with cheese, other ingredients, pizza
   b. covered, added, put
   c. with cheese, into the oven, added pepperoni

8. In sentence #6, each parallel verb has at least one object. What are these objects?
   a. sauce, pepperoni, onions, ingredients, pizza
   b. sauce; pepperoni, onions, other ingredients, pizza
   c. sauce, with cheese, other ingredients

9. In sentence #7, four verbs begin a series of parallel phrases. What makes these phrases parallel?
   a. Each one includes a verb and nothing more.
   b. Each one includes a verb and an adjective.
   c. Each one includes a verb, object, and prepositional phrase.

10. In sentence #8, what two adverbs are parallel?
    a. was coming, was tossing
    b. out of the oven, joined the other person
    c. magically, gracefully

11. In sentence #8, what verb is parallel to "was coming"?
    a. joined
    b. was tossing
    c. out of the oven

12. In sentence #9, what phrase is parallel to "grabbed an order"?
    a. started a delivery
    b. just as quickly
    c. drivers grabbed

13. In sentence #10, what two verbs are in parallel form?

   a. minute, people

   b. stayed, kept

   c. no one, working

B. Dangling and Misplaced Modifiers

Read through this second paragraph about the pizza parlor, and then answer the questions that follow.

(1) Suddenly, among all this productivity, pressure began to build.

(2) Tossing the pizza dough in the air, it suddenly flew out of the young man's reach and landed on the floor. (3) Glancing at the floor, flour and a couple of pepperoni stared back at him. (4) He quickly pushed the dough under the table that had also fallen near a pile of flour. (5) Just then, an older woman with extra toppings came in and ordered ten pizzas to go.

(6) Noticing that the stack of folded boxes was almost gone, there was no place to slide the cooked pizzas. (7) At the same time, someone yelled that the several pizzas near the oven were ready to come out.

(8) Not even the manager panicked at the store. (9) Working together, everything was corrected and production soon became smooth again.

In the above paragraph, all of the sentences except the first one have either a dangling modifier or a misplaced modifier. Circle the letter of the best correction for each sentence.

1. This sentence is correct as written.

2. a. Tossing the pizza dough in the air, it suddenly flew out of the young man's reach and landed on the floor.

    b. Tossing the pizza dough in the air, the young man missed the dough, and it landed on the floor.

    c. Tossing the pizza dough in the air, the dough flew out of the young man's hands and landed on the floor.

3. a. Glancing at the floor, flour and a couple of pepperoni stared back at him.

    b. Glancing at the floor, the flour and pepperoni lay on the floor.

    c. Glancing at the floor, he noticed flour and a couple of pepperoni staring back at him.

4. a. With his foot, he quickly pushed the dough under the table near a pile of flour that had also fallen.

   b. He quickly pushed the dough under the table near a pile of flour that had also fallen with his foot.

   c. He quickly pushed the dough with his foot under the table near a pile of flour that had also fallen.

5. a. Just then, an older woman with extra toppings came in and ordered ten pizzas to go.

   b. Just then, an older woman came in with extra toppings and ordered ten pizzas to go.

   c. Just then, an older woman came in and ordered ten pizzas with extra toppings to go.

6. a. Noticing that the stack of folded boxes was almost gone, the cooked pizzas had no place to go.

   b. Noticing that the stack of folded boxes was almost gone, the associate had no place to slide the cooked pizzas.

   c. Noticing that the stack of folded boxes was almost gone, there was no place to slide the cooked pizzas.

7. a. At the same time, someone near the oven yelled that several pizzas were ready to come out.

   b. At the same time, several pizzas near the oven were ready to come out someone yelled.

   c. At the same time, someone yelled that several pizzas were ready to come out near the oven.

8. a. Not even the manager panicked at the store.

   b. Not even the manager at the store panicked.

   c. The manager did not even panic at the store.

9. a. Working together, production became smooth again and everything was corrected.

   b. Working together, everything was corrected, and production soon became smooth again.

   c. Working together, the crew corrected everything, and production soon became smooth.

 Writing Assignment

Write a paragraph on one of the following topics. Be sure to start with a topic sentence. Then add support sentences, and end with a concluding sentence. Brainstorm or freewrite at length to have enough details to use in your support sentences. Be sure to have good examples of parallel form. Look for any dangling or misplaced modifiers and revise accordingly.

1. Who or what gives you your greatest feeling of security?

2. What has changed in your life because of a threat of terrorism?

3. What can individuals or the government do to prepare for a national disaster?

4. What can parents do to create a sense of patriotism in their children?

5. What are the negative or positive outcomes for a high school athlete who skips college to go directly into professional sports?

6. What can people do to prepare themselves when a spouse or partner is called to active duty?

7. What can parents do to prepare their children when one of the parents is called to active duty?

8. Describe a favorite family event.

9. Describe a favorite state or national park.

Chapter 7

Editing for a Final Version

Part 1

Punctuation

Objectives

- Review the uses of a comma.
- Review the use of quotation marks.
- Review the use of the apostrophe.
- Review the use of underlining or italics.
- Review the use of parentheses.
- Review the use of dashes and hyphens.
- Review ways of punctuating simple, compound, and complex sentences.

As you write papers, you will want to be sure that you punctuate your sentences and paragraphs correctly. This means paying close attention to all types of punctuation. Punctuation helps your reader follow your ideas clearly. Often in verbal communication, you use tone of voice or facial expressions or even hand signals to help you say what you mean, but in writing, you have to rely on punctuation marks.

Using Commas Correctly

Using commas correctly is not a matter of speculation. Though you can sometimes tell by a natural pause whether or not you need a comma, that may not be the best way to decide because not all pauses take a comma. Learning the simple rules for using commas and using commas only when you know the rules will help you edit your paragraphs to be more effective. Following is a summary of the uses of commas.

- Items in a series
- Introductory material
- Clarity
    - Identifying and non-identifying expressions
    - Interrupters
    - Misunderstandings
- Addresses and dates
- In direct address

Items in a Series

- Commas are used to separate three or more items in a series of words, phrases, or clauses.

  Three or more words in a series are set off by commas.

  > They purchased **bananas, apples,** and **oranges** at the farmers' market.
  >
  > **Fire trucks, police cars,** and **two helicopters** arrived at the accident.
  >
  > My friend Amy is **bright, motivated,** yet often **sarcastic.**
  >
  > Phil entered the room **slowly, sadly,** and **dejectedly.**

  Three or more phrases in a series are set off by commas.

  > I looked for the missing papers **in the closet, on the shelf,** and **under the stairs.**
  >
  > Rodney **planned the trip, made reservations,** and **bought airplane tickets.**
  >
  > Robin needs to **make an appointment, get her tax information together,** and **see her tax attorney.**
  >
  > Even to be considered for the job, applicants must have **completed a college degree, worked in a medical facility,** and **volunteered at a hospital.**

  Three or more dependent clauses in a series are set off by commas.

  > I know **where I am going, how I am going to get there,** and **whom I will see.**
  >
  > I like **who you are, how you act,** and **what you say.**

- Commas are *not* used to separate words, phrases, or clauses in a series if they are all separated by coordinate conjunctions. You might intentionally use coordinate conjunctions in this way to emphasize each word or phrase.

  > I especially liked his smile **and** his wit **and** his enthusiasm.
  >
  > My girlfriend did not like my haircut **or** my clothes **or** my car.
  >
  > He was so nervous that he could not eat **or** sleep **or** concentrate.

- Use a comma between two equal adjectives or adverbs if the words can be reversed or when they sound acceptable when a coordinate conjunction separates them. The first sentence below sounds correct when you reverse the words: "beautifully and softly." It also sounds correct when you say "softly and beautifully."

  > **Softly, beautifully,** she hummed as she worked.
  >
  > She worked as she hummed **softly and beautifully.**
  >
  > I wore my **old black boots.**

  The last sentence does not sound right if you say "my old and black boots" or "my black old boots."

Exercise 1

Punctuate the following sentences correctly. Look for items in a series, and add commas as needed. If a sentence is correct, put a **C** in the left margin.

Example:

The vending machine sold peanuts, candy, and gum.

Version A

1. We restocked the shelves refilled the gum machine and turned out the lights.

2. Lucille wanted to see the Grand Canyon Bryce Canyon and Death Valley.

3. When looking for our little brother, we looked down the street around the corner and up the hill.

4. At the hardware store, we bought brushes paint and tape.

5. My neighbor was thoughtful and generous and patient.

6. The manager seems upbeat and organized.

7. When David goes to his parents' house, he leaves with home-cooked food clean laundry and gas money.

8. Before my next class, I need to read the assignment answer the questions and write a summary.

9. My mother was not at all pleased with my boyfriend his tattoo or his purple hair.

10. The old couple seemed resourceful content and quick-witted.

Version B

1. The children spent the afternoon playing marbles jacks and cards.

2. At the bank, Tony cashed a check opened a savings account and ordered new checks.

3. Tom was so frustrated that he closed the book left the room and turned on the television.

4. Heather Tammy and Marsha are all involved in student government.

5. The peahen guided her two chicks across the parking lot down to the classroom and onto the tree limb.

6. He dreamed of earning his degree starting his own business and buying a home.

7. At the crafts fair, we saw paintings jewelry and other handmade items.

8. The memorial service was inspirational and dignified and reassuring.

9. Helping with experiments writing reports and cleaning equipment were Sandra's primary responsibilities in the lab.

10. After hunting for a parking space waiting to see an advisor and registering for classes I still had time to buy my books.

Introductory Material

Commas are used to set off introductory items.

- **Single words**

    Unfortunately, I cannot find my debit card.

    Yes, I need to reschedule the appointment.

    Suddenly, the door flew open.

    Well, we could always do this differently.

- **Phrases**

    In the summertime, we love to walk along the edge of the river.

    After the movie, Gerard and I went out for pizza.

    Watching the squirrel dart up the tree, I forgot about all my problems.

    After eating lunch, Tom walked back to the library to study.

    Sickened by the pollution, most people had to stay inside their homes.

    To get into the art exhibit, even the members had to have a ticket.

- **Dependent clauses**

    When the sun goes down, the music begins.

    After Sam enters pharmacy school, he will have four years to complete his degree.

    Because the traffic signals were not working, the drivers had to be extremely cautious.

Note Often when these expressions are placed somewhere else in the sentence, they are not set off by a comma.

    The door **suddenly** flew open.

    Gerard and I went out for pizza **after the movie.**

    The music begins **when the sun goes down.**

Exercise 2

Punctuate the following sentences by setting off introductory words, phrases, and dependent clauses with commas.

Example:

Unexpectedly the door of the car flew open.

Version A

1. Because Rob left his car with the engine running an opportunistic thief jumped in and drove it away.
2. Fortunately I had an adequate supply of bottled water.
3. Yes I do want to come to visit you in St. Louis.

4. Before leaving would you be sure the appliances are all off?

5. Shocked by the news I called my family in Wisconsin.

6. Realistically I do not think I can make it home on time.

7. All right I was wrong about the score of the game.

8. To file a police report Ed had to go down to the station and fill out several forms.

9. At the end of the conference we all exchanged e-mail addresses.

10. Personally I like classical music better than jazz.

Version B

1. In spite of the ice storm emergency room doctors and nurses had to report to the hospital.

2. While sitting at a sidewalk cafe I had my purse stolen.

3. Before the game the entire team warmed up in brand-new shoes.

4. Most likely we will get a flight out of New York tomorrow.

5. By putting up the wallpaper herself Abby saved several hundred dollars.

6. No I do not want to call a cab at this time.

7. Being courageous I was the first one in line to donate blood.

8. Stung by a spider I immediately went to the hospital emergency room.

9. Unless you have any more questions we will move on to the next chapter.

10. Well where do you want to go for lunch?

Commas for Clarity

- ### Identifying and non-identifying expressions

An **identifying expression** is one that is needed in the sentence to identify the noun that comes before it. You do not use commas to separate this kind of expression from the rest of the sentence.

The college students **who have not had their vaccinations** may not register for classes.

The father **who coached his daughter's ball team** also helped her with her homework.

I needed to stop at the store **that had the best sales.**

A **non-identifying expression** simply adds more information to the sentence but is not needed to identify the noun that comes before it. Because it is not needed to identify the noun, you can leave it out of the sentence without changing the meaning. For this reason, you **do use** commas to separate these expressions from the rest of the sentence.

Brenda, **the youngest child in her family,** is learning to play the piano.

I need to pick up my mother, **who just got off work.**

Sonic, **which is on the way home,** has great milkshakes.

- **Interrupters**

A comma is used before and after an interrupter, a word or phrase that interrupts the flow of the sentence. If an expression is not really a part of the structure of the sentence, then it is most likely an interrupter. The word or phrase could be taken out of the sentence and still leave a complete idea. On the other hand, these interrupters are often transitional in nature and add to the overall effectiveness of the sentences within a paragraph.

I do not, **for example,** wish to reschedule my appointment.

I called my neighbor, **a very helpful person,** and asked her for advice.

Colin Powell was, **after all,** competent to take care of the situation.

Everybody in my family, **especially Jan,** loves to get up early in the morning and work in the yard.

Words or Phrases That Are Often Used as Interrupters

as a matter of fact	however
by the way	in fact
for example	nevertheless
especially . . .	of course
for instance	that is

- **Misunderstandings**

Sometimes a comma is needed to avoid confusion and misunderstanding in a sentence. A comma may also help to clarify the precise meaning of a sentence. Without commas, the following sentence is confusing.

Sue Ellen is going to meet you at the student union.

The girl's name is Sue Ellen, so no comma is needed. In the next sentence, however, the comma clarifies that someone is talking to Sue about Ellen.

Sue, Ellen is going to meet you at the student union.

Exercise 3

In the following sentences, look for identifying and non-identifying expressions, interrupters, and misunderstandings. Then add commas as needed. If the sentence is correct, put a C in the left margin.

Example:

The taxi driver ∧of course ∧needs a suitable tip.

Version A

1. We left our road map by the way at the last rest stop.

2. Dr. Hernandez who teaches math will be in charge of the seminar.

3. All of my employees especially those attending college are outstanding.

4. The nurse who dispenses medication must be very efficient.

5. The administrators not the teachers wanted to implement a new program.

6. A dog without proper training is not pleasant to have around.

7. The office attendant as a matter of fact was not courteous to the pets or their owners.

8. The math instructors who are all from the local university offered a seminar.

9. The book that I read for extra credit was an exciting novel.

10. The waitress of course earned a generous tip.

Version B

1. The credit union as a matter of fact has lower interest rates than the bank.

2. The long drive however was not as tiring as we expected.

3. Shawn who grew up with a pet learned responsibility early.

4. The cats in the show especially the Himalayans were laid back and cooperative.

5. A child who grows up with a pet will learn responsibility early.

6. Stan Wagner who has excellent experience is our new college president.

7. The applicant who has the best qualifications will be our new dean.

8. The auto dealers who advertised on television had many new customers.

9. Islam by the way has millions of followers throughout the world.

10. The pet supermarket of course carried an unusually large variety of food.

Addresses and Dates

- Use a comma to separate the elements in a street address used in a sentence: the name of a city, county, state, and zip code. You do not use a comma between the name of the state and the zip code, but you do put a comma after the zip code.

  The package that Mom sent me at **530 Park Avenue, Flagstaff, Arizona 85261**, did not arrive on time.

  My trip to **Pike's Peak, Colorado**, was much too short.

- Use a comma to separate the parts of a date. Also, put a comma after the year.

  On **April 6, 2003**, we began our trip across the United States.

  On **Tuesday, April 6, 2003**, we visited the Jelly Belly factory.

- However, you do not use a comma if the day is not included along with the month.

  Our trip that began in **April 2003** was very educational.

- When you use the following format for a date, do not use a comma.

We began our trip across the United States on **6 April 2003**.

Direct Address

- Use a comma to set off a person's name when you are speaking directly to someone, whether you use that person's actual name, nickname, or another word in place of a name, like **Mom** or **Dad.**

If you do not mind, **Carrie**, could you please pick up a book for me?

Well, **Dad**, I need some information about growing roses.

- Do not use a comma when you are talking about someone rather than directly to someone.

Please ask **Carrie** to pick up the book.

Exercise 4

Add the commas needed in the following sentences. Look for addresses, dates, and direct address. If no punctuation is needed, put a C in the left margin.

Example:

On May 10ˏ2004ˏwe have reservations for the Forest Houses Resort.

Version A

1. The last place we lived was 32 East Columbus Avenue Mesa Arizona.
2. My dog is registered in San Diego County.
3. Tom can you fix my flat tire this evening?
4. If you think about it Jim you will probably make the right decision.
5. If you do not mind Susan I would rather stay home tonight.
6. The package that I shipped to 711 North Townley Alameda California 94501 arrived safely.
7. If you would like to Fred we could paint the garage tomorrow.
8. We went to Canada Mom on 10 July 2003.
9. Please ask Cathy if she wants to go with us.
10. Everybody who has an April birthday will be honored at the potluck.

Version B

1. Steven applied for the police academy in September 2003.
2. We completed our tour on 14 August 2003.
3. Beth completed her degree on May 22 2002.
4. We left on June 10 2002 for San Francisco California.
5. Some day Barbara we will go to Alaska and see the wildlife refuge.
6. Marita why don't we call Mack and see if he wants to go out for pizza?

7. My old address at 4309 W. Phillips Drive Hoover Alabama 35216 is being changed.

8. At the last count Bill we had collected enough money to help the family.

9. John the house we considered buying is at 1400 Wilder Road Taos New Mexico.

10. The trouble my friend is that we have no gas in our truck.

Using Quotation Marks (" ") Correctly

Quotation marks enclose the exact words that someone says or writes. Capitalize the first word of a direct quotation unless it is a continuation of a sentence.

- Use a comma to set off the direct quotation from the rest of the sentence. Capitalize the first word of the direct quotation.

    My mom wrote, "The winters seem to get colder every year."

    Robert said, "That new red Chevy truck has lots of extras."

- If the quotation is interrupted, put quotation marks only around the actual words that someone says or writes. Use commas to separate the quoted words from the rest of the sentence.

    "The winters," my mom wrote, "seem to get colder every year."

    "You know," said Robert, "I would like to buy a new truck."

- Do **not** use quotation marks if you use an indirect quotation or simply summarize someone else's words.

    My mom said that the winter weather gets colder all the time.

    Robert said that the new Chevy truck has lots of extras.

- If you put some of the quotation in your own words and use some of the exact words as well, you still need quotation marks around the exact words you use. If the quotation is a continuation of your own sentence, no comma is used. In this case, do **not** capitalize the first word of the direct quotation.

    My mom said that the winter weather seems "a little colder every year."

Words Used as Words

Quotation marks, italics, or boldface are used to designate words that are being discussed as words.

    When I think of the word "courageous," I think about Tom.

    When I think of the word *courageous*, I think about Tom.

    When I think of the word **courageous**, I think about Tom.

Quotation within a Quotation

Sometimes you will need to put one quotation inside another. **Use single quotation marks inside the double ones.**

> Nerida said to her mother, "I want you to hear the baby say 'Mama' just as she did for me."

Titles Contained within Larger Works

Use quotation marks around the title of any selection that has been published within a larger work. Underline or *italicize* the name of the larger work.

> "His Separate Shadow" is the title of the second chapter in Leif Enger's book *Peace Like a River.*

> Nikki Giovanni's poem "Beautiful Black Men" shows a positive attitude toward men.

Punctuation with Quotation Marks

- **Commas** and **periods** always go **inside** the quotation marks.

> "I am hungry," said Andrew, "so I hope we can go out to eat."

- If you combine quoted material with a sentence that is not a quotation, you may have to use a **semicolon.** Semicolons go **outside** the quotation mark.

> The restaurant advertises "the best hot corned beef and pastrami in the city"; we wholeheartedly agree.

- If you ask a question, you need to think clearly about what the exact question is. For example:

> Dan said, "I am busy Saturday night." (This is obviously not a question.)
> Did Dan say, "I am busy Saturday night"?

You are quoting Dan, but Dan did not ask the question. The **question mark** goes **outside** the quotation mark because the whole sentence is a question.

- In a similar way, if you say something that needs an exclamation point, but you are also quoting something, the exclamation mark goes outside the quotation mark.

> The legislature wants to cut school budgets "by twenty-five percent"!

Exercise 5

In this exercise, use quotation marks and other punctuation marks where needed.

Example:

The mechanic said ~~your~~ "Your car is in top shape."

Version A

1. All at once, everyone yelled get the ball.

2. My aunt wrote I hope you can visit with us this summer.

3. Justin said that he was looking for a new condominium.

4. Did you hear your mother say I am proud of you?

5. When I think of the word crook, I think about the executives at Enron and the Baptist Foundation.

6. Cathy Queen of Cats is one of my favorite stories in The House on Mango Street.

Version B

1. Stephanie yelled we won the National Collegiate Volleyball Championship.

2. Come when you can he said and it is all right to bring your dog.

3. I find I am offended when people use the words honey and sweetie when they are talking to customers.

4. My instructor said that we could leave after we finished the test.

5. The hotel reservations read thank you for choosing our hotel.

6. My psychology professor recommended that I read the chapter called Coming Around in Dave Pelzer's book The Lost Boy.

Using Apostrophes Correctly

Apostrophes are used in writing to show **ownership or possession.** When you are speaking and you want to show that somebody owns something, you add an *s*. When you want to show that Tony owns a car, you would say "Tony's car." As you can see in this phrase, when you want to show **in writing** that Tony has a car, you add **an apostrophe and an *s*.** The apostrophe and the s show the difference in writing between a regular plural noun and a noun showing possession or ownership. You always need an s sound to show ownership.

Singular Possessive Nouns

- **If a singular noun does not end in *s*, add an apostrophe and an *s* ('s) to show the possessive.**

   Study the following to become familiar with the singular possessive form of nouns.

A boy	has or owns	a car.	=	boy's car
A car	has	an engine.	=	car's engine
A painter	has	a contract.	=	painter's contract
A dog	has	a personality.	=	dog's personality

- **If a singular noun ends in *s*, add an apostrophe and an *s* ('s)**

   We always go to Louis's house on Friday nights.

   I would love to ride in James's car.

Note Some writers use only an apostrophe if adding both an apostrophe and an **s** would seem odd. For example, to use the form "Alexis's" might look odd, and some writers elect to simply use the apostrophe. Instead of writing "Alexis's book," they write "Alexis' book."

Plural Possessive Nouns

When you want to show ownership or possession for a plural noun, you always need to know what the **correct plural** form of the noun is.

- **If the plural ends in s, just add an apostrophe after the s.**

   Study the following to become familiar with the most common way of forming plural possessive nouns.

Boy<u>s</u>	have	cars.	=	boys' cars
Car<u>s</u>	have	engines.	=	cars' engines
Painter<u>s</u>	have	contracts.	=	painters' contracts
Dog<u>s</u>	have	personalities.	=	dogs' personalities

- **If the plural form does not end in s, you add an apostrophe and an s.**

Children	have	toys.	=	children's toys
Women	have	golf clubs.	=	women's golf clubs
Men	have	golf clubs.	=	men's golf clubs
Deer	have	antlers.	=	deer's antlers

Work through the following exercises to help you practice writing the possessive forms of singular and plural nouns.

Exercise 6

In each blank, write the possessive form for each <u>underlined</u> singular noun.

Example:

A girl has a bike.   _girl's_____ bike

Version A
1. The <u>cat</u> has a kitten.   _____ kitten
2. The <u>neighbor</u> has canaries.   _____ canaries
3. The <u>oven</u> has temperature.   _____ temperature
4. The <u>counselor</u> has a new schedule.   _____ new schedule
5. The <u>heater</u> has a switch.   _____ switch

Version B
1. The <u>cart</u> has wheels.   _____ wheels
2. The <u>store</u> has advertising.   _____ advertising
3. The <u>magazine</u> has a cover.   _____ cover
4. The <u>shovel</u> has a handle.   _____ handle
5. The <u>book</u> has pages.   _____ pages

Exercise 7

Using the same words as in Exercise 6, write the plural possessive form for each noun. First, make the noun a regular plural form. Second, make the plural a possessive form.

Example:

Singular	Regular Plural	Plural possessive	
girl	*girls*	*girls'*	**bikes**

Version A

1. cat	_____	_____	kittens
2. neighbor	_____	_____	canaries
3. oven	_____	_____	temperatures
4. counselor	_____	_____	problems
5. heater	_____	_____	switches

Version B

1. cart	_____	_____	wheels
2. store	_____	_____	advertising
3. magazine	_____	_____	covers
4. shovel	_____	_____	handles
5. book	_____	_____	pages

- **If the plural does not end in an *s*, add an apostrophe and an *s*.**

In English, there are several common nouns that do not add an -s to make the plural form.

Singular	Plural	Singular	Plural
child	children	tooth	teeth
man	men	goose	geese
woman	women	ox	oxen
foot	feet	mouse	mice

To make each noun above into the plural possessive form to show ownership, you would add **an apostrophe and an *s*.**

Plural	Plural possessive
children	children's
men	men's
women	women's
feet	feet's (possessive not often used)
teeth	teeth's

geese	geese's
oxen	oxen's
mice	mice's

A few nouns have the same form for both singular and plural.

Singular and plural	**Singular and plural possessive**
deer	deer's
moose	moose's
sheep	sheep's

The next exercise will give you practice in using plural possessive nouns that are not regular plurals, that is, do not end in *s*.

Exercise 8

Underline the plural noun that should show ownership or possession. Then write the correct plural possessive form in the blank.

Example:

<u>*children's*</u>   **The <u>childrens</u> mothers were classroom aides.**

Version A

1. _____ The mens locker room was closed for repairs.
2. _____ Ellen worked in the childrens section of the library.
3. _____ The womens designer clothes attracted the most customers.
4. _____ The geeses honking sounds filled the air.
5. _____ Their baby teeths roots were not very deep.

Version B

1. _____ We saw the mens sport utility vehicle stuck in the sand.
2. _____ Few womens colleges still limit enrollment to women only.
3. _____ The oxens harness made slight jangling noises as they moved.
4. _____ The childrens stories also caught the attention of adults.
5. _____ The mices tails were all we saw disappearing into the hole.

Remember that it is important to determine whether the noun showing ownership is singular or plural. If the noun is plural, then determine whether the noun has a regular *s* ending or not. To form the possessive, you may have to add just an apostrophe or both an apostrophe and an *s*.

The following exercise will give you practice in finding nouns that show ownership or possession and then will give you practice in making these nouns possessive.

Underline the noun that shows ownership or possession. Then write the correct possessive form in the blank.

Example:

_____ *dog's* _____   **A dog<u>s</u> howl sounded through the neighborhood.**

Version A

1. _____ The waffle irons cord was missing.
2. _____ The mama and papa quails babies marched between them.
3. _____ The senators districts were worried about their voting records.
4. _____ The shredders basket is now full and needs to be emptied.
5. _____ The diners roofs were damaged in the hurricane.
6. _____ Four students books were stolen.
7. _____ Julio's six daughters weddings were all expensive.
8. _____ The mayor wants to lower the citys property taxes.

Version B

1. _____ I might need to buy a new jacket because my jackets zipper is broken.
2. _____ I could not find my art history book. I wanted to check my books index of photographs.
3. _____ Both of the flat screens images were extremely sharp.
4. _____ All the applicants resumes were in on time.
5. _____ Most of the parks employees are volunteer workers. (one park)
6. _____ All the soaps fragrances made her ill.
7. _____ Though he was fired from his job, he still received his two months bonus.
8. _____ Londons castles are well marked on the map.

Using Underlining or Italics Correctly

When you are drafting a paragraph of your own, you should mark titles correctly.

- With published material, **italics** or underlining is used for **titles** of **books, magazines,** and **newspapers.** When you use titles in a draft you are writing by hand, underline them to indicate italics. On the computer, either underline them or use the italics function.

    Sharon loaned her favorite mystery, *Black Notice,* to a friend.

    I decided to subscribe to *Newsweek,* a respected news magazine.

    Every Sunday morning, they read *The New York Times.*

- In addition, italics or underlining is used for titles of **plays, movies, newsletters**, and **bulletins.**

> Kathy went to New York to see a revival of *Death of a Salesman.*
>
> Daniel takes a financial newsletter called *Mutual Funds.*
>
> The elementary school publishes *The Osborn Voice* for the community.
>
> We watched *Harry Potter and the Sorcerer's Stone* on our DVD player.

- Italics are also used for names of **ships, airplanes,** and **space shuttles.**

> The *Queen Mary* is anchored at Long Beach, California.
>
> The *Columbia* broke apart over Texas on February 1, 2003.
>
> The last surviving crew member of the *Enola Gay* died in February 2003.

Work through the following exercises for practice in marking titles correctly.

Exercise 10

Underline each title below.

Example:

The <u>Los Angeles Times</u> has a crossword puzzle every day.

Version A

1. Hannah could not find the current issue of People.
2. Arizona Highways is known worldwide for its beautiful photographs.
3. The article in Personal Finance recommended buying bonds.
4. We sent a subscription to TV Guide to our mother for her birthday.
5. The Mayo Clinic Health Letter has an excellent index.
6. Two American space shuttles have been named Endeavor and Atlantis.
7. We wanted to see the drama department's production of Hamlet.
8. The Desert Botanical Garden publishes a bulletin called The Sonoran Quarterly.
9. Rita reads Prevention for its articles on health and fitness.
10. My National Geographic subscription ends next month.

Version B

1. Our newspaper publishes a weekly entertainment guide called The Rep.
2. The college drama department is presenting Agatha Christie's famous play The Mouse Trap.
3. Of all the books I checked out of the library, A Naturalist Buys an Old Farm was the best.
4. If you own mutual funds, you ought to take The Independent Advisor for Investors.

5. Most people still vividly remember where they were on January 28, 1986, when the Challenger exploded shortly after takeoff.

6. Gerald is currently reading Adam Smith's The Money Game.

7. The class read the play Waiting for Godot.

8. My brother-in-law enjoys a magazine called The Retired Officer.

9. The sinking of the Titanic is an internationally known event.

10. Every afternoon after work, Shawn drinks a cup of coffee and reads The Gazette.

Using Parentheses ( ) Correctly

- Use parentheses to separate words, phrases, or sentences that interrupt the flow of thought.

> Those four boys (without doubt the guilty ones) damaged my lawn several times.

> When I get into town for the wedding (and I hope I can arrive a few days early), I will call you immediately.

Note In the above sentence, a comma is needed after the introductory dependent clause and comes after the closing parenthesis.

- If a whole sentence is inside the parentheses, the end punctuation is inside the last parenthesis. If only part of a sentence is inside the parentheses, then the end punctuation is outside the last parenthesis.

> I am sure you understand my position. (See my earlier note.)

> Please send your application early (in triplicate).

- Use parentheses around letters or numbers indicating items in a series.

> Before I leave the house, I always (1) turn off the lights, (2) set the alarm, and (3) lock the door.

- Use parentheses around numbers that clarify words used as numbers.

> We need to pack four (4) shirts, two (2) pairs of pants, and one (1) extra pair of shoes.

- If the material inside the parentheses is a question, whether or not it is a complete sentence, it requires a question mark inside the parentheses.

> The concert (wasn't it exciting?) was the best one I have ever attended.

- Use parentheses sparingly.

Exercise 11

In the following sentences, add the missing parentheses where needed. Also, add a question mark if appropriate.

Example:

We need to call ahead (if we even go) so that Grandmother can plan for us.

Version A

1. The movie we watched wasn't it boring was too long.

2. The pecan trees in fact all the trees are suffering from the drought.

3. We invited her was this a mistake to come for lunch.

4. The women's basketball team what a surprise this is has not lost a game this year.

5. When you come to the reunion, bring three 3 apple pies, two 2 rum cakes, and four 4 batches of oatmeal cookies.

Version B

1. The Arena Football League games Channel 30 are attracting a large audience.

2. The floodwaters can you believe they have finally subsided damaged the entire city.

3. The instructions with the seeds specify to 1 prepare the soil, 2 sow the seed, and 3 water well.

4. I had to borrow money what else could I do to prepare for our vacation.

5. For your overseas vacation, pack one 1 extra pair of glasses or several pairs of disposable contact lenses and one 1 extra prescription for each medication you are taking.

Using Dashes (–) Correctly

Dashes mark strong pauses to separate material that sharply interrupts the flow of the sentence. Such material might also go inside parentheses, but dashes provide stronger emphasis. Just as you do not want to overdo the use of parentheses, be sparing in your use of dashes.

> Lorraine—in spite of her counselor's support—has not yet solved her problem.
>
> Jason, Robert, and Al—all three—graduated with honors.
>
> Jason, Robert, and Al (all three) graduated with honors.

When you write by hand, use a longer mark for a dash than for a hyphen. Your computer will have a dash key or combination of keys that will equal a dash.

Work through the following exercise to practice using dashes.

Exercise 12

Put a caret (∧) between words where a dash should be. Put the dash above the line.

Example:

The yacht club͟∧out of bounds for non-members͟∧was having a party.

Version A

1. The family members mother, father, and children are all musicians.

2. The state parks every one of them operate on smaller budgets.

3. Someone broke into our cabin perhaps someone lost and hungry and stole food.

4. The Picasso paintings on loan from New York will be at our museum for one month.

5. The gourmet dinner never mind the enormous cost was delicious.

Version B

1. I will not test-drive let alone buy a sport utility vehicle.

2. Vacationers are flocking to Florida and Arizona the two states with baseball spring training to watch their favorite players.

3. The summer college class offered over the Internet stressed creative thinking skills.

4. The alligator pond now empty of gators will shortly have a new inhabitant.

5. The Japanese visitors dangerously close to the edge of the cliff were taking pictures.

Using Hyphens (-) Correctly

- Use a hyphen between two or more words used as a single adjective to describe a noun. The descriptive words must come directly before the noun.

  He wrote a two-page essay for his class.
  He wrote a two-and-a-half-page essay.

- Do not use a hyphen or hyphens between the words if they follow the noun.

  He wrote an essay that was two and a half pages long.

- Do not use a hyphen between an **-ly** adverb and the word it describes.

  The student government was on a severely limited budget.

- Use a hyphen in two-word numbers from twenty-one to ninety-nine.

  Diana just celebrated her twenty-first birthday.

- If you wish to divide a word at the end of a line, you need to use a hyphen to divide the word between syllables. However, you want to avoid having only a one- or two-letter syllable at the end of a line or at the beginning of the next line. If you are not sure where to divide a word, check the dictionary. (Many computers will automatically hyphenate your sentences and paragraphs if you wish.)

  Because I want to decorate my new home, I need to look at several exquisitely decorated homes to get ideas.

The following exercise will give you practice in using hyphens correctly.

Exercise 13

Put a caret between the words where a hyphen is needed. Put the hyphen above the line.

Example:

The deadline for mail in registration is January 3.

Version A

1. We wanted a blue sky day for our picnic.

2. The barbershop always took walk in customers.

3. We shopped for the twenty four children in the homeless shelter.

4. The fifteen year old soprano sang the national anthem at the World Series.

5. The new shirt was made of easy care cotton.

Version B

1. The catalog advertises wrinkle free cotton blouses and skirts.

2. The weight training attendants in the fitness center were very helpful.

3. The groom was sixty seven, and the bride was forty five.

4. One of my favorite songs is "Seventy six Trombones" from *The Music Man*.

5. We were all amazed by the story of the four year old child who fell from a third floor window and survived.

Punctuating Sentences Correctly

Simple Sentences

All sentences must end with a period (.), a question mark (?), or an exclamation mark (!). Most of your sentences will end with a period, but questions end with a question mark, and sentences with strong feeling end with an exclamation mark.

- **Period**

   Elizabeth spent eight months planning her wedding.
   Phillip hopes to compete in the Olympics some day.

- **Question Mark**

   Why are you feeding all of these cats?
   What makes your job so interesting?

- **Exclamation Mark**

   Watch out for the snake!
   I just won the lottery!

Compound Sentences

Punctuation marks used between compound sentences include a semicolon; a comma and a coordinate conjunction; or a semicolon, a conjunctive adverb, and a comma.

- **Semicolon**

    Sheila traveled throughout the country; she kept her cell phone handy.

- **Comma and a Coordinate Conjunction**

    Sheila traveled throughout the country, so she kept her cell phone handy.

- **Semicolon, a Conjunctive Adverb, and a Comma**

    Sheila traveled throughout the country; therefore, she kept her cell phone handy.

Complex Sentences

A complex sentence includes one independent and one or more dependent clauses. When the dependent clause comes first, put a comma after it. When the dependent clause comes at the end of the sentence, do **not** use a comma before the dependent clause.

- **Dependent Clause at the Beginning of the Sentence**   (Use a comma.)

    When Sheila traveled throughout the country, she kept her cell phone handy.

- **Dependent Clause at the End of the Sentence**   (Do not use a comma.)

    Sheila kept her cell phone handy **when she traveled throughout the country.**

Exercise 14

Punctuate the following simple, compound, and complex sentences correctly. Do not add any extra words or unnecessary punctuation.

Example:

Ivan loved to work on cars‸so he became a mechanic‸

Version A

1. I really am interested in learning about art history but I cannot take a class right now

2. Unless I am notified of a change in plans I will be there tomorrow

3. Fran's house is on fire

4. We wanted to sell our car therefore we put an ad in *Auto Trader*

5. The bouquet of red carnations on the table slowly wilted
6. I have enough credits to graduate from college so I will apply for graduate school
7. I would rather go swimming before I eat lunch
8. Why are you inviting the entire neighborhood
9. Early this morning, the telephone rang I did not get to it on time
10. If the telephone rings again I will be sure to pick it up promptly

Version B

1. My new little ferret burrowed under the rug however I found him right away
2. When did you say you could go for lunch
3. I will probably buy a new car if I get a pay raise
4. If I get a pay raise I will probably buy a new car
5. Call the police immediately
6. Harvey trained thoroughbred horses he also raced them
7. The cartons of pop fell onto the street when the truck slid around the corner
8. Last night, a light drizzle fell in the morning, I saw a beautiful rainbow
9. Jack spent his weekend playing tennis
10. I found my purse in the trash can but my credit cards were gone

---

 Summary

A very important part of writing is punctuating your sentences. Because you do not have the opportunity to vary your tone of voice or facial expression to help get your meaning across to your reader, you have to rely on punctuation to do this for you.

- Using commas
    - Items in a series
    - Introductory material
    - Clarity
    - Addresses and dates
    - Direct address
- Using quotation marks
- Using apostrophes
- Using underlining or italics
- Using parentheses
- Using dashes
- Using hyphens
- Punctuating simple, compound, and complex sentences correctly

Practice Test

Read the following paragraph, and then answer the questions that follow by circling the letter of the correct answer.

(1) On July 13 2003 during the four-and-a-half hour flight on Southwest Airlines to Kansas City Missouri the passengers all used their time wisely. (2) One mother tended her five month old baby who wanted nothing more than to get down on the floor and crawl around. (3) Another mother who was traveling with her young kids seemed well prepared and entertained them throughout the entire time playing math games and reading *Harry Potter and the Order of the Phoenix*. (4) An older couple spent the entire flight playing cards. (5) She sat by the window he sat by the aisle, and they folded down the table in front of the empty seat between them, brought out a deck of cards, and played game after game of gin rummy. (6) Across the aisle from them a young man who was obviously a student pulled out his Dell laptop computer and worked on his business course. (7) Another student pulled out her *Psychology for Today* textbook and started highlighting as she read the chapter "Abnormal Psychology." (8) Another passenger pulled out his Palm organizer checked his appointments and then arranged his schedule. (9) One middle aged man played war games on his laptop Game Boy. (10) Several passengers read books but one lady seemed especially interested in reading *Living History* by Hillary Rodham Clinton. (11) Several other passengers dozed off and caught up on their sleep until they heard the stewardess ask, What would you like to drink? (12) She then walked up and down the aisle and delivered their drinks, including Minute Maid orange juice Sprite and diet Coca Cola. (13) She also passed out a snack pack that included Nabisco fruit snacks, Oreo cookies, and Ritz crackers with real cheese. (14) Before the flight was over almost everyone headed for the front or the back of the airplane to use the tiny, water-efficient bathrooms. (15) As the flight came to an end, Captain Tom Lewis, announced, "Welcome to Kansas City, Missouri. (16) He then said, "Thank you for flying with us on Southwest Airlines. (17) The temperature is currently 72 degrees." (18) The passengers seemed relieved and ready to continue their day.

1. In sentence #1, choose the correct punctuation.
   a. July 13 2003
   b. July 13, 2003,
   c. July 13, 2003

2. In sentence #1, choose the correct punctuation.
   a. Kansas City, Missouri,
   b. Kansas City, Missouri
   c. Kansas City Missouri,

3. In sentence #2, choose the correct punctuation.
   a. five-month old
   b. five month-old
   c. five-month-old

4. In sentence #3, choose the correct punctuation.
   a. Harry Potter and the Order of the Phoenix
   b. "Harry Potter and the Order of the Phoenix"
   c. Correct as written

5. In sentence #4, choose the correct punctuation.
   a. couple, parent
   b. flight, playing
   c. Correct as written

6. In sentence #5, choose the correct punctuation.
   a. window; he sat
   b. window, he sat
   c. Correct as written

7. In sentence #6, choose the correct punctuation.
   a. across the aisle from them; a
   b. across the aisle from them, a
   c. Correct as written

8. In sentence #7, choose the correct punctuation.
   a. "Psychology for Today"
   b. *Abnormal Psychology*
   c. Correct as written

9. In sentence #8, choose the correct punctuation.
   a. passenger, pulled
   b. organizer, checked his appointments, and then arranged his schedule
   c. Correct as written

10. In sentence #9, choose the correct punctuation.
   a. man, played
   b. middle-aged
   c. Correct as written

11. In sentence #10, choose the correct punctuation.
   a. books, but
   b. books, but,
   c. books. But,

12. In sentence #11, choose the correct punctuation.
   a. ask, what would you like to drink?
   b. ask, "What would you like to drink"?
   c. ask, "What would you like to drink?"

13. In sentence #12, choose the correct punctuation.
   a. the aisle, and delivered
   b. the aisle and, delivered
   c. Correct as written

14. In sentence #12, choose the correct punctuation.
   a. orange juice, Sprite and diet Coca-Cola
   b. orange juice, Sprite, and diet Coca-Cola
   c. Correct as written

15. In sentence #13, choose the correct punctuation.
    a. snacks, Oreo cookies, and Ritz crackers with real cheese
    b. snacks, Oreo cookies and Ritz crackers with real cheese
    c. snacks, Oreo cookies, and Ritz crackers, with real cheese

16. In sentence #14, choose the correct punctuation.
    a. over; almost everyone
    b. over, almost everyone,
    c. over, almost everyone

17. In sentence #15, choose the correct punctuation.
    a. end, Captain Tom Lewis announced,
    b. end Captain Tom Lewis announced,
    c. end, Captain Tom Lewis, announced,

18. In sentence #15, choose the correct punctuation.
    a. announced, "welcome
    b. announced "Welcome
    c. announced, "Welcome

19. In sentence #16, choose the correct punctuation.
    a. to, Kansas City, Missouri
    b. to Kansas City, Missouri
    c. to Kansas City, Missouri."

20. In sentence #17, choose the correct punctuation.
    a. degrees".
    b. degrees.
    c. Correct as written

Writing Assignment

Write a paragraph on one of the following topics. Be sure to start with a topic sentence. Then add support sentences, and end with a concluding sentence. Try to use a variety of sentence structures. Edit carefully for punctuation.

1. Home schooling
2. Playing a card game like blackjack, gin rummy, or bridge
3. Advantages or disadvantages of being an only child, oldest child, or youngest child
4. The worst advice I ever heard
5. The worst educational experience I ever had
6. Favorite hobby
7. How jealousy affects a relationship

Something to Think About, Something to Write About

Professional Essay to Generate Ideas for Writing

This Student Marches to His Own Drumbeat

Larry Bohlender, *Professional Journalist, Department Chair of English, Journalism, and Reading at Glendale Community College*

1   One of the many benefits of teaching at a community college, especially one with the size and diversity of Glendale Community College (GCC), is the closeness with the students. Community college students are special. They are a combination of many things: practicality and idealism, student and parent, student and worker, young and old.

2   One of the students people might see on the GCC campus on any given day is Gabriel Ramiro Cruz. In the morning, he is most likely getting his second wind since he has just finished his shift at the Hyatt Regency. For the past four years, since he was 18, Gabe, as he is known, has been a valet parker for the downtown Phoenix hotel. He has also been a student at GCC for three semesters.

3   It's hard to say what anyone would notice first about Gabe. It could be any of several special qualities. Probably it will be his smile. He sports a full-time smile. It is infectious, unaffected, and garnished with a perpetual fingers-in-the-cookie-jar twinkle flashing from his dark eyes. He offers a quick response to greetings. Gabe walks fast and purposefully. He stands tall, his back straight, with no slump. He often comes to campus wearing black dress pants and a white shirt. Sometimes black suspenders provide a rakish contrast to the white shirt. They are all part of his valet uniform, but on those days, Gabe seems to be making a statement: he is bodacious. Occasionally he adds a wide-brimmed 1930s hat, à la Al Capone. On other days, he might be spotted wearing a Che Guevara T-shirt.

4   Gabriel Cruz wants to be a writer, probably for a newspaper, but mainly he wants to be a writer. Of course, he was not always sure he could be one. Before completing his senior year at Glendale High School, he left because of some problems with the school. Like many others, he spent some time uncertain about his future, but he finally returned to graduate from high school at Chris-Town Academy. He was just a few days away from joining the Army when his mother reminded him, as only mothers can, that he not only liked to write but also was pretty good at it. He dropped his Army plans and enrolled at GCC.

5   He likes sports, but it was not a sports story that first brought him attention and praise from others on the newspaper staff in October of 2002.

It was the passionate opinion story he wrote about child abuse, a story he wrote between visits to the funeral home and his own home, helping his family prepare for the burial of 21-month-old Liana Sandoval, a source of great joy for Gabe's immediate and extended family in the old Glendale neighborhood just east of downtown. Liana, along with her sister, Isabella, was the apparent victim of abuse from her mother and her mother's boyfriend. For Liana, it was fatal. Her body, weighted by a rock, was found in a canal. Gabe wrote:

6   "Liana and Isabella were the light of the eyes of the Sandoval family. The father, Anthony, who had been separated from the mother for quite some time, is my cousin and one of my role models. When he lost his child, it was as if I had lost one of my own. I thought a lot about Liana at her funeral. I asked myself, 'What kind of mother would be involved in the death of her child?' I wondered if anyone would ever again recollect Liana's cute little dimples as she had always constantly smiled, her beautiful brown sparkling eyes, and the joy she brought to all the family when we spent time with her."

7   Later, Gabe was able to focus more on other topics. Among his stories is a feature on former GCC baseball star Paul LoDuca, the Los Angeles Dodgers hard-hitting catcher. In the spring of 2002, he took his enthusiasm and personality into politics. Working with the Chicano student group, M.E.C.H.A., and other groups, Gabe was the driving force behind a candidates' forum that brought several Arizona gubernatorial hopefuls to the GCC campus. Recently, Gabe worked behind the scenes when former President Clinton made a fund-raising speech in Phoenix. Not surprisingly, Gabe now proudly flashes a photo of the two.

8   In the spring of 2002 at Arizona State University, many 22-year-olds graduated. In the fall of 2002 at Glendale Community College, 22-year-old Gabe will be back for his fourth semester. He will be sports editor of the newspaper. He is thinking about quitting his job and going to school full time. If so, he will take more than the one or two classes he has taken so far each semester. He has goals, and he is on track to meet those goals.

9   Gabe has that combination of practicality and idealism that is among the traits that make community college students special as well as different from most university students. He knows about being both a student and a worker. He has a number of special qualities, and he has a wide range of interests. He also has a wide range of responsibilities. It's not surprising then that he is on track to meet his goals. He is a community college student.

Understanding Words
Briefly define the following words as they are used in the selection.

1. diversity
2. valet
3. garnished
4. perpetual
5. rakish
6. bodacious
7. gubernatorial

Writing Assignment

Write a paragraph on one of the following topics. Be sure to start with a strong topic sentence. Add specific examples and details for support, and end with a strong concluding sentence.

1. How would you characterize a community college student?
2. Other than money, what has been your greatest challenge as a community college student?
3. What role does attitude have to do with being a successful student?
4. What qualities does Gabe have that will probably make him successful?
5. What responsibilities do you have in addition to attending college?
6. Explain in what way a family can provide support for college students. (You might use one of the following: money, encouragement, child care, transportation.)

Part **3**

Student and Professional Paragraphs

I Am the King of P

John McMurray, *Student*

Being the king of procrastination, I know the consequences that it can have on college. The first regal mistake is always thinking that there is enough time to finish my assignments at least two or three days before the due date. I banish the thought of doing homework for a while. After my noble compromise, I grant myself leisure time in the royal garden of video games. I sit on my throne before a computer and command the mouse to do my bidding. When the time comes to do my stately duties, a decree is sent out that college work will be done for the next two days. I charge on the academic battlefield with my Papermate sword high and Mead shield close. It will be a long and fierce battle. The first day is slow and tough as I gather my sources to support my claims. The opposing forces are ahead of me. There is Duke Disaster and Prince Poor Paper at the far side of the combat zone. I begin to wonder if there is enough time to create a worthy essay. It is day two, and I have fought all night to keep my lines orderly. The end of my crusade is in sight. I expect a victory. Then there is the final surge. I send forth Sergeant Spellchecker for the final rush. Looking back at my work, my sentences look scattered like soldiers who have lost their morale in battle. When a college student like myself waits for the last minute to turn in work, it is like fighting a battle. When I think that I am in control of my work and procrastinate, it always turns into an academic defeat. Postponing my homework leads to inadequate papers. Being King Procrastination is not a noble title for college.

Understanding Words

Briefly define the following words as they are used in this selection.

1. procrastination
2. stately
3. crusade

Questions on Form

1. What is the topic sentence?
2. What main example does the author use to support his topic sentence?
3. What is the point of view in the paragraph?
4. Identify a complex sentence.

Questions on Content

1. What does he do instead of his homework?
2. What is it like to wait until the last minute to turn in work?
3. How does he make fighting the battle humorous?

School

Nereyda Martinez, *Student*

When I first came to this country from Mexico, school was very difficult for me because I did not know English. We first moved to Nogales, Arizona, but back then there were no English-as-a-second-language (ESL) classes. Even though my teacher was bilingual, the whole class was in English, and it was very difficult for me to keep up with the rest of the class. I cried every day because I felt left out, and every time the boys and girls laughed at something that happened in class, I thought they were talking about me. Then my parents decided to move to Tucson, but things at school only got worse. I had ESL classes, but they made me different from the other students. Now the name calling was worse and more offensive. These people did not even know me. They had never talked to me before, but on the way to and from school and during recess, they enjoyed making fun of me. This really hurt me, and I would pray every day to learn English faster. Now, I might not be the best English speaker, but I understand almost everything. I thank God every day, but I still pray to learn better English.

Questions on Form

1. What are the topic and direction in this paragraph?

2. What examples support the main idea?

3. Identify a compound sentence.

4. Identify a simple sentence.

Questions on Content

1. How did the other kids treat the author when she was in ESL classes?

2. Where was the author born?

3. What is her goal today?

Four-Wheeling

Mark Sanchez, *Student*

Going four-wheeling up in the mountains near Payson is a favorite weekend activity for our family. The wide open country is full of forest trails for quading. The forest service has cut roads through this region for logging and fire protection. Some of the trails are wide enough for two-way traffic, and others are wide enough for only smaller vehicles. After my children load up on water and snacks for one of our outings, we will use these trails to go four-wheeling. Depending on which direction we want to go, from the trails we can see many different types of vegetation from high desert to tall ponderosa pine trees. We thoroughly enjoy ourselves, but we must be careful when we go out on the trails because we will be away from any phone service. If one of us is injured, this would create a real problem. Also, the changing weather can happen very quickly, so we must be vigilant. Most important of all, when my children and I go quading, it is to enjoy ourselves and this beautiful country.

Understanding Words

Briefly define the following word as it is used in this selection.

quading

Questions on Form

1. Identify the topic and direction.

2. What point of view is used in the paragraph?

3. List some concrete details that support the main idea.

Questions on Content

1. What kind of vegetation do they find near Payson?

2. What are two problems they have to consider?

3. Where do they go four-wheeling?

Excerpt from Housekeeping in the Klondike

Jack London

A certain knowledge of astronomy is required of the Klondike [Yukon Territory in Canada] cook, for another task of his is to keep track of the time. Before going to bed, he wanders outside and studies the heavens. Having located the Pole Star by means of the Great Bear, he inserts two slender wands in the snow, a couple of yards apart and in line with the North Star. The next day, when the sun on the southern horizon casts the shadows of the wands to the northward and in line, he knows it to be twelve o'clock, noon, and sets his watch and those of his partners accordingly. As stray dogs are constantly knocking his wands out of line with the North Star, it becomes his habit to verify them regularly every night, and thus another burden is laid upon him.

Questions on Form

1. What is the topic sentence in this paragraph?
2. In what order is this paragraph organized?
3. What word in the concluding sentence reinforces the topic idea?

Questions on Content

1. How does he know when it is twelve o'clock?

2. Why is it important for him to know when it is twelve o'clock?

3. Who keeps messing up his lines?

Excerpt from Healing Harmonies

Tim Wendel

1 When the images [from September 11, 2001] became too difficult to watch, many of us turned to music to stir our souls, to heal us from unimaginable wrong, to inspire us to open our hearts. In the days following [Denyce] Graves' uplifting performance [at the National Cathedral in Washington], a who's who of musicians performed on network television in an unprecedented show of unity to raise money for victims and their families. Thousands of strangers held hands at Yankee Stadium as the Harlem Boys and Girls Choir performed *We Shall Overcome* and Bette Midler sang *Wind Beneath My Wings*. The sounds of music seem to summon a new sense of patriotism and purpose for a nation in shock.

2   Surprisingly, acknowledgment of music's profound capacity to move us comes not only from politician and preacher, but also from the unexpected recesses of today's high-tech research laboratories. . . . New studies indicate that listening to and playing music actually can alter how our brains, and thus our bodies, function. Scientists use the sound of music to do everything from battling cancer and mining the memories of Alzheimer's patients to relieving severe pain and boosting kids' test scores. Doctors believe music therapy in hospitals and nursing homes not only makes people feel better, but also makes them heal faster. (It's a budding field: From 1998 to 1999, the job market for music therapists jumped 30 percent.) Across the nation, a growing number of nursing homes have hired music therapists to help geriatric patients maintain motor coordination and socialization skills. Among the beneficiaries: Some stroke and Parkinson's patients have recovered more rapidly with musical accompaniment during physical therapy. "We're only beginning to understand the value of music," says Deforia Lane, a music therapist at Cleveland's University Hospital. "We're tapping into the fundamental ways our brain interprets [it] and drinks it in." Researchers say nothing enthralls the brain more than music.

Understanding Words
Briefly define the following words as they are used in this selection.

1. unprecedented

2. summon

3. geriatric

4. enthralls

Questions on Form

1. What is the main idea in the first paragraph?

2. List some concrete examples that support the topic sentence in the first paragraph.

3. What is the main idea in the second paragraph?

Questions on Content:

1. In the first paragraph, what does the author point out about the healing power of music?

2. In the second paragraph, Wendel points out that recent studies show how music can actually "alter how our brains, and thus our bodies, function." What specific examples does he give?

3. How have nursing homes used music to help geriatric patients?

Part 4

Capitalization

Objectives

- Review the rules of capitalization.
- Practice capitalization in sentences and paragraphs.

As you edit your sentences and paragraphs, you will want to be concerned with the mechanics of capitalization. Knowing the basic rules will make it easier for you as you write. Later on, if you are not sure about a certain word, you can look it up in the dictionary to determine whether or not it needs to be capitalized. First, however, become familiar with the following rules. This text has organized the rules for capitalization by first words, names, things, and places.

Capitalize First Words

- Capitalize the first word in every sentence:

   > Individuals are the ones who can create happiness in their own lives.

   > The sunshine coming through the window always makes me feel positive.

- Capitalize the first word in a direct quotation if it is a complete sentence, not just the continuation of a sentence.

   > My boss said, "You need to work overtime this weekend."

   > My sister told him, "No, I cannot work because I do not have a babysitter."

- Do **not** capitalize the first word in a quotation if it is part of another sentence.

   > My psychology instructor told us that people who work overtime "shortchange their families."

   > Juan let him know that he loved his family, but he still needed to "pay the bills each month."

- Do **not** capitalize an indirect quotation.

   > My boss said that we needed to work overtime this weekend.

   > My sister said that she does not have a babysitter.

Capitalize Names

- Capitalize proper names and nicknames, including initials.

   > Ask Sara if she heard the telephone ring. She is expecting a call from Tiny.

   > My friend R. G. Simmons works as a bank teller.

- Capitalize words, including *mother, grandmother, dad,* and *grandfather,* when they are substituted for a person's name. Do not capitalize them when they are preceded by the word "my."

> Could you please give Mom a call and tell her we are on the way over?
>
> If you send Grandmother your address, she will write you a letter.

- Capitalize titles when they appear before a person's name, including such titles as *aunt, uncle, mother, grandmother, father,* and *grandfather.*

> The college gave an award to Professor Collins.
>
> Next week, Grandmother Beach will take all the children to the movies.
>
> Someone needs to give Aunt Bertha a ride to the football game this evening.

- Do not capitalize these above words when they are preceded by the word "my" **unless** they are used as titles.

> My uncle has been very generous to me and my brothers and sisters.
>
> My Uncle Fred has been very generous to me and my brothers and sisters.
>
> I need to call my grandmother and tell her about my classes.

- Always capitalize the word *I* as well as the names of individual people.

> Sasha and I plan to rent an apartment together.
>
> Whenever it rains, Robin and I look for a rainbow.

- Capitalize the word *president* only when it refers to the President of the United States or is used as someone's title.

> The President will address the nation at 2:00 p.m. today.
>
> After the luncheon, President Sanchez greeted all the visitors.

- Capitalize all references to God, the Bible, and all religious books.

> Every morning, I read my Bible and pray to God.
>
> When a tragedy hits the country, people seldom complain when the President asks God to keep the country safe and to provide His guidance.
>
> In the Koran, Allah speaks of peace.

Exercise 1

Correct the following sentences by capitalizing according to the above rules.

Example:

Please send ͏alicia the recipe for ͏aunt ͏carol's famous bread pudding.

Version A

1. yesterday, i met my sister anne at the airport.

2. mr. johnson enrolled his son adam in school.

3. i heard president bush speak at the rally.

4. the celebration of diversity included prayers to god and allah.

5. my aunt delores thought that i should call her.

6. the reporter interviewed vice president cheney before he boarded the helicopter.

7. the new director is a brother of peter lynch.

8. jackie took her dog katrina to the vet.

9. she asked doctor crane about special food for katrina.

10. the basketball players followed coach wilson's advice.

Version B

1. my mother said, "take dad the extension cord."

2. after the concert, angelica said, "let's go out to eat."

3. When grandpa stays with us, he reads his bible and prays to god every morning.

4. stephanie and i helped professor rivers tutor his beginning math students.

5. the students listened as president randolf said that the college is "reaching out to the community."

6. president randolf said, "the college is reaching out to the community."

7. my aunt josie just got a new job working for a government agency.

8. before tamar left for college, she hugged mom and told her, "I love you."

9. uncle pablo asked angelica and fred to take care of his new baby daughter.

10. the person i enjoy being around the most is aunt mary.

Capitalize Things

- Capitalize the names of the days of the week, names of the months, and holidays.

> On the first Friday of each month, we have afternoon meetings.
>
> The shortest day of the year is in December; the longest day is in June.
>
> My children look forward to Thanksgiving because of the delicious food.
>
> Every year, we make New Year's resolutions as a family.
>
> My father still loves to celebrate Valentine's Day.

- Do not capitalize the names of the seasons: **summer, fall, winter, spring.**

> Every summer, I spend two weeks at my aunt and uncle's farm in Wisconsin.
>
> Sully enjoys all the seasons of the year, but she looks forward to winter the most.

- Capitalize names of specific schools and colleges.

  > North Dallas High School has an excellent academic program.
  >
  > The University of Arizona has an outstanding medical school.
  >
  > My cousin attends the University of California at Berkeley.

- Capitalize names of particular groups or organizations.

  > Every year, the Girl Scouts sell their famous cookies.
  >
  > The Nature Conservancy works hard to maintain wildlife preserves.
  >
  > The primary political groups of the United States are the Democratic Party and Republican Party.

- Capitalize names of businesses.

  > The Bank of America has branches all over the United States.
  >
  > He plans to send a letter to the Better Business Bureau.

- Capitalize brand names or commercial products, but not the name of the product itself.

  > The little boy insisted on buying Nike shoes so he could run fast.
  >
  > The Spalding golf clubs proved to be quite good.
  >
  > I forgot to buy Windex and Kleenex tissues.

- Capitalize abbreviations that stand for words that are capitalized.

  > Many young boys wish to play ball for the NFL when they grow up.
  >
  > The effectiveness of NAFTA has been debated.

- Capitalize specific historical events.

  > My neighbor fought in World War II.
  >
  > The Trojan War occurred in 1265 B.C.
  >
  > My brother served our country during Operation Desert Storm and in Operation Iraqi Freedom.

- Capitalize words in the titles of newspapers, books, chapters from books, magazines, plays, movies, short stories, poems, literary articles, pictures, and works of art. Do not capitalize *a, an, the,* and short prepositions unless one of these words is the first word in the title.

  > I enjoyed reading "A Clash of Cultures," a chapter in David J. Peck's book, *Or Perish in the Attempt.*
  >
  > The *Mona Lisa* has been admired by many people.

- Capitalize specific college courses that are numbered, but not general courses unless they are language classes.

  > My English 101 course and my Math 107 course are challenging.
  >
  > Next semester I plan to take psychology, French, and algebra.

- Capitalize the opening and closing of a letter.

  > Dear Stacy,
  >
  > Sincerely, Rosa

Exercise 2

Correct the capitalization in the following sentences.

Example:
     M   *M*
The michelin tires were on sale during the month of march.

Version A

1. cassy loves the summers because she has time to read books like *white oleander.*
2. many people look forward to friday afternoons rather than monday mornings.
3. the *new york times* featured an article about the girl scouts one week and the boy scouts the next week.
4. the battle of trenton was part of the American revolutionary war.
5. while I was attending newberry college, I took english, physics, and psychology.
6. my communications 101 course was quite interesting.
7. last april, the usda recalled kraft cheese.
8. harvard medical school is doing extensive research on dna.
9. the folgers iced cappuccino tasted very good.
10. on valentine's day, the phi theta kappa honorary group sold single red roses as a fund-raiser.

Version B

1. the family met on sunday to celebrate my birthday.
2. samantha saw an advertisement in *time* for a new macintosh computer.
3. sharon traded in her old truck for a new nissan altima.
4. he ordered an easter lily from the jackson perkins catalog.
5. my sister joined the audubon society last summer.
6. in 2003, the number one-pick in the nba draft was a high school senior.
7. every year in november, macy's sponsors a parade on thanksgiving day.
8. last summer, martin graduated from florida state university.
9. the civil war caused a great deal of destruction.
10. we picked up hunt's tomato paste for our spaghetti sauce.

Capitalize Places

- Capitalize *north, south, east,* and *west* when they refer to specific parts of the country, but **not** when they are directions.

    They built a new home somewhere in northwest Oregon.
    Before he moved to the South, he had spent seven years in New York.
    Two miles past the railroad tracks, turn south.

- Capitalize the names of specific places such as streets, cities, towns, states, countries, parks, buildings, oceans, and mountains.

> The new Westside Park at 3459 West Utopia Road includes a wildflower display.
>
> I love spending time at Revere Beach near Boston, Massachusetts.
>
> We loved vacationing in the Rocky Mountains.

- Capitalize the names of all races, tribes, nations, and nationalities as well as adjectives derived from a particular country.

> In my English class, we have students from Korea, Mexico, Bosnia, Italy, and Vietnam.
>
> We bought a new Persian rug for the computer room.
>
> The Cherokee people endured a 116-day march called the Trail of Tears.

Exercise 3

Correct the capitalization in the following sentences.

Example:

                N   *N*   *A*

I bought a new ~~n~~avajo rug from the ~~n~~avajo reservation in ~~a~~rizona.

Version A

1. many homeless people have taken up residence at balboa beach in california.
2. I enjoyed going through mammoth cave in kentucky.
3. we moved to 1625 west aspen drive in pueblo, colorado.
4. many people want to leave the midwest when cold weather comes.
5. clearwater beach, florida, has beautiful beaches.
6. the restaurant specialized in spanish omelets.
7. last summer we followed the direction of the oregon trail all the way to the west coast.
8. if you turn north on the interstate highway, you will eventually get to the canadian border.
9. The hopi tribe is one of the few tribes who do not have gambling on their reservation.
10. my little sister went on a field trip to the metropolitan museum of art.

Version B

1. i always look forward to eating my aunt's french toast.
2. dan lives at 25 north traceside drive in fargo, north dakota.
3. the challenger space center caters to school-age children.
4. We took a steamboat up the mississippi river to st. louis, missouri.

5. I drove my car across the country from the atlantic ocean to the pacific ocean.

6. because of the threat of terrorism, people can no longer tour the white house.

7. the blue ridge mountains are famous for their beauty.

8. when we lived in the south, we loved to go to the french quarter in new orleans.

9. the college hosted a get-together for students from all countries, including bosnia, mexico, el salvador, and cambodia.

10. golden gate park in san francisco attracts people from all over the world.

Summary

Paying attention to mechanics includes using capitals correctly. Learning the basic rules will make writing easier for you.

- Capitalize first words

    First word in all sentence

    First word in a direct quotation unless it is part of another sentence

- Capitalize names

    All words used as names

    All titles when they are used as part of a name

    I and all names of individual people

    All references to the deity

- Capitalize things

    Days of the week, names of the months, and holidays

    Names of specific schools

    Particular groups or organizations

    Names of businesses and commercial products

    Abbreviations that stand for words that are capitalized

    Historic events

    Literature and art titles

    Specific titles of college courses

    Opening and closing of a letter

- Capitalize places

    Specific sections of the country

    Specific places

    All ethnic groups

    All adjectives that come from the name of a particular country

- Do not capitalize
    Indirect quotation
    Seasons of the year
    General product names
    Academic subjects, except language classes
    Compass directions

Practice Test

Capitalize words in the following paragraph according to the rules you have reviewed. Make your corrections on the page.

(1) Last summer, professor lyle and I hosted a small group of visitors from china and australia. (2) They arrived at hartsfield international airport in atlanta, georgia, on a tuesday morning for a two-week visit. (3) We picked them up at the airport and drove them to the hyatt regency hotel at 1702 peach tree street. (4) though they were not here to learn english, they enjoyed practicing their english skills while they were here. (5) In the afternoons and evenings, we had special events. (6) We went to visit the cnn studio and the famous cyclorama about the civil war. (7) We also attended an atlanta braves baseball game and toured the coca-cola company. (8) They liked stone mountain park and took many pictures there. (9) They also toured the spelman college campus, where they were especially impressed by the library. (10) They often commented on the peach trees that were in full bloom, and one afternoon one of the women asked, "can we stop to take pictures?" (11) on the last friday they were here, we had a farewell party and served papa john's pizza and coca-cola. (12) We presented each person with a bag of mementos, including atlanta braves key chains, atlanta hawks T-shirts, hershey chocolate bars, jergen's lotion, and crest toothpaste. (13) Our visitors said that they had really enjoyed their stay in atlanta.

Writing Assignment

Write a paragraph on one of the following options.

A. Write your own paragraph about a city you have visited, and include places you went to, such as theaters, museums, parks, beaches, or historic sites. Be sure to use words that begin with capital letters. Include specific names of the places you saw, people you were with, and events you attended. Be sure to have a topic sentence, support sentences, and an ending sentence.

B. If you have not visited another city that you remember well, go into the Internet to find information about a city you would like to visit, and write about the places there that sound interesting.

Confusing Words

Read through the explanations of the following words that people often confuse. Sometimes these short words will give you more problems than longer, more complicated words. With perseverance, you can prevent these types of errors from occurring in your writing.

Work through the exercises, and mark any words that create problems for you. Try the following tips.

- Write these words with their definitions in a special section of a notebook.
- Write them on 3 × 5 cards so that you can learn how to review them easily.

Perhaps you should concentrate on one word at a time, and then consciously practice using that word at least ten or twenty times in one day until you are sure you have it mastered. By the end of the day, you are ready to add a new word. If a particular word just seems impossible, continue to refer back to your notebook or your 3 × 5 card when you are writing.

1. *a, an, the*

A and *an* are indefinite articles that are used before *singular generic words.*
a: used when the word following the *a* begins with *a consonant sound*

> singular noun
> We attended *a lecture.*

> singular noun
> We had *a wonderful* appetizer.

an: used when the word following the *an* begins with *a vowel sound*

> singular noun
> He brought me *an* apple.

> singular noun
> I had *an* excellent time.

the: definite article used before *singular or plural words* that refer to a specific person or thing

> plural noun
> He brought me *the* apples.

plural noun
We attended *the* long lectures.

plural word but not specific
We had wonderful *times* together.

singular word that is specific   *singular word that is specific*
The President of *the* United States will arrive shortly.

singular word that indicates any tree
He planted *a* **b**eautiful tree.

singular word that indicates a specific tree
He planted *the* beautiful tree.

plural word
He planted *the* beautiful trees.

The indicates that one particular emerald hummingbird feeds there.
She saw *the* emerald *hummingbird* at the feeder.

No article indicates she saw many emerald hummingbirds, but they are not always the same ones.
She saw emerald *hummingbirds* at the feeder.

A or **an** indicates a one-time appearance of an emerald hummingbird.
She saw *an* **e**merald hummingbird at the feeder.

> Remember:
> **A** and **an** are used only before singular generic words.
>   **A** goes before a word that begins with a consonant sound.
>   **An** goes before a word that begins with a vowel sound.
> **The** is used before both single and plural words that are specific.

One important bit of information that you need to remember about using these articles, or using no articles at all, is that the article changes the meaning in a sentence. These slight differences in meaning can create problems for you.

Look at the following sentences:

- I ate chicken for lunch. (indefinite)

The above sentence means that you ate some amount of some chicken.

- I ate the chicken for lunch. (definite)

The above sentence means that you ate some part of the particular chicken that was prepared for lunch.

- I ate a chicken for lunch. (indefinite)

The above sentence means that you ate a whole chicken, any chicken, for lunch.

Now look at four more sentences.

- I do not like oranges. (indefinite)

The above sentence means that you do not like any type of oranges.

- I do not like the oranges in my backyard. (definite)

The above sentences means that you do not like the particular oranges in your backyard.

- I do not like oranges in my backyard. (indefinite)

The above sentence means that you do not like to have oranges growing in your backyard or being thrown into your backyard.

- I do not want to eat an orange. (indefinite)

The above sentence means that at this particular time you do not want to eat any orange. You might want to eat one later.

Exercise 1

Complete the following sentences by writing in the correct choice (*a, an,* or *the*).

1. George wanted to buy _____ American car for his parents.

2. Please buy _____ stereo that we saw at _____ store.

3. We saw _____ eagle as we hiked the trail.

4. Please buy me _____ new stereo.

5. By refinishing _____ back patio, he made _____ backyard more attractive.

6. She saved _____ wheat pennies for her grandchildren.

7. He wanted to hire _____ accountant to help with his taxes.

8. After breaking _____ cup, I washed _____ dishes more carefully.

9. Before becoming _____ high school teacher, Tom worked as _____ teacher's aide.

10. I do not have _____ concern in _____ world about _____ test that we have on Monday.

11. He did _____ exceptional job of planning the retreat.

12. America's First Ladies have always left _____ mark on _____ country.

13. Please bring _____ better picture of yourself to _____ immigration office nearest you.

14. We plan to stop at _____ Grand Canyon on _____ way to California.

15. J. K. Rowling's Harry Potter is _____ amazingly imaginative character.

2. *a lot, allot, alot*

a lot: many

> I have a lot of beautiful neon-blue tropical fish.

allot: To assign to as a share

> They will allot three hours to each person.

alot: NOT a word

Exercise 2

Complete the following sentences by writing in the correct choice (*a lot, allot*).

1. We have _____ of work to do before Friday.

2. Several recipes called for _____ of sugar.

3. The young parents had to _____ their time for their children.

4. They learned to _____ time for each child.

5. The children also learned _____ from their parents' efforts.

---

3. *accept, except*

accept: agree to, take something that is offered

> I accept your invitation.

except (*preposition*): other than, with the exception of

> Everyone finished except me.

Exercise 3

Complete the following sentences by writing in the correct choice (*accept, except*).

1. All the dogs _____ Blazer went to the veterinarian today.

2. All the dogs _____ the little one have learned to walk on a leash.

3. At first, Stormy did not _____ the trip very easily.

4. The attendants at the office _____ their jobs with good cheer.

5. Jason _____ his supporting role as a bench player for the coach.

---

4. *advise, advice*

advise (*verb*): recommend or suggest

> Could you advise me on what classes I need to take?

advice (*noun*): opinion or suggestion

> Her advice was excellent.

Exercise 4

Complete the following sentences by writing in the correct choice (*advise, advised, advice*).

1. Experienced students take _____ with good humor.

2. In study groups, they are used to giving _____ tactfully to each other.

3. Helen went searching for _____ when she needed it.

4. My dad always _____ me to invest my money carefully.

5. I can still hear his wise words of _____ .

5. *affect, effect*

affect (*verb*): bring about change, influence

> Her understanding affected the behavior of the students in her classroom.

effect (*noun*): result

> The effects of not sleeping well showed on his face.

effect (*verb*): to accomplish or bring about

> The manager refused to effect any change in policy.

Exercise 5

Complete the following sentences by writing in the correct choice (*affect, affected, effect, effected*).

1. The snowstorm _____ the traffic the next morning.

2. I do not know what _____ this program will have on students.

3. The stench of his cologne _____ everyone around him.

4. The conductor's pink sequined tuxedo _____ the attitude of the audience.

5. Working so many hours at his job _____ his grades.

6. The _____ of working many hours did not appear until later.

7. The parents and teachers _____ a compromise.

6. alright, all right

alright: incorrect word
all right: satisfactory or correct

It is all right to park behind the bank.

Carol feels all right today.

Exercise 6

Complete the following sentences by writing in the correct choice (*alright, all right*).

1. After the storm, the airplane landed _____ .

2. I think the painter's estimate is _____ .

3. Is it _____ to take my car to that shop?

4. My dad said it was _____ to borrow a little money for college.

5. The solution to the problem was _____ with everybody.

7. all ready, already

all ready: fully or completely ready

We were all ready to go fishing.

already: previously or before

I have already packed for the trip.

Exercise 7

Complete the following sentences by writing in the correct choice (*all ready, already*).

1. The bill had _____ been paid.

2. Kelly has _____ planned her next remodeling project.

3. Samaki and his brothers were _____ for the new semester.

4. We have _____ been there.

5. When everyone is _____ , please give me a call.

8. are, our

are: verb form to be used with *you, we,* and *they*

Sandy and Harry are often in Phoenix.

our: possessive pronoun or adjective expressing ownership

We did our laundry this morning.

Exercise 8

Complete the following sentences by writing in the correct choice (*are, our*).

1. We hope to have _____ garage sale soon.

2. _____ baby chickens _____ eating well.

3. Saturdays _____ often busy days for _____ family.

4. _____ supply of dog food is dwindling.

5. The wildfires in Colorado _____ burning near Denver.

---

9. by, buy

by: near or beside; not later than

We stood by the door for an hour.

Be ready to go by next week.

buy: to purchase

I hope to buy a new car before the end of the year.

Exercise 9

Complete the following sentences by writing in the correct choice (*by, buy*).

1. I need to _____ new carpeting for my house.

2. Would you like to stop _____ after the concert?

3. We stood _____ the bridge as the steamer went past.

4. The intruder was bitten _____ the dog.

5. The parents agreed to _____ their kids a ferret.

10. could of, must of, might of, should of, would of

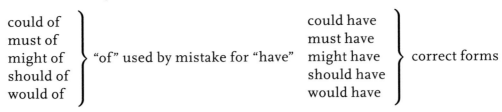

could of ⎫
must of ⎪
might of ⎬ "of" used by mistake for "have"
should of ⎪
would of ⎭

could have ⎫
must have ⎪
might have ⎬ correct forms
should have ⎪
would have ⎭

Exercise 10

Complete the following sentences by writing in the correct choice (*could have, must have, might have, should have, would have*).

1. We should _____ bought our tickets for the play ahead of time.

2. I must _____ done this a hundred times.

3. Steve might _____ been called away on business.

4. I would _____ planned differently if I had known your schedule.

5. I wish I could _____ gone to the party.

---

11. good, well

good: better than the usual (describes a noun or pronoun); enjoyable

Larry is a good driver.

We had a good time at the concert.

well: in a way that is pleasing; in good health; thoroughly

My future is going well.

I am well.

Stir it well.

Exercise 11

Complete the following sentences by writing in the correct choice (*good* or *well*).

1. That was an extremely _____ movie.

2. The vacation was _____ for all of us.

3. We usually work _____ together.

4. The students and teachers planned the field trip _____.

5. Their trip to Canada went _____.

12. *quite, quiet, quit*

quite: one-syllable word that means *completely;* rather

> I have not quite finished planting my garden.
> It is quite hot outside today.

quiet: two-syllable word that means *not loud*

> The teenagers were unusually quiet at the dinner.

quit: to stop; to give up

> I quit smoking last year
> Please quit treating me as if I were stupid.

Exercise 12

Complete the following sentences by writing in the correct choice (*quite, quiet, quit*).

1. That was _____ a _____ group of students.

2. They wanted to _____ playing cards, but I was not _____ ready.

3. On the drive home, I became _____ and thoughtful.

4. The receptionist was _____ abrupt.

5. If you will just be _____, I will give you the information.

13. *use, used*

use: present tense verb meaning to *consume;* to bring into action or service

> I do not want to use all of the hot water.
> I use his financial advice often.

used: past tense of *use*

> I used to go to the fitness center every day.
> I used all of the water last night.
> Last year, I used his financial advice.

Exercise 13

Complete the following sentences by writing in the correct choice (*use, used*).

1. I _____ to go dancing every Saturday night.

2. Sam _____ to have an iguana for a pet.

3. Benny knows how to _____ his money wisely.

4. The chiropractor _____ gentle pressure on his neck.

5. The retired couple _____ to drive across the country every year.

14. *than, then*

than: used in comparisons

>   Rachel is younger than her sister.

then: time word that means *next, soon after;* at that particular time

>   Once you get off work, then we can go to the movies.
>   The class ended, and then I went to the library to do research.
>   The house was new then.

Exercise 14

Complete the following sentences by writing in the correct choice (*than, then*).

1. Our new truck is larger _____ the old one.

2. The twins are more energetic _____ they used to be.

3. The dust storm subsided; _____ the rains came.

4. _____ we can plant the trees.

5. He often eats fresh fruit and vegetables rather _____ fried foods.

15. *weather, whether*

weather: outside conditions in regard to temperature, sunshine, rainfall; to pass through safely

>   The weather outside is perfect.
>   We weathered the storm.

whether: used to introduce one or more alternatives

>   I doubt whether it really matters.

>   Whether or not he comes, I plan to go swimming.

Complete the following sentences by writing in the correct choice (*weather, whether*).

1. _____ or not we will go depends on the _____.

2. I do not know _____ to vacation in California or in Florida.

3. Unless the _____ clears, the beach will be closed.

4. The monsoon brings wet _____.

5. I had to pay my bills _____ I wanted to or not.

16. were, where

were: verb form of *be* used to show past time with *we, you,* and *they*

> We were first in line.

where: in, at, or to a place

> Where are all my flowers? Where does it hurt?
> I know where you are.
> We are only an hour from where the Joshua trees grow.

Exercise 16

Complete the following sentences by writing in the correct choice (*were, where*).

1. _____ _____ all the people?

2. _____ you there when the fire broke out?

3. We _____ able to fix the flat tire without having to buy a new one.

4. Exactly _____ _____ you going?

5. Do you know _____ we should go to pan for gold?

17. to, too, two

to: preposition showing direction toward; first word in an infinitive phrase

> We walked to the pond.
> Steven loves to jog around the lake.

too: also; too much or too many

    I would like to go, too.

    I can never have too many books.

two: the number 2

    They left only two brownies.

Exercise 17

Complete the following sentences by writing in the correct choice (*to, too, two*).

1. He consumed _____ Krispy Kreme doughnuts as he waited in line.

2. The batter's count was _____ balls and one strike.

3. _____ many people crowded into the elevator.

4. We all went _____ the lake _____ go fishing.

5. We went out _____ eat _____ many times.

---

18. *their, they're, there*

their: ownership

    The couple drove their new car into the garage.

they're: contraction for *they are*

    Hopefully, they're going to have a good vacation.

there: in or at that place; to introduce a sentence

    You can catch a train there.

    There are three baby pigeons in the nest.

Exercise 18

Complete the following sentences by writing in the correct choice (*their, they're, there*).

1. _____ he is!

2. They put on _____ backpacks and climbed Mt. McGregor.

3. Unfortunately, _____ usually late for class.

4. _____ sure that they can come to _____ class reunion.

5. When I got _____, the store was closed.

19. *hear, here*

hear: to listen to, to perceive sound

I can hear the music in the background.

here: in or at this place

We are here at last.

Exercise 19

Complete the following sentences by writing in the correct choice (*hear, here*).

1. They did not _____ about the hurricane until it was too late.

2. They often _____ the noise of jets flying overhead.

3. _____ comes my bus.

4. I always _____ the train before I see it.

5. Maria moved _____ from Brooklyn.

---

20. *know, no, knew, new*

know: to have information in the mind, be certain, realize

Jason knows how to program the computer efficiently.

no: negative response

I have no news of the plans.

knew: past tense of *know*

Heather knew all the shortcuts.

new: recently created or acquired

She needs to buy a new computer.

Exercise 20

Complete the following sentences by writing in the correct choice (*know, no, knew, new*).

1. I _____ that my boyfriend would say _____ .

2. If you get to _____ him well, you will realize his potential.

3. We have _____ neighbors next door.

4. Ray _____ he wanted to marry his girlfriend.

5. I have _____ use for whiners.

---

21. *passed, past*

passed: successfully completed; went by or beyond

I passed all my classes last semester.

The mail carrier passed my house.

past: ended, over, gone by; further than, beyond

We had done it that way in the past.

Jim often works past ten o'clock every day.

Exercise 21

Complete the following sentences by writing in the correct choice (passed, past).

1. Six cars _____ me before someone stopped to help.

2. We drove _____ the ancient redwood forest.

3. As they _____ through the tunnel, the light faded.

4. Joe has visited his grandparents for the _____ five summers.

5. Angela _____ all her courses last year.

---

22. *your, you're*

your: pronoun showing ownership

Your tattoo is quite attractive.

you're: contraction for *you are*

You're going the wrong way.

Exercise 22

Complete the following sentences by writing in the correct choice (*your, you're*).

1. _____ sense of humor is greatly appreciated.

2. We hope _____ having a good time.

3. It is illegal to park _____ car on the street.

4. _____ going to have to trim _____ trees soon.

5. If _____ in a hurry, please go on without me.

ESL: Gaining Confidence in Using English

Count Nouns

Count nouns refer to people, places, and things that you can count one by one. These nouns most often refer to concrete objects. Their plural forms end in **s** or **es**; however, a few of them have irregular plurals. (See Chapter 7 for irregular plural forms.) Just remember that you can **always** count individually the people or objects they refer to. Study the following examples to see how count nouns are used correctly.

Concrete Count Nouns

Singular	car	The **car** ran the red light.	(correct)
Plural	cars	The **cars** ran the red light.	(correct)
Singular	book	We ordered the **book** online.	(correct)
Plural	books	We ordered the **books** online.	(correct)
Singular	box	We packed the **box** carefully.	(correct)
Plural	boxes	We packed the **boxes** carefully.	(correct)

Although most count nouns refer to concrete things, some common ones refer to abstract or non-concrete things. However, you can still count them one by one. Study the following examples.

Abstract Count Nouns

Singular	decision	He made his **decision** quickly.	(correct)
Plural	decisions	He made two important **decisions**.	(correct)
Singular	dream	Kim's **dream** was to become a chemist.	(correct)
Plural	dreams	Kim hoped to fulfill her **dreams**.	(correct)

Noncount Nouns

Noncount nouns refer to things that are wholes. You cannot count them one by one. Sometimes they are concrete and specific, but **there is no plural form with an s.** Study the following sentences to see how these nouns are used correctly.

Concrete Noncount Nouns

butter	Do you want **butter** on your pancakes?	(correct)
No plural with *s*	Do you want **butters** on your pancakes?	(incorrect)
sugar	The **sugar** is damp and in a lump.	(correct)
No plural with *s*	The **sugars** are damp and in a lump.	(incorrect)

Although you cannot count the butter, you may still want to express an amount of it. You might want to use one of the indefinite pronouns you have previously studied. (Remember, though, that when the describing word comes right before the noun, it functions like an adjective.)

Do you want **more** butter on your pancakes?

Do you want **some** butter on your pancakes?

We need to buy **more** sugar.

We need to buy **some** sugar.

If you want your meaning to be clearer, you can use a **count** noun to make the meaning more specific. For example, you could say, "Do you want two **pats** of butter on your pancakes?" or "We need to buy five **pounds** of sugar."

Abstract Noncount Nouns

	The **music** from the concert could be heard for miles.	(correct)
No plural with *s*	The **musics** from the concert could be heard for miles.	(incorrect)
	Winning the lottery brought no **happiness** to Nora.	(correct)
No plural with *s*	Winning the lottery brought no **happinesses** to Nora.	(incorrect)
	At ninety-one, she had the **courage** of a fifty-year-old.	(correct)
No plural with *s*	The newspaper recorded the people's **courages**.	(incorrect)

Nouns That Are Either Count or Noncount

Some nouns can refer to things that can be counted one by one and can also refer to something that cannot be counted one by one. The meaning needed in the sentence determines which kind of noun you need. Note the following examples.

Count	The **lights** came on throughout the house.	(the individual lamps)
Noncount	We wanted more **light** in the kitchen.	(light in general)
Count	Jay wrote two **papers** for his English class.	(individual essays)
Noncount	Jay uses good-quality **paper** for his assignments.	(paper in general)

Count   The banging **noises** from the dishwasher worry me.

(individual kinds)

Noncount   The **noise** from the traffic woke Gerald early.   (noise in general)

Exercise 1

Determine whether the underlined noun is a count (C) or noncount (N) noun. Circle the C or the N at the beginning of each sentence.

Example:

Ⓒ N   **The <u>game</u> began just after 10:00 a.m.**

C Ⓝ   **She admired her son's <u>courage</u>.**

Version A

C N   1. The hospital patient struggled for <u>survival</u>.

C N   2. People continue to hope that <u>humanity</u> will learn religious tolerance.

C N   3. The lawn mower damaged a <u>brick</u> in the fence.

C N   4. My sister takes <u>calcium</u> every day.

C N   5. The health <u>magazine</u> recommends yearly mammograms.

Version B

C N   1. Terri expressed <u>relief</u> at the end of the test.

C N   2. We remodeled the house to have more <u>room</u> in the kitchen.

C N   3. Because of her diabetes, Sharon could not eat any of the apple <u>pie</u>.

C N   4. I forgot my <u>appointment</u> at the dentist.

C N   5. After growing up, my cat did not like <u>milk</u>.

Using Indefinite Articles with Count and Noncount Nouns

A and **an** are indefinite articles. If English is not your native language, you may have had trouble using the correct indefinite articles with count and non-count nouns. To become more fluent in English, you will want to work on using these articles correctly. They do not refer to any specific or clearly identified person, place, or thing. **They are used only with singular count nouns.**

A is used with singular count nouns that begin with a **consonant.**

An is used with singular count nouns that begin with a **vowel.**

When you are trying to choose between **a** or **an,** consider the beginning **sound** of the next word. For example, the word **hour** does not begin with the same sound as the word **house.**

Study these examples:

We waited for **an** hour to get into the movie.	(no particular time)
I looked at **a** house to rent.	(no specified house)
I bought **a book** to read on my trip.	(book not specified)
She ate **a sandwich** for lunch.	(kind not identified)
He mailed **an invitation** to his sister.	(not any particular invitation)
After the accident, Jeri rented **an automobile**.	(not any one specified)

A and *an* are **not** used with noncount nouns.

We listened to **a music** last night.	(incorrect)
We listened to **music** last night.	(correct)
Rene saw **a snow** for the first time this winter.	(incorrect)
Rene saw **snow** for the first time this winter.	(correct)

Exercise 2

Use **a** or **an** correctly in the sentences below. If the sentence is correct as it is, mark a C in the left margin.

Example:

Carl wanted ___*a*___ motorcycle for his graduation present.

Version A

1. I poured my water into _____ glass from the cupboard.

2. The Bryans wanted their new house to be made of _____ brick.

3. To increase her strength, Leta enrolled at _____ gym.

4. My neighbor collects antique bottles made of _____ glass.

5. The elderly gentleman ordered _____ egg and some toast for his breakfast.

Version B

1. My father made _____ error in his taxes this year.

2. After Raye worked out for _____ month, her shoulders were stronger.

3. Stanley wanted to take a course in _____ geography this semester.

4. We sent _____ compliment to the chef for his delicious appetizer.

5. The parents had to learn _____ new method for disciplining their child.

Using the Definite Article "the" before Singular and Plural Count Nouns

In contrast to indefinite articles, you should use the definite article **the** if a **particular person, place, or thing is specified**. This particular meaning can be in the sentence itself or in the context of your paragraph. You can use **the** before both **singular** and **plural count** nouns. Study the following correct examples.

I bought **the** new magazine on my way home from work.

(a particular magazine)

Rory used **the** cell phone you loaned him.   (a particular cell phone)

The handyman very quickly washed **the** windows of my house.

(particular handyman;
particular windows)

The computers in our lab are usually dependable.   (particular computers)

Using the Definite Article "the" before Noncount Nouns

You can use the definite article **the** before **noncount** nouns if there is a particular meaning specified within the sentence or within the context of your paragraph. When no particular meaning is expressed, do not use **the**.

After the race, I was surprised at **the relief** on her face.   (**particular** relief)
I found **relief** from the heat in the shade.

The light from the ball field shines into my house.   (**particular** light)
I do not like **light** coming into my house.

We liked **the music** played by the orchestra last night.   (**particular** music)
I enjoy **music** more than my brother does.

Work through the following exercise to get more practice in using **the** with count and noncount nouns.

Exercise 3

Consider the use of **the** in each sentence below. Write **C** for correct or **I** for incorrect in each blank.

Example:

___*I*___ **When we are on vacation, I am happy when he shows the enthusiasm.**

___*C*___ **When we are on vacation, I am happy when he shows enthusiasm.**

Version A

_____ **1.** He experienced failure last Saturday.

_____ **2.** He was saddened by the failure of his business.

_____ **3.** He showed the nervousness before his wedding.

_____ **4.** The nervousness he felt before his wedding soon disappeared.

_____ **5.** He lacked the courage needed to become a soldier.

_____ **6.** Becoming a soldier requires the courage.

Version B

_____ **1.** She does not have the sympathy.

_____ **2.** She does not have the sympathy her neighbor needs right now.

_____ **3.** In New Orleans, cafés have live jazz every weekend.

_____ **4.** In New Orleans, cafés have the live jazz every weekend.

_____ **5.** Melanie appreciates the beauty.

_____ **6.** Melanie appreciates the beauty of Renaissance art.

Knowing whether to use count or noncount nouns comes fairly naturally to native speakers of English, but if English is not your native language, try to get lots of experience talking with fluent speakers and reading as much English as you can. Try to benefit from your mistakes, and, as often as you can, practice using what you have learned. This is also good advice for the next section concerning verbs.

Verbs

English verbs may be troublesome for you if English is not your native language. To help you gain confidence in using English, study and then practice using the following verb forms.

Phrasal Verbs

These verbs are two-word verbs that are very common in English, especially in popular usage. They are made up of a verb plus a preposition and have special meaning when used together. Study the following examples:

The mother **checked on** her sleeping child.　(She looked at the child closely to see if she was all right.)

The words "checked on" function as a verb. "On" seems like a preposition, but it does not function as a preposition in this sentence.

Margaret **put off** her education.　(She postponed her education.)

"Put off" functions as a verb, so "off" is not a preposition in this sentence.

Partial List of Common Two-Word Verbs (Phrasal Verbs)

ask out	ask a person to go on a date
call off	cancel
call on	ask someone to answer in class
	formal usage—make a formal visit to someone
check on	attend to the needs of someone
cheer up	make somebody feel happy
check out	investigate
	officially take a book out of the library
come across	meet by chance
drop off	leave something or someone at a certain place
figure out	find an answer
fill out	put answers in the blanks of a form, such as an application
find out	get information
give up	quit; do not try anymore
go over	reread carefully
hand in	submit a paper or a document to a person or an office
look over	review or check again
make up	invent (for example, a story)
	complete missed work in school
pass out	distribute (as tests in a class)
	become unconscious
pick out	choose (perhaps an article of clothing in a store)
point out	show or call attention to
put up with	tolerate
run out (of)	use all the supply of something
tear down	destroy, as the confidence of a person
	demolish, as a building
turn down	lessen sound on a stereo or television set
turn off	stop a machine, such as an appliance in a house
	close a faucet or touch the off switch for a light

Exercise 4

Do you know any other "preposition-like" words that can be used with the verb **turn?**

turn _____, which means _____

turn _____, which means _____

turn _____, which means _____

Now try using some of these verbs in sentences of your own.

Exercise 5

Write three sentences, using any three of the above phrasal verbs. Underline the verb.

Example:

I *handed in* **my research paper to the English Department.**

1. _____

   _____

2. _____

   _____

3. _____

   _____

Modal Verbs

A modal is a helping verb that has its own meaning. When a modal is used with the main verb, it adds meaning to the main verb. Study the following examples.

The baby **can** walk.   (The baby knows how to walk.)

Zito **might** walk to work.   (We do not know for sure that he is going to walk.)

He **will** walk tomorrow.   (We know this for certain.)

He **should** walk.   (It is advisable for him to walk, perhaps for his health.)

Points to Remember about Modals

- When you use a modal, do not use an s on the main verb
- The modal form does not use an s for *he, she,* or *it* (the third-person singular)

- Most modals are **not** followed by **to**-plus-a-verb (an infinitive); common exception is "ought." Example: "She **ought** to go."
- Modals function like other helping verbs in questions and in negative sentences. "**Should** he go?" "He **will** not walk tomorrow."
- Modals are **not** immediately followed by **-ing** verb forms. Incorrect: "He must washing his car." Say instead, "He must wash his car."

Partial List of Modals and the Meanings They Add to Main Verbs

can	has the ability; has permission
could	had the ability in the past
have to	expressing obligation or necessity
may	expressing possibility or uncertainty
might	expressing some uncertainty
must	expressing obligation or necessity
should	expressing obligation
would	expressing preference

Work through the following exercise to help you use modal verbs.

Exercise 6

Write a **C** for correct or an **I** for incorrect in the blank before each sentence.

Example:

_____*I*_____ **Rhonda has to making a deposit at her bank.**

_____*C*_____ **Rhonda has to make a deposit at her bank.**

Version A

_____ 1. The student can buys her supplies at the discount store.

_____ 2. We have to go tomorrow morning.

_____ 3. Sonya must seeing the doctor after all.

_____ 4. He might jogs around the lake in the morning.

_____ 5. Walter may study at the library.

Version B

_____ 1. After lunch, we could going to the mall to shop.

_____ 2. If you prefer, I will enroll immediately.

_____ 3. The church bells should to ring at noon.

_____ 4. Gerald might mows the lawn next week.

_____ 5. Clara may not read the newspaper before breakfast.

Verb Plus -ing Verb Form (Gerund)

As you have already learned, an **-ing** verb form (gerund) is a noun that can be either a subject or an object. Certain verbs in English are usually followed by these **-ing** forms. The sentences below show how these commonly used verbs are followed immediately by an **-ing** form of another verb.

I **advised** *paying* bills on time.

Ralph **appreciated** *going* to college.

He **avoided** *rushing* into the new business.

We **considered** *borrowing* money to buy our furniture.

We **discussed** *painting* our house.

Glenda **enjoys** *going* to school.

Elena **finished** *decorating* her cousin's home.

I **keep** *working* on the project even though I am tired.

Matthew **quit** *smoking* two years ago.

The agent **suggested** *selling* the house as soon as possible.

These kinds of expressions are so common in English that it would benefit you to practice them and use them whenever you can. The next exercise will help you use these verbs with suitable **-ing** verb forms after them.

Exercise 7

Add an appropriate **-ing** verb form (gerund) to each subject and verb below. Use other words and phrases to make your sentences meaningful and complete.

Example:

The instructor discussed _____ *revising our essays* _____.

Version A

1. The counselor suggested _____.

2. We will discuss _____.

3. Sharon quit _____.

4. Ken kept _____.

5. Mom enjoys _____.

Version B

1. My grandfather advises ————————————————————————.

2. The customers appreciated ————————————————————————.

3. The nurse avoided ————————————————————————.

4. The builder finished ————————————————————————.

5. The senior citizens will consider ————————————————————————.

Note   It is important to remember that the above verbs are not followed by an infinitive verb form. It is incorrect to say, "We discussed to go on vacation." On the other hand, it is correct to say, "We discussed going on vacation."

Verb Followed by "to" Plus a Verb Form (Infinitive)

Many common verbs are followed by an infinitive—the word **to**-plus-a-verb. For instance, someone might say, "Jean plans to babysit for us next Saturday." The verb **plan** is one of these common verbs. Study the examples below to see how these verbs work.

Raymond **expects** *to get* a raise next month.

Lindsay **refused** *to go* to Hawaii with me.

The newly married couple **decided** *to take* a honeymoon later.

Partial List of Verbs That Can Be Followed by an Infinitive

agree	forget	refuse
appear	need	try
decide	plan	want
expect	promise	

These verbs cannot be followed by an **-ing** verb. For example, you cannot say, "I will decide asking for a raise." Rather, say "I decided to ask for a raise." The next exercise will give you a chance to use these verbs correctly.

Exercise 8

Put a **C** or an **I** in each blank below. Use the list above to help you.

Example:

___*I*___ **We forgot paying our electric bill.**

Version A

_____ **1.** She promised going to the store tomorrow.

_____ **2.** Larry refused to lend him any more money.

_____ **3.** Her tax advisor needed having other records.

_____ **4.** The coach promised helping him apply for a college scholarship.

_____ **5.** We tried to drive across town to a special store.

Version B

_____ **1.** I wanted learning to play the piano.

_____ **2.** They expect enrolling in the fitness center.

_____ **3.** The supervisor agreed to hold a meeting with the new employee.

_____ **4.** The cashier forgot putting away the checks.

_____ **5.** The flight attendant refused serving the unruly passenger.

More Help with Prepositions

When using certain common words and expressions, you may have had trouble choosing the correct preposition that native speakers and writers of English expect you to use. You want to be able to choose the correct preposition, but you have to choose the one that is right for the meaning you intend. You may just have to practice and learn as many of these commonly used expressions as you can. Following are some of these common expressions that require prepositions.

Agree on (a plan)	We agreed **on** outcomes for the class.
Agree to (an offer)	They agreed **to** the salary offer from the company.
Angry about (a problem)	We were angry **about** the loss of the money.
Angry with (someone)	Mom was angry **with** me for losing my jacket.
Capable of	The child was surprisingly capable **of** doing math.
Contrast with	This assignment contrasts **with** the previous one.
Differ from (some thing)	This computer differs **from** that one.
Differ with (a person)	He differed **with** me about the possible result.
Impatient with (a person)	I was impatient **with** the sales associate.
Responsible for (someone or something)	They are responsible **for** themselves.

In addition to the above expressions, the common prepositions **at**, **in**, and **on** are sometimes confusing. Consider the following uses for these prepositions:

For a specific place or specific time, use **at**.

Come to my office **at** 50 W. State **at** 3:00 P.M.

For a length of time, use **in**.

I went to college **in** the sixties.

Dana's birthday is **in** April.

For names of streets and days of the week or month, use **on**.

The house for sale is **on** 15th Street. We saw it **on** Monday.

On April 22, we want to offer to buy it.

The following exercise will give you practice in using the above prepositions.

Exercise 9

Determine whether the underlined preposition in each sentence is correct. Put **C** or **I** in the blank.

Example:

___*I*___ **He agreed <u>to</u> me about the movie.**

Version A

_____ **1.** We live <u>in</u> 2701 N. 10th Street.

_____ **2.** Our boss was angry <u>for</u> us.

_____ **3.** I am capable <u>in</u> doing the homework.

_____ **4.** My last trip is <u>at</u> Tuesday.

_____ **5.** I found my lost purse <u>on</u> June 10, 2003.

Version B

_____ **1.** Kiko's birthday is <u>on</u> May.

_____ **2.** The voters cannot agree <u>for</u> a plan to raise taxes.

_____ **3.** My last test is <u>on</u> Thursday.

_____ **4.** I will meet you <u>at</u> the entrance to the shopping center.

_____ **5.** We agreed <u>to</u> you about the suggestion.

The material in this appendix may not cover all the problems you are having with English, but they may help you use English more fluently and confidently.

Spelling

When you write a paper, it is important that all the words are spelled correctly. When you submit a paper with misspelled words, it appears as though you did not bother to take the time to proofread carefully or run a spell checker. You probably know some people who are excellent spellers and others who are extremely poor spellers. Research has shown that spelling skills have nothing to do with basic intelligence. On the other hand, since correct spelling is one of the characteristics of public writing, you need to spend time doing whatever is necessary to improve your spelling. If spelling is a problem for you, you will be happy to learn that it can be improved with practice. If you are willing to put in some time to review these pages and use the **Keys to Better Spelling**, your spelling should improve. Remember, though, that spelling is something that should not be a preoccupation until you do your final editing. To begin understanding spelling, you need to be aware of a few basic terms that follow.

Basic Terms

The main part of the word without a prefix or a suffix is the **root word.**

un **manage** able

One or more letters of a word that together form a unit for pronunciation is a **syllable.**

va ca tion

A **vowel** forms the prominent sound in a syllable.

a e i o u

Any letter of the alphabet that is **not** a vowel is identified as a **consonant.**

b, c, d, f, g, h, j, k, l, m, n, p, q, r, s, t, v, w, x, y, z

A syllable or syllables attached to the beginning of a word to extend the meaning of the root word is a **prefix.**

undo, **anti**government

A syllable or syllables attached to the end of a word to extend the meaning of the root word is a **suffix.**

govern**ment**, ski**ing**

Keys to Better Spelling

Here are a few basic patterns that can help with spelling. Read and study the keys, but more important, look at and pronounce the examples so that you can understand them. Then begin incorporating them into your spelling habits.

Key 1. If a one-syllable word ends in a consonant-vowel-consonant pattern, double the final consonant before adding a suffix that begins with a vowel.

Here are some words to study.

wrap	+er	=	wrapper
ton	+age	=	tonnage
hop	+ed	=	hopped

If the final consonant is an "x" or is not pronounced, do not double it.

| box | +ing | = | boxing |
| row | +ing | = | rowing |

Practice 1

To practice, add "ed" to the following words.

star _____

tag _____

drug _____

wrap _____

ship _____

Practice 2

To practice, add "ing" to the following words.

brag _____

swim _____

hum _____

chat _____

lug _____

Key 2. If a two-syllable word ends in a consonant-vowel-consonant pattern and is accented on the second syllable, double the final consonant before adding a suffix that begins with a vowel.

Here are some words to study.

refer	+ed	=	referred
transmit	+er	=	transmitter
begin	+ing	=	beginning
admit	+ance	=	admittance

Practice 3

To practice, add "ed" to the following words.

defer   _____

allot   _____

control   _____

omit   _____

remit   _____

Practice 4

To practice, add "ing" to the following words.

occur   _____

repel   _____

extol   _____

unwrap   _____

acquit   _____

Key 3. If a word ends in "e" preceded by a consonant, drop the "e" before adding a suffix that begins with a vowel.

Here are some words to examine that follow the pattern of a suffix that begins with a vowel:

hope	+ing	=	hoping
excuse	+able	=	excusable
cope	+ed	=	coped
scarce	+ity	=	scarcity

Keep the "e" if the suffix begins with a consonant.
Here are some words that follow this pattern.

move	+ment	=	movement
tire	+less	=	tireless
remote	+ness	=	remoteness
strange	+ly	=	strangely

Practice 5

Practice by combining each root word with the suffix given.

judge	+	ment	=	_____
believe	+	able	=	_____
compose	+	ing	=	_____
delete	+	ing	=	_____
write	+	ing	=	_____
relate	+	ing	=	_____

replace	+	ment	=	_____
devote	+	ing	=	_____
forgive	+	ness	=	_____
encourage	+	ment	=	_____

Key 4. After a soft "c," write the "e" before the "i" when these two letters appear in sequence, or keep this jingle in mind: "i" before "e" except after "c."
  Here are some examples that follow this pattern:

deceive   receive   conceive

The "e" also goes before the "i" if the sound is like an "a" as in *neighbor* and *weigh*.

Practice 6

Practice on these words as you insert either "ie" or "ei" in each blank:

unbel____vable	r____gn
fr____ght	shr____k
gr____f	br____f
rec____pt	misch____vous
rel____ve	n____ce

Key 5. If a word ends with "y" preceded by a consonant, generally change the "y" to an "i" before adding a suffix other than "ing."

Here are some words that follow this pattern:

worry	+er	=	worrier
worry	+some	=	worrisome
hurry	+s	=	hurries
lazy	+est	=	laziest
company	+s	=	companies

The "y" is kept to preserve the "y" sound in the proper pronunciation of words such as the following:

carry	+ing	=	carrying
worry	+ing	=	worrying
hurry	+ing	=	hurrying

Practice 7

Practice on the following words:

happy	+ness	=	_____
merry	+est	=	_____
vary	+s	=	_____
tasty	+er	=	_____
jury	+s	=	_____
baby	+ing	=	_____
study	+ing	=	_____

Spelling List

As you create your personal list of spelling words, you may want to add some of the following words to your list.

absence	category	envelop (verb)	labeling
absorption	ceiling	exaggerate	legitimate
accede	cemetery	exceed	leisure
accessible	changeable	exhaust	license
accommodate	clientele	exhilaration	likable
accumulate	collateral	existence	litigation
achieve	color	extraordinary	loneliness
acoustics	committee	fallacy	loose
acquittal	comparative	familiar	maintenance
advantageous	competitor	flexible	mathematics
affiliated	concede	fluctuation	mediocre
aggressive	connoisseur	forty	minimum
alignment	connotation	gesture	misspelling
all right	conscience	grammar	necessary
aluminum	consensus	gratuity	necessity
analyze	convenient	grievous	negligence
anoint	convertible	haphazard	negotiable
apostrophe	corroborate	hemorrhage	newsstand
apparent	criticism	holiday	nickel
appropriate	definitely	hosiery	noticeable
argument	description	hypocrisy	occurrence
asphalt	desirable	illegible	omission
assistant	despair	immigrant	opponent
asterisk	development	incidentally	oscillate
athletics	dilemma	indelible	pageant
auditor	dilettante	independent	panicky
bachelor	disappear	indispensable	parallel
balloon	disappoint	inimitable	paralyze
bankruptcy	disbursement	inoculate	pastime
believable	discrepancy	insistent	peaceable
benefited	discriminate	intermediary	penicillin
bicycle	dissatisfied	irresistible	permanent
brilliant	dissipate	irritable	perseverance
bulletin	drunkenness	jewelry	persistent
calendar	ecstasy	judgment	personnel
campaign	eligible	judicial	persuade
canceled	embarrassing	khaki	physician
canvass (verb)	endorsement	kindergarten	plagiarism

possesses	questionnaire	sergeant	technique
potato	receive	sheriff	tenant
precede	recommend	stationary (fixed)	tranquilizer
predictable	repetition	stationery (paper)	truly
preferred	rescind	succeed	tyrannize
privilege	rhythmical	suddenness	unanimous
procedure	ridiculous	superintendent	until
proceed	sacrilegious	supersede	vacillate
professor	salable	surgeon	vacuum
pronunciation	secretary	surprise	vicious
psychology	seize	tangible	weird
pursue	separate	tariff	

Tips for Improving Spelling

1. One very common, practical, and logical activity to improve your spelling is to read. Time spent reading is a reinforcement of spelling words, vocabulary, and writing models.

2. Personal spelling lists help you focus on troublesome words. Post the lists on your refrigerator so that you see the list frequently, or perhaps you can make a plan and work on just five words a week. Carry the list of five words on a three-by-five card and look at the words any time, especially during the time you spend waiting for traffic lights to change, buses to come, or classes to begin.

3. As you study your words, be sure to pronounce all the syllables carefully.

4. A computerized dictionary such as a Franklin can be a handy aid to use while writing. Some models contain thousands of words, and the computer can bring the word up instantaneously, so if you can afford the extra purchase, your money might be well spent. Some models allow you to customize your dictionary by adding specialized words that you need for your job.

5. The purchase of a handy paperback dictionary is another very practical option. Most college bookstores have various publications, and your writing instructor could suggest one for you.

6. If you do your writing on the computer, run the spell checker before you submit your final draft to your instructor. Also, use your "find" function for your personal "troublesome word list." "It's," "its," "there," "their," "they're," "your," and "you're" can be searched easily so that you can double-check the spelling for your use of the word.

Answers to Odd-Numbered Exercises

Chapter 1, Part 1

Exercise 1 (Page 12)

Answers will vary.

Exercise 2 (Page 16)

Version A

1. How many times did you call me yesterday?

3. We wanted to have a picnic at sunset tonight, but a storm is coming.

5. During spring break, Nikki wants to go to the mountains.

7. After breakfast, Sandy went shopping but came home soon after she bought a pair of shoes.

9. Wilbur's big dog Jake always has his dinner in the middle of the afternoon.

Exercise 3 (Page 16)

Version A

___1___ I will always remember helping my grandfather feed his chickens.

___6___ While I did this, Granddad always cleaned up and got everything organized for their next meal.

___7___ Then he would take my hand in his, and we would go back into the house.

___5___ As soon as I scooped out the first spoonful and put it down for them, they began to peck at the mash.

___2___ Though I was only four years old, I remember his calling my name and leading me to the backyard to see his chickens roaming around.

<u>_3_</u>   I still remember the sweet smell of the corn and wheat as he mixed the dry chicken feed with water.

<u>_4_</u>   Then my job was to put the feed on a long log, spoonful by spoonful.

<u>_8_</u>   Today, I remember these events as though they were yesterday.

Chapter 1, Part 4

Exercise 1 (Page 44)

Version A

1. Tiger Woods is an incredibly talented athlete.

3. Uncle Mike made a delicious pie.

5. Many people prefer natural foods.

7. Kevin likes apple pie.

9. The computers in the lab were all busy.

Exercise 2 (Page 45)

Version A
Answers will vary.

Exercise 3 (Page 46)

Version A

1. Jeremy bought a new CD player. He played it nonstop for a week.

3. Katrina made three runs on the giant roller coaster. It roared down the steep dips and hurled her around the curves.

5. With so many homes being built, the wildlife are being forced from their habitat.

7. Tom has a test tomorrow. He expects it to be difficult.

9. The owls were nesting in the tree. They kept me awake at night.

Exercise 4 (Page 48)

Version A

1. Henry dropped the pizza before <u>_he_</u> could put <u>_it_</u> into the oven.

3. Angela is taking a class in college. <u>_She_</u> asked <u>_her_</u> son to help <u>_her_</u> with more tasks around the house.

5. Two women and one man refereed the first game of the new basketball season. The crowd booed _them_ only twice.

7. My grandmother is learning to use a computer. _She_ wants to use _it_ to keep track of stocks and bonds.

9. Tarya went to her senior prom with Dan. _They_ had pictures taken that night.

Exercise 5 (Page 49)

Version A
Answers will vary.

Exercise 6 (Page 50)

Version A

1. Yesterday, I worked with (each) of my brothers.

3. A (few) of the restaurants closed early.

5. Richard lost (everything) in the fire.

7. He was not able to save (anything) from the flood.

9. The detectives asked (everyone) at the scene to describe the crime.

Exercise 7 (Page 51)

Version A

adj. 1. We went to **several** computer stores and compared prices.

pro. 3. We watched **all** of the movie before going to bed.

pro. 5. **Most** of the children are playing in the backyard.

Exercise 8 (Page 51)
Answers will vary.

Exercise 9 (Page 53)

Version A

1. The ribbon curled back on (itself) and became tangled.

3. He (himself) wanted to change the oil in his car.

5. The dirty clothes are not going to wash (themselves) today.

7. The young child called 911 (herself) for her mother.

9. I gave (myself) a reward for graduating from college.

Exercise 10 (Page 54)
Answers will vary.

Exercise 11 (Page 55)

Version A

1. (This) is the last vacation we have planned.

3. (That) is the puppy who could be a champion.

5. (This) is the street where we can catch the subway.

7. Do you really want to give (this) to your instructor?

Exercise 12 (Page 56)
Answers will vary.

Exercise 13 (Page 58)

Version A

1. ~~Before the game,~~ the players stretched ~~for half an hour.~~

3. ~~Without a doubt,~~ Jeff became an excellent president ~~of the school.~~

5. Everyone ~~in my family~~ will be home ~~within an hour or two.~~

7. ~~At the beginning of the meeting,~~ the leader ~~of the organization~~ spoke ~~to the members.~~

9. ~~Because of its action,~~ the movie thrilled the audience.

11. Investing money ~~in the stock market~~ should provide income ~~during retirement.~~

13. I do some of these tasks ~~on a daily basis.~~

15. The tallest player ~~on our basketball team~~ stood a full foot ~~above the coach.~~

17. ~~On Saturdays,~~ my family and I often go ~~to the zoo.~~

Exercise 14 (Page 59)
Answers will vary.

Exercise 15 (Page 62)

Version A

1. On her eighty-eighth birthday, Polly <u>sang</u> a solo.

3. They immediately <u>could walk</u> into the ocean.

5. Two peanuts <u>rattled</u> in the bottom of the can.

7. Roxanne <u>should be</u> happy with the concert.

9. Eric <u>has been chosen</u> captain of the team.

11. The famous poet <u>will arrive</u> on Friday and <u>will read</u> her poetry the same night.

13. The eager visitors <u>hiked</u> into the Grand Canyon and <u>camped</u> overnight.

15. I <u>would like</u> to finish my project today.

Exercise 16 (Page 63)

Version A

1. Tourists ___*find*___ Holiday Inns in most states in America.

3. Working out at the gym ___*gives*___ people energy.

5. The newspaper ___*provides*___ people a lot of important information.

7. The little lizard often ___*scurries*___ across my morning path.

9. Searching for seashells ___*keeps*___ the kids busy.

Exercise 17 (Page 68)

Version A

1. We ___*asked*___ for a table by the window.

3. The boiling water almost ___*burned*___ the chef.

5. The cat on the chair just ___*blinked*___ at me.

7. The college class ___*planted*___ a tree in memory of their classmate.

9. This morning, I ___*stumbled*___ on the broken step.

Exercise 18 (Page 69)

Version A

1. Without planning ahead, I ___*went*___ to the grocery store.

3. I ___*bought*___ a birthday present for my brother.

5. The server ___*did*___ his best to please the customers.

7. My neighbor ___*rang*___ my front door bell at dinnertime.

9. The geraniums ___*grew*___ in the raised flowerbed near my patio.

Exercise 19 (Page 70)

Version A

1. Before lunch, I had ___eaten___ an apple.

3. Have you ___chosen___ your suit for the wedding?

5. I was ___taking___ my lunch break early.

7. The wasps had ___stung___ me several times.

9. The sun has already ___set___ .

Exercise 20 (Page 71)
Answers will vary.

Chapter 2, Part 1

Exercise 1 (Page 79)

Version A
Answers will vary.

1. biographies
   calendars
3. manicure
   permanent
5. going to a fitness center
   watching movies/television

Exercise 2 (Page 81)

Version A
1. carrots, green beans, potatoes   ___vegetables___
3. pants, shirts, socks   ___clothes___
5. *Arizona Republic, USA Today, New York Times*   ___newspapers___

Exercise 3 (Page 82)

Version A

Part 2

Cluster #1: Fire, cooking, marshmallows, and hot dogs
   a. part of cooking on an open fire.
Cluster #3: Telling stories, looking at the stars at night, and reading a book
   a. a relaxing part of camping.
Cluster #5: Hiking and fishing
   b. activities campers enjoy.

Exercise 4 (Page 84)

Version A

1. Topic: _Mary Elizabeth_ Direction: _enjoys shopping for shoes_ .

3. Topic: _adult children_ Direction: _showed appreciation for their parents_ .

5. Topic: _ceremonies_ Direction: _featured the state's Native American people_ .

Exercise 5 (Page 86)

Version A

1. Topic: Little League baseball

_TS_ c. Little League baseball can be fun for children.

3. Topic: petting zoos

_TS_ e. Children can benefit by going to a petting zoo.

5. Topic: old houses

_TS_ a. Old houses often provide spacious living conditions.

Exercise 6 (Page 88)

Version A

_F_ 1. My cell phone fits into my pocket.

_TS_ 3. My cell phone is quite convenient.

_F_ 5. Jeremy painted his house last week.

_TS_ 7. My new computer is outstanding.

_TS_ 9. His ex-girlfriend is having lots of fun.

Exercise 7 (Page 90)

Version A

1. Topic: Successfully recovering from surgery means
   Direction: _√_ following the doctor's instructions carefully.

3. Topic: Successful college students
   Direction: _√_ have good study habits.

5. Topic: Living outside a city
   Direction: _√_ provides a quieter environment.

Exercise 8 (Page 91)
Answers will vary.

Version A

1. School _helps children learn to cooperate with each other_ .

3. Graduating from college _brings pride_ .

5. My cousin _is good at using computers_ .

7. Snowboarding _____*can be dangerous*_____ .

9. Listening to a CD _____*puts me in a good mood*_____ .

Exercise 9 (Page 92)

1. Topic Sentence: When I was a child, my older brother often played tricks on me.
    c. Whenever my brother got candy or a cupcake at school, he saved it until he got home and shared it with me.

3. Children can learn kindness from examples set by adults.
    d. Parents discuss with their children how to save money.

5. Being the parent of young children gives parents many responsibilities.
    b. The parents need to teach the children how to make brownies.

Exercise 10 (Page 95)
Version A

_a_ 1.

_a_ 3.

_a_ 5.

Exercise 11 (Page 98)
Answers will vary.

Exercise 12 (Page 98)
Answers will vary.

Chapter 2, Part 4

Exercise 1 (Page 114)
Version A

1. The strong wind blew the rain into the new carport.

3. Summer weather in Phoenix is usually hot.

5. Up on the mountain, the anxious skiers waited to fly down the steep slope.

7. Kay wanted new blinds in the living room.

9. James bought flowering shrubs for the front yard.

Exercise 2 (Page 115)

Version A

1. *The dirty rug needed to be cleaned.*
3. *The fallen pine needles crunched under my feet.*
5. *I spilled my chocolate milkshake.*
7. *We went to the last concert.*
9. *I worked at the new Burger King.*

Exercise 3 (Page 117)

Version A

1. *The proud gardeners set out healthy plants.*
3. *The old white rhino has a cancerous tumor on his front leg.*
5. *The hot weather required us to use all our fans.*
7. *Madison started a well-planned pizza restaurant.*
9. *Rosa applied for an exciting new job.*

Exercise 4 (Page 120)

Version A

1. *Students went to their campus bookstore to buy books.*
3. *The new neighbors are replacing their old roof.*
5. *The traffic jam lasted for two hours.*

Exercise 5 (Page 121)

Version A

1. *quicker*
3. *fuller*
5. *cooler*
7. *kinder*
9. *greater*

Exercise 6 (Page 122)

Version A

1. *more surprising*
3. *more suitable*
5. *more tragic*
7. *more dangerous*
9. *more talkative*

Exercise 7 (Page 123)

Version A

1. *spongier*

3. *sootier*

5. *craftier*

7. *easier*

9. *classier*

Exercise 8 (Page 124)

Version A

1. *quickest*

3. *fullest*

5. *coolest*

7. *kindest*

9. *greatest*

Exercise 9 (Page 125)

Version A

1. *most surprising*

3. *most suitable*

5. *most tragic*

7. *most dangerous*

9. *most talkative*

Exercise 10 (Page 126)

Version A

1. *spongiest*

3. *sootiest*

5. *craftiest*

7. *easiest*

9. *classiest*

Exercise 11 (Page 128)

Version A

1. The parents <u>proudly</u> watched the ceremony.

3. The winter weather <u>repeatedly</u> cracked the pavement.

5. <u>Quietly</u>, the springer spaniel waited by the front door.

7. The child waited <u>patiently</u> for her breakfast.

Exercise 12 (Page 129)

Version A

1. We looked ___carefully___ at the new furniture before buying any.

3. ___Unexpectedly/Quickly___, the new puppy ran around the living room.

5. The ceiling fan did not turn as ___quietly___ as we had hoped.

Exercise 13 (Page 130)

Version A

1. My paper was ___extremely___ easy to write. (extreme)

3. The exhibits were ___equally___ well done. (equal)

5. His ___harshly___ spoken words upset me. (harsh)

Exercise 14 (Page 131)

Version A

1. The mother spoke ^_harshly_ to her daughter.

3. Before lunch, Heather ^_quietly_ sat down in the snack bar.

5. _Immediately,_ ^Jose joined the band at school.

7. Jim ^_spontaneously_ bought a red convertible.

Exercise 15 (Page 132)

Version A

1. The directions were not written very ___clearly___. (clear, clearly)

3. Our football team is not a ___nationally___ ranked team. (national, nationally)

5. Our vacation went ___quickly___ last summer. (quick, quickly)

Exercise 16 (Page 133)

Version A

1. The child sat ___quietly___ in the car. (quiet)

   The child was ___quiet___ in the car.

3. My friend Beth was never a ___patient___ person. (patient)

   My friend Beth waited ___patiently___ for her friends.

5. Candice ___courageously___ walked up the stairs for her diploma. (courageous)

   Walking up the stairs to get her diploma, Candice looked ___courageous___.

7. David was prepared for the ___mental___ job ahead of him. (mental)

   David was ___mentally___ prepared for the job.

9. The children played ___nicely___ together. (nice)

The children were ___nice___ to each other.

Exercise 17 (Page 134)

Version A

1. I did ___well___ on the test.

3. Anita is always a ___good___ friend when I need one.

5. Anne's students follow instructions ___well___.

7. After surgery, Matt did not look ___well___ for a week.

Exercise 18 (Page 135)

Version A

1. I felt ___bad___ about missing my mother's wedding.

3. The food from the sidewalk vendor tasted ___bad___.

5. On the night I saw the play, it was ___bad___.

Chapter 3, Part 1

Exercise 1 (Page 143)

Version A

1. Booking airline tickets over the Internet <u>saves</u> money.

3. They <u>produce</u> healthy stems with beautiful yellow roses.

5. Jasper <u>played</u> the piano beautifully.

7. <u>Balancing</u> a checkbook at the beginning of the month <u>is</u> a worthwhile habit.

9. The <u>dog</u> in the yard <u>dug</u> under the fence.

Exercise 2 (Page 143)
Answers will vary.

Exercise 3 (Page 144)

Version A

1. The <u>tourists</u> and their <u>guide</u> <u>became</u> friends.

3. <u>Rain</u> and <u>sleet</u> <u>fell</u> for several hours.

5. <u>Firefighters</u> and police <u>officers</u> often <u>work</u> together.

7. My <u>brother</u> and <u>sister</u> <u>left</u> for school together.

9. <u>To plant</u> seeds and <u>to see</u> growth <u>excited</u> the children.

Exercise 4 (Page 145)

Answers will vary.

Exercise 5 (Page 145)

Version A

1. We <u>played</u> in the snow and <u>made</u> snowmen.

3. The old <u>car</u> <u>rattled</u> and <u>rumbled</u> down the street.

5. The <u>chef</u> <u>whistled</u> and <u>hummed</u> in the kitchen.

7. Every morning <u>Alan</u> <u>exercised</u> with his son and then <u>read</u> to him at bedtime.

9. <u>Reading</u> that book <u>relaxed</u> me and <u>helped</u> me sleep.

Exercise 6 (Page 146)

Answers will vary.

Exercise 7 (Page 146)

Version A

1. My <u>daughters</u> and <u>I</u> <u>went</u> to the library and <u>read</u> the books until 6:00 P.M.

3. <u>Yowling</u> and <u>barking</u> <u>came</u> from the backyard and <u>woke</u> Elijah.

5. <u>Natasha</u> and her <u>mother</u> <u>laughed</u> and <u>cried</u> together.

7. <u>Mike</u> and his <u>friends</u> <u>walked</u> slowly and <u>chatted</u> in low voices.

9. <u>Laughing</u> and <u>crying</u> <u>can relieve</u> stress and <u>can erase</u> bad feelings.

Exercise 8 (Page 147)

Answers will vary.

Exercise 9 (Page 148)

Version A

1. They <u>flew</u> their (kites) in the afternoon.

3. The strong <u>wind</u> <u>pushed</u> the (child) along the street.

5. The fruit <u>trees</u> <u>withstood</u> the freezing (temperatures).

7. The <u>coach</u> and her <u>students</u> <u>enjoyed</u> their (trip) to the tournament.

9. The <u>pitchers</u> and <u>catchers</u> <u>met</u> the (deadline) for training camp.

Exercise 10 (Page 150)

Version A

1. The freshest <u>apples</u> <u><u>were</u></u> (red).

3. My childhood <u>dream</u> <u><u>was</u></u> (to play) professional golf.

5. <u>To play</u> in the NBA All-Star Game <u><u>is</u></u> (rare) and (profitable).

7. He always <u>felt</u> (proud) of his work.

9. The pumpkin <u>pie</u> <u>tastes</u> (delicious).

Exercise 11 (Page 152)

Version A

1. The *black and white* kittens wanted to play with the *yellow tennis* balls.

3. We *quietly* sat at the *worn wooden* desks.

5. The *frisky, tumbling* kittens played *roughly* with each other.

7. The *busy* airport was filled with *chattering, excited* people.

9. He dropped the *cornbread* crumbs into his *homemade vegetable* soup.

Exercise 12 (Page 154)

Version A

1. *After school, Tori practiced her guitar lessons.*

   Tori practiced her guitar lessons after school.

3. *Joseph and Ron planned a fishing trip to Lake Pleasant.*

5. *The young driver ran into the parked truck near the fence.*

Exercise 13 (Page 156)

Version A

1. My family wants to buy a new (car). *red Mustang*

3. My best friend loves (music). *rap, hip-hop, jazz, classical*

5. My sister's (clothes) fit me nicely. *blouses, pants*

7. The classroom has many (resources) for students to use. *computers, books*

9. The new (appliance) in the kitchen did not work. *oven, dishwasher*

Exercise 14 (Page 157)

Version A

1. She _sipped, slurped, gulped_ her hot chocolate.
3. The grocery cart _dented, scratched, smacked_ my car.
5. I _dropped, slammed, gently placed_ my schoolbooks onto the large wooden table.

Exercise 15 (Page 158)

Version A

1. _The rainstorm damaged the mobile home._
3. _The librarian stacked the magazines._
5. _The desperate motorist flagged down a sheriff._
7. _My brother took the wedding pictures._
9. _The judge sentenced the shoplifter to two years of probation._

Exercise 16 (Page 160)

Version A

1. This is easy as _pie / falling off a log_ .
3. He was last but not _least_ .
5. You are worth your weight in _gold_ .

Exercise 17 (Page 161)

Version A

1. _Don't just apply for one job/Don't have just one child._
3. _We are unable to move forward._
5. _I can't see the larger picture for the details._

Chapter 3, Part 4

Exercise 1 (Page 175)

Version A

1. The dogs _want_ their dinner right away.
3. Each Saturday, Marta _looks_ forward to working in her yard.
5. Carita and her sister _like_ to travel in the city on the new subway.
7. Jogging slowly and humming quietly _help_ Sandy forget her problems.
9. Coming upon stray dogs or cats always _bothers_ Veronica.

Exercise 2 (Page 176)

Version A

1. The loaves ~~of bread~~ __*were*__ hot and delicious.

3. His notes ~~for the test~~ __*were*__ soaked ~~in the downpour.~~

5. Her regret ~~over the forgotten lunch dates~~ __*seems*__ to be genuine.

7. CDs ~~under the bed~~ __*collect*__ dust.

9. The income ~~of the cooperating countries~~ __*has*__ risen recently.

Exercise 3 (Page 177)

Version A

1. Most ~~of my neighbors~~ __*go*__ ~~on vacation in June.~~

3. Some ~~of them~~ __*are*__ sober.

5. Some ~~of it~~ __*is*__ missing.

7. One ~~of us~~ __*has*__ to go ~~to the store.~~

9. All ~~of the desserts~~ __*look*__ delicious.

Exercise 4 (Page 178)

Version A

1. We __*were*__ just hanging out at the mall.

3. She __*does*__ not want to go with us tonight.

5. I __*am*__ not the one to do this job.

7. Studying for exams __*was*__ always easy for Sam.

9. He __*does*__ the best on his math tests.

Exercise 5 (Page 180)

Version A

__*past*__ 1. We moved into a new apartment last month. It ~~is~~ *was* a good move because
it ~~brings~~ *brought* me closer to my job.

__*present*__ 3. The throat lozenges soothe my scratchy throat. I ~~liked~~ *like* their assorted
citrus flavors.

__*present*__ 5. In January in Arizona, the sun shines almost every day. Some out-of-
state travelers ~~came~~ *come* to visit and ~~ended~~ *end* up staying a month or two.

past **7.** Two of the goldfish grew too large for the tank. We ~~have~~ to buy a new

      tank for them.

      had

past **9.** Yesterday, the weather caused a ten-car pileup on the freeway. Traffic

      was

      ~~is~~ backed up for two miles.

Chapter 4, Part 1

Exercise 1 (Page 187)

Version A

            s   v   v

S **1.** Kyle played baseball in college and won most of the games.

            s   v   v

S **3.** Brett drove to school and parked his car in the north lot.

                s   v   v

S **5.** The firefighter proudly carried the flag in the memorial service and held

      it throughout the ceremony.

              s   v   v

S **7.** Sandra drove to the mall and spent the afternoon window shopping.

            s   v   s v

C **9.** Josh played on the college baseball team, and he hit several home runs.

Exercise 2 (Page 190)

Version A

1. *Jason studied for his math exam, so he passed it easily.*

3. *Kyle and Josh wore their raincoats, for they knew it was going to rain.*

5. *The patient needs to take the doctor's advice, or the illness will not be cured.*

7. *Americans showed respect for their country, and they flew their flags.*

9. *Sandra gathered a bouquet of flowers from her garden, for she wanted to decorate her dining room table.*

Exercise 3 (Page 192)

Version A

1. *Heather made brownies; they were delicious.*

3. *The United States and Russia developed the International Space Station; they now share responsibility for it.*

5. *The quarterback threw four touchdown passes; his team won the game.*

7. *The pizza delivery driver took his time; he made his deliveries safely.*

9. *Some college expenses can be as high as $25,000 a year; financial aid can help ease the burden.*

Exercise 4 (Page 195)

Version A

1. *Mr. Lewis is open-minded; therefore, he is likely to succeed as a manager.*

3. *Fatima had saved enough money to buy a new stereo; nevertheless, she wanted to wait for a sale.*

5. *All the gate receipts were donated to charity; in addition, even more pledges came from television viewers.*

7. *Tony fertilized the tomato plants; as a result, the tomatoes grew to be large and flavorful.*

9. *Anthony just lost his job; however, he still has to make his house and car payments.*

Exercise 5 (Page 197)
Answers will vary.

Chapter 4, Part 4

Exercise 1 (Page 212)

Version A

1. There is always plenty of food (there) are many types of main dishes and desserts.

3. I like the park extremely well (I) can see the birds fly free.

5. Making mistakes is a part of life (that's) why children learn from their mistakes.

7. The players need to receive cheers (for example), they will respond by playing well.

9. Seeing a doctor can be expensive (in some cases) many ill people cannot pay their medical bills.

11. Teenage girls are not mature (they) do not know how to be good parents.

13. Eddie called her on the telephone (then) he asked her for a date.

15. Parents buy pets for their children (this) is a great way to keep an only child company.

17. The nicotine in tobacco is addictive (people) just cannot seem to stop smoking.

Exercise 2 (Page 214)

Version A

1. Jessie fell behind on the assignments . She ~~she~~ worked hard to catch up.
   $\wedge$

3. I enjoy spending time with my family . In ~~in~~ fact, we plan to go on vacation together.
   $\wedge$

5. I will finish all my assignments ~~then~~ *. Then* I will have a good chance to pass my classes.

7. William hopes to graduate from college soon ~~he~~ *. He* has only four more classes to complete.

9. Alex wanted to rest after work ~~he~~ *. He* turned off his cell phone.

Exercise 3 (Page 215)

Version A

1. The military pays for my tuition and books *, so* I do not have to pay for anything.

3. My wife is excited *, for* we are going to be parents.

5. Mariah received a puppy for her birthday *, and* she loves him very much.

7. Thirty years ago, picking up a hitchhiker was not unusual *, but* it's very dangerous today.

9. They needed to earn money for the band tour *, but* they did not have enough time.

Exercise 4 (Page 217)

Version A

1. Sara applied for the nursing program *;* she wanted to change careers.

3. Temptations were everywhere *;* he refused to buy any drugs.

5. Kurt saw the bus coming *;* he sprinted down the street.

7. The old bridge withstood the flood *;* the newer one washed away.

Exercise 5 (Page 219)

Version A

1. I got caught up on all of my bills *; however,* then my car stopped running.

3. Being thirty pounds overweight is harmful *; in fact,* it can cut years off a person's life.

5. Paddling the kayak proved to be dangerous *; in fact,* he almost drowned.

7. Tanya quit her job *; furthermore,* she had to drop out of school.

Chapter 5, Part 1

Exercise 1 (Page 226)

Version A

__F__ **1.** After we watch both of the movies.

__S__ **3.** Seventeen times he locked and unlocked the door.

__S__ **5.** One of my favorite teams will be playing a game this afternoon.

__S__ **7.** The tourists provide needed income for the small town.

__S__ **9.** Caring parents protect their children.

Exercise 2 (Page 227)

Version A

    dependent   *independent*

1. Once I have eaten my lunch, I will have time to work in my garden.

    dependent

3. While people ran down the stairs to escape the fire,

    independent

firefighters went upstairs to fight the fire.

    independent   *dependent*

5. I do not wish to go to the concert unless you come with me.

    dependent

7. After the World Trade Center was destroyed,

    independent

Americans became more aware of their freedom.

    dependent   *independent*

9. Even though Barb was late, she showed up for class.

Exercise 3 (Page 230)

Version A

1. *Because I was hungry and short on time, I went to a fast-food restaurant.*

I went to a fast-food restaurant because I was hungry and short on time.

3. *We will eat in the cafeteria as long as the food is good.*

As long as the food is good, we will eat in the cafeteria.

5. *Josh and Tara have separate checking accounts even though they are married.*

Even though Josh and Tara are married, they have separate checking accounts.

7. *Although I have a headache, I need to take the test.*

I need to take the test although I have a headache.

9. *As long as Justin attends college, he can stay on his parents' insurance.*

Justin can stay on his parents' insurance as long as he attends college.

Exercise 4 (Page 232)

Version A

1. I have paid for the magazines that we delivered.

3. Harry wanted to watch the concert that was in the park.

5. I took the pictures of the dog that won the ribbons.

7. We met in the building which had no windows.

Exercise 5 (Page 234)

Version A

1. b. The park where we play during the day becomes eerie and scary late at night.

3. b. Several students who were ready to write their papers did their research in Spain.

5. b. The little girl whose mother took her to the circus laughed at the silly clowns.

7. b. I drove my sister's car to the shopping center that was an hour away.

9. c. The residents of the care center adopted the baby kittens whose mother had died.

Exercise 6 (Page 238)

Version A

1. My cousin Leo, who likes to swim, spent his summer at the lake.

3. David, who had taken his friends for granted, went to a movie by himself.

5. My youngest sister, who wanted to repay a favor, gave me a present.

7. Richard, whose car was stolen, was angry.

9. My clothes dryer, which was only one year old, needed to be repaired.

Exercise 7 (Page 239)

Version A

1. *We bought the hand lotion that was on sale.*
   We bought the hand lotion because it was on sale.

3. *Jim wants to buy a new car that gets good gas mileage.*

5. *After Andrea invested money in Enron, the company went bankrupt.*
   Andrea invested money in Enron, which went bankrupt.

7. *The bookmobile that traveled to isolated little communities needed volunteers.*
   The bookmobile that needed volunteers traveled to isolated little communities.

9. *The letter that he was waiting for was in the mailbox.*
   He was waiting for the letter that was in the mailbox.

Exercise 8 (Page 241)
Answers will vary.

Exercise 9 (Page 242)
Answers will vary.

Chapter 5, Part 4

Exercise 2 (Page 258)

Version A

1. Keeping track of receipts. ~~It~~ is important when doing income tax. Being prepared makes the job easier.

3. Andrew spoke about the harmful results of violence. *He said* ~~Said~~ violence can only lead to trouble.

5. Every summer, the children went to the Boys and Girls Club. By summer's end, they had planted and nurtured their vegetable garden. Picking the tomatoes, corn, carrots, and green beans had been fun. Then *they* made soup.

7. I am thankful for many things. Sometimes I think about how little others own. To have a warm house and loving family. ~~That~~ makes me feel secure.

9. Everyone looks forward to going on vacation. Going on cruises or going camping. ~~It~~ can be exciting.

Exercise 3 (Page 261)

Version A

1. If you are away from other people and you need help. A cell phone could
   save your life.
   , a (above "help. A")

3. Wal-Mart built a new shopping center. Which was just down the street from
   me. I finally shopped there last weekend.
   , which (above "center. Which")

5. Going out and having a good time is important to many people. Who spend
   many hours at their jobs. This way, they can relax and return to work
   refreshed.
   who (above "people. Who")

7. After one year of marriage, they talked about buying a house. That was
   outside the city. For the next year, they saved as much money as they could
   for a down payment.
   that (above "house. That")

9. I told him that I did not want to go. That I was busy. He understood and
   thanked me for being truthful with him.
   , that (above "go. That")

Chapter 6, Part 1

Exercise 1 (Page 267)

1. Leo and __I__ love to play soccer.

3. Marsha and __I__ saw the yard sale sign.

5. _She_ and __I__ went to the video store.

Exercise 2 (Page 268)

Version A

1. The girls and _he_ spent many hours practicing with the band.

3. _She_ and __I__ both decided to go to church.

5. My cat and __I__ lounged on the sofa in front of the fire.

Exercise 3 (Page 269)

1. Mom bought my sister and _me_ some new school shoes.

3. The wind seemed to blow right through _her_ and _me_ .

5. Mario gave tickets to _them_ and _us_ .

Exercise 4   (Page 270)

Version A

1. My neighbor offered Paul and _me_ a summer job.

3. She had a wonderful surprise for Zach and _me_.

5. Sam was pleasantly surprised when the city honored _him_ and Jake.

Exercise 5   (Page 271)

Version A

_b_   1.   Steven read the story to him and me.

_a_   3.   Hiking the canyon was a thrill for her and me.

_a_   5.   The wasps at the picnic stung both my brother and me.

_a_   7.   My teacher urged my parents and me to plan for college.

_b_   9.   The surgeon explained the operation to him and me.

Exercise 6   (Page 274)

Version A

1. a.   When a student arrives on campus, ~~they~~ *he or she* will need to attend orientation.
   b.   When a ~~student arrives~~ *students arrive* on campus, they will need to attend orientation.

3. a.   A good nurse wants ~~their~~ *his or her* patients to feel comfortable while in the hospital.
   b.   ~~A good nurse wants~~ *Good nurses want* their patients to feel comfortable while in the hospital.

5. a.   A teenager often sees ~~their~~ *his or her* younger brothers and sisters as needing a lot of guidance.
   b.   ~~A teenager~~ *Teenagers* often sees their younger brothers and sisters as needing a lot of guidance.

7. a.   A child may need friends, but ~~they do~~ *he or she does* not know how to make them.
   b.   ~~A child~~ *Children* may need friends, but they do not know how to make them.

9. a.   A doctor may not realize that ~~their~~ *his or her* patients do not have insurance.
   b.   ~~A doctor~~ *Doctors* may not realize that their patients do not have insurance.

Exercise 7   (Page 278)

Version A

1. **Everyone** on the men's basketball team earned _____*his*_____ letter.

3. **Each** of the teachers volunteered _*his or her*_ time after school.

5. **Everyone** put _*his or her*_ best effort into the class project.

Exercise 8   (Page 280)

Version A

2nd person plural **1.** Students, **you** will find out about **your** books on the first day of class.

3rd person singular **3.** **She** is really enjoying **her** new high-speed Internet modem.

1st person plural **5.** **We** asked **our** neighbor to take in **our** mail.

Exercise 9   (Page 281)

Version A

1. When students miss school, ~~you~~ *they* miss out on a lot of important things.

3. Young people like the thrill of driving fast. However, driving fast is scary because ~~you~~ *they* are in a chunk of metal going at high speeds.

5. I realized that I do not need to know ~~your~~ *my* major to enroll in college.

7. At a party, people have a chance to meet new friends. ~~You~~ *They* can even dance with new people.

9. Hikers are usually very polite. As ~~you~~ *they* pass each other, ~~you~~ *they* exchange greetings.

Exercise 10   (Page 284)

A. **1st person point of view**

Every morning, I get up and read the newspaper so ~~you~~ *I* can get information on different events in the city. ~~You~~ *I* can read about all the violence happening in schools, communities, and homes. It seems as though every day ~~you~~ *I* read about a child drowning in a swimming pool or in a freezing lake. One morning, ~~people~~ *I* read about a computer virus that hits the banks, and ~~you are~~ *I am* not able to make withdrawals from many banks, including the Bank of America ATMs. Another morning, I read about a drug bust where police seize a thousand pounds of marijuana.

B. **2nd person point of view**

Every morning, ~~I~~ *you* get up and read the newspaper so you can get information on different events in the city. You can read about all the violence happening in schools, communities, and homes. It seems as though every day you read about a child drowning in a swimming pool or in a freezing lake. One morning, ~~people~~ *you* read about a virus that hits the banks, and ~~I am~~ *you are* not able to make withdrawals from many banks, including the Bank of America ATMs. Another morning, ~~I~~ *you* read about a drug bust where police seize a thousand pounds of marijuana.

C. **3rd person plural point of view**

Every morning, Americans get up and read the newspaper so ~~you~~ *they* can get information on different events in the city. ~~You~~ *They* can read about all the violence happening in schools, communities, and homes. It seems as though every day ~~you~~ *they* read about a child drowning in a swimming pool or in a freezing lake. One morning, people read about a virus that hits the banks, and ~~I am~~ *they are* not able to make withdrawals from many banks, including the Bank of America ATMs. Another morning, ~~I~~ *they* read about a drug bust where police seize a thousand pounds of marijuana.

Chapter 6, Part 4

Exercise 1   (Page 297)

Version A

1. The buffet featured <u>blueberry muffins</u> and <u>bread pudding</u>.

3. The players were <u>nervous</u> but <u>happy</u> before the game.

5. Jim <u>saved money</u> and <u>followed a budget</u>.

7. At the drugstore, Tim bought toothpaste and shaving gel.

9. The chef rapidly but efficiently prepared the entrée.

Exercise 2 (Page 298)

Answers will vary.

Exercise 3 (Page 300)

Version A

1. The sun shone through the window and onto the carpet.

3. Across the street and down the alley, his voice carried unbelievably far.

5. We walked underneath the bridge and around the lagoon to reach the picnic area.

7. Whenever I have a little extra time in the spring, I hike over the bridge and through the beautiful meadow.

9. We need to put the groceries in the refrigerator but not on the counter.

Exercise 4 (Page 301)

Version A

1. The puppy seemed happy just chewing on toys and sleeping in the sun.

3. Marilyn liked filling the feeder and watching the hummingbirds.

5. Chewing tobacco and smoking cigarettes will lead to major health problems.

7. Seeing the lightning and hearing the thunder upset the young children.

9. Eating but not overeating can be a challenge for some people.

Exercise 5 (Page 303)

Version A

1. Jodi spent her Saturday mornings playing CDs, doing laundry, and cleaning her room.

3. My mother asked for a blue scarf, a red jacket, and a white hat.

5. The innocent, sweet, but impish little girl stole everyone's heart.

7. The strong winds battered the power lines, splintered the oak tree, and destroyed the roof.

9. The robbers entered the bank quietly, swiftly, but dangerously.

Exercise 6 (Page 304)

Version A

1. We opened the box and _____unpacked_____ the books.

3. The water covered the yard and _____filled_____ the flower beds.

5. We found the golf course _____*difficult*_____ but beautiful.

7. We sensed the excitement of the concert as we came into the theater and _____*walked to our seats*___.

9. We put the directions on the computer file and ___*in the desk drawer*___.

Exercise 7   (Page 308)

Version A

1. Either the dog needs to stay outside, or he needs to get a bath.

3. He missed neither a meal nor a conference.

5. The car not only had a flat tire but also had a damaged fender.

Exercise 8   (Page 310)

Version A

1. b. Being very spicy, the hot Mexican food was delicious.

3. a. Built in 1800, the house had to be restored.

5. b. After having a second serving of spaghetti, the man fed his dog leftover spaghetti.

7. b. Making a routine traffic check, the police officer confiscated ten bags of marijuana.

9. b. To save money, the company carefully planned a budget.

Exercise 9   (Page 312)

Version A

Answers will vary.

1. Lost for two days, *the exhausted dog found his way home.*

3. Painted with bright colors, *the picture seemed perfect for the baby's room. / the picture seemed too busy for the baby's room.*

5. Brushing my dog, *I noticed that she needed to have her toenails clipped.*

7. Arranging the food on the picnic table, *we noticed an entire swarm of bees coming in our direction.*

9. Enjoying the sale, *we bought several items for our home.*

Exercise 10   (Page 314)

Version A

1. b. The children with happy faces were outside playing on the swings.

3. b. The house with the three-car garage burned to the ground.

5. a. The singer winning the Grammy Award declined an interview.

7. b. The movie made on location in the Rockies won an Academy Award.

9. a. The young couple getting married in Las Vegas planned a Hawaiian honeymoon.

Chapter 7, Part 1

Exercise 1   (Page 324)

Version A

1. We restocked the shelves, refilled the gum machine, and turned out the lights.

3. When looking for our little brother, we looked down the street, around the corner, and up the hill.

C   5. My neighbor was thoughtful and generous and patient.

7. When David goes to his parents' house, he leaves with home-cooked food, clean laundry, and gas money.

9. My mother was not at all pleased with my boyfriend, his tattoo, or his purple hair.

Exercise 2   (Page 325)

Version A

1. Because Rob left his car with the engine running, an opportunistic thief jumped in and drove it away.

3. Yes, I do want to come to visit you in St. Louis.

5. Shocked by the news, I called my family in Wisconsin.

7. All right, I was wrong about the score of the game.

9. At the end of the conference, we all exchanged e-mail addresses.

Exercise 3   (Page 327)

Version A

1. We left our road map, by the way, at the last rest stop.

3. All of my employees, especially those attending college, are outstanding.

5. The administrators, not the teachers, wanted to implement a new program.

7. The office attendant, as a matter of fact, was not courteous to pets or their owners.

C   9. The book that I read for extra credit was an exciting novel.

Exercise 4   (Page 329)

Version A

1. The last place we lived was 32 East Columbus Avenue͵Mesa͵Arizona.

3. Tom͵can you fix my flat tire this evening?

5. If you do not mind͵Susan͵I would rather stay home tonight.

7. If you would like to͵Fred͵we could paint the garage tomorrow.

C 9. Please ask Cathy if she wants to go with us.

Exercise 5 (Page 331)

Version A

1. All at once, everyone yelled͵ᵛ͓get the ball.ᵛ

C 3. Justin said that he was looking for a new condominium.

5. When I think of the wordᵛcrook,ᵛ I think about the executives at Enron and the Baptist Foundation.

Exercise 6   (Page 333)

Version A

1. *cat's* kitten

3. *oven's* temperature

5. *heater's* switch

Exercise 7   (Page 334)

Version A

1. *cats/cats'* kittens

3. *ovens/ovens'* temperatures

5. *heaters/heaters'* switches

Exercise 8   (Page 335)

Version A

1. ____*men's*____ The <u>mens</u> locker room was closed for repairs.

3. ____*women's*____ The <u>womens</u> designer clothes attracted the most customers.

5. ____*teeth's*____ Their baby <u>teeths</u> roots were not very deep.

Exercise 9   (Page 336)

Version A

1. ____*iron's*____ The waffle <u>irons</u> cord was missing.

3. ____*senators'*____ The <u>senators</u> districts were worried about their voting records.

5. _diners'_ The <u>diners</u> roofs were damaged in the hurricane.

7. _daughters'_ Julio's six <u>daughters</u> weddings were all expensive.

Exercise 10 (Page 337)

Version A

1. Hannah could not find the current issue of <u>People</u>.

3. The article in <u>Personal Finance</u> recommended buying bonds.

5. The <u>Mayo Clinic Health Letter</u> has an excellent index.

7. We wanted to see the drama department's production of <u>Hamlet</u>.

9. Rita reads <u>Prevention</u> for its articles on health and fitness.

Exercise 11 (Page 338)

Version A

1. The movie we watched ⋀(wasn't it boring⋀)was too long.

3. We invited her ⋀(was this a mistake⋀)to come for lunch.

5. When you come to the reunion, bring three ⋀3⋀( ) apple pies, two ⋀2⋀( ) rum cakes, and four ⋀4⋀( ) batches of oatmeal cookies.

Exercise 12 (Page 339)

Version A

1. The family members ⋀—mother, father, and children⋀— are all musicians.

3. Someone broke into our cabin ⋀—perhaps someone lost and hungry⋀— and stole food.

5. The gourmet dinner ⋀—never mind the enormous cost⋀—was delicious.

Exercise 13 (Page 341)

Version A

1. We wanted a blue ⋀-sky day for our picnic.

3. We shopped for the twenty ⋀-four children in the homeless shelter.

5. The new shirt was made of easy ⋀-care cotton.

Exercise 14 (Page 342)

Version A

1. I really am interested in learning about art history ⋀, but I cannot take a class right now ⋀.

3. Fran's house is on fire ⋀!

5. The bouquet of red carnations on the table slowly wilted ⋀.

7. I would rather go swimming before I eat lunch⌄

9. Early this morning, the telephone rang⌄I did not get to it on time⌄
,

Chapter 7, Part 4

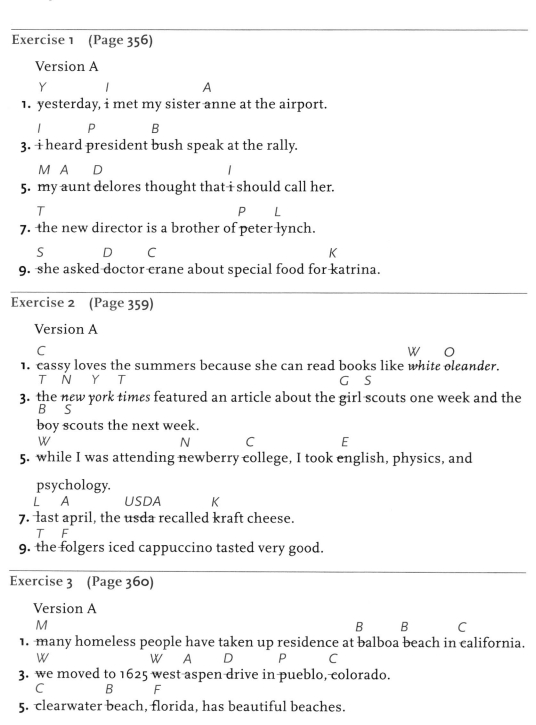

Exercise 1   (Page 356)

Version A

    Y   I   A
1. yesterday, i met my sister anne at the airport.

    I   P   B
3. i heard president bush speak at the rally.

    M A   D   I
5. my aunt delores thought that i should call her.

    T   P   L
7. the new director is a brother of peter lynch.

    S   D   C   K
9. she asked doctor crane about special food for katrina.

Exercise 2   (Page 359)

Version A

    C   W   O
1. cassy loves the summers because she can read books like *white oleander.*
    T   N   Y T   G   S
3. the *new york times* featured an article about the girl scouts one week and the
    B   S
    boy scouts the next week.
    W   N   C   E
5. while I was attending newberry college, I took english, physics, and

    psychology.
    L   A   USDA   K
7. last april, the usda recalled kraft cheese.
    T   F
9. the folgers iced cappuccino tasted very good.

Exercise 3   (Page 360)

Version A
    M   B   B   C
1. many homeless people have taken up residence at balboa beach in california.
    W   W   A   D   P   C
3. we moved to 1625 west aspen drive in pueblo, colorado.
    C   B   F
5. clearwater beach, florida, has beautiful beaches.

7. $\underset{L}{\cancel{l}}$ast summer we followed the direction of the $\underset{O}{\cancel{o}}$regon $\underset{T}{\cancel{t}}$rail all the way to the $\underset{W}{\cancel{w}}$est $\underset{C}{\cancel{c}}$oast.

9. The $\underset{H}{\cancel{h}}$opi tribe is one of the few tribes who do not have gambling on their reservation.

Answers to Appendix A (Confusing Words)

Exercise 1 (Page 367)

1. George wanted to buy __an__ American car for his parents.

3. We saw __an__ eagle as we hiked the trail.

5. By refinishing __the__ back patio, he made __the__ backyard more attractive.

7. He wanted to hire __an__ accountant to help with his taxes.

9. Before becoming __a__ high school teacher, Tom worked as __a__ teacher's aide.

11. He did __an__ exceptional job of planning the retreat.

13. Please bring __a__ better picture of yourself to __the__ immigration office nearest you.

15. J. K. Rowling's Harry Potter is __an__ amazingly imaginative character.

Exercise 2 (Page 368)

1. We have __a lot__ of work to do before Friday.

3. The young parents had to __allot__ their time for their children.

5. The children also learned __a lot__ from their parents' efforts.

Exercise 3 (Page 368)

1. All the dogs __except__ Blazer went to the veterinarian today.

3. At first, Stormy did not __accept__ the trip very easily.

5. Jason __accepted__ his supporting role as a bench player for the coach.

Exercise 4 (Page 369)

1. Experienced students take __advice__ with good humor.

3. Helen went searching for __advice__ when she needed it.

5. I can still hear her wise words of __advice__.

Exercise 5 (Page 369)

1. The snowstorm __affected__ the traffic the next morning.

3. The stench of his cologne __affected__ everyone around him.

5. Working so many hours at his job __affected__ his grades.

7. The parents and teachers __effected__ a compromise.

Exercise 6   (Page 370)

1. After the storm, the airplane landed __all right__ .

3. Is it __all right__ to take my car to that shop?

5. The solution to the problem was __all right__ with everybody.

Exercise 7   (Page 370)

1. The bill had __already__ been paid.

3. Samaki and his brothers were __all ready__ for the new semester.

5. When everyone is __all ready__ , please give me a call.

Exercise 8   (Page 371)

1. We hope to have __our__ garage sale soon.

3. Saturdays __are__ often busy days for __our__ family.

5. The wildfires in Colorado __are__ burning near Denver.

Exercise 9   (Page 371)

1. I need to __buy__ new carpeting for my house.

3. We stood __by__ the bridge as the steamer went past.

5. The parents agreed to __buy__ their kids a ferret.

Exercise 10   (Page 372)

1. We should __have__ bought our tickets for the play ahead of time.

3. Steve might __have__ been called away on business.

5. I wish I could __have__ gone to the party.

Exercise 11   (Page 372)

1. That was an extremely __good__ movie.

3. We usually work __well__ together.

5. Their trip to Canada went __well__ .

Exercise 12   (Page 373)

1. That was __quite__ a __quiet__ group of students.

3. On the drive home, I became __quiet__ and thoughtful.

5. If you will just be __quiet__ , I will give you the information.

Exercise 13   (Page 374)

1. I _used_ to go dancing every Saturday night.

3. Benny knows how to _use_ his money wisely.

5. The retired couple _used_ to drive across the country every year.

Exercise 14   (Page 374)

1. Our new truck is larger _than_ the old one.

3. The dust storm subsided; _then_ the rains came.

5. He often eats fresh fruit and vegetables rather _than_ fried foods.

Exercise 15   (Page 375)

1. _Whether_ or not we will go depends on the _weather_.

3. Unless the _weather_ clears, the beach will be closed.

5. I had to pay my bills _whether_ I wanted to or not.

Exercise 16   (Page 375)

1. _Where_ _were_ all the people?

3. We _were_ able to fix the flat tire without buying a new one.

5. Do you know _where_ we should go to pan for gold?

Exercise 17   (Page 376)

1. He consumed _two_ Krispy Kreme doughnuts as he waited in line.

3. _Too_ many people crowded into the elevator.

5. We went out _to_ eat _too_ many times.

Exercise 18   (Page 376)

1. _There_ he is!

3. Unfortunately, _they're_ usually late for class.

5. When I got _there_, the store was closed.

Exercise 19   (Page 377)

1. They did not _hear_ about the hurricane until it was too late.

2. _Here_ comes my bus.

3. Maria moved _here_ from Brooklyn.

Exercise 20   (Page 377)

1. I _knew_ that my boyfriend would say _no_.

2. We have _new_ neighbors next door.

3. I have _no_ use for whiners.

Exercise 21 (Page 378)

1. Six cars __passed__ me before someone stopped to help.

3. As they __passed__ through the tunnel, the light faded.

5. Angela __passed__ all her courses last year.

Exercise 22 (Page 378)

1. __Your__ sense of humor is greatly appreciated.

3. It is illegal to park __your__ car on the street.

5. If __you're__ in a hurry, please go on without me.

Answers to Appendix B (ESL)

Exercise 1 (Page 381)

Version A

C Ⓝ 1. The hospital patient struggled for <u>survival</u>.

Ⓒ N 3. The lawn mower damaged a <u>brick</u> in the fence.

Ⓒ N 5. The health <u>magazine</u> recommends yearly mammograms.

Exercise 2 (Page 382)

Version A

1. I poured my water into __a__ glass from the cupboard.

3. To increase her strength, Leta enrolled at __a__ gym.

5. The elderly gentleman ordered __an__ egg and some toast for his breakfast.

Exercise 3 (Page 383)

Version A

_C_ 1. He experienced failure last Saturday.

_I_ 3. He showed the nervousness before his wedding.

_C_ 5. He lacked the courage needed to become a soldier.

Exercise 4 (Page 386)

Answers will vary.

turn __in__ which means __hand in or submit__

turn __down__ which means __reject__

turn __around__ which means __change__

Exercise 5   (Page 386)
   Answers will vary.

Exercise 6   (Page 387)

   Version A
_I_ **1.** The student can buys her supplies at the discount store.

_I_ **3.** Sonya must seeing the doctor after all.

_C_ **5.** Walter may study at the library.

Exercise 7   (Page 388)
   Answers will vary.

   Version A
1. The counselor suggested _studying harder._

3. Sharon quit _smoking cigarettes._

5. Mom enjoys _having us around._

Exercise 8   (Page 389)

   Version A
_I_ **1.** She promised going to the store tomorrow.

_I_ **3.** Her tax advisor needed having other records.

_C_ **5.** We tried to drive across town to a special store.

Exercise 9   (Page 391)

   Version A
_I_ **1.** We live <u>in</u> 2701 N. 10th Street.

_I_ **3.** I am capable <u>in</u> doing the homework.

_C_ **5.** I found my lost purse <u>on</u> June 10, 2003.

Answers to Appendix C (Spelling)

Practice 1 (Page 394)

star	_starred_
tag	_tagged_
drug	_drugged_
wrap	_wrapped_
ship	_shipped_

Practice 2 (Page 394)

brag _bragging_ occur _occurring_

swim _swimming_ repel _repelling_

hum _humming_ extol _extolling_

chat _chatting_ unwrap _umwrapping_

lug _lugging_ acquit _acquitting_

Practice 3 (Page 395)

defer _deferred_

allot _allotted_

control _controlled_

omit _omitted_

remit _remitted_

Practice 4 (Page 395)

occur _occurring_

repel _repelling_

extol _extolling_

cunwrap _umwrapping_

lacquit _acquitting_

Practice 5 (Page 395)

judge	+	ment	=	_judgment_
believe	+	able	=	_believable_
compose	+	ing	=	_composing_
delete	+	ing	=	_deleting_
write	+	ing	=	_writing_
relate	+	ing	=	_relating_
replace	+	ment	=	_replacement_
devote	+	ing	=	_devoting_
forgive	+	ness	=	_forgiveness_
encourage	+	ment	=	_encouragement_

Practice 6 (Page 396)

unbel _ie_ vable   r _ei_ gn

fr _ei_ ght   shr _ie_ k

gr _ie_ f   br _ie_ f

rec _ei_ pt   misch _ie_ vous

rel _ie_ ve   n _ie_ ce

Practice 7 (Page 396)

happy	+ness	=	_happiness_
merry	+est	=	_merriest_
vary	+s	=	_varies_
tasty	+er	=	_tastier_
jury	+s	=	_juries_
baby	+ing	=	_babying_
study	+ing	=	_studying_

Index